Femme Fatale

Femme Fatale

❧❧

LOVE, LIES, AND THE
UNKNOWN LIFE OF
MATA HARI

❧❧

Pat Shipman

Weidenfeld & Nicolson
LONDON

First published in Great Britain in 2007
by Weidenfeld & Nicolson

1 3 5 7 9 10 8 6 4 2

A CIP catalogue record for this book
is available from the British Library.

ISBN-13   978 0 297 85074 8

Printed in Great Britain by Butler & Tanner Ltd, Frome and London

Weidenfeld & Nicolson

The Orion Publishing Group Ltd
Orion House
5 Upper Saint Martin's Lane
London, WC2H 9EA

An Hachette Livre UK Company

www.orionbooks.co.uk

The Orion publishing group's policy is to use papers that are natural, renewable
and recyclable products and made from wood grown in sustainable forests.
The logging and manufacturing processes are expected to conform to the
environmental regulations of the country of origin.

To Alan

Contents

Acknowledgments

Mata Hari first came to my immediate attention because of a newspaper article in 2000. At that time, the Institute of Anatomy museum in Paris announced that the head of Mata Hari— in the museum's collections since her death in 1917—was missing. A curator speculated that the head might have been stolen by an admirer in the 1950s, the last time the collection had been moved. This seemed to me an extraordinary suggestion bordering on the fantastic. The thought of an aging admirer stealing a woman's head thirty years after her death was both ludicrous and macabre. I soon came to realize that, for Mata Hari, many unbelievable things were possible.

As I investigated the books about and documentary evidence of her life, I felt that previous biographers had neglected her married years in the Dutch East Indies. Because I had researched the colonial period in Indonesia extensively for another book, *The Man Who Found the Missing Link*, I was convinced that the roots of the later, better-known part of her life lay in her years in the Indies. This approach has led me to a new understanding and some important discoveries.

I have used terms popular in the later 1800s and early 1900s for the racial and social classes of people in the Dutch East Indies. Some of these are now offensive or derisory. I wish to make clear that I do not use them because I wish to impugn the people to which they refer but simply as a matter of historical accuracy.

I have relied heavily on available correspondence to or from Mata Hari. Letters are often irregularly punctuated, with dashes and underlinings used instead of more conventional punctuation. In quoting these, I have inserted more modern punctuation and used italics instead of underlinings for emphasis, but otherwise the words stand as written. Because I am writing for English-speaking readers, I give the names of all publications in English in the text. The full references in the original language can be found in the notes.

Translation has been a major issue in researching and writing this book. Translations from the French are my own, with the able assistance of Marc Godinot and Catherine Helgeson. Translations from the Dutch have been done either by my remarkable colleague and research assistant, Dr. Paul Storm, or by myself with assistance from Chiara Bols and Ida In't Veldt. I am very grateful for such friends. In this book as in previous work we have done together, Paul Storm has demonstrated his invaluable ability to discover long-lost or -overlooked information. I cannot thank him enough for his inspired efforts.

Nonetheless, I am solely responsible for any errors in translation.

I wish to express my gratitude to the curators, scholars, and institutions that have kindly provided access, assistance, or information, and I apologize if I have overlooked any. Thanks to librarian Mrs. M. Gaspar-Raven of the Museum Bronbeek; Gerk Koopmans and Evert Kramer of the Fries Museum in Leeuwarden; Michiel van Halem of the Gemeente Archief, Leiden; and the Haanstraschool in

Leiden. I am grateful for the invaluable assistance of Philippe Fernandez in obtaining permissions from France. My appreciation also goes to the Algemeen Rijksarchief, the Centraal Bureau voor Genealogie, the Nationaal Archief, and the Stichting Indische Familie Archief, all in The Hague; Gina Houwer at the Tropeninstituut in Amsterdam; Liesbeth Ouwehand of the KITLV, which housed a photograph of Mata Hari that is, to my knowledge, previously unpublished; the Legermuseum and its excellent library in Delft; the Public Record Office at Kew; Emmanuel Penicaut of the Service Historique de l'Armée de la Terre at Vincennes; Tristan Boos; Glenn Bruce; Tineke Hellwig; Christine Ruggere of the Institute of the History of Medicine, Johns Hopkins University School of Medicine; Ann Laura Stoller; and Julie Wheelwright.

As always, my closest friends and family have offered me a great deal of support and encouragement, without which I can never write. You know who you are. Thank you.

Femme Fatale

The most important thing to know about Margaretha Zelle is that she loved men. The most crucial thing to know about her is that she did not love truth. When it was convenient, she told the truth. When it was not, or when she found the truth tedious, she invented what might be kindly called "alternative truths"—and unkindly, "lies." For her, what was factually true never seemed as essential as what should have been true. By the time she had transformed herself into Mata Hari, she was highly skilled at fashioning the world to her liking.

She was a creation from beginning to end, a character in a play that she continuously rescripted. She changed her name as often as some women change hairstyles.

Only once in her life did she acknowledge this fact about herself, and it was when she was in prison, in imminent danger of being convicted of espionage and sentenced to death. The severe conditions of her imprisonment, the catastrophic collapse of the world she had created, and the brutal destruction of her identity had driven her very near to madness. With painful insight sharpened by her teetering on the edge of the abyss, she wrote to the man who was her captor, accuser, and interrogator, trying to explain:

> *There is something which I wish you to take into consideration, it is that Mata Hari and Madame Zelle MacLeod are two completely different women.*
>
> *Today, because of the war, I am obliged to live under and to sign the name of Zelle, but this woman is unknown to the public.*
>
> *I consider myself to be Mata Hari. For 12 years, I have lived under this name. I am known in all the countries and I have connections everywhere.*
>
> *That which is permitted to Mata Hari—dancer—is certainly not permitted to Madame Zelle MacLeod.*
>
> *That which happens to Mata Hari, they are the events which do not happen to Madame Zelle. The people who address one do not address the other.*

This was probably the moment of her greatest self-understanding. In this telling of her life I have steered as close to the truth as I am able—but in her case, the truth is an ever-shifting and elusive wind.

The Little Orchid

HE TAUGHT HER to think of herself as special. She was his little princess and he loved to show her off. He bought her wonderful dresses in vivid, flamboyant colors—once a dress of scarlet velvet that she wore to school. She twirled to show her father how the skirt flared out, and he beamed and told her she was beautiful. She did the same for her friends at Miss Buys's exclusive school, and they looked at her with wide eyes. They pretended to be shocked, to think it was a scandalous dress for a girl her age, but she knew they were only jealous. They were better suited to the subdued colors they habitually wore. They could have afforded a dress like hers easily, but they never could have worn such a garment with her flair. Their pallid skin and colorless hair and lack of personality condemned them. Only someone like her, with thick, darkly waving hair, compelling eyes, and café au lait skin—only someone whose very essence cried "Look at me!"—could get away with it.

One of her school friends in a moment of genius called her an orchid in a field of dandelions, and she was, even then. And

Adam Zelle was the prosperous and handsome father of Margaretha Geertruida Zelle, the future Mata Hari, and her three brothers. She was his favorite child. (The Mata Hari Foundation/ Fries Museum)

she knew it. She knew it because she was different from everyone else. She knew it most of all because of the way her father treated her, as if she were infinitely precious. His love gave her a wonderful feeling.

She was born on August 7, 1876. Her younger brother, Johannes, was born two years after her, on November 26, 1878. Then in 1881, on September 9, came twin boys, Arie and Cornelius. The birth of her brothers never displaced Margaretha from her place in their father's affection; she was always the favored child in his eyes. She probably believed he loved her more than he loved her mother.

On her sixth birthday, her father surprised her with a goat cart, a *bokkenwagon*. It was the most marvelous gift she had ever received. The vehicle was an exquisite miniature phaeton as fine as the ones the rich drove with their superb horses. Hers was pulled by a matched pair of stout goats with fine horns. All her friends clamored to go for a drive in it, and she loved indulging them. The neighbors clucked their tongues at the extravagance of such a gift, and for a little girl too! It would only make her vain and give her ideas about her own importance. They should have known that she already had those ideas, that she had learned them at her father's knee.

The extraordinary goat-drawn phaeton was remembered by Margaretha's former classmates and many others in the town decades

I n 1882, on Margaretha's sixth birthday, her father gave her a goat carriage—a magical and extravagant gift. (The Mata Hari Foundation/Fries Museum)

later. "It was an *amazing* bit of foolhardiness, which put Margaretha absolutely in a class by herself!" So said one of her former friends in 1963, when she was well over eighty years old and Margaretha was long dead. Others spoke of the gift of the *bokkenwagon* as the most unforgettable event of their childhood years.

But that was typical of Adam Zelle: he loved to be noticed. His daughter was in some ways his most becoming accessory. He was vain about his full beard and his good looks. He always dressed well, in a top hat and flowered waistcoat that flattered him, to advertise the quality of the goods produced by his hat factory and for sale in his haberdashery. Some people called him "the Baron," as a jibe at his pretension and posing, but he rather liked the nickname, assuming it was a recognition of his natural superiority.

In 1873 he had his greatest social triumphs, the first of which was marrying Antje van der Meulen from nearby Franeker. Although

Antje was thirty-one years old, only two years his junior, and not a young woman in her first flush of marital eligibility, she was from a family with higher social standing than his. He felt the marriage was a major step up for a rising young merchant in a provincial capital in northern Holland. Later that year, Zelle was selected to be in the mounted Guard of Honor when King Willem III visited their town, Leeuwarden, in the province of Friesland. Zelle prided himself on his horsemanship and was honored to be selected to represent his town. He had his own portrait painted, showing him on horseback and in full uniform. Many years later Zelle presented it to the new Fries Museum as an important work it ought to display. It is a mediocre piece of art but an excellent example of Zelle's personality.

Ten years after these triumphs, in 1883, Zelle's haberdashery business was doing so well that he moved his growing family into a beautiful old brick house at 28 Groote Kerkstraat. It was a fine residence and doubtless he felt himself established as one of the most important burghers of Leeuwarden. He hired more servants and sent his pretty daughter to learn elegant manners, music (both singing and piano), exquisite handwriting, and French at Miss Buys's school; his sons were growing into strong and good-looking boys, and he planned a good education for them, too. Although Amsterdamers might claim that Leeuwarden was rural and unsophisticated, Zelle felt the town in which he had been born and raised was an excellent place. It boasted nearly 27,000 inhabitants.

After another six years of acting the baron, Zelle found that Leeuwarden no longer seemed so splendid. His investments and business ventures went so far wrong that on February 18, 1889, he was forced to declare bankruptcy. The failure must have been a bitter comedown to a proud man. The news was probably a great shock to his family, for men of his background did not discuss financial matters with their wives and children. Leeuwarden was no longer a place where Zelle could live and hold up his head.

He left for The Hague on July 15 to look for work. His family was left behind, crowded into a cheap upstairs apartment on the Willemskade, a much less fashionable address than Groote Kerkstraat, with little money to live on. It was the family who had to face the pitying looks and whispered words about their sudden turn of fortune.

For Margaretha, her father's departure for The Hague less than a month before her thirteenth birthday must have felt like a desertion. Didn't Papa love her any-

In 1889, Adam Zelle went bankrupt and divorced his wife, who died two years later of shame and poverty. The adolescent Margaretha was sent to live with relatives who found her difficult, with few prospects for a good marriage or a useful career. (The Mata Hari Foundation / Fries Museum)

more? How could her birthday come with no goat carriages, no fancy dresses, no gifts from him at all? She was by then honing her excellent linguistic skills on English and German as well as French, but there was no loving Papa to applaud her academic triumphs or to admire her pretty dresses. He had left her, and the effect must have been shattering.

After ten months, on May 31, 1890, Zelle returned to Leeuwarden and his family. Margaretha may have expected the golden days she remembered from her younger years to resume, but Zelle was unable to support his family and equally unable to reconcile with his wife. The neighbors overheard violent quarrels. By the end of the summer, the couple filed for a legal separation, which was granted on September 4. In conservative Friesland in the nineteenth century, a legal separation was a scandalous act, fuel for gossip and smug or knowing nodding of heads. A decent man and his wife would simply have come to an unspoken agreement and lived apart. But a legal separation? Even in disgrace, they might have said, that man Zelle had to call attention to himself.

Zelle moved to Amsterdam, nearly ninety miles away, where he was soon living openly with another woman. His wife stayed in Leeuwarden trying to hold her family together. On May 10, 1891, Antje Zelle died. The announcement in the newspaper read:

> *This day it pleased the supreme architect of the universe, to take away from this earth, after a grievous suffering from February 21, 1889, my dearly beloved wife, loving mother of four helpless children, Mrs. Anna van der Meulen Zelle, at the age of 49 years. Adam Zelle Corneliszoon [son of Cornelius].*

The date mentioned—February 21, 1889—was three days after the public declaration of Adam Zelle's bankruptcy. There is no evidence of what happened on this date; perhaps it took three days for the word to spread throughout Leeuwarden that "the Baron" was bankrupt. Perhaps Antje had only enough courage to hold her head up for three days against the titters and snubs that plagued her. The intertwined causes of Antje's "grievous suffering" were almost certainly humiliation and poverty.

On the afternoon of Antje's funeral, piano music was heard issuing from the Zelle household by those passing in the street. People in Leeuwarden were surprised, even shocked. Music was considered an entertainment and hence indecorous in a house of mourning. "*I* was playing; it was the *pain* I felt," Margaretha told a friend solemnly, enjoying the opportunity to dramatize her sorrow just a bit.

Neighbors looked after the Zelle children for some weeks while more permanent arrangements were made. In November, Johannes, the older boy, was sent to Antje's family in nearby Franeker. The twins were sent to their father in Amsterdam, but Margaretha—M'Greet as she was usually called by then—was not. Instead she was sent to live with her uncle and godfather, Mr. Visser, and his wife, in the small Friesian town of Sneek.

The depth of M'Greet's feelings of outrage and betrayal can only be imagined. She had always been her father's favorite; she was now almost a woman, nearly fifteen years old, and she had suffered what were to her terrible deprivations because of the family's sudden poverty and social downfall. Why didn't Papa come and take *her* to Amsterdam? *Why did he take the twins and not her?*

The answer can never be known, but it would not be surprising if Zelle's new woman refused to have M'Greet in the house. The girl was vain and self-centered and used to having her father indulge her. Money was still tight; the couple did not live in a good section of Amsterdam. It was less onerous to take on twin ten-year-old boys than a spoiled teen-aged girl who loved extravagant clothes and being the center of attention.

From M'Greet's point of view, her mother had died and her beloved father—the handsome papa who had made life magical and fun, the man she bent every energy to please—had rejected her twice. She felt she was practically an orphan. In all likelihood, she was sulky, petulant, and angry, not an easy guest in her godfather's home. Sneek was a small town in which respectability and conformity were of paramount importance to everyone except, perhaps, M'Greet. There was little to distract her from her misery.

What seems clear is that the Vissers tried hard to reform the headstrong girl. Within weeks, they told her she was unlikely ever to attract a husband. She was dark and flat-chested; she had grown to five feet nine inches tall, an awkward height in an era when the minimum height for men in the military was five feet; she had no dowry; and her family name had been disgraced. No one would ever want to marry her. The Vissers felt she had best begin thinking of how she was going to earn her living. Fancy languages, a fine hand, and piano playing were not very marketable skills. One obvious alternative, domestic service, was unthinkable to a proud girl like M'Greet. Since her grandmother van der Meulen had allotted five thousand florins for the education of the Zelle children after Antje's death, perhaps she should attend some sort of training school.

Early in 1892 the Vissers packed M'Greet off to a boarding school in Leiden where all the newest educational innovations were being taught to young women wanting to become kindergarten instructors. The school later became famous for the "Leiden kindergarten method" of encouraging children's natural love of learning through play and practical exercises rather than attempting to make them sit down and listen to lectures. In all probability, the real reason the Vissers sent M'Greet there was that they found her trying to live with and they knew the headmaster, Wybrandus Haanstra. Haanstra had earned his teaching credentials in Sneek, where his father was a pastor and a teacher. The Vissers may have felt more at ease passing the responsibility for this awkward poor relation of theirs to a well-thought-of fellow Frieslander.

When M'Greet arrived at the Leiden school, Haanstra had been headmaster for ten years. He was a very well respected educator and apparently liked by the students. There is now a plaque on the school wall dedicated to him by his "grateful students." It shows a bas-relief of Haanstra with a walruslike moustache and a full head of hair; his profile vaguely resembles that of Albert Einstein.

Although the then-radical approach of teaching children through play might have appealed to M'Greet's sense of fun and spontaneity, it is difficult to envision a career less appropriate for her character. She never in her life exhibited any particular fondness for children or any nurturing instincts. In the assessment of one of her former school friends, choosing such a career for M'Greet was an obvious error: "Such a job was good for a 'motherly' girl, and M'Greet was a *personality*." This appraisal must be weighed carefully, for it was made long after the fact, but the sentiment rings true. As both child and woman, Margaretha Zelle was rarely concerned with anyone but herself.

The oft-repeated story of M'Greet's brief stay at the Leiden school is that Haanstra fell in love and had a sexual relationship with her. She was sixteen; he was fifty-one and married. She was clever academically and, judging from later reports of her life, exceedingly charming and attractive. She had learned very early that pleasing men was the way to find happiness.

In 1893 she was sent home from the school in shame, while Haanstra remained in his position of power and esteem until his death in 1925. Whatever happened, M'Greet was blamed for the scandal, not Haanstra. Today his behavior would be considered criminal sexual exploitation of a minor. He was a mature man in a position of authority over children; she was a girl who had been placed in his care. But in 1893 she was considered the one without morals and was disgraced.

The Vissers did not take M'Greet back. They were probably deeply embarrassed; M'Greet had proved herself to be her father's scandalous daughter. Everyone in Sneek would know of this wild young woman's dishonor. If they were unwilling to try to reform M'Greet further, who could blame them?

It is impossible to verify the story of M'Greet's love affair with Wybrandus Haanstra. In January of 2005 a representative of the school, now known as the Haanstraschool, confirmed that

Margaretha Zelle was on their list of former students. The school itself has no further information, not even archives that might shed light on her classes, grades, or reason for dismissal. The General Leiden Archive (Gemeente Archief Leiden) holds three linear meters of material from the Association for the Professional Training of Female Nursery School Teachers (Vereniging tot opleiding van bewaarschoolhouderessen) for the period 1867 to 1972, looked after by archivist Michiel van Halem. Mysteriously, there are no documents from the Haanstraschool for the period 1890–1900, the decade that includes M'Greet's attendance there. Were these documents deliberately lost or withheld because there was something in them that someone wished to conceal? Or is their lack of preservation another one of the odd twists of fate that haunt the story of the life of Mata Hari? There is no way to be certain.

After she left Leiden, M'Greet was shuffled off to yet another set of relatives, Mr. and Mrs. Taconis, in The Hague. She was seventeen, without family or prospects and with little to do. But The Hague was not as boring as small-town Friesland; it was the seat of the Parliament and boasted many chic shops and magnificent buildings. With its broad, tree-lined avenues, it had a much more cosmopolitan air than Leeuwarden. The scenic dunes and popular promenade at Scheveningen were enticingly near. The Hague was full of people returned from the Dutch colonies, who clustered together close to the Ministry of the Colonies. Their homes, their speech, and their possessions often recalled the *tempo doeloe*, the golden past when they lived like kings in the Dutch East Indies or Suriname. Above all, The Hague was full of colonial soldiers on leave.

Margaretha was young and restless and longing for romance and excitement. If she were to create in her mind a man who would restore her *tempo doeloe*, he would be an older man, a handsome man in uniform, like her father on his horse in the painting that hung in their home on Groote Kerkstraat in Leeuwarden. He would be a man who would treat her like a princess, a precious creature to be spoiled and indulged and petted.

Was she consciously looking for such a man? Almost certainly; girls of seventeen and eighteen with too much time on their hands often daydream about handsome lovers. A town full of young soldiers on leave in their best uniforms was a rich background for such fantasies. Did she realize she was seeking to re-create her father's magical love during her childhood? Probably not. But an adored and adoring father who disappears, as Adam Zelle did, can leave his daughter with a nearly insatiable longing for male attention.

The pity is that she found the man she sought.

Different Lives

WHEN M'GREET MET THE MAN she was to marry, he had spent as many years in the Dutch East Indies as she had lived on earth: seventeen. Their experiences during those seventeen years were utterly different.

Rudolf MacLeod was a hard man—hard-living and hard-drinking, sure of himself, and used to command. He was born into a proud Scottish family that had lived for generations in the Netherlands and produced several military officers. His father was a retired Dutch infantry captain; his uncle had reached the rank of general and been an adjutant to King Willem III. His mother, Dina Louisa, Baroness Sweerts de Landas, had been born into an impeccably aristocratic family that, sadly, had lost most of its fortune.

Rudolf was born March 1, 1856, which made him a full twenty years older than M'Greet. Following the family tradition, he entered a military academy, or *battalion d'instruction*, at Kampen in the Netherlands on August 15, 1872, when he was sixteen. He wanted to become an infantry officer and was an excellent cadet. In his first year, he was promoted twice: to brevet corporal and then corporal.

Like other cadets, Rudolf followed the ongoing war in the Atjeh province of the island of Sumatra, part of the Dutch East Indies where the Royal Dutch Indies Army (Koninklijk Nederlands Indisch Leger, or KNIL) played a major role. A man who had graduated at the end of Rudolf's first year at Kampen, Johannes van Heutsz, won great glory—medals and rapid promotions—for his heroism there. From a distance, and with the optimism of youth, Rudolf saw Atjeh as a promising post. The cadets at Kampen had no more idea than the Dutch government that the Atjeh War would prove to be the bloodiest, most viciously fought colonial war of the era. It lasted

Rudolf's portrait was taken at or near the time of his graduation from Kampen. Picture Collection Halwasse, Central Bureau of Genealogy, The Hague, The Netherlands. Originally published in Herinneringsalbum 1850–1890, copyright 1891, Kampen, The Netherlands.

for forty long years. At any point in its duration, about one-fifth of the total Indies army forces were fighting in Atjeh. Approximately 7,700 officers and men of the Indies army were killed; an even greater number died of disease aggravated by the fetid tropical conditions, poor food, heavy drinking, and frequenting of brothels. As well as decimating the army, the bitter fighting of the Atjeh War killed between 30,000 and 100,000 Indonesian "rebels," who viewed themselves as freedom fighters, before it ended in 1903.

The war had begun, ostensibly, because pirates controlled by Sultan Mahmoud Shah of Atjeh regularly attacked Dutch and British trading ships. More truly, though, the war was about establishing

Dutch control over the so-called Outer Districts of the Indonesian islands. Atjeh was a rich province that produced half the world's supply of pepper, and the sultan, who was believed to rule the province as if it were a nation, had firm religious and trading connections to Persia, India, and beyond. He was entirely too powerful for Dutch liking.

The "glorious war" that the young cadets at Kampen followed in the newspapers was far from glorious on the ground. The initial attack had come in 1873. A force of 3,000 Indies army soldiers had sailed from Batavia—now known as Jakarta—on March 22, intending to land in Atjeh and to take the fortified palace, or *kraton*, inhabited by the sultan. Neither the government nor General J. H. R. Kohler, the experienced officer in command of the troops, knew two crucial facts that predetermined the war's long duration and difficulty. First, Atjeh was lush and heavily vegetated, with terrain nearly impossible for marching, moving huge cannon, and transporting heavy wagons full of food, smaller artillery, and ammunition. Second, the sultan was assumed to be the leader of a state but was in fact only a figurehead at the head of a loose coalition of local groups in Atjeh. Thus, even when the army took the *kraton* and the sultan died, the rebellion did not end.

The Indies army warships had landed in Atjeh on April 8 and had met the guerilla fighters in fierce combat. Their artillery and rifles had proved to be not terribly effective against small bands of fighters armed with razor-sharp *klewangs* (curved Indonesian swords). The guerillas attacked by stealth out of the tall grass or struck without warning from the dark greenness of the forest. The Indies army had shelled and attacked the mosque and the *kraton* in Banda Atjeh but could not take either. Eighty Indies soldiers and officers, including General Kohler himself, had been killed outright in the battle. Pushed back, unable to grapple with an elusive foe with a much better knowledge of the terrain and local resources, the Indies troops had retreated under the command of Colonel van Daalen. In addition to the dead, there had been 408 wounded and an unrecorded but very large number of men ill with malaria, syphilis, dysentery, cholera, foot rot, beriberi, and other medical problems. The defeat had been bitter and humiliating for the Dutch, who vowed to return and root out the rebels. The rebels, who felt they were protecting their own territory from an invading force, had been equally determined to rout their enemies.

The second Atjeh expedition had left Batavia in November of 1873. Even before they had landed in Atjeh, Indies army soldiers were dying of cholera in large numbers. The commanding officer, General J. van Swieten, later wrote: "December 6, already 302 sufferers were being nursed, 133 of them died, and 169 were still being treated. In the 24 hours from December 5 to 6, 22 died." Nonetheless, the invasion had begun on December 9. Indies army soldiers had invaded Atjeh, armed with modern Beaumont rifles, two machine guns—useless under the field conditions—and eighteen pieces of artillery. Their intent was to end the Atjeh War once and for all. With a vast force of more than 8,000 soldiers, supported by 4,300 native servants, convicts, and coolies and 200 women, they had expected to accomplish their goal.

During the late nineteenth century, at least three-quarters of the enlisted men in the Indies army were Indonesian, some of them from other regions or tribes of Sumatra with traditional hostility to the Atjehers. Most of the officers were Dutch or European; they comprised about 20 percent of the total force. Some of the other nationalities in the Indies army included Germans, the odd African, and some Ambonese, natives of the island of Ambon, now part of the Molucca Islands of Indonesia. Both Africans and Ambonese were officially "European" through a bizarre legal quirk.

In the second expedition, the Indies army again had failed to take local conditions into account and had foolishly attacked in the middle of the rainy season. One cannon, a twelve-foot-long behemoth weighing 4,700 kilograms, had been brought all the way from the Netherlands by ship. Almost immediately, it had bogged down in the mud and could not be moved further.

During the rainy season in the Dutch East Indies, about 60 percent of deaths could be attributed to illness rather than fighting, and medical treatment was minimal. J. A. Moor sums up the situation recorded by army medical officers in their diaries and reports:

> *An expedition in the Outer Districts was primarily a desperate, often futile battle against nature and climate. Officers and men were pushed to their furthest limit, physically and mentally. Everyone who took part fell ill at least once, if not several times, and some remained more or less ill for the duration of the campaign. More of the military were disabled, temporarily or for good, because of the merciless physical conditions during a march or in camp, than because of actual combat.*

Fighting against native insurgents in the Dutch East Indies had relied on a scorched-earth policy. The army burned and destroyed everything: crops, *kampongs* (villages), granaries, and mosques. In 1862, M. van Adringa, a young health officer, described a military expedition in which he had taken part; though he had been in Borneo, the description is equally applicable to the fighting in Atjeh a decade later: "So every day we would get up steam and then halt to destroy everything that belonged to the enemy." Soon the annihilation did not stop at structures and tangible resources but included native men, women, and children. As the war ground on, the fighting grew more savage.

The *kraton* in Banda Atjeh had been finally captured on January

24, 1874, but the Atjeh resistance to Dutch rule did not end. The sultan had died—allegedly but improbably of cholera—on the day of capture. Instead of surrendering, as the Dutch had expected, the Atjehers had appointed another sultan and continued their incessant and ruthless raids on the Indies army. The army force had been decimated during the second Atjeh expedition as during the first. The second expedition had officially ended on April 20, 1874. A total of 1,052 men had died (almost 13 percent of the expeditionary force); another 764 were wounded, and an additional 877 had to be evacuated because of illness. Sixty-nine percent of the dead had fallen victim to disease.

The Indies army had settled into the heavily fortified *kraton,* which soon became known as the Kota Raja—city of the raja or sultan—as their base for a prolonged "pacification" of Atjeh. Their aim was "to remain in Atjeh for ever" in order to establish and secure Dutch sovereignty. The fighting had continued as the army marched inland, trying to root out the rebels. Contemporary photographs preserve scenes of the wholesale slaughter of Indonesian men, women, and children, their bloody bodies lying in twisted disarray in ruined *kampongs*. Even hardened officers sometimes had to turn away from what they and their men had done.

A letter from a young second lieutenant in the Atjeh War, Hendrikus Colijn, who later became prime minister of the Netherlands, showed graphically what the fighting was like:

> *I have seen a mother carrying a child of about 6 months old on her left arm, with a long lance in her right hand, who was running in our direction. One of our bullets killed the mother as well as the child. From now on we couldn't give any mercy, it was over. I did give orders to gather a group of nine women and three children who asked for mercy and they were shot all together. It was not a*

pleasant job, but doing anything else was impossible. Our soldiers
attacked them with pleasure with their bayonets. It was horrible.
I will stop reporting now.

No more could be written to send home to a loving wife who
could not understand the horrors of bitter battle.

As for the Indies rank-and-file soldier—known by the nickname
"Jan Fusilier"—he suffered dreadfully throughout the long Atjeh
War. His uniform was wool too thick and warm for the stifling,
humid climate; he was required to wear a heavy helmet known as a
shako; and he carried weighty weapons and a pack. If he had foot-
wear, which the native troops did not until 1908, it deteriorated almost immediately in wet conditions. The food was monotonous and
spoiled quickly. Jan Fusilier lived on rice, coffee, dried or salted
meat, dried fish, bacon, pepper, and vinegar, supplemented with
bread and tinned potatoes when he was in garrisons. Europeans were
issued a tot of gin each morning, and native soldiers were given arak
(a local liquor) or watered cognac. Invalids received "fortifying provisions," which included bouillon, arrowroot, cans of meat and vegetables, tea, and red wine.

After the taking of the Kota Raja, the war continued guerilla-
style. As the Indies army marched single file through the rice paddies, fields, and glowering forests, Atjeh warriors picked them off
one by one. During battles, the Indies army wounded were routinely abandoned to be retrieved later if they were still alive by the
time the native convicts, who served as orderlies to shorten their
sentences, got to them. The orderlies put the wounded on *tandus*—
homemade stretchers—and carried them from the front to the
medical station. There, young medical officers with an average age
of about twenty-seven, and no previous experience of warfare, did

what they could. They worked in the open air or in hastily constructed thatched huts, cleaning and bandaging wounds, removing bullets or amputating limbs, and administering opium or quinine if there was any. Field medical stations and even the military hospital that was set up at Kota Raja routinely ran out of these vital medicines.

Many of the sick and wounded died of infection, since antibiotics had not yet been invented, and the infections were compounded by poor sanitation, dysentery, and inadequate nutrition. Not only the enlisted men suffered. In the first half of the nineteenth century, only 50 percent of the medical officers survived their first five years. A mere 10 to 15 percent of officers lived long enough to achieve twenty years of service in the Dutch East Indies. Conditions did not improve markedly throughout the nineteenth century. Few of the horrors, hardships, and dangers of the Atjeh War were known to any but the soldiers themselves.

Rudolf graduated from Kampen on July 22, 1877, as a second lieutenant. A photograph taken of him at this time shows a very handsome young man, proud of his uniform with its new badges of rank. He looked at the camera with more than a touch of arrogance and great self-confidence.

After graduation, Rudolf accepted a posting to the Indies and sailed on the packet boat *Conrad* on November 3, 1877. After a brief stint in Padang, the twenty-one-year-old officer was plunged into the brutal hell of the Atjeh War. For the first time, he came face-to-face with war as it was fought instead of war learned from books in Kampen.

The men he commanded and lived with were either native troops or the roughest sort of Dutchman who had been pressed into service, often while drunk, in Harderwijk in the Netherlands. The colonial recruiting depot there was colloquially known as the sink-hole or sewer of Europe. The men recruited in Harderwijk were rarely better than the place. Jan Fusilier was crude, ill educated, often drunken, and an incurable gambler. Yet if properly led, he was a ferocious and loyal warrior. Discipline was harsh and immediate. Officers did not show fear or indecision lest they lose the respect of their men.

Rudolf soon learned to dispense orders without hesitation, to react immediately to the terrifying warning *"Orang Atjeh datang!"* (The Atjehers are coming!) and never, ever to flinch. He did as he was told and badgered, bullied, and inspired his men into doing as he told them.

Soon after arriving, Rudolf fought at Samalanga, one of the bloodiest and most notorious battles of the war. The rebels were holed up in a native fort, or *benteng,* surrounded by earthworks and bamboo palisades and too strongly held to be taken. The Indies troops retreated and then returned with more men and cannon. What they did not know was that the *benteng* was connected by underground tunnels to a second fort, from which more rebel troops had been funneled in. It was a sharp defeat for the Dutch, killing about 30 Indies soldiers and wounding another 150.

The commanding officer, General Karel van der Heyden, was wounded twice during the battle, once by a bullet that grazed his forehead and again by a bullet that entered his left eye. As soon as his wounds were bandaged, he returned to the front line to lead his men. Van der Heyden's act of raw heroism was commemorated in a famous painting now on display in the Bronbeek Museum in Arnhem, the Netherlands, which houses both a museum devoted to the Indies and an old soldiers' home.

Van der Heyden was a brilliant soldier but an inflexible man. An observer described the way he left those around him

stunned by the rapidity of his decisions and his incredible energy.
The General does not recognize any obstacles, he said to me, he
knows nothing but to advance. The officers who can be checked
[delayed] do not last long in his army. It can be seen when he is
stopped because an order was not carried out, about which he was
not informed at the time: then he is terrible! Otherwise, he is full of
heart, he loves his men, and also loves those who are in fear of him.
One sees large tears roll down his cheeks when he visits the hospi-
tal, which he frequents, and where the wounded or ill soldiers call
him familiarly and ask him to come to their bedside.

Rudolf fought in Atjeh for seven long years, until 1884. He earned
the Atjeh expeditionary cross for military actions between 1873 and
1880 and was promoted to first lieutenant at the end of 1881. His
career was going well.

In the early 1880s, Rudolf was one of the officers engaged in trying to eliminate the enemy from a zone surrounding the Kota Raja.
After a certain rough control had been established by 1882, a strategy known as the "concentrated line" was put into effect in Atjeh.
Kota Raja would be encircled by a series of sixteen forts, linked by
good roads or tramlines, thus demarcating a zone that the Indies
army hoped to control. First the roads had had to be constructed
and the forts had had to be built, miserable labor that was carried
out in the stifling heat, with the fear of guerilla attacks.

Eventually more than 5,059 square kilometers were encircled,
but eradicating native resistance within the circle was very difficult. Small mobile units consisting of one or two officers and fifteen to seventeen men were sent out on patrol for two to four
weeks at a time with orders to search out and kill rebel forces.
These patrols carried all their supplies with them from the garrison. If tropical diseases and rancid food didn't kill them, they

were often picked off by invisible attackers. It was grueling and disheartening work.

Rudolf was transferred out of Atjeh in 1884 and sent to Magelang in Java and then to Banjermassan in Borneo, where he spent five years. His career then became choppy and uncertain, with many transfers and no promotions. For reasons unexplained in his military records, in 1889 he was transferred from one battalion to another on May 4 and promptly transferred to yet another battalion on May 23. These were the first two of four rapid transfers within the space of a year. In May 1890 he received two years' leave of absence to return to Europe, but his leave was retracted "by request" a little over a month later. Why? Did he suddenly recover—or did he hope for a more congenial posting? A mere nine days after the retraction he was transferred again to become adjutant to yet another battalion. That posting proved no more suitable, because he was transferred again two months later, on August 26.

This record suggests that he made himself unwelcome rather quickly at each posting. He stayed nowhere very long and was not promoted, in contrast to his marked successes during his first six years in the Dutch East Indies. Something was blocking Rudolf's advancement, quite possibly something of his own doing. He admitted freely to drinking, gambling, and going with women. Was he living so wild a life that his superiors thought him unsuitable for further promotion? Was he too harsh on his men, or not harsh enough? For seven years, Rudolf's career stagnated.

In 1890 Rudolf returned to action in Atjeh and then his record changed for the better. During his second year back in Atjeh, he was promoted to captain (April 7, 1892); on December 9 he was awarded the Officer's Cross, a medal for long patriotic service. Against considerable odds, he had survived twenty years of service since his cadet days, much of it in vicious combat. He always claimed

he had deserved a Willem's Cross but that his superiors had "finagled" not to give it to him.

Rudolf's situation in 1892 was vastly different from M'Greet's.
By 1892, her father had declared bankruptcy, her parents had separated and then divorced scandalously, and her mother had died. She
had been shuffled off to reluctant relatives. At the time of Rudolf's
promotion to captain, M'Greet was at the teacher training school in
Leiden, seducing or being seduced by Heer Haanstra. She longed to
experience life, to have romances and adventures; Rudolf had seen
too much of the dark side of life and had had altogether too many
adventures to indulge in romantic fantasies at that point.

Yet it would be wrong to assume that Rudolf spent his years in
the Indies without female companionship. He coyly asserted to one
writer that during his bachelor years in the Dutch East Indies he
had never gone with native women but that he had loved women
often and very much. Rudolf almost certainly had not had affairs
with "Pures," or full-blooded European women, because they were
in very short supply in the Indies before 1900. Women comprised
less than 20 percent of the European-born population in the entire
Indies. The sex ratio among Europeans was even less favorable to
romance in Sumatra, where Rudolf was posted most of the time.
Between 1877 and 1883, women comprised only about 14 percent of
the European-born population in Sumatra, and during his second
posting there in 1890–1893, the percentage of European women
was still only about 26 percent. The odds of finding an attractive
and unmarried European woman to woo were very long. Romanc-
ing married ones almost always led to great trouble.

If Rudolf followed the normal pattern for Indies officers, he took
a mistress of Indonesian or mixed Indonesian-Dutch ancestry, a
population known as mestizos, *métis,* "half-castes," or most commonly Indisches or Indos. Until 1895, nearly half of the soldiers in

the Indies—most of whom were officers—lived with Javanese or Indo concubines. Those without concubines were almost invariably enlisted men who found the salary too low to support even a native "wife." For officers like Rudolf, a mistress was an officially acknowledged privilege of rank.

The Indies army had many official regulations pertaining to long-term concubines and prostitutes. Prostitution and concubinage were regarded by the military as necessary evils and, in some circumstances, conveniences. This official stance had an enormous effect on Indies society in general because, until 1895, most of the male Europeans in the Dutch East Indies were in the military.

The army had formally recognized the right of a soldier to have a native or half-caste mistress, known as a *nyai* or *muntji*, in 1836. By 1872, military regulations permitted formal, legal marriage for officers or noncommissioned officers (NCOs) but only with permission; marriage was absolutely prohibited for men below the rank of sergeant major. Yet sexual activity was considered necessary for a man's health, since the government was convinced that the hot climate and spicy food of the Indies increased a man's libido. Prostitutes living in the barracks were common. The military was not opposed to the practice of concubinage, for their statistics showed that fewer men who cohabited with *nyais* were infected with venereal diseases (0.7 percent) compared with men who went with prostitutes (6.64 percent). Similarly, men who cohabited with *nyais* were more rarely punished for drunkenness (14.4 percent) versus those who frequented prostitutes (40.9 percent).

One government official wrote: "The moral standards of the soldier can be so elevated that his conduct is excellent and he refrains from drink. Yet no matter what height he may attain the woman remains indispensable to him, and thus the degree of abstinence is more a question of natural inclination and financial circumstances than moral standards."

"Unnatural vice," or homosexuality, was feared by the government more greatly than use of prostitutes, the infection of soldiers with venereal disease, or the birth of children out of wedlock, so there were army brothels. The belief was that the girls in military brothels were less likely to have syphilis than prostitutes elsewhere. They ranged in age from about twelve to perhaps thirty-five or forty. The youthfulness of the concubines is not so shocking in light of the age of legitimate marriage in the Indies, which was fourteen or fifteen. At the end of the nineteenth century, a single visit to the brothel cost Jan Fusilier more than one quarter of the pay he received every five days.

European NCOs whose salaries were higher than enlisted men's might set up a regular relationship with an Indo concubine, who then lived in the barracks with him in a sort of marriage. Theoretically a European NCO might be given permission to marry, but this was very uncommon. To get some privacy within the barracks, both European lower ranks and native soldiers with concubines created "rooms" by hanging cloths on cord or wire to separate their bed from the others. In 1888, only a little more than 1 percent of the European soldiers (mostly officers) in the Indies army were married.

A soldier normally handed over at least half of his pay packet and his rations to his woman, who somehow managed to produce better and tastier meals than the canteen. This was so usual that setting up "women's sheds" where the wives and concubines cooked for their men was a priority when a new camp was built. The children resulting from these relationships generally slept underneath the platform on which the couples' straw mattress rested. Both concubines and

children could eat in the mess halls, and in the later part of the nineteenth century, schools were established on some military bases for
the mestizo children fathered by the soldiers. The lower ranks were
inspected weekly for signs of venereal disease; their concubines were
inspected only when the soldiers showed symptoms. Unfortunately,
there was no effective cure for syphilis until 1922, though treatments
involving doses of mercury and mercury compounds were routinely
given to "cure" syphilis.

As an officer, Rudolf lived in much better quarters than the
lower ranks, usually in a small house of his own or in a small house
divided down the middle and shared with another bachelor officer.
Like Indies planters, civil servants, or merchants who had reached
high enough status and income, most Indies officers had a *nyai*—a
term that was politely translated as "housekeeper" but that was understood to include sexual access. A *nyai* always addressed her man
as *tuan,* a term of respect that translated roughly into "lord" or
"master." For discretion's sake, an officer did not take his *nyai* out in
public, and she was rarely seen when he was entertaining fellow
Europeans at home. As a well-known novel of Dutch colonial life
expressed the situation:

> For that [discretion] is prescribed by adat [traditional law or cus-
> tom]. The white tuan may keep a nyai but officially nobody should
> know about it. That would be too indiscreet and would shock the
> few white women who are here. For a man's prestige, too, it is desir-
> able to keep silence on that score; a white man may keep a black
> [native] servant girl, but strictly speaking ought not to sleep with
> her in one bed.

Whether she was seen or not, a *nyai*'s influence on the home was
obvious to all in terms of the beauty of its furnishings, the quality of

its food, the cleanliness and good repair of her man's clothing, and the quietness and obedience of the servants. *Nyais* ran the kitchens in the officers' quarters at home and received field rations when they accompanied their men on field duty to cook for them, do their laundry, and nurse them.

Having a *nyai* was considered the most effective way for a European man to learn local languages and customs, to the point that Indo mistresses were known as "walking dictionaries." Plantation owners openly favored their European employees' taking *nyais*. In a well-known fictional treatment of plantation life in Sumatra, a newly arrived Dutchman is urged by his superior: "And now, hurry up; you should learn Malay, even better if you have Javanese too, and there's no better classroom than the square with the white mosquito net [the bed]."

Some *nyais* had children by their masters, but other men demanded that their *nyais* have abortions if they became pregnant. Even a *nyai* of long standing had no legal rights whatsoever; she could be dismissed at the man's whim at any time. And if her *tuan* legally recognized the children of the union, their mother had no further rights to them. The *tuan* could break with her and keep the children with him, could send them to a boarding school or back to Europe for an education without consulting their mother. When soldiers left the Indies, most simply abandoned their *nyais* and children to be absorbed back into the *kampong*. Others tried to provide for their *nyais* and offspring by turning them over to another soldier, in hopes that he would treat them kindly. A very few men sent or took light-skinned Indo children back to Holland for an education, but their mothers were rarely taken to Europe. Some *nyais*, considered extraordinarily faithful, waited patiently for their *tuans* to return from home leave, which was often a year or more in duration.

A *nyai*'s existence was rarely recorded in official documents unless her *tuan* legally recognized her child. As Lieutenant Colonel J. I. de Rochemont characterized the situation, "The *nyai* are numerous and belong to all strata of our Indo-European society. Not only the soldiers in the barracks, but also most of the generals, field and other officers, governors of the territories, residents, senior and other officials, have a *nyai* if they are not married."

Thus, though there is no documentary proof that Rudolf took a *nyai* during his unmarried years in the Dutch East Indies, his situation would be extraordinary if he had not. He was a young and virile officer in the Indies, and he liked women. Since he asserted that he never touched native women, the overwhelming probability is that his *nyai* was an Indo woman.

Circumstantial evidence of the influence of a wise *nyai* can be read into the changing pattern of Rudolf's career. A long-term *nyai* might have helped Rudolf achieve rapid promotion and success when he was first in Sumatra between 1877 and 1884 by encouraging him, advising him subtly, keeping him from excessive gambling or drinking, and making his home comfortable. Then in 1884, when he was transferred to Borneo, there was no real possibility of taking his *nyai* with him there; to insist on doing so would have been unseemly and embarrassing. In Borneo, Rudolf's career foundered. When he was transferred back to Sumatra for the period 1890–1894, his success resumed, as if he had come once again under the beneficial influence of a good *nyai* who managed his household well, kept him content and out of trouble. Of course, other explanations can be generated for the changes in his military record and confirming evidence is lacking, but the likelihood remains strong that a man of his tastes and personality performed better with a happy home life.

On January 9, 1894, Rudolf was granted two years' home leave, with continued employment, "because of illness." He left the Indies

five months later, a little more than three weeks after an official document was issued ensuring his "promotion during leave." He probably had not delayed his departure waiting for the assurance of
promotion but was simply too ill to travel. Similar prolonged periods
of in-hospital convalescence in the Indies prior to being sent home
are recorded for others. On June 27 he was carried on a stretcher
onto the steamship *Prinses Marie* for the journey home.

Precisely what illness Rudolf suffered from is not recorded in
surviving documents. All medical records from the Indies during
this period were destroyed in 1900. According to MacLeod family
legend, Rudolf suffered from diabetes and rheumatism, but this
story may not be accurate.

Diabetes was spoken of in the nineteenth century, but there was
neither a reliable means of diagnosing the disease nor an effective
treatment for it until decades later. One of the usual nineteenth-
century treatments for diabetics was to restrict their carbohydrate
intake and put them on a high-fat, high-protein diet—not at all
what Rudolf's military life permitted. If Rudolf had what is now
recognized as diabetes, his life was rampant with risk factors that
would have increased its severity: he was a hard drinker; he smoked;
his diet was heavy with starchy carbohydrates and low on protein,
vegetables, and fruits; his meals occurred at irregular intervals; he
spent many hours marching through tropical terrain under conditions ripe for contracting foot funguses or infections, which often
lead to amputation in diabetics; he was unable to maintain good
hygiene under field conditions; and he was at constant risk of other
illnesses that might aggravate diabetes, such as malaria, cholera,
typhoid, typhus, and tropical parasites.

The facts of Rudolf's life do not suggest severe diabetes suffered
under extremely unfavorable circumstances. Though Rudolf took
extended medical leave to return to the Netherlands, he did so only

once in seventeen years, and by the time he retired from the Indies army, he had survived twenty years' service in the Indies, a rare event. There is no indication that he ever had a leg, foot, or toes amputated, nor was his life span noticeably shortened: he died at the age of seventy-two at home. The sum total of evidence suggests strongly that Rudolf did not have diabetes as it is recognized now.

However, along with the more familiar symptoms of diabetes related to excessive thirst and the passing of "sweet" urine due to inadequate sugar metabolism, the disease also often commonly provokes joint problems, stiffness, and pain, such as rheumatoid arthritis, osteoarthritis, and osteopenia.

The other condition from which family legend says that Rudolf suffered was "rheumatism": a vaguely defined ailment involving joint and bone pain, stiffness, or similar orthopedic problems. In fact, the joint symptoms that Rudolf suffered from may have been the reason that the family believed he suffered from diabetes. Rheumatism was common among military men. One study of medical complaints in the Indies army concluded: "Everyone, including the few who survived for more than twenty years, suffered more or less from complaints of the liver, frequent stools, rheumatism, etc., and everyone remained susceptible to acute illnesses."

Symptoms of rheumatism as it was understood in the nineteenth century included "pain in the bones, joints, rheumatic complaints, arthritis." All of these are well-documented symptoms of early stages of syphilis. Could venereal disease have been the cause of Rudolf's medical leave and the true source of his medical problems?

Though specific medical records pertaining to Rudolf are not preserved, information about Dutch military hospitals in the Indies tells us about medical ailments in the Indies army in general. Initially hospital wards were organized into two types: W (wounded) and F (fever). In the last half of the nineteenth century, the diseases that killed the largest number of European patients in the Indies were, in order of severity, dysentery/diarrhea (28–35 percent), leprosy (14–22 percent), and malaria (3–5 percent). Malaria constituted 90–95 percent of the "fevers" reported in medical records concerning the European Indies population. Recurrent or chronic malaria is an extremely debilitating disease that caused lifelong ill health in many Europeans who had spent years in the tropics, and it is highly likely that Rudolf suffered from it. Rudolf was not wounded but he almost certainly had fevers.

Other major causes of illness among Indies soldiers are shown in the designations of the wards that were added later to military hospitals: V (venereal), O (ophthalmic)—which might include syphilitics who suffered from iritis or irritation of the iris—and C (contagious), which would have included leprosy.

Statistically, syphilis or some form of venereal disease must be considered a strong possibility for the source of Rudolf's medical leave, aside from the fact that its symptoms coincide with those of "rheumatism" and diabetes as it was then known. This hypothesis has never been suggested previously, although circumstantial evidence— which is presented in chronological order in this book—suggests strongly that he suffered from syphilis. This scenario would explain much that has remained mysterious about the married life of the woman who became Mata Hari.

Syphilis was the third most common cause of European soldiers' being invalided home from the Indies, surpassed only by malaria and nervous breakdown. Army commandant de Bruyn identified the two greatest enemies of battleworthiness in the Indies army as alcoholism and venereal disease, of which syphilis was the most common. Syphilis was "rampant" in the Indies and was twice as common in towns with naval or army garrisons as in rural towns. The impression of the high prevalence of syphilis in the Indies is borne out by hard statistical data. For example, in one hospital in Surabaya, where there was a large naval garrison, an average of 127 prostitutes were treated for venereal disease every day between July 1, 1868, and the end of June 1869. During a later four-year span (1909–1913) for which there are good military records, an astonishing 29.4 to 35.9 percent of the European Indies army soldiers were treated for "venereal disease" and another 10 to 14 percent were specifically treated for "syphilis," the distinction between the two not always being clear in the records. Thus, it is plausible that Rudolf contracted syphilis during his first tour of duty in the Indies, a likelihood rendered still more plausible because he was a known womanizer and because the symptoms of the diseases he was publicly alleged to have correspond closely to those of syphilis.

Rudolf might also have suffered from beriberi. This vitamin-deficiency disease was first recognized in 1652 in a young man recently returned from the Indies. Early signs of beriberi are irritability, weakness, fatigue, bowel irritation, numbness or twinges, burning sensations, and aches in the hands, feet, and legs—all symptoms that could be attributed to "rheumatism," syphilis, or many other ailments. Patients with advanced beriberi become either paralyzed in the hands or feet or suffer extreme edema of the limbs. Sufferers may die of heart failure caused by the deterioration of the cardiac muscle.

The number of cases of beriberi in the Indies increased suddenly and dramatically starting in the 1870s, while Rudolf was stationed there. In 1886, the alarmed Dutch government made determining the cause of beriberi one of the main charges of its medical research institute in Batavia. Finally, in 1896, Charles Eijkman was able to demonstrate that beriberi was caused by a deficiency of vitamin B, or thiamine, related to the processing of rice, the staple food of the Indies. The rice-polishing machines that had been brought to the Indies in the 1870s removed the outer husk of the rice where the thiamine was found. Thus the technological shift to mechanized rice processing was directly to blame for the epidemic rise in beri-beri. Both locals and Europeans found polished rice tastier and preferred its whiter appearance, so polished rice was what the military bought, if it was available. Rudolf might well have been among the many soldiers who suffered from beriberi, but the fact that his illness persisted for years after he returned to the Netherlands mitigates against this diagnosis.

When Rudolf was carried helplessly onto the *Prinses Marie* to go home to the Netherlands in 1894, he took with him seventeen years of hard experience as an officer in the Dutch East Indies. He had led his rough troops into some of the worst battles of the Atjeh War and had seen his men die of bloody wounds and insidious diseases. He had made difficult decisions and developed a self-protective vigilance against sneak attack in the terrible guerilla war he fought under grueling conditions. He had marched long hours in the monsoon rain and enervating heat over rough terrain so thickly vegetated that a man hiding five feet away was invisible.

Rudolf was a soldier's soldier. Even on leave, he always wore his uniform and insisted that subordinate soldiers he passed in the street salute him properly. He still spoke "soldier's language" after returning to the Netherlands. The manners and polish he had learned as a child were so foreign to him after he returned to the Netherlands that he actually told a salacious story in the presence of ladies, not realizing how offensive it would be. Yet in the Indies, his was not a purely masculine world. He whiled away happy hours in the arms of one or more Indo *nyais* who kept his quarters clean and pleasant, cooked his food, taught him languages, and warmed his bed. He also contracted diseases that made him too weak to fight any longer, that gave him fever and skin rashes and caused his joints and limbs to ache unbearably.

In 1894, his future bride was a mere seventeen years old to Rudolf's thirty-nine. He had spent years in the jungles of the Indies, whereas she had traveled no farther than the relatively short distance from Leeuwarden to Sneek, and then to Leiden and The Hague. He was a sexually experienced man, who had wooed and apparently bedded a number of women; despite M'Greet's affair with her headmaster in Leiden, she had little experience of men or life. Rudolf was cynical, confident, and tough, a true officer. He had faced and beaten death time and again; and now that he was back in the Netherlands, he wanted more than ever to enjoy drinking parties and attractive women.

M'Greet knew nothing of bloody ambushes, desperate night marches, vicious fighting, malaria, or syphilis; she thought being forced to live with prim relatives as a poor relation was suffering. She was in an odd way innocent. She still expected a magical love to transform her world. Still she knew instinctively how to flirt and please a man. At seventeen, M'Greet was deeply romantic, frivolous, and terribly vain. She longed for experience—to burst out of the strict world of propriety and regulation so she could have fun— and she craved admiration from an older man.

She loved officers and Rudolf was an officer to the core. He loved pretty, flirtatious women and she was one.

Their meeting was disastrous for both.

Object *Matrimony*

RUDOLF ARRIVED IN HOLLAND on August 14, 1894, and after a few weeks in the hospital went to his sister Louise's flat in Amsterdam to recuperate. Soon he was bored, though not yet entirely well. Then he met J. T. Z. de Balbian Verster, a journalist working for the *News of the Day*. De Balbian Verster was anxious to talk to officers recently returned from the East Indies who would be able to interpret the reports that were filtering back to the Netherlands about fierce fighting on Lombok, the island east of Bali. Rudolf had never visited Lombok, but he had many years of experience in the Indies and was very knowledgeable and opinionated. He and the journalist became friends and drinking companions.

In 1894, Lombok was causing almost as much trouble as Atjeh province on Sumatra. Lombok was a semi-independent kingdom of largely Muslim tribal peoples who had been ruled for two centuries by Hindu Balinese rajahs. These differences meant that the Hindu crown prince in charge of the province of Mataram treated the locals harshly, leading to riots, rebellions, and appeals by the tribesmen for Dutch intervention. This unrest gave the Dutch a perfect excuse to invade and take control of the whole island.

In March of 1894, an Indies army force led by General Vetter landed at Ampenan on Lombok's west coast. The troops marched east into the provincial capital, leaving massive destruction in their wake. When they arrived in the capital, they found that the prince had committed suicide. Theoretically the Indies army had invaded only to protect the tribes from the prince's cruelties, and he would dispense no more. But the army was there, and the opportunity to establish Dutch control and drive out the Balinese aristocracy was irresistible. Realizing the Dutch had no intention of leaving the island without conquest, the Balinese forces attacked at night, killing more than 250 soldiers and wounding many more.

The massacre was a shocking blow to Dutch forces and Dutch pride. In the Indies and at home, the Dutch newspapers dubbed this battle the "Treason of Lombok" and demanded revenge. Finally, ten thousand Indies army troops attacked Cakranegara, where the rajah resided. He was captured and banished to Batavia, where he died in the spring of 1895. The rest of the Balinese rulers committed ritual suicide by facing the Dutch troops weaponless and dressed in their best white clothing. Rudolf, like most career soldiers, was shocked by the Treason of Lombok and proud of the great victory won at Cakranegara, which helped erase the stain of the sneak attack.

By the beginning of 1895, Rudolf was restless. He and de Balbian Verster met often at the stylish American Café on the Leidseplein overlooking the canal, under the shade of the great sycamore trees. During the day they'd drink coffee and discuss the news; at night they'd drink alcohol and carouse with other friends. Though his health was still intermittently poor, Rudolf was looking for something exciting and entertaining to do.

Half jesting, de Balbian Verster placed an ad in *The News of the Day* on Rudolf's behalf:

Officer on home leave from Dutch East Indies would like to meet a girl of pleasant character—object matrimony.

Marriage was not such a ridiculous proposition as it might seem. Rudolf liked women, very much. If he was promoted to major—and his promotion was more or less guaranteed—then when he returned to the Indies, he could expect a prestigious posting. As a senior officer, he would be expected to entertain. Certainly neither military nor civilian society could be entertained with a *nyai* as one's hostess; there were even rumors that men known to live with *nyais* might no longer be promoted as quickly as others.

The attitude toward *nyais* was beginning to change. Ever since 1888 when the minister for the colonies, Levinus T. Keuchenis, had declared that concubinage must be gradually done away with, it was clear that poor Jan Fusilier would soon no longer enjoy his most basic comfort. The disapprobation for soldiers who kept concubines was growing stronger every day. If Rudolf were to get a straitlaced superior officer, keeping a *nyai* would be out of the question unless he chose to give up on his ambitions. The best choice for Rudolf was to acquire a European wife; second best would be a beautiful Indo wife, but half-castes were still greatly looked down upon in many circles. Yes, a pretty Dutch wife would be a very useful accessory to Rudolf.

Though the Indies army recognized a senior officer's need for a wife, he was still required to obtain permission before marrying, a regulation apparently intended to ensure that the wife of a senior officer had a suitable social background and was presentable in society. Lower-class wives, such as the enlisted men or NCOs might wed, were viewed by the high command with a sort of disgust. Such wives, they feared, would provide endless difficulties within the camps: more expense on passages to and from Europe; more complaints about food and conditions; more children who would require an education; greater need for pensions for widows and orphans; and more immorality, since the opportunities for adultery and jealousy were abundant in the Indies, where men heavily outnumbered women. For enlisted men or NCOs, *nyais* were a better choice—far more tractable—and they could always be shipped back to the *kampong* if they made trouble. For any soldier of any rank, contracting an unapproved marriage would bring official disapproval and would not entitle the man to the usual increase in pay and upgrade in housing.

There were two great questions for Rudolf. The first was, where was he to find a wife? Like many officers home on leave after long service in the colonies, he had virtually no acquaintances in Holland anymore, much less among suitable young ladies. He called upon the families of a few of his fellow officers, perhaps hoping to meet an attractive younger sister, but his manners had deteriorated during his military service in the Indies. Finding a suitable prospect for marriage was not an easy task.

The second question was, was Rudolf "fit to marry"? If he had contracted syphilis during his years in the Indies, he would infect a young, virginal wife who was innocent of any licentiousness. While only a pure girl would suit Rudolf's purposes in marrying, if he infected her with syphilis and it became known, he would have done himself irreparable social damage. Catching syphilis—the pox— was recognized to be the consequence of leading an immoral life, and there was a widespread dread in Victorian society that an entirely innocent wife (or occasionally husband) could be infected because of the sins of her partner.

Attempting to diagnose syphilis or any other disease in the late nineteenth century was a task requiring considerable skills. There was no laboratory test for syphilis at the time, and the pox was notorious for its varied symptoms and manifestations. The disease was known as "the Great Imitator" following a speech to the British Medical Society in 1879 by Jonathan Hutchinson. In addition to the chancres or sores that were often the first sign of syphilis, recorded symptoms included "rheumatism, arthritis, gout, eczema, hypertension, epilepsy, headache, stomachache, jaundice, mania, depression, dementia, schizophrenia, deafness, 'nerves,' also smallpox, measles, psoriasis, lupus vulgaris, and iritis."

Diagnosing syphilis in a historical figure from this period is, of course, even more uncertain. In her book *Pox: Genius, Madness, and the Mysteries of Syphilis*, Deborah Hayden offers a series of ten clues that suggest someone had syphilis. Rudolf showed at least four of these: he was known to engage in high-risk sexual behavior and visit prostitutes; he had high fevers and chronic relapsing illness, accompanied by baldness; he said he intended not to marry; he visited numerous physicians; he had a long list of ailments including pain in the joints, rheumatism, and arthritis. Thus, there is considerable circumstantial evidence that Rudolf had caught syphilis as a young soldier in the Dutch East Indies, as so many did. Could he, then, marry?

The wisdom and ethicality of a man's marrying once he had been diagnosed with syphilis was a subject of intense discussion in medical circles in the late 1800s. Alfred Fournier, who in 1857 had published *Research on the Contagion of the Chancre*, was the first professor to hold the chair of syphilogy and dermatology that had been created at the Hospital of Saint-Louis in Paris, the leading center for the treatment and study of venereal disease. In 1890 he addressed the vexatious question of whether or not a man with syphilis might marry following a "cure" with mercury treatments and a period ranging from six months to two or three years without symptoms. He wrote, "So yes, a hundred times yes, you can marry after you have had the pox, and the consequences of such a marriage can be, medically speaking, entirely happy ones."

But prolonged treatment was seen as an essential prerequisite to such a happy marriage.

Another of the foremost medical texts on syphilis in the latter half of the nineteenth century was Paul Diday's *Treatise on Syphilis in New-Born Children and Infants at the Breast*. Diday pronounced unflinchingly, "An individual actually affected with primary or constitutional syphilis, and who has not undergone any general treatment, ought to be declared unfit for marriage."

He offered the following rules of thumb for advising patients who wished to marry. Those who had had only simple chancres and who had experienced no recurrence for eight months were marriageable. Those who had had indurated chancres and been treated with mercury for three or four months were also marriageable *if* there had been no recurrence of general symptoms and *if* he waited to marry until six to eight months after the induration. For those with "constitutional symptoms, however slight and however treated," marriage was unsafe unless the patient underwent a new course of mercury treatment (if the first had been incomplete), unless at least two years passed without any new symptoms, or unless he modified his constitution, through various exertions and sanitary changes.

The all-important treatment that rendered a man fit for marriage involved compounds of mercury, which were not only ineffectual but poisonous if administered in too-large doses. Mercury compounds did not cure syphilis, though they were believed to do so because syphilis so often goes into long latent stages where there are no overt symptoms.

Was Rudolf such a cad that he would marry while he knew he

was still infected with syphilis? It is most unlikely. But more than a year had elapsed since the beginning of his medical leave in January 1894 and the appearance of the matrimonial ad in March 1895. There was plenty of time for him to have been treated with mercury compounds for three or four months, as prescribed, and then passed more than the suggested eight months without symptoms. He would be entirely entitled to believe he was cured and "fit to marry"—if only the newspaper ad produced some pretty and willing young women.

Rudolf received fifteen or sixteen letters during the two weeks following the appearance of the matrimonial ad in *The News of the Day*. Most were forwarded from the newspaper office by de Balbian Verster, but the last two came directly to Rudolf, as his friend was out of town. One of these two was from a lovely young girl who had the wit to include a photograph of herself: Margaretha Zelle. Something about that particular letter struck Rudolf, perhaps the photograph and the elegant copperplate handwriting that bespoke the girl's expensive education. He wrote back, saying he wanted to meet her. It is unclear whether he answered any of the other letters he received.

The correspondence with Margaretha continued, and his fascination with this young girl grew. He called her Griet or Greta, contractions of Margaretha, and she called him Johnie, a family nickname. He confided to de Balbian Verster at some point that "now he had an affair that was enormous," indulging in hyperbole as was typical of him.

Rudolf's poor health prevented his meeting with Griet on several occasions; he was still plagued with fevers and "rheumatism" and was under a doctor's care for his ailments. After a few letters, Griet boldly offered to come to meet him, writing "I know well it is not *'comme il faut'* [proper social behavior] but we find ourselves in a special case, no?" She boldly signed herself "your future little wife" in her letters. The two arranged to meet at the Rijksmuseum in Amsterdam on March 24, 1895.

Their attraction was sexual, mutual, and very strong. In his fine soldier's uniform, with his erect posture, square shoulders, and splendid moustache, Rudolf was a handsome man. From the time of her childhood, Griet had always found strongly built men very attractive, and she favored officers. As she said much later in her life,

> *Those who are not officers . . . do not interest me. An officer is another being, a sort of artist, living outdoors with sparkles on his arms in a seductive uniform. Yes, I have had many lovers, but it is the beautiful soldiers, brave, always ready for battle and, while waiting, always sweet and gallant. For me, the officer forms a race apart. I have never loved any but officers.*

Griet was striking rather than pretty, with flirtatious dark eyes, an exotic "dark" complexion (by Dutch standards), and luxuriant black or very dark brown hair. She was tall and elegant, with magnificently regal posture. She had an extraordinary personal charm.

After that first meeting, their future was sealed. She signed her next letter to Rudolf, "your future little wife who loves you already." The cliché of a whirlwind romance is exemplified by the truth in this case: they became formally engaged a mere six days after first meeting. In the Netherlands in the nineteenth century, a formal engagement legally bound the affianced to each other. Had Rudolf backed out of the marriage thereafter, he would have been liable for a breach-of-promise suit.

There was no chance of such a suit. Rudolf was thoroughly, crazily in love, and so was Griet. Soon after their engagement was announced, Griet began to address her letters "My dearest Johnie" and filled them with pet names such as "my sweet angel" and "my treasure." Her signature shifted, becoming "your loving little wife," which, with the daring content of some letters, suggests that the couple were physically intimate. Though few of Rudolf's letters are preserved, Griet's show clearly that she was answering his inquiries and suggestions. In a letter in late March she wrote in a romantic passion,

> *You ask me if I am longing to do crazy things? Well, Johnie, rather ten times than only one. Go on, you know, in several weeks I will be your wife. What luck that we both have the same ardent temperament. No, I do not believe either that all these pleasures can ever end. Yes, my dear, I wish very much to wear everything that you find beautiful. The rose silk suits me very well, because I am so brown[-skinned] and have dark hair. Surely, I find these nightgowns beautiful.*
>
> *Pardon my ignorance, but tell me, should such a chemise end above or below the knee? I will make sure that they are very low cut . . . ! And the underdrawers, should they be the same style as my white ones? . . .*
>
> *Ah! How we will play! . . . Be amorous, my treasure, for I will be also, and be strong when I come [to you].*

A few days later, she wrote to him saying she was uneasy about their rapid decision to marry. Was it wise? He replied on March 30, dated "the day of our engagement": "I thank you for your very sweet letter but I'm sorry you have any doubts. Let these go and trust in me completely, trust in me like a rock, and I promise you on my word of honor as a Dutch Indies officer that I will love you and protect you without reservations, my darling."

She wrote a few days later: "Do not believe that I am indisposed,

I go exactly by the date [I am very regular in my menstrual periods] and naturally it is past by several days. You know you can ask me whatever you wish. . . . I dare to hope that once married, I will respond to your beautiful expectations in my chemise of rose silk."

She dreamed in writing that they would make a beautiful, magnificent couple, that she would be exquisite in her lovely wedding gown.

The correspondence was so suggestive and so intimate that Griet was harshly scolded by her aunt Mrs. Visser, who found some of MacLeod's letters. Griet responded furiously. Was her aunt trying to ruin her best chance at happiness by coming between her and her fiancé? Griet countercharged that the Vissers were stingy tightwads who had never wanted her in the first place. She had then and for the rest of her life a horror of frugality that doubtless arose after her father's bankruptcy.

As the wedding approached, several problems arose. Rudolf was still very ill intermittently. In one of her letters, Griet wrote:

> *Oh darling, I feel such pity for you, and I am so terribly sorry that our plan once again has gone wrong. All accidents happen at once, don't they? Well, John, don't feel too bad about it, tootie. When I come to see you on Sunday I hope the pain will be gone.*
>
> *Did you suffer much, and couldn't you write me yourself?— I guess not, for otherwise you would have done so. Do you think you'll be able to walk again on Sunday? I do hope so, darling, but try not to overdo it. . . .*
>
> *Louise wrote me: "I hope for both of you that in a few weeks at the city hall everything will be floating in sunshine." Well, I hope so too, and you, John? What do you think? You'd better be brave and gay, for that brings the best results. Your little*

wife always does that, and if I had not, my gaiety would have
worn off a long time ago. Do you expect me Sunday?

When you are able to, will you write me and let me know
how you are feeling? Just give me a wonderful kiss, and just
imagine that I am with you, that's what I do too.

Well, Johnie, adieu with a delicious kiss from your so very
loving wife— Greta.

The letter is full of the sort of romantic babbling that appeals
mostly to young lovers themselves, but two points are evident. First,
Griet was blithely sympathetic to his ailments but had no doubt his
physical problems would be short-lived. She did not think she was
marrying an invalid who would infect her. The nursemaid role was
not one for which she had any talent or taste. Second, she had little
forewarning of the interference in their lives that would be forthcoming from Rudolf's sister, Louise. Before the wedding, their
married future looked bright and promising and Louise was apparently in favor of the marriage. Once they were married, Louise's
attitude was conspicuously different.

Another difficulty to be overcome was that Griet had to be approved by Rudolf's superiors. In the MacLeod family, this meant
taking the girl to meet the family patriarch, Rudolf's uncle the retired general Norman MacLeod. Uncle Norman was apparently a
shrewd judge of character and wielded considerable power within
the family. His assessment was, "Young but good-looking, damn
good-looking." Griet was certainly young and immature; she was
also clearly very attractive, and Norman MacLeod seemed to feel
those qualities were sufficient.

By military regulation, Rudolf also had to obtain permission
from his superior officer to marry. Because he was home on leave,
that meant applying to the Ministry of Colonial Affairs in The

Hague, who would charge someone with determining the suitability of the girl. Surprisingly, Rudolf's military records contain no evidence that he ever applied for permission to marry, nor was there much time for such an application between his meeting of Griet on March 24 and their engagement, announced on March 30. No previous biographer has noticed this point or considered its implications.

The cost of not asking permission was serious. Aside from the military's condemnation of those who did not follow the rules, there were financial consequences to an unapproved marriage. If indeed he did marry Griet without such approval, he was then personally liable for her fare to and from the Indies, instead of its being paid by the army. Further, he would not receive the higher salary and larger quarters to which a married officer was entitled. It was downright foolhardy of Rudolf to marry without obtaining permission unless, among the network of officers, the approval of his uncle the general would suffice. But marry they did, come what might.

Griet was not the only one who had to be approved. Although she had told Rudolf she was an orphan—a romantic lie—her father was still living. And because she was under the age of consent, Adam Zelle's permission had to be obtained for her to marry Rudolf. How exactly she broached the subject is unknown, but the third Mrs. MacLeod recounted a family story about the occasion to one Mata Hari biographer, Sam Waagenaar. She said that Griet finally blurted out that she had a father, and Rudolf replied, in jest, "That happens in the best of families."

"But," Griet replied, "he is *alive*!" Her lie became apparent.

Zelle was living with his second wife at 148 Lange Leidsewarsstraat in Amsterdam, a poor neighborhood. At first Griet offered to meet with Zelle alone, probably to spare Rudolf the embarrassment of being judged by a man far his social inferior—or to spare herself the embarrassment of having her fiancé meet her ne'er-do-well father. But Zelle, of course, insisted on meeting his daughter's intended and felt that having such an important officer call upon him was an opportunity to improve his social standing with his neighbors. However, Griet refused to call on her father at home, where he lived with the woman who had replaced her mother and who had taken in Griet's brothers but not Griet herself. Clearly Griet and her stepmother were not fond of each other. Griet offered to meet Zelle at the station, promising Rudolf that she would keep her temper and quickly "dispose" of her father—"that is what I continue to call him," she said, despite his neglect of her—before joining Rudolf elsewhere. Again, Zelle insisted: they must both come to meet him, and in a grand, two-horse carriage.

"I will give my consent," Zelle bargained, "but I wish to attend the wedding and I wish that someone brings me there in a carriage." He had what he wanted.

Griet and Rudolf were married in a civil ceremony at the City Hall in Amsterdam on July 11, 1895. Rudolf wore his full-dress uniform, with gold braid, medals, and a tall shako helmet. Griet was resplendent in a glorious silk gown with a long train and floor-length veil. Instead of the traditional white, which might not have flattered Griet's complexion, she selected a vibrant yellow silk for her gown. She had two bridesmaids. Two of Rudolf's fellow officers were witnesses, and de Balbian Verster and the publisher H. J. W. Becht attended, along with Rudolf's widowed sister, Louise. Though Louise was seemingly polite at the ceremony, that very morning she had pleaded with her brother, "Johnie—don't do it."

Rudolf did not listen. He was determined to marry this lovely

In March of 1895, Margaretha impulsively answered an ad for a Dutch army soldier seeking a wife. She and Rudolf MacLeod became engaged six days after meeting. They were wed on June 7, 1895, shortly before Margaretha's nineteenth birthday. (The Mata Hari Foundation/Fries Museum)

young creature who fascinated and tantalized him, and did so. Zelle must have attended the ceremony, but when it came to the luncheon and reception at the American Hotel, he was absent. Griet and Rudolf had pulled a rather cruel trick, telling Zelle's carriage driver to take him somewhere else so he would not embarrass them at the reception.

Their honeymoon was spent in Wiesbaden, a popular spa town

in Germany. As ever, Griet's striking good looks and regal carriage drew the attention of a number of young men, to Rudolf's displeasure. "Gentlemen," he snapped at her admirers haughtily, "that lady is my wife." An ugly jealousy was already brewing. Nonetheless, later Griet remembered her honeymoon as an idyllic time: "We went to Wiesbaden and we lived like people who can spend one hundred thousand guilders in one year . . . I love luxury. It was just the right thing for me; I was proud of him, and he of me, we could do what we wanted."

They soon had to return to the Netherlands, and the only place they could afford to live was with Louise—now known to Griet as Tante (Aunt) Frida—at 79 Leidsekade, just down the street from the American Café. Finances quickly became an issue. Rudolf was on part pay during his sick leave and had accumulated substantial debts through heavy drinking and high living. He also had borrowed money in the Dutch East Indies, as many soldiers did, and was still paying back those loans. For her part, Griet knew nothing about housekeeping and was hardly inclined to frugality. Newly wed to a military officer from an old aristocratic family, she had no expectations of living carefully within limited means. The marriage began to deteriorate almost immediately.

Griet's feelings during this period can be glimpsed in two sources: a book her father published in 1906, which was clearly aimed at casting all the blame for the failure of the marriage on Rudolf, and an interview she gave to journalist G. H. Priem shortly after the publication of her father's book. In the former, the period of living with Tante Frida was described as unbearable, with no privacy for the newlyweds and a busybody, interfering sister-in-law who disapproved both of the marriage and of the young woman her brother had chosen to marry. In the interview with Priem, given years after the emotion of the situation had faded, Mata Hari (as she called

herself by then) was more moderate in her criticisms of Tante
Frida:

> Have you ever heard of a young married wife that got on very well
> with her mother-in-law? No, well? Now, in the same way I did not
> get on very well with Tante Frida. As an isolated event this means
> little; she was helpful, but—as she was dealing with a young wife
> who knew little of housekeeping—she was perhaps too censorious,
> something that I naturally did not like.

As for the deterioration of the marriage after the honeymoon,
Mata Hari told Priem: "Well, [the marriage] did alter, from the moment that there was no more money. . . . I had not married to go
without luxury and . . . I was flirtatious and he did not like that. He
was jealous."

Priem remarked that Rudolf's jealousy was a kind of compliment, and Griet replied,

> Certainly, but it was also difficult. He was so much older than I
> am. . . . He could have been almost my father. And then, a woman
> with my temperament. . . . I want to confess truly and openly, that
> seeing a handsome young man made my heart start to beat quicker.
> And that is very natural, that is something that one can't help. . . .
>   I was very temperamental. I had also artistic aspirations. . . . I
> [had] inclinations that made it impossible for a woman like me to
> be a good housewife. . . . I was not like that [content at home], I
> confess frankly; I wanted to live like a colorful butterfly in the sun,
> rather than in the calmness of the inside of my room.

As for their continual financial difficulties, with the distance of
time Mata Hari admitted that she spent as recklessly as Rudolf.

Marriage did not reform Rudolf's manners or his way of living. About two weeks after their return from their honeymoon, Rudolf was already seeing other women. One day he explained boldly to de Balbian Verster that he had a date with two women and asked if his friend would go keep Griet company that evening, as he would be home late. De Balbian Verster spent an evening with Griet, listening to her play the piano and sing, which she did well and charmingly. Griet, young and innocent as she was, did not yet suspect her husband. When Rudolf returned some hours later, he posed as the perfect husband, greeted his friend, gave Griet a loving kiss, and apologized for being detained. De Balbian Verster was disgusted with him.

Soon Griet realized what was going on and started complaining that Rudolf left her home alone too often while he went out with his friends. One who heard the complaints was interviewed by writer Sam Waagenaar in the late 1920s; he identifies her only as "Mrs. V." Rudolf had called upon her when he first arrived in the Netherlands, bringing greetings from her son, a fellow officer. But Rudolf had offended Mrs. V. and her mother by telling an off-color joke and they thought very little of him. Following his engagement to Griet, Rudolf took his fiancée to call on Mrs. V. After seeing the couple together, Mrs. V. wondered if the marriage would survive. Griet was very pretty and very naïve and expected a lot of life, she felt, while Rudolf had crude manners and would hardly provide his young bride with "the right guidance." Perhaps the Indies—where women went to parties with their husbands rather than staying demurely home—would suit Griet. She hoped so.

During either their brief courtship or early marriage, the couple attended the 1895 Hotel and Travel Sector Exposition in Amsterdam, which was open between May 11 and October 31. Somehow they had made the acquaintance of N. A. Calisch, the chairman of the executive committee, who had organized the event. Calisch made the couple his personal guests, ensuring they had a wonderful time at the exposition. It was an extraordinary event attended by more than one million people. The exhibits included a re-created seventeenth-century Dutch village, complete with canal; a life-sized model of the ship *Prins Hendrick* afloat in a specially dug basin; a huge papier-mâché construction depicting an Indian elephant, with a mahout and a three-story howdah on its back. There were also ornamental gardens to stroll in and myriad smaller pavilions flying bright flags.

As a result of their acquaintance, Calisch loaned Rudolf three thousand guilders sometime between 1895 and 1897. He was never repaid; the loan note, signed by Rudolf, was found among Calisch's possessions after his death some years later. Three thousand guilders was a very substantial sum—about half a year's pay for a married officer in the Dutch Indies army in 1896 and the equivalent of more than twenty thousand dollars in today's currency. When Rudolf later retired from the army as a major with almost thirty years of service, his annual pension was only twenty-eight hundred guilders, less than the amount loaned to him by Calisch. One of the outrages with which Zelle charged Rudolf in his book about his daughter's life was humiliating her by asking her to "be nice" to Mr. Calisch, so he would not demand payment of his loan. The clear implication is that Rudolf was urging his wife into something very like prostitution in order to clear his debts.

Zelle's book featured a heartrending story of spending the last evening in the Netherlands with his daughter, before she and her husband left for the Indies. He described her shame as moneylenders pounded on her door demanding payment of Rudolf's notes, about which she knew nothing. Whether or not Zelle and his wife actually witnessed the arrival of moneylenders cannot be determined; Zelle is the only source to mention it, and his book is clearly contrived to heap maximum blame on Rudolf. But the unpaid loan from Calisch is documented, as is the large amount of money owed in the Indies, for letters from Rudolf and Griet often complain about the amount of the regular payments they must make.

On March 16, 1896, almost a year after Griet and Rudolf first met, Rudolf's leave was extended because of his still-precarious health. His drinking and carousing had done nothing to improve his physical situation and had sabotaged his financial circumstances. The couple moved out of Tante Frida's apartment into their own place on Jacob Lennepkade to diminish the domestic conflict, but Tante Frida visited frequently and continued to criticize all too freely.

A few weeks later, on April 23, Griet and Rudolf went to a reception at the Royal Palace given by the queen regent Emma, mother of the young queen Wilhelmina, in honor of the queen's upcoming sixteenth birthday on April 30. The MacLeods were privileged to be invited. Griet dressed in her yellow silk gown, and, as at their wedding, Rudolf wore his best dress uniform. Many at the reception commented what a beautiful couple they were, the lady so dark-haired in her vivid gown, the gentleman so upright and dignified, with his gold braid and medals. This was the sort of high-society life Griet had doubtless envisioned for herself, far from staying home and cooking frugal meals! Proud and happy with their social triumph at the reception, the couple drew closer again. Within days, Griet was pregnant with their first child.

On September 17, Rudolf was given another six months' extension of his leave, this time because of Griet's pregnancy. Taking a woman to the Indies was risky enough without expecting her to travel in an advanced state of pregnancy. Their financial situation was precarious. Griet suspected that Rudolf saw other women; they

Rudolf, Margaretha, and their infant son, Norman, set sail for the Dutch East Indies on the S.S. *Prinses Amalia* in 1897. Margaretha is in the first row at the left; Rudolf is the second man from the left standing behind his wife. Norman is not seen. (The Mata Hari Foundation/Fries Museum)

quarreled frequently. Yet he was very pleased when she delivered a baby boy on January 30, 1897, and proudly named him Norman John—Norman in honor of the retired general, John in honor of Rudolf's paternal grandfather. After the child's birth, Rudolf was absent more often than ever, leaving Griet home alone with the baby. According to her father's biased account, Griet grew certain that Rudolf was spending all their money on "ladies" from the "ice skating club."

On May 1, 1897, Rudolf, Griet, and baby Norman left on the steamboat S.S. *Prinses Amalia* for the Dutch East Indies. They were accompanied by a detachment of raw troops direct from Harderwijk for which Rudolf was responsible. The young MacLeod family was about to experience life in the colonies in the military service. Although the procedures, duties, and conditions were certainly familiar to Rudolf, Griet had little or no idea what to expect.

As was customary, a group photograph was taken of those leaving on the *Prinses Amalia* that day. In the foreground are seated four young women, including Griet, and an older matron in black bombazine. Two small children sit at the women's feet, while one clings to a woman seated next to Griet—presumably the child's mother. Norman does not appear in the picture. Behind the seated women stand the men—two officers in uniform including Rudolf, a man who is probably the captain, two well dressed civilians who might be planters or civil servants, and another officer. Interspersed among the men are three other young women, one of whom is clearly Eurasian, and a Eurasian child. Elsewhere on the ship, but not of a social status to be included in this photograph, were the new recruits from Harderwijk.

Griet looks the youngest and freshest-faced of the women; she has an expectant half smile on her face. She had wed impulsively and her marriage was not entirely happy, but she was a young matron of high social standing going to a new life in a new land. Promise was in the air. Contrary to her optimistic expectation, what transpired in the Indies was a tragedy that grew directly out of the practices of the Dutch colonials. It was a tragedy that would strongly influence the rest of her life and the formation of her famous persona, Mata Hari.

4

Indies Life

FIVE WEEKS LATER, on June 7, 1897, the S.S. *Prinses Amalia* carried the MacLeod family into the harbor at Tanjung Priok near Batavia. The harbor was full of extraordinary sailing ships painted in vivid hues with terra-cotta-colored sails. The ships' crews were made up of natives from a dozen islands, small men in bright sarongs that showed off their muscular builds. All had bronzed skin and dark hair. They moved on bare, calloused feet with an athletic ease that spoke of years on ships. The men called to one another in exotic languages as they tossed lines, hauled goods, furled sails, or vied for the attention of the women on the docks who were selling food and drink. Rudolf had seen all this before—the ships, the busy harbor, the strange and wonderful cargos being unloaded by the natives of the Indies—but Griet drank in the new sights and smells and sounds as if she had been starved for color her whole life. A new existence was opening up for her.

Griet had been ill during the voyage to the Indies. She may have been seasick, as many were on such voyages. The descrip-

tion in Zelle's book—purported to be Griet's own words—is am-
biguous as to the exact cause of her misery: "Physically and morally
I suffered enormous complaints; the terror of fever haunted me day
and night; my weary brains hammered in my poor head until it burst
and the appalling heat, which even in the middle of the night gave no
cooling, held me steady as if in a bath of sheer flames."

By saying she suffered from moral complaints, Griet (or Zelle)
may have been hinting that she had caught a disease that originated
in immorality: in other words, a venereal disease. Without the evidence of Griet's later letters, which indicate unmistakably that Rudolf had given Griet syphilis, the clue in this passage would be
flimsy indeed.

The impact of arriving in the Indies and discovering a world of
light, heat, lush vegetation, and social freedom was enormous on
Griet, as it was on most of the Dutch colonials. The brilliant colors,
the abundant flowers, the spicy food, the succulent fruits, the volca-
nos that loomed above the rice paddies, the intricate patterns of native Indonesian music, clothing, art, design—all these were worlds
away from staid, dull, carefully controlled Holland. The Indies were
exuberant, wild, exotic, and very beautiful. Going there was trans-
formational; the old life of the Netherlands, the old identity, the old
rules of behavior, fell away. To symbolize the change in herself, she
sometimes called herself Gretha—another common nickname derived from Margaretha—rather than Griet.

In those days, all the colonials who went to the Dutch East Indies
to live were altered irrevocably by the experience. For example, one
of the characters in Madelon Székely-Lulofs's novel *Rubber* says:

> *You get acclimatized here. Acclimatized and standardized. . . . Here*
> *everybody loses his particular personal characteristics, forgets what*
> *he has learned, forgets what his mother taught him in the nursery.*

All of that is let go here . . . and a new type of man emerges. . . . Here
you became transformed into an isolated human being without con-
nection with your family and your youth.

Similarly, journalist W. L. Ritter wrote in 1856: "A European,
no matter where he may have been born, becomes an entirely different creature in the Indies than he would have been had he stayed
home. . . . The European man who goes to the Indies removes his
old self, as it were, in order to assume a new self."

Gretha probably hoped for a transformation of her quarrelsome,
overcrowded marriage into a freer, happier arrangement. She was
beautiful and young—only twenty years old—but in the Indies,
she was the wife of a very important man, a captain soon to be a
major. Here Gretha's bankrupt father and her precocious affair with
the headmaster at the Leiden school were unknown to anyone. Here
she and Rudolf could and did live like royalty, with servants and a
grand house: no more penny-pinching, no more sharing an apartment with a sister-in-law. Here Tante Frida and her censorious remarks were thousands of miles away, and so was their former friend
Mr. Calisch, with his ugly demands for repayment of loans.

After a week in Batavia, Rudolf was posted to the Eighth Battalion at Willem I, a military fort in Ambarawa near Semarang in
Central Java. The MacLeod family boarded the S.S. *Speelman* to
travel from Batavia to Semarang and then went on horseback and
oxcart to Ambarawa, where Rudolf would train raw recruits. Ambarawa was a small place and not a particularly good posting for
Rudolf. There Gretha began to learn about housekeeping and society in the Indies.

If there was something a *totok*, or newcomer, to the Indies learned
quickly, it was the importance of reinforcing European superiority
and prestige at every turn. Though morals were looser in the Indies

than in the Netherlands, the hierarchical separation between Indonesians and Europeans was maintained with the utmost seriousness. Even a modest household employed half a dozen Indonesian servants—a cook, a houseboy, a nursemaid, or *babu*, a ladies' maid, a gardener, a laundress and seamstress, for example—who would generally be treated as if they were invisible until summoned with a shout or a clap of the hands. Yet these servants and their families lived at the back of the compound that housed the European family they served; their cooking smells, the cries of their children, the crooning songs of mothers, the low men's voices talking into the night, formed an integral backdrop to colonial Indies life. The servants were there and yet not there, socially unrecognized and yet essential to daily life for the Dutch.

As a *totok*, Gretha was in danger of acting inappropriately in her new social milieu. Most newly arrived women were thought too familiar with their servants, not commanding enough in their orders, and not demanding enough in the standards of cleanliness, hygiene, and subservience they expected. Some were criticized for being "indecorous in their speech and dress," as the tropical climate of the Indies prompted them to abandon their corsets (and sometimes their morals) to wear looser, more revealing clothing made of lightweight fabrics. As Jean Gelman Taylor noted in her study of Dutch colonial life:

> *It was precisely when the immigrants were able to keep in close touch with the homeland, by furlough, telegraph, libraries, and so forth, that they ostentatiously adopted Indonesian practices [in food, bathing, clothing, napping]. . . . Starting from the late nineteenth century, the Dutch civil servant wore colonial whites, left the office at two in the afternoon, and donned batik pyjamas after a siesta and an Indonesian meal.*

Gretha's regal bearing probably served her in good stead as she began to assume the role of captain's wife and slowly integrated Indies ways into her life. The most important hire, which she made immediately, was of a *babu* to look after Norman. Not to have one was unthinkable.

For any child raised in the Indies, the *babu* was a central figure, a beloved and loving person devoted solely to that child for his entire life (a *liifbabu*, or nanny-for-life). Rob Nieuwenhuys, a Dutch writer raised in the Indies, wrote of his *babu* with tremendous love and affection when he was in his seventies:

Nènèk Tidjah was my liifbabu *at least until I was five, and therefore my first mother. I have been told that the first words I spoke were Javanese. Later I talked with her in a strange lingo of Javanese and Malay, interspersed with Dutch words. She always called me Lih, pronounced with a long drawn-out vowel, which was an abbreviation of* lilih, *which means darling in Javanese. When my parents were out visiting or went to the opera . . . Nènèk Tidjah had to take care of us. That was always a party. She installed herself in front of our beds with her* sirih *apparatus (oh that sharp scent of bruised* sirih *leaves, chewing tobacco,* gambir *and* pinang *I can still smell them in my mind) and she began her breathtaking stories about gods and goddesses, about petrification and metamorphoses. Sometimes she performed long sections from the* Ramayana *using two different voices, and when it began to rain during the west monsoon, accompanied by thunder and lightning, I knew that "up there" the powers of good and evil were engaged in noisy combat with one another. Then I was allowed to sit in her lap. I must have inhaled the smell of her body and her clothes, especially her sarong, quite intensely, a sort of preeroticism. She caressed me by pressing me close to her and by stroking me. . . . And thanks to Nènèk*

Tidjah's stories, Indies nature is angker *to me, that is to say holy, alive, peopled by living creatures which you learn to manipulate by murmuring holy formulas or by giving* selamantan *[religious offerings of food]. I was raised as a child in a magic world—and that means a lot.*

Sirih leaves, chewing tobacco, *gambir,* and *pinang* were considered the essential ingredients to be added to betel nuts when they were chewed; these accoutrements were usually carried in a small, special box with compartments for each item. Betel-nut chewing turned the saliva red and was regarded by Europeans as disgusting, but Indonesians embraced the habit as a mild vice as enjoyable as smoking.

Though Gretha was not raised in the Indies, she too was raised in a sort of magic world, and her innate belief that somehow her life could be transformed into the fairy tale she longed for never left her.

Despite the *babu*'s intense and constant intimacy with the child, she was distinctly subordinate to any member of the family, even the youngest. Her name was usually forgotten or never learned by her white master and mistress; she was known simply as "*babu* Norman." But the Dutch who tried so hard to keep themselves aloof and superior from the natives undermined their own efforts by turning their children over to *babus* to be raised. They rarely saw that the generations born in the Indies and raised by *babus* would be so deeply imbued with the customs, sounds, beliefs, tastes, and smells of the Indies that the Netherlands would be forever foreign to them. The children of the Indies were neither native nor Eurasian nor Dutch but something wholly new born of the colonial situation.

Race played a major role in Indies life and influenced Gretha's experiences strongly. In his previous years there Rudolf had learned the intricate social calibrations based on race that characterized Indies society, but to Gretha the crucial influence of race came as a shock. The Indies were a minefield of racial categories, the distinctions among which were fraught with emotional and social importance.

By 1897, when Gretha, Rudolf, and Norman arrived in the Indies, the legal and social category of "European" was a strange and motley collection of people of various ethnic ancestries. In Java particularly there were a great many families—even very prominent ones—comprising a complex mixture of Dutch and Indonesian or sometimes Chinese ancestry. Since 1854 no one had attempted to determine who was a pure-blooded European and who was of mixed blood, but at that time, more than half (9,360) of the 18,000 Europeans had "the characteristic skin color" that was seen as indicative of mixed blood, while another 5,600 Europeans born in the Indies did not have a darker skin color but were nonetheless also of mixed blood. By 1900, the estimated number of mestizos, or mixed bloods, was in the tens of thousands and amounted to about three-quarters of the legally European population.

Van Marle, who made an extensive study of the question of Europeans in the Dutch East Indies, explained:

> *Most of the* blijvers *[those Europeans who settled in the Indies] were thus of mixed blood.... Passage into the legal European grouping was possible only through: 1. Legal adoption, which had been replaced in 1867 by recognition [a legal claim by a European father to a child born of a non-European mother]; 2. registration in the registers of the registry of births, deaths, and marriages; 3. equalization by Governor-General.*

Moving from a non-European legal status to a European status carried with it substantial political, social, and financial advantages. "Equalization" was a legal ruling that a particular individual was equivalent to a European and should therefore be considered one. The conditions for such a judgment in 1897 were quite specific. An individual must be a Christian and must:

> (a) *have enjoyed a European education (as [if] educated in Europe) or in European surroundings such as those in which a European has been raised;*
>
> (b) *move well in European society (i.e., be socially or behaviorally European—facility in the Dutch language and style of dress were relevant); and*
>
> (c) *feel no longer at home in the society (or legal grouping) from which he comes.*

The year before the MacLeods went to the Indies, another legal method for moving from a non-European status to a European status was established. In 1896, Article 275 of the Civil Code was modified so that a child born out of wedlock could be legitimized without the father's marrying the mother "if important objections existed—in the judgment of the Governor-General—against the marriage of the parents." A Dutchman's marrying an Indonesian woman was generally seen as objectionable, and the European's rights to the child always prevailed. Under this law, a mixed-race, illegitimate child could be legitimized as a European.

The objection to European-Indonesian marriages was based on the belief that, through sexual contact with native women, European men contracted "disease as well as debased sentiments, immoral proclivities, and extreme susceptibility to uncivilized states." Prejudice against mixed-race children was so strong that the extent of criminality or delinquency among youths in the European category was seen as directly reflecting the percentage of Indonesian blood that ran in their veins.

All of the elaborate gradations of racial admixture and how they were to be treated according to Indies society might have been little more than a new and complex set of social rules to learn but for one thing: Gretha's distinctive skin color, dark eyes, and dark hair gave her the appearance of being part Indonesian. She had been teased about this even as a child in Friesland. Ironically, her coloring was probably a major part of Rudolf's immediate sexual attraction to her, since it is highly likely that all of his previous sexual encounters had been with Indo women.

Gretha's appearance was extremely important in the Indies, much more so than any previous biographer has appreciated. When she walked into a room full of strangers in the Indies, people would not wonder who Captain MacLeod's new Dutch wife was. Instead, they would be surprised that such a proud and haughty officer, one so concerned with his social status, had married an Indo. Those who presumed he had gotten permission to marry her probably speculated how he had managed that; those who suspected he had not obtained permission would assume it had been denied because of her obviously mixed ancestry. And yet, Gretha was as fully Dutch as any blond, blue-eyed woman from the Netherlands could be.

The issue of race certainly arose during Gretha's first days in Java. The MacLeod family stayed first in Batavia, where large families with mixed blood were common and socially acceptable, but there was still an open prejudice against Indos in some circles. A contemporary writer remarked:

I cannot bear the arrogance of the Dutch ladies and gentlemen to-wards the sinyos *[Eurasian men classified as Europeans]. I have witnessed it for years in Batavia. You cannot imagine anything more heartless or conceited than the arrogance of the Hollanders vis-à-vis the colored. If a* sinyo *becomes even slightly prominent,*

the true Hollanders immediately close ranks to work against him.
They find their greatest amusement in treasuring up the linguistic
errors of the sinyos, *so that at night on the front verandah they can*
crack all kinds of jokes at their expense.

An apparently Indo woman, whose youth, beauty, and husband's position provoked jealousy and envy, would be subjected to
pointed jibes and snubs. Gretha must have faced inquiring looks
and catty remarks behind her back, even if her husband's status offered her some protection. Fortunately, Gretha had an excellent
command of the Dutch language and social graces that proclaimed
her to be fully European, but she was too clever not to notice she
was being constantly tested.

The social discomfort she felt then was but a foretaste of what
would happen when the MacLeods later moved to East Java and still
later to Sumatra. As they relocated from the busy cosmopolitan capital to remote towns with smaller and smaller European communities,
Gretha's appearance would have drawn more and more comments
and snubs. There was even a term for her precise skin coloring: *kulit*
langsep, which refers to a native fruit of a pale pink-tan color. While
such a complexion was much admired by Indonesians, it was seen in
European society as an unmistakable sign of being a half-caste.

Gretha's coloring brought with it a set of expectations about her
behavior and morals. Tineke Hellwig, in her study of the representations of women in the Dutch East Indies, wrote: "[Indos] had an
image of being indolent, unreliable, oversubmissive or, on the other
hand, incredibly reckless, and they all spoke poor Dutch and with a
heavy accent. The women were known to be sensual, coquettish
and seductive."

Gretha met these expectations in many ways. She was a woman
practiced in flirting, who very much enjoyed male attention.

Doubtless the two-to-one ratio of men to women in the Indies at that time suited her very well; she had plenty of admirers. Her languid, graceful style of moving, her seductive dark eyes and luxuriant hair, telegraphed her sexuality to any male in her presence. And her ability to attract men simply reinforced the stereotype that her looks won her; she was seen as a morally dangerous, selfish, and frivolous woman who enjoyed clothes and jewels.

After six months in Ambarawa, on December 29, 1897, Rudolf was promoted to major and sent to Tumpang, a very good posting indeed. Gretha was a few months pregnant and very pleased at this improvement in their circumstances. Tumpang was on the outskirts of Malang, one of the most pleasant and beautiful hill towns in Java, high enough in altitude to be nicely cool and full of gracious colonial houses with beautiful gardens. Malang housed Fort Van Den Bosch and the First Reserve Battalion, of which Rudolf was in charge. A huge river, the Sungai Brantas, wound its way through the town and provided lovely views. The lower reaches of the nearby mountains, Gunung Bromo and Gunung Semeru, were the sites of rich coffee plantations, so there was a good-sized population of Europeans, both civilian and military. And there were proper shops, chic restaurants, and theatrical and musical performances, albeit sometimes a trifle amateurish. Here was a society in which Gretha hoped to shine as the first lady of the battalion.

They lived in a lovely house with large, open rooms and a spacious verandah, front and back. There was room for Norman to walk and play under his *babu*'s watchful supervision in the garden, where Gretha promenaded to admire the whitewashed pots of flowers and the lush bushes and trees that the gardener nurtured. Rudolf gave her a lovely suite of furniture in blue and brown plush for her boudoir; he set up a masculine office in the house where he did most of his work. Sometimes in the evening they would stroll arm in arm,

Military officers in the Dutch East Indies lived in colonial houses like this, with a spacious verandah front and rear filled with flower pots and casual furniture. This photo shows Dutch army physician Dr Johan Kunst, his wife, Betty Meeter Kunst, and their child, Fritjof, in 1902. The sign says that his medical office is at the rear. (Collectie KIT Tropenmuseum)

looking back with contentment on their house as the servants lit the lamps. Gretha enjoyed enormously being high in rank—a military wife assumed her husband's rank—and more beautiful than the other wives.

On May 2, 1898, Gretha gave birth to her second child, a daughter named Jeanne Louise to honor the hated Tante Frida, whose real name was Louise. Probably because Gretha so disliked Tante Frida, the child was never called Jeanne or Louise. She was soon referred to only by the Indies nickname "Non," which was a contraction of the Javanese word *nonna,* meaning "little miss." Rudolf may have been disappointed that his wife had not produced another son and future soldier, like Norman, upon whom he doted, but he soon grew

European children in the Indies were cared for by devoted Indonesian *babus*. The subjects in this image are unknown. (Collectie KIT Tropenmuseum)

very fond of his dark-haired, dark-eyed daughter. By custom, another *babu* would have been promptly hired to look after Non.

In September came several days of celebration to honor the crowning of Queen Wilhelmina at home in the Netherlands, some six months after her eighteenth birthday. There were races, a banquet, a gala ball, and—best of all—an amateur theatrical production of *The Crusaders*, a musical written by two young lieutenants in the battalion. Gretha shone in the starring role of the queen, to great applause and a favorable notice in the local newspaper. Rudolf had sent to Europe for expensive dresses for his wife, perhaps to emphasize that she was Dutch. During the dinners, parties, and dances that marked the celebrations, she was ravishingly beautiful in a yellow silk costume embroidered with camellias and an extremely low-cut gown in purple velvet, decorated with pearls. From the stage to the ballroom, Gretha's performance was a triumph. She drew every man's eye and lustful admiration, every woman's envy. Rudolf's pride at his lovely wife was spoiled by his jealousy and his fury at those who made remarks about Gretha's skin color. His mood fluctuated wildly.

Immediately after the celebrations, Gretha took the children and three servants and went to spend three weeks at a coffee plantation on the slopes of Gunung Semeru, the highest mountain on Java. To reach it, they took a train and then a carriage, up and up along winding roads. The last part of the ascent was so difficult that they were carried in *tandus*—sedan chairs or stretchers—by porters. The air at three thousand feet was bracing and clear, the scenery of Semeru and its brother, the active volcano Gunung Bromo, was breathtaking. At night the coolness of the air was delicious after the sultry heat of the lowlands. One night they were awakened by the deep, earth-shaking rumbling of Gunung Bromo, which coughed out flame-colored lava from time to time. Gretha found the sight magnificent but a bit frightening.

There is no evidence about whether the trip to the coffee plantation was planned as a simple holiday or as a rest cure. Perhaps the children had been ill; European children often were in

In September of 1898, Margaretha made her stage debut in a play called *The Crusaders,* performed in Malang as part of the celebrations of Queen Wilhelmina's coming-of-age. She caught every man's eye in her low-cut purple velvet gown decorated with pearls. (Collection of the KITLV, Leiden, The Netherlands, #41797)

the Indies. Certainly Gretha had been in her glory during the coronation celebrations and obviously not ill at all. When Gretha and the children returned to Tumpang, the rainy season hit in full force. Every day the rain poured down in blinding sheets for several hours, battering the tin roofs and splattering mud everywhere. Everything inside the house was damp; the verandahs—such lovely places to sit and read or chat in the dry season—were slippery and dank. The furniture and clothes mildewed. Creeping and crawling insects of every description thrived and invaded the house. Tinker birds sang their infuriating song, shrieking ever higher and higher notes that grated on listener's nerves—and then fell suddenly silent, which was even worse. It was impossible to go out without getting covered in mud and equally impossible to stay in. The brilliant tropical sun Gretha had come to love was replaced by overcast skies and a feeling of claustrophobic gloom.

Rudolf was short-tempered and irritable. Perhaps he had been brooding on the admiring looks Gretha had received during the coronation celebrations; perhaps it was merely that the weather was putting him out of sorts as it did most people. The happiness Gretha and Rudolf had enjoyed in the earlier part of 1898 deteriorated into sharp quarrels, too much drinking, heavy spending, and suspicions of infidelity.

Rudolf accused Gretha of cheating on him with the many men who admired her so openly. If his accusations were accurate, his anger at her lax moral standards was ironic. Most European men in the Indies—certainly all of the upper-class unmarried ones and many of the married ones, too—had *nyais*. Out-of-wedlock sex was everywhere. Even though *nyais* were kept more discreetly than formerly, Gretha soon learned to recognize them on the street by their mannerisms and gold jewelry, but most especially by their slippers and the characteristic color (white) of their *kebayas*. The *kebaya* was a long, lacy overblouse worn slightly open over a slip or camisole, the two sides fastened together with fine chains anchored to filigreed gold brooches. It was a comfortable and flattering garment, worn at home or on casual occasions by Javanese, Indo, and European women alike. To wear slippers and a white *kebaya* if you were a Javanese or Indo woman was to announce that you were a white man's mistress.

If she thought about the question, Gretha would have surmised that Rudolf had had a *nyai* before marrying her; he had certainly been no virgin when they met, and he had spent virtually his entire young manhood in the Indies. She was grateful to have been spared the humiliation experienced by many *totok* wives, who arrived in the Indies to be immediately confronted by her husband's resentful "housekeeper" and their brood of mixed-race children.

Rudolf acquitted himself well at Fort Van Den Bosch. On December 21, 1898, he was transferred to be head of the garrison battalion in Medan, Sumatra. Though Medan was a far less comfortable and civilized place for a European than Malang, to be garrison commander was a significant step up for Rudolf. From the moment of his arrival in Medan, he would be one of the most important men in the region. Sumatra had been the scene of his early military successes, and he hoped to repeat his triumphs there.

The quarrels between Rudolf and Gretha, the slurs on her racial identity, the hypocrisy of the superficially proper Indies society, which was rife with illicit sex, weighed on Gretha. Late in 1898 or early in 1899, she wrote to her father and stepmother back in the Netherlands: "No, I have no more beautiful illusions about the Indies because if you really look at it, it is not a nice country. It has without doubt many good things but also many nasty ones. If I could I would come back tomorrow."

The Fatal Move

RUDOLF LEFT FOR MEDAN on March 17, 1899, on the S.S. *Carpentier,* going via Batavia. He took his horse, King, and his dog, Blackie, with him but left Gretha and the children behind in Tumpang. While Rudolf went ahead to find a new house for the family and start his command, Gretha was to see to auctioning off all of their household goods. It was considered thriftier to do this than to try to transport furnishings. Rudolf and Gretha had been quarreling ever since the coronation celebrations, so this arrangement provided a way to separate and let tempers cool.

Arriving in Medan, Rudolf settled into a very different social milieu from that in cosmopolitan Malang. Medan was the only major city in the plantation region of Deli. A mixed group of Europeans—British, Belgians, Germans, Dutch—came to Deli with the intention of making a fortune and retiring back to Europe in a decade or so—a hope not often fulfilled. But in 1899 the Europeans in Medan (not counting enlisted men) numbered a mere 385 out of a total population of 12,984.

The great majority of Europeans were men involved with the military, the plantations, or the civil service. Few men were married and there were very few European women and children. For example, in 1905 only 3.6 percent of the male civilians over the age of nineteen in Sumatra were married. The region had one of the lowest percentages of married men of any in the Dutch East Indies.

One reason for this paucity of European families was the policies of the employers. Precise statistics on the percentage of married men in the military stationed in Sumatra in 1899 are not available, but it was at most 2 percent. Similarly, the major tobacco or rubber companies that ran plantations flatly refused to hire married men. Many prohibited their employees from marrying while in service, though occasionally plantation employees were allowed to marry after six years of service in Sumatra, if they could demonstrate financial solvency. The third major group of men in the province of eastern Sumatra, civil servants, had little or no chance to marry until they reached the highest ranks. As a result, the society was predominantly male and rather wild; drinking, gambling, prostitution, and concubinage thrived. Ironically, the social rules for the few European women who lived in eastern Sumatra were much stricter than those in Java. If the men were freer in their behavior, the women were more restricted in theirs.

Racial barriers and distinctions were more strictly demarcated in this part of Sumatra than in Java, perhaps because of the overwhelming number of Indonesians relative to Europeans. Lily Clerkx, writing about European colonials in Deli, described the situation:

The white group defended its privileges tooth and nail. Its position was strong because [it was] predicated on white group solidarity. Facing the Asians, the community always behaved as a closed

*group. Its organization was impeccable, and one acted in a disci-
plined way, army-like, including distinctive external features such
as dress. . . . [The* totok*] was permitted to do nothing that might
impair prestige and endanger the security of the group. An aggres-
sive act of a single Asian towards a white person caused the entire
group of whites to turn against the assailant, if necessary assisted
by the police corps or the armed forces which were at their service.*

Medan in particular and the Deli region in general were notorious for the rowdy drunken parties that took place when the planters
were in town. Plantation employees got two days off a month,
known as *hari besar* (big day). During *hari besar*

*almost everyone went to the club or, even better if the distance was
not prohibitive, to the famous—or infamous—Hotel De Boer in
Medan. There were none there but menfolk, not a single woman
could be seen in the whole hall. . . . Women, planters' wives, were
still rather rare at that time and those who were there avoided the
neighborhood of the hotel on* hari besar *day. The planters are
coarse people, their mirth and their jokes are not fit for a woman's
ear. The evening would start with an extensive dinner and even
during the meal the rowdiness began. Somebody would climb on
the table, breaking plates and dishes; others poured beer all over
each other; a table would topple over and so on.*

Another Dutch colonial writer, H. Veersema, concurred: "A
Delian *hari besar* was always something special, Medan turning into
a seething cauldron, the walls of the Hotel Medan were bulging and
at the de Boer Hotel personnel brought out their coarsest crockery,
in anticipation of breakage once people took to spinning plates on
the marble floor."

Far away from his wife and children, Rudolf would have found this just the sort of raucous party he had enjoyed so much in his bachelor years.

A more hidden part of Deli European society was the unmarried women, either Indo or Javanese, who were kept as *nyais*. Most of them had been brought to Sumatra as contract coolies and had then been offered the position of *nyai*, with little real chance to refuse. Most of Rudolf's senior military colleagues kept concubines, and so did the plantation men and the civil servants in Deli he drank and partied with. No one would have been surprised if Rudolf took a *nyai* to look after him and keep him company until Gretha and the children arrived in Medan; they would have been more surprised if he had not.

In considering the relationship between Rudolf and Gretha, it is key to recognize that going without sexual companionship was not believed to be an option for men in the Indies. In 1899, the year Rudolf went to Medan, ninety-six Dutch Indies army officers were polled about the wisdom of continuing barracks concubinage; Rudolf might have been among those polled. Eighty-eight of them (almost 92 percent) were in favor of continuing officially sanctioned concubinage within the barracks.

The women had little choice about becoming a *nyai*, even if they were already married, because of the dual handicaps of being female and being poor. Few female coolies turned down the opportunity for light work and a life of luxury in exchange for becoming the sexual partner of a white man who might or might not be kind, clean, or good-looking. The alternative was the coolie's life of grinding poverty, meager food, and exhausting labor.

While Rudolf was alone in Medan, he almost certainly took a *nyai* and may have resumed a relationship with an Indo *nyai* he had kept when he was in Sumatra before his marriage. When he arrived in Sumatra in 1899, the identity of the new garrison commander was the subject of much gossip in both the Asian and European communities. Any former *nyai* of Rudolf's would have learned almost immediately of his return in an elevated position. The resumption of a sexual relationship with a former *nyai* may have caused a devastating event that occurred not long afterward.

There were two crucial new variables. First, Rudolf was now married—a husband and father—and sooner or later his European family would join him in Sumatra. This meant that, if he took up with a *nyai*, a crisis was inevitable. Of course, he could dismiss the *nyai* when his European wife appeared; this is a common plot in Dutch colonial literature. And, as often happened in such literature, the *nyai* might well turn vindictive, threatening to tell Gretha of Rudolf's infidelity and provoke an enormous row. Alternatively, Rudolf could try to keep both a wife and a *nyai*, an extremely difficult deception in a very small community but one some men attempted. Maintaining both a family and a *nyai* would require a significant outlay of money, which in Rudolf's life was always in short supply.

Second, and most important, the laws pertaining to mixed marriages and children of mixed race had changed markedly between Rudolf's departure from the Indies on sick leave in 1895 and his return to Sumatra in 1899. In 1898 a mixed-marriage law had been passed that gave European status to the wife and recognized children of any European man, regardless of the wife's race or country of origin. The underlying premise was that the family was the emblem of state authority and that all members of a family must be subject to the same laws. For an Indo or native *nyai*, particularly one who had borne children to a European man, the law was a godsend. If she could persuade the man to marry her, she would become legally European; even if he would not marry, if he recognized her children, then they would be guaranteed the privileged legal status of Europeans.

Children posed the most troubling social problem that attended the widespread keeping of *nyais*. Though *nyais* were sometimes forced to have abortions or were dismissed for becoming pregnant, a significant number of children resulted from concubinage. Just how many mixed-race children were produced at this time is unknown, but one authority, Robert E. Park, wrote: "One man, a Hollander, who was very free with the native women on his plantation and who kept track of his children had over 1400 descendants in thirty years. . . . There are *kampongs* that are known to be full of mixed bloods."

Statistics gathered by the Dutch government suggest the magnitude of the issue. During the year 1900, 1,746 children who had been sired by lower-level soldiers were legally recognized and hence reclassified as European or the equivalent. In the entire Dutch East Indies between 1891 and 1900, a total of 7,000 Indo children were recognized by their European fathers. Every year, one European man out of every thirteen or fourteen chose to recognize a mixed-race child whom he had fathered. Fully 28 percent of the Indo children born in the decade at the end of the nineteenth century achieved both recognition and legitimacy through the marriage of their mothers to European men.

The great majority of Indo children born of concubinage were neither recognized nor legitimized. At the end of the nineteenth century, most mixed-race children were sent into the *kampongs*, which in the common metaphor of the day absorbed these unwanted children as a sponge absorbs water. There was a widespread European fear, perhaps prompted by guilt, that the *kampongs* were the breeding grounds of rebellion, criminality, and hostility toward full-blooded whites. Braconier, writing early in the twentieth century, expressed a common view: "This category of children, left behind by their European fathers, whether or not they were recognized, are *par droit de naissance* [by their birthright] European-haters. . . . In the future, they will be the anarchists and extremists of Indische society if Dutch lawmakers do not intervene in a timely manner to extend their protective hand to these 'outcasts.'"

Where racial tensions were higher, due to the smaller number of Europeans and the greater competition between Indonesian and European men for a limited number of sexual partners, Eurasians were viewed with great suspicion and hostility. Though in Java mixed-race men were typically employed in numerous lower-level professional jobs, few Deli planters would employ *sinyos* as accountants, scribes, or clerks. White-collar jobs were reserved for Europeans. As Van Marle explained, "Already I have spoken of the misplaced shame some felt concerning their 'Indies blood.' Nevertheless it is not surprising, if you hear how others thought about this Indies blood. The remark was repeated into a lot of ears, very clearly, that 'The Indo-European is a profoundly unfortunate product of Dutch sexual abuse and Inlandsche [Indonesian native] selling [prostitution].'"

When Rudolf entered Deli society as garrison commander, he probably worried that Gretha's Indo appearance would cause him considerable embarrassment. If he were also involved with an Indo *nyai*, his tension must have been nearly unbearable. Rudolf's letters to Gretha during their two-month separation in 1899 are harsh and critical. They reveal his increasing agitation over the necessity that their household—and her behavior—be impeccably European.

While Rudolf enjoyed the raucous, masculine atmosphere of Medan, Gretha and the children had been thrust upon Mr. and Mrs. van Rheede in Tumpang. Van Rheede was the government comptroller of the province. According to an interview given by the van

Rheedes around 1927, the arrangement was effected rather peremptorily by Rudolf. He rode up to their house at about seven one morning and, without dismounting, proceeded to announce that in a few hours his wife and children would be coming to stay with the Van Rheedes "for about a week. That is all right, isn't it?" Indies hospitality was legendary, and although the MacLeods and van Rheedes were not especially close friends, the latter agreed, never dreaming that their guests would stay with them for more than two months. Rudolf may have felt that putting his wife into a respectable household, with little spending money, would keep her from seeing other men while he was gone.

On March 28, after he had been in Medan about a week, Rudolf wrote to his wife, describing Medan in enthusiastic terms that were somewhat undercut by the realities he could not help but mention: "It is strange to see this city with its many multiple-storied homes and its excellent roads: electric lights, beautiful *tokos* [shops] that outshine those in Batavia, wonderful horses and carriages. They have had to kill 739 dogs during two days on account of rabies, but Blackie is inside the house and feels fine; and now, dear Griet, adieu! and be sure to give my regards to the van Rheedes."

As the "week" grew into more than a month, Gretha ran so short of money that, as Mrs. van Rheede expressed it, the situation was "becoming quite embarrassing." Gretha's everyday clothes were a *kebaya* and *sarong*, and even these were worn. Gretha had no money to buy new ones, much less new European garments.

Finally, Mrs. van Rheede wrote to her sister who lived in Medan, asking her to make Rudolf aware that his wife urgently needed money. To receive such a message from an outsider must have humiliated Rudolf. What would happen to the prestige and respect he enjoyed as garrison commander if people learned he kept his wife so short of funds that distant acquaintances had to beg him to send money to her? Mrs. van Rheede apparently felt rather sorry for her guest, describing Gretha as intelligent, charming, and nice, "if a little bit frivolous." Gretha regularly went to the local club where she was always surrounded by a crowd of admirers. But Mrs. van Rheede believed Gretha suffered primarily "from being married with a much older man, who was extremely jealous and who did not guide her along, but on the contrary was in some way her enemy."

On April 11, Rudolf wrote to Gretha saying: "Wire me if you need money." It is a peculiar communication that was probably meant to be made public, because he knew she needed money and yet did not send any. On April 24, he urged again, "You know always that you do not have to worry about expenses, I will send more [money] quickly when you ask for it, but 150 guilders, that is not sufficient [for the fares?]."

Other parts of this letter reveal the tension between Rudolf and Gretha, whom he often still called Griet. He had complained in a previous letter that she wrote too infrequently; she had replied that she was waiting for a response—a letter or money?—to her last letter. He blamed the problem on her foolishness. "You mention that 'after having written me two letters, you are waiting for my answer from Medan.' Come now, Griet, I bet that by now you are laughing about your stupidity. 'To wait for an answer from Medan'—but Griet, that takes about sixteen days, and you mean to say that you intended not to write during all this time? That is really typical of you!"

Elsewhere in the same long letter, he complained: "The thing that makes me so often inwardly complain is the fact that we absolutely never have any financial luck, and what a great many rotten things we have been obliged to do on account of all that lack of money."

The lack of "luck" may be an oblique reference to the fact that

Rudolf was spending more money than ever on drinking, gambling, and another woman.

His letter then turned to a certain lieutenant she had mentioned in her letter. He quizzed her jealously about his identity.

> *Who is that naval lieutenant you wrote about, who photographed the children, and how did he happen to be in Tumpang? You never explain things of that sort, Griet, and you can perfectly well understand that when I read this, I start thinking, now, who is that again, and how did he get to Tumpang? It's funny you suddenly jump from [Norman's] sailor suit and [Non's] affectionate nature to that lieutenant and then I do not hear a word about him any more! . . . Yes Griet, just try to understand that when I rave and swear, this is caused principally because I am afraid for the children, for do not forget that our characters differ tremendously.*

In response to this, or another one of Rudolf's rambling and insulting letters, Gretha remarked to her hostess bitterly one evening when she came in from a walk, "I wanted to be bitten by a snake tonight, so I would not have to go back to him." She had no real alternative but to go back to Rudolf.

When Gretha did write, Rudolf was abusive and completely dissatisfied with the quality of her correspondence. In another letter, he chastised her mercilessly:

> *A puerile letter such as that of yesterday does me no good at all and if you don't know how to write better you might as well abstain from writing. . . . If you knew how your silly and superficial letter irritated me yesterday, you would be ashamed. . . . But in the face of your stupidity you have no*

sense of honor, happily for you. In effect, there is not a single word that is worth the pain of reading it. . . . You are satisfied when you have filled a page of foolishness with your scribbles, with nothing of your interior life playing the least part. . . . You are too limited, too stupid and superficial to ever write an interesting letter, you can speak only of beautiful dresses, of hairdos and other banalities, for outside of this nothing interests you and everything is strange. Do you understand now why I am always in a bloody temper because of you?

On May 2, Rudolf still had not made the reservations for Gretha and the children to join him, probably because he could not pay the fare. He wrote her bitterly:

I await your telegram, the money is at your disposition, but you have only to ask. . . .

For the love of God, think to note your expenses, because I swear to you, we do not have a lot and all the cares fall upon me, because you are not capable of identifying them [expenditures] when I ask you what this is.

You will always have what it takes to live, but the good God must be ashamed of having created a creature without a single value like yourself. We live in a bizarre world: one of us has all the worries, must work hard and unhappily, and the other doesn't do a thing with her ten fingers and is allowed to live without concerning herself with anyone or anything.

But believe me, Griet, when I will have disappeared and you are the same useless creature as now, you will cry tears of blood for not having done your duty better in your life and for not having passed the precious time doing anything except dressing yourself, eating, and sleeping, and when, then, you are

dragging your poor children down into your misery—but stop
there. Truly, I had thought for a moment that you would have
an identical reasoning to mine, and now I make myself laugh: I
know better than you what I keep to myself. Upon people with
no sentiment of honor, with neither refinement nor education,
similar logic has no effect. . . . Believe me, my soul is dark and
somber, when I think of the future of my poor children. Ah! If
I am not there, then sail the ship *[rush headlong to disaster]*
and après moi le déluge!

May 2 being Non's birthday, he added an anxious wish: "May
God see that the little dear one has a happy life and that I may yet
see her grow up and prosper."

Rudolf worried obsessively about his children because they were
not with him. He knew very well how quickly an adult, much less a
child, could fall ill and die in the tropics. He was also gripped by a
tremendous fear that was increasingly common in the Indies: that
the servants were not to be trusted with the care of the children.
Unfortunately, he did not believe his wife was to be trusted with
them either. He wrote:

God knows what is going on with Norman or little Louise
[Non]. . . . Norman is always so exuberant and takes great
risks, and good God, what will I do if he comes to harm?

I am anxious: I know well that you do not concern yourself
with these things; you give yourself airs, but you are insensible
to everything. You know me, therefore you know that I am tor-
mented at present. At last, I have nothing to do, other than
wait, hope, and pray . . . I give myself all sorts of black ideas and
I am anxious more and more. All in writing, I never stop
thinking: when will it come?

*Perhaps Norman has been killed by a serpent or he has
eaten poison!*

That Rudolf despised and mistrusted Gretha was obvious. His
fears for his children were also based on an acute awareness that
they were genuinely at risk. If Rudolf had contracted syphilis and
given it to Gretha, she would have passed it to the children during
childbirth. This interpretation makes sense of many of his extreme
and vehement emotional responses. His extreme, almost rabid jealousy of Gretha may have been based on the fact that he believed she
had caught syphilis from someone else early in their marriage. He
would not want to believe she had caught it from him because he
had been treated for months by doctors before their marriage. She
in turn would have been deeply resentful that he had given the disease to her—a despicable act. Thus the deep cruelty and vicious
anger in their marriage may have drawn its venom from their common affliction for which each blamed the other.

Rudolf's exaggerated concern about his children's health was
less bizarre if the children suffered from congenital syphilis, a common killer in the late nineteenth century. Even today, about 40 percent of children with untreated congenital syphilis die perinatally.
What greater guilty terror might a father experience than to fear he
had condemned his own children to illness and death?

Is there evidence that little Norman and Non suffered from congenital syphilis? What would their symptoms be?

Paul Diday, in his authoritative 1859 work on the topic, explained:

*A child born with the germs of syphilis, and which will present in a
short time the most marked manifestations of that disease, may
come into the world with every appearance of health and even of a
vigorous constitution. . . .*

In the generality of cases, however, this is not the usual course
of things. From their very birth, and although as yet without any
distinctly syphilitic symptoms, the subjects of hereditary taint may
often be recognized. There is a certain habitus, *a general physiog-*
nomy, about the expression about which parents already taught by
a previous accident of the same nature, or an experienced physi-
cian, are rarely deceived . . . as Doublet has more simply expressed
it, "they present a miniature picture of decrepitude." . . .

Next to this look of little old men, *so common in new-born*
children doomed to syphilis, the most characteristic sign is the color
of the skin. . . . Before the health becomes affected, the child has
already a peculiar appearance; the skin, especially that of the face,
loses its transparency; its rosy color disappears, and is replaced by a
sooty tint, which resembles that in Asiatics. It is yellow, or like cof-
fee mixed with milk, or looked as if it had been exposed to smoke;
it has an empyreumatic color, similar to that which exists on the
fingers of persons who are in the habit of smoking cigarettes. It ap-
pears as if a layer of coloring matter had been laid on unequally; it
sometimes occupies the whole of the skin, but is more marked in
certain favorite spots, as the forehead, eyebrows, chin, nose, eye-
lids, in short, the most prominent parts of the face; the deeper parts,
such as the internal angle of the orbit, the hollow of the cheek, and
that which separates the lower lip from the chin, almost always re-
main free from it. Although the face is commonly the part most af-
fected, the rest of the body always participates more or less in this
tint. The child becomes pale and wan.

Any child of Gretha's might have inherited her swarthy skin.
Was it a sign of syphilis? It is easy to imagine Gretha and Rudolf
inspecting their children daily, agonizing over whether their skin
color was symptomatic or normal. Sometimes syphilitic symptoms

showed up immediately and children died at birth; sometimes, cruelly, syphilitic children seemed healthy for two or three years and were then struck down. As Diday commented, even when a father had undergone treatment, there was no guarantee that the child would be spared: "Experience shows that, in spite of the most prolonged latency of the poison [that caused syphilis], and of the absence of any constitutional symptoms for four, six, and ten years, an individual may beget syphilitic children."

Even if both Rudolf and Gretha had been treated for syphilis in the Netherlands, the first years of their children's lives would be a time of torture as they watched and waited for symptoms to appear.

This special anxiety had to be concealed from the rest of society at all cost. Extreme parental caution was somewhat more ordinary in the late nineteenth century in Indies society than now. Hygienic and racial vigilance—protecting white prestige and white health—was a growing fixation, and nowhere was it stronger than in Deli. European wives were tacitly charged with redefining and enforcing moral and racial boundaries by their irreproachable behavior, while, paradoxically, European women were also seen as being more delicate, having finer sensibilities, and needing extra protection from the crudeness and sexual rapacity of the natives. The worst segment of European society was the poor whites, who were regarded as being in imminent danger of "going native" and sinking into the moral morass of the *kampongs* with a horde of illegitimate Indo children. Modern historian Ann Laura Stoler explains beliefs at the end of the nineteenth century:

> Good colonial living now meant hard work and physical exercise
> rather than sexual release, which had been one rationale for condoning
> concubinage and prostitution in an earlier period. The debilitating

climate could be surmounted by regular diet and meticulous personal hygiene over which European women were to take full charge. . . . Adherence to strict conventions of cleanliness and cooking occupied an inordinate amount of time of colonial women and those who served them. Cleanliness itself served as a "prop to a Europeanness that was less than assumed." Both activities entailed constant surveillance of native nursemaids, laundrymen, and live-in servants while demanding a heightened domesticity for European women themselves.

Indeed, such hypervigilance was just what Rudolf demanded that Gretha exert. In the last letter he wrote to her before she went to Medan, Rudolf's alarm over the children's health was rampant:

I am glad to have received your letter of 25 April this morning, with your description of the children's illness. There is a lot of work waiting for you here, Griet, for these houses are dangerous to live in if one is not constantly clean. If one is not continuously busy with sweeping, moving of flowerpots and tarring of the premises, all kinds of vermin crawl around. Thus last night I saw a scorpion the size of which I had never before seen in my life. Although the bite of such a beast is not immediately fatal, it does cause a high fever and for small children it is very dangerous. Therefore you'll have to inspect the rooms every day yourself, clean the children's beds and move the flowerpots. I am glad to note from your letter that you are perfectly aware of your heavy responsibility with the children and that you take care of them with devotion.

At the time, Norman, his favorite, was just a few months over two years old and Nonnie had just turned one. Either still might

The commandant's house in Medan was outside of the garrison and overlooked the river. (Collection of the KITLV, Leiden, The Netherlands, #3501)

suddenly show signs of congenital syphilis and die. Rudolf's demands that Gretha become a more diligent and careful household manager can be read as a desperate attempt to control at least some of the dangers that threatened his family. Fear for the children was overlaid with a poisonous mixture of guilt, anger, and jealousy.

At long last, Rudolf sent money and booked the tickets for Gretha, Norman, and Nonnie to join him. It was usual in the Indies for the children's *babus* to accompany the family on such a relocation, so in all probability they came too. They sailed from the port city of Surabaya on the S.S. *Reijniers*, commanded by Captain Haye. Gretha took advantage of the money Rudolf had sent and spent much of the day before departure shopping. Rudolf was outraged, ostensibly because she left the children with their *babus*. However, since the *babus* took care of the children all day every day, this seems a flimsy pretense. More probably he was upset by the expen-

R udolf presided over military ceremonies like this one at the government office in
Medan. (Collectie KIT Tropenmuseum)

diture. Having had no money to spend on herself in months, Gretha
saw this as perhaps her last chance to refresh her wardrobe (she
bought dresses and gloves) before the great unknown of Medan.
And she was, undeniably, a vain woman who loved clothes.

The family arrived in Medan on May 26. After a brief stay in the
Hotel de Boer, they moved into the splendid house Rudolf had se-
cured for them in one of the finest areas of Medan. A few days after
moving in, on May 31, the MacLeods hosted a farewell party for
General Reisz, who had preceded Rudolf as garrison commander.

Gretha had already received some cruel insults from some of the
other women in Medan, so she took advantage of their first official
entertainment to exact revenge. Exquisitely dressed, young and beautiful and dark-skinned, she insisted on rank and formal ceremony in
greeting the guests. As the older officers' wives arrived, she refused
to move forward to greet them graciously but stood imperiously by

Rudolf's side and made them come to her. Rudolf was angered by her actions, but doubtless Gretha felt the women were merely getting what they deserved: a pointed reminder that, despite her dark skin, she was superior to them in every way.

Real disaster came swiftly.

6

Death of a Child

PREDICTABLY, RUDOLF WAS FURIOUS with Gretha as soon as he saw the children. He thought they looked thin, pale, and neglected—just what he had feared during the two-month separation. He called the garrison doctor to examine them. According to MacLeod family stories, the doctor advised a special diet for Norman, who was in worse health; apparently a potion or medicine was also prescribed. Ominously, the children's condition deteriorated during the first days of the doctor's regimen. But after about a week, Rudolf noted that Norman's color was better and he was playing with his toys with more enthusiasm.

The bitter misery of the MacLeod marriage had returned in full force almost as soon as the couple were reunited. On June 10, Rudolf wrote a long letter to his sister, Tante Frida, about Gretha.

> *How she makes me suffer! I am spending all my days without saying a single word to her, she has nothing to do*

except for her pleasure and was scandalously negligent of the poor little ones. . . .

And how am I to disentangle myself from such a floozy, while keeping the children? This will be very difficult, Louise. Ah! If I had the money to buy her consent, for this debauched woman would do anything for money. . . . If I could get rid of her, I would think myself rich, but to lay myself open to one such as she, the sort who would press the law, she looks out for herself well. . . .

If I have not written enough, it is because at every moment I am thinking of my children and each day I give thanks to God, that I have hastened their return. This vain and egotistical creature would have killed them, by not thinking of them. It is thus that I pray that God gives me a long life, because I would be in a frightful agony thinking what would come to pass concerning the honor of my name, under her wicked influence, if this creature were to raise my children. . . .

P.S. If I could deliver myself of this bitch, I would be happy. Sometimes, I cannot bear to have this creature around me; but what can I do to get rid of her? With or without scandal, it is the same to me.

These are the words of a tormented man trapped in a dreadful marriage.

Suddenly the children's health worsened precipitously. On June 20, Norman began violent vomiting and was taken to the household of Lieutenant Adjutant Baerveldt, which was better suited for frequent visits from the doctor. Probably the lieutenant lived on the base, unlike the MacLeods.

The most detailed account of the children's illness is given by Charles Heymans, whose source was Rudolf, Rudolf's letters, and

Rudolf's third wife. No mention is made of Non in Heymans's account, perhaps indicating how strongly Rudolf favored his son over his daughter. Other sources indicate that both children were ill and vomiting; probably Nonnie was also transferred to the Baerveldt house.

The children improved slightly after a few days, and on June 27 Rudolf visited at lunchtime to bring a favorite toy to his son. At 12:30 P.M. Norman and Non began again to vomit repeatedly, painfully retching up a terrible black liquid with thick clots in it. Rudolf stayed by his son's bedside, holding the tiny, hot little hand in his own. Between bouts of vomiting, Norman bravely asked to put on his sailor suit and go for a ride in a carriage with his papa. He also asked for his medicine, so he could get well again.

Slowly the boy sank into unconsciousness, mumbling and then falling silent, though he still appeared to be in great pain. At 12:30 A.M. Norman died. He was only two years and five months old. Rudolf lifted the small body and placed it on a wheeled stretcher. With the aid of two soldiers, he took his son home and put him in his office. Abandoning his small daughter, who was still very ill, Rudolf spent the night keeping watch over his dead son. As the boy lay in his coffin the next morning, Rudolf cut a lock of his hair. Six months later, he sealed the lock of hair into an envelope on which he wrote: "Hair of my only son, cut in his little coffin on 28 June, 1899, enclosed on 27 December, 1899." Rudolf saved the leaves of the calendar from June 27 and 28, writing on them, "Day of the death and day of the burial of my dear Norman."

The funeral was held the day after the boy's death, at 5 P.M., with full military pomp and splendor. All the officers of the garrison attended. In the days before refrigeration, funerals in the tropics could not wait. According to Heymans, Rudolf and his third wife said that the garrison doctor had thought the cause of death was criminal

Rudolf adored his son, Norman, who died of poisoning a few months before his third birthday. Rudolf wrote to his sister, "He was my darling, the little one, and my life is empty and arid without him." Norman probably died of treatment for congenital syphilis. (The Mata Hari Foundation/Fries Museum)

poisoning and wanted to conduct an autopsy. The garrison pharmacist examined the vomitus and was not so sure. Rudolf refused to permit an autopsy.

A few days later, on July 4, Rudolf again wrote to his sister in anguish.

Ah, Louise, I am profoundly unhappy and miss my little dear every minute of day and night. I have prayed and supplicated that he would be saved but in vain. . . . Oh great God, I have suffered enough and I feel so old. I have no other resort. . . . He was my darling, the little one, and my life is empty and arid without him. He was everything on earth to me, my illusion and the point of my life. I am stricken and there is nothing I possess dearer than he was, and I will never see him again. It is why I am happy to quit the service.

And thus, if I were dead myself and my wife had to continue his education, it would be all and badly turn out; also God alone knows if it is not for the best this way.

Of his wife, he says simply: "Gretha is at the end of her resources with care and sorrow."

The most direct evidence of Gretha's reaction to Norman's death was a terse postcard she wrote to her father and stepmother on July 27: "The 28th of June my lovely little Norman has died and I am not in a state to write much about it. Concerning sorrow, the Indies doesn't spare anything. I thank God that on the 29th of December we are going to ask for a pension and come back to Holland. I cannot write any more. The passing of my dear Norman has taken everything out of me."

Zelle painted a poignant vision of Gretha's sorrow in his novelized account of her marriage. The narrator's voice, meant to reflect Gretha's thoughts and feelings, spoke of crippling despair and grief over the death of such a young and innocent child:

My child had been poisoned!

Why or by whom was initially an unfathomable riddle; and this it would probably have always remained, when at the hour of death the perpetrator herself confessed. It was one of our babus!

And what was the reason of this dishonorable act? I have to recognize that I have never been able to feel certain about this, never sure, although it seems highly likely that revenge has been the most important motivation for the murder. It was said that the babu *was the lover of a lower soldier in the army who, in his opinion, had been unjustly and wrongfully punished by my husband. To cool his rancor about this, [the soldier] must have used his lover the* babu *to strike back at the wife and child of his enemy. Others added to this that MacLeod maybe had had an affair with the infamous* babu *after which one of his inferiors, a soldier, fell in love with her. If these were the facts, it would not be surprising in military circles in Java, but I could not swear to the truth of this because I have no proof.*

Heymans also reported the story that, fifteen days after Norman's death, the *babu* was struck down with cholera and on her deathbed confessed to poisoning the children. Waagenaar's biography repeated the versions of the death that blame the *babu*.

A slightly different account of the cause of the poisoning appeared in a 1964 reminiscence by the Balkstra sisters, Louise and Laura, who had known Gretha in Java late in the nineteenth century. Their father, G. P. Balkstra, had started a coffee plantation called Kemloko on the slopes of Kloet, a volcano in Central Java, not far from Malang. Gretha was a frequent visitor to Kemloko after being introduced to the Balkstras by their good friend Mary Greve, whom she had met on the boat over. As the Balkstras recounted the story, using the nickname Greta instead of Griet or Gretha,

> *Greta was a high-spirited young thing, her spouse a quiet and withdrawn character. In Atjeh, the first duty station of the major, took place a drama that cost the life of the older of the two children from this unequal marriage.*
>
> *Out of revenge for a disciplinary sentence, which the major had imposed on his orderly, the woman of the orderly who served as cook at the MacLeods' poisoned Norman, then four years old, apple of his father's eyes and the picture of his mother, whose splendid eyes he had inherited.*
>
> *MacLeod never recovered from that blow. He grew more and more somber, withdrew into himself more each Tuesday—the deathday of his little son—with his portrait. His grief took on a pathological character. He blamed himself shockingly: he should not have punished the orderly, then Norman would be still alive. . . .*
>
> *With each day, the gap widened between the lively young woman and the dark, much older man. Each time for longer periods Greta withdrew from his presence. When the family MacLeod was*

stationed in Banjoe Biroe, the always welcoming atmosphere of Kemloko with its bright and lively family life became a sanctuary, where she sometimes months stayed. Her best friend at Kemloko became Louise, who was first the girlfriend of Mary Greve, the link between Greta and the Balkstras.

The Balkstras' reminiscences are demonstrably inaccurate in detail, since Norman was only two years old when he died, not four, and Rudolf's first posting was to Ambarawa, not Atjeh. But the essence of the story—that Norman was poisoned by a female servant in revenge for an act of Rudolf's—is consistent with other versions.

Despite the repetition of similar stories, the idea that Norman was poisoned by his *babu* is extraordinary, almost unbelievable. Undoubtedly these stories were circulated at the time, but their veracity is suspect. For a *babu* to thus attack her charge is virtually unknown in fiction or fact about the Dutch East Indies. For the *babu* to then die so conveniently fifteen days later, after confessing the crime on her deathbed, strains credulity.

In all probability, the children's *babus* came with the family to Sumatra and were therefore as newly arrived in Medan as Gretha and the children themselves. From the time of their arrival in Medan, the children were unwell— witness Rudolf's insistence that they be examined by a doctor. They began vomiting and showing serious signs of illness a mere seventeen days after their arrival. If this vomiting was caused by one of the *babus* who was seeking revenge for Rudolf's punishing her soldier boyfriend, she had acquired a devoted lover very rapidly and Rudolf had punished him severely in a short period. Even if it was the cook, not the *babu*, who poisoned the children, nothing about these stories explains why it was the children, not Rudolf himself, who were poisoned. Would not poisoning the harsh garrison commander—or the sexual assaulter—himself make a more fitting revenge than killing his innocent children?

Poisoning in and of itself is easily believed. In Indies novels and memoirs, poisoning of Europeans by natives was widely thought to occur. However, in these sources, *babus* were not the poisoners and the children they cared for were not the victims. In Indies literature, *nyais* poison or otherwise kill either their masters or their masters' wives.

Though greatly feared, poisoning was not a common cause of death. According to official documents, between 1894 and 1899, only fifteen Europeans and thirteen natives in the Dutch East Indies were treated for poisoning, and none of these died. The opportunity to poison someone was always present, because every adult Indonesian man whose family could afford it owned a kris, a singularly Indonesian, wavy-edged dagger. By tradition, once a year a kris should be cleaned and reconsecrated. Part of the ceremony is bathing the kris in a substance called *warangan*, mixed with water, to bring out the intricate pattern of the different metals in the blade. *Warangan* is a potentially fatal arsenic compound (arsenic trioxide), and it was (and is) available in almost any Indonesian household or any market.

How much *warangan* would have to be administered to cause death? Fatal doses are tiny, on the order of one to fifteen milligrams of arsenic trioxide or sodium arsenate for a toddler.

Would *warangan* poisoning fit the crime as it is reported? The main symptoms of acute arsenic poisoning—severe nausea, vomiting, bloody diarrhea, abdominal cramping—are consistent with those of the MacLeod children. Additional symptoms of arsenic poisoning not mentioned in Norman's case are a dry, burning mouth, a metallic taste in the mouth, garlicky breath, headache, and cold, clammy extremities, followed by hair loss after two to three weeks (if the patient survives so long). Neuropathies in the extremities, renal damage or failure, or dermatologic problems may also be found among survivors.

Other traditional means of poisoning relied on the considerable number of plant-derived poisons that were well known in the Dutch East Indies. *Guna-guna*, or black magic, was widely feared by the native population and many of the Europeans as well. The most commonly used native poison was a decoction prepared from the leaves, sap, or fruit of *Datura fastuosa*. In Indonesia, the poison was administered either by mixing an extract with food or by creeping into the house at night and blowing a dried powder of *Datura* into the nostrils of a sleeping victim.

Symptoms of *Datura* poisoning are caused by its two main pharmacologic ingredients, hyoscamine (an antispasmodic and antisalivation drug) and scopolamine (used in ophthalmic preparations to dilate the iris). *Datura* is also a hallucinogenic. A vivid description of the effects of *Datura* ingestion is given in an anonymous ditty: "Red as a beet, dry as a bone, blind as a bat, mad as a hatter, hot [sexually aroused] as a hare." These symptoms do not match those described of the MacLeod children.

Another way of examining Norman's death is in the context of its being an attack on a white person by an Indonesian, a circumstance that in Sumatra raised extreme anxieties at the time. The poisoning (or suspected poisoning) of the son of one of Medan's most prominent citizens would surely have caused an uproar and a thorough investigation. Yet none of the four major Indies newspapers of the day and none of the three more local Sumatran newspapers carried anything about inquiries into Norman's death.

A discreet official death notice appeared in the *Deli Current* (*Deli Courant*) on June 28:

Our darling
NORMAN JOHN MAC LEOD
passed away this night.
R. MAC LEOD
M.G. MAC LEOD—ZELLE
MEDAN, JUNE 28, 1899

On July 1, the bereaved parents put in another formal notice thanking people for their expressions of sympathy. There was no other acknowledgment of Norman's death in these newspapers.

The striking absence of newspaper coverage of Norman's death cannot be attributed to delicacy. During the same year, Indies newspapers included a long, rather graphic account of a colonial housewife who shot herself with her husband's revolver in a fit of despair and another account of a planter who was attacked by natives with machetes and agricultural tools. The Deli newspapers were so local and gossipy in character that almost any event was reported. In early June of 1899, for example, there was a series of articles and letters debating the quality of a musical concert that had been given by a visiting professor who had been accompanied by local amateurs. That Norman's death featured in not a single article or letter shows clearly that it was not considered a suspicious death or potential poisoning in Medan.

Other potential sources of information are the *Colonial Report* and the *Government Almanac for Netherlands-Indies 1899–1901*. The first is an annual report compiled by the provincial governor on all of the happenings in his province, reported numerically; the latter summarizes several years from all of the provinces. While these reports are sometimes inaccurate with regard to native Indonesians, the number of Europeans in eastern Sumatra in 1899 was so small that nothing pertaining to them was likely to be missed.

Appendix E of the *Colonial Report* lists the deaths of Europeans in eastern Sumatra in 1899, divided by age, sex, and place of origin (Indies-born or not Indies-born). In 1899, Norman was the only European child born outside of the Indies and between the ages of two and ten years to die; eight Indies-born children of similar age also died. Norman was not identified by name, nor was there any comment on the cause of his death. This lack of remark is flatly impossible if there had been anything suspicious about his death. There is no remark about Norman's death in the *Almanac*.

What alternative hypotheses would account for Norman's death and the lack of comment upon it? And what motivation or action would account for the children, rather than Rudolf, falling ill when Rudolf at the time was widely held responsible for provoking the attack?

The first and most obvious explanation is some sort of accidental food poisoning, which is reasonably common even in modern Indonesia. Children ate separately from their parents, so food poisoning affecting Norman and Non would not necessarily strike the senior MacLeods. Were that the case, Norman's death was simply another tragedy of life in the tropics. The MacLeods would mourn, the friends and colleagues would offer sympathy, and nothing out of the ordinary would have occurred.

The second hypothesis is that the garrison physician who was treating Norman and Nonnie was attempting to cure congenital syphilis. This hypothesis, which traces the death back to Rudolf's contracting syphilis, has never before been evaluated. Indeed, no previous writer concerned with Mata Hari's life ever noticed the glaring lack of newspaper coverage and comment on Norman's death.

Is this hypothesis probable? Certainly, if the garrison physician miscalculated the dosage of the mercury compounds he was giving the children, because he was used to treating grown men, then he would have poisoned them inadvertently. Further, the children's symptoms of violent vomiting, incoherence, diarrhea, and abdominal cramping match those of mercury poisoning as well as they do those of arsenic poisoning, both mercury and arsenic being heavy metals.

According to modern medical texts, ingestion of 0.5 grams of mercuric chloride (the most common preparation used in treating syphilis then) usually produces serious symptoms within about ten to fifteen minutes; fatal doses are recorded after ingestion of 1 to 1.5 grams. Modern mortality rates are much improved since the use of chelating agents, which were not available in 1899. However, in eighteen relatively recent cases of a single ingestion of mercuric chloride, all patients experienced severe symptoms and nine individuals died. The fatal doses in these cases ranged from 29 milligrams per kilogram of body weight to 50 milligrams per kilogram of body weight. Children are notoriously more susceptible to poisoning with mercuric chloride than adults.

Overdosing a very young child during treatment for congenital syphilis must have occurred fairly commonly. The standard advice in the late nineteenth century for the treatment of congenital syphilis was to increase the dosage of "bichloride of mercury"—the usual name for mercuric chloride then—dissolved in syrup (to facilitate swallowing) until excessive salivation appeared. Iodide of potassium dissolved in syrup was a second choice of treatment. However, Diday warned that

> *[a child's] gastrointestinal mucous membrane may be too suscepti-*
> *ble to bear the irritating contact of preparations of mercury or io-*
> *dine. There is even need of greater vigilance here to forestall the*
> *inflammation before it breaks out, and to meet it on its earliest in-*
> *dication by the suspension of the internal treatment. . . .*

*Employment of remedies internally irritates the stomach and
occasions diarrhea, a tympanic condition of the abdomen, cries,
and an expression of suffering remarked during the first hours which
follow the ingestion of them—if vomiting supervenes under the
same circumstances, and especially if emaciation be observed, do
not wait for more serious derangements before changing your plan
of treatment. The substitution of topical remedies for internal ones
then becomes imperative and cannot be adopted too soon.*

Contradicting this caution, he also advised that syphilis pro-
ceeds rapidly and the dose must be increased equally rapidly to a
maximum tolerable dose.

Salivation was a sign that the effective dose was being reached,
according to Diday, and he argued that a degree of inflammation of
the gums and intestines must be endured and used as a guide that
the physician was giving a big enough dose. In this, Diday was disastrously wrong. Excessive salivation is one of the signs that a toxic
dose has been reached.

Diday continued:

*So long as strength, sleep, and plumpness are absent, [we] must
persist in the treatment and increase the doses rapidly. . . . I will
say that we may commence by administering one tenth of a grain
[6.5 milligrams] of bichloride or three twentieths of a grain of
Hahnemann's soluble mercury, in three doses, in the course of the
twenty-four hours. This quantity may be augmented one twentieth
of a grain every three days until it produces a sensible effect either
upon the mouth, or upon the syphilitic symptoms. The daily quantity may then be diminished, as is done for the adult, so as to keep
up a slight action on the gums, or rather so as to reproduce it, several times in succession, during the whole course of the treatment.*

If the garrison physician who treated the MacLeod children followed the treatment protocol prescribed by Diday in his standard textbook, he began their treatment with 6.5 milligrams of mercury bichloride and increased that amount by 3.25 milligrams every three days. After about a month of such treatment, each child would have ingested 175.5 milligrams of mercury bichloride, a dangerous amount for small children. If the children had been treated previously with mercuric chloride, their total chronic ingestion would have been much higher.

The timing was right. In the case of the MacLeod children, vomiting began less than two weeks after treatment by the garrison physician began, worsened and became fatal to Norman after three to four weeks. If the children were poisoned by the garrison doctor, their death soon after arrival in Medan was related directly to the onset of his medical care. The strength of this hypothesis is that it explains why Norman died so soon after his arrival in Medan, it accounts for the children's symptoms, and it explains the fact that the children, not Rudolf, were poisoned.

Why, then, was there no public comment on the death in the newspapers? The MacLeods and the physician had good reasons to suppress any suspicions. All would have been ruined had the cause of death come out. Thus, those most intimately involved in the death had a vested interest in preventing further inquiry, such as an autopsy. Instead, they spread a flimsy story that blamed the death on a vengeful native who died most conveniently. The story had the added benefit of playing into the colonists' fears and distrust of Indonesians.

The third and least likely possibility is that an Indo woman was involved, but instead of being the *babu,* the poisoner was Rudolf's former *nyai.* If Rudolf had resumed his relationship with her without telling her of his changed marital status, her hopes of obtaining European status for herself and/or any child she had borne Rudolf previously would have been cruelly dashed when Gretha and the children arrived. Poisoning Rudolf's European children would have been vengeance for his preferring them and Gretha over the *nyai* and her children. The *nyai* may even have hoped that, once Norman and Nonnie were dead, Rudolf would turn to her child or children and officially recognize him/them. This scenario also explains why the children were attacked, not Rudolf, and why the attack occurred so rapidly after the arrival of Gretha and the children in Medan. However, it does not explain the lack of comment on the death or the lack of an investigation. It is wildly improbable that a poisoning *nyai* would be permitted to get away with her crime when the ruling class in society was so anxious to maintain its superior status. At the very least, a serious and ruthless criminal investigation would have been initiated—and it was not.

Analyzed in this way, the bulk of the evidence indicates that Norman died either of random causes, which required no public comment and had nothing to do with the family's recent arrival in Sumatra, or of inadvertent poisoning during treatment for congenital syphilis shortly after his being placed under the care of a new physician. The lock of hair that Rudolf cut at the time of Norman's death still exists, in the care of his descendants. If the living family would permit a few hairs from the lock to be analyzed for traces of mercury or arsenic, definitive proof of his cause of death might be forthcoming. Unfortunately, the family is wary of publicity and has declined repeated requests to provide hairs for examination.

There is one additional piece of pertinent evidence: Rudolf's career trajectory tips the favor toward the congenital-syphilis hypothesis. On July 24, less than a month after Norman's death, Rudolf was abruptly transferred back to Java to a posting of much lesser significance. Rudolf had been in the Indies with his family since 1897 and rising rapidly in his promotion and postings, yet immediately after the death of his son, and only four months after his arrival in Medan, his career turned sour once again. If his performance as garrison commander in that short time had been less than perfect, Rudolf would have been accorded pity and sympathy from his colleagues because his only son had died. Instead, he was removed from his post, sent away from Sumatra, and effectively demoted. This transfer suggests serious official disapproval, perhaps resulting from a suspicion or rumor about Norman's death.

The MacLeods remained on Sumatra for another few weeks until Rudolf's replacement, Major P. A. Gallas, formally assumed command on September 1. Then the devastated family left for Batavia on the S.S. *Riebeek* with Captain Koppeschar. From there, they were sent to Banjoe Biroe, a small village near Semarang. The transfer was a bitter disappointment to Rudolf and, probably, to Gretha. Leaving Norman's grave behind, where they could never visit it again, was deeply painful.

After Norman's death, the MacLeods' marriage deteriorated still further and more disastrously. Rudolf blamed Gretha for the boy's death, and she blamed him. Whatever the cause of his death, the tragedy deepened their vicious hatred for each other. Rudolf's jealousy and brutality flared up in ugly ways; Gretha's resentment and disgust took still crueller forms.

While they lived in Banjoe Biroe, Gretha sometimes sought refuge at Kemloko, the coffee plantation owned by the Balkstra family. She would go there for prolonged visits, to get away from the atmosphere at home.

The Balkstra sisters characterized the woman they called Greta thus:

She was not beautiful, but had a pronounced individuality, full of charm, full of grace; she danced like a goddess. In the evenings she was a complete dancer, mastering the most intricate steps. She gladly dressed herself with much refinement and flirtatiousness. Her mouth was too large; her body too short to call her "beautiful," but she had splendid legs.

Greta outraged Mother Balkstra on numerous occasions [by her behavior toward men, yet she had a] . . . deep affection for the woman, who she started to call "mother" in confidential moments.

"If you had been my mother, I would never have become bad . . . ," Greta said once, though Louise did not yet understand what she could mean by that. Louise had not then the slightest suspicion that Greta was already having affairs with other men.

When Louise went to Banjoe Biroe to visit, then Greta's spouse appeared, although a withdrawn and somber man, he was nevertheless always pleasant and obliging towards his wife: there was no brawling. But there was an immeasurable distance between these two people, whose ideas of life, character and age were particularly badly matched.

Gretha said to Louise and Laura once, "half joking, half serious: 'I will be celebrated . . . or notorious.' And then that prophecy, which essentially came true: 'I will die eventually on the scaffold.'"

The letters Gretha wrote from Banjoe Biroe tell a much more terrible story than the Balkstra sisters' saccharine recollections. Though these letters are clearly self-dramatizing and intended to evoke sympathy, her words reveal her emotions. On December 2, 1899, she wrote to her father and stepmother:

More than ever I am longing for Holland. Good lord, what a lot of problems and sadness in my life. And why all this?

How could one be worried about a rank and a name when one is so deeply unhappy? Don't think that I have a good time with such an old, severe man who does nothing other than watching me, punishing me and telling me one hundred times a day that I am inferior to him, that I should be happy with his name and good family—family who do not even look at me and behave as if I don't exist.

I really have no life. He has all the money in his hands, pays for the milk and the meat and only gives me what is needed for the market (a maximum of 50 cents per day). And if I want to buy needles or thread, then I have to beg him for 10 cents. He doesn't give me clothes because he is afraid that I will look too good. Oh I can't really bear it. And if then you see all these young lieutenants around me, who are always so amorous—then it is very difficult to behave so that he can't reproach me. Thus the Indies is a typical country; isn't Holland the same?

This morning he was looking again for a brawl, so he thumps into me and last week he hit me with his cat-o'-nine-tails, because he thought that I had painted myself; it wasn't true my lips are always that red.

It is impossible to stand this situation any longer. In a moment I will go to his office and I will propose to him that we get a divorce. I will study theater in Amsterdam, and I may become something, but this I don't want any more.

Goodbye, dear parents! Maybe it is better for Norman that he is resting in his grave and does not know what he has been saved from. I do not know one happy person that I would wish this fate on.

Rudolf was disheartened, grieving, and enraged by the injustices of life. He wrote long letters to a cousin and to his sister in Amsterdam, and kept copies for some reason; they were full of

complaints and anguish. He had
lost his taste for the military life
and wanted only to hang on
long enough to earn his pension.

He was convinced that General Reisz, his predecessor in
the Medan garrison and his superior officer, would never promote him to lieutenant colonel
and thus he might as well resign. Life with Gretha was in-
sufferable. He accused her of
squandering money on every
worthless trifle offered by passing merchants and of complaining endlessly. Only little Non

Non MacLeod, here about four years
old, was poisoned at the same time
as Norman but recovered. She died suddenly at age twenty-one, shortly before
she was to leave for Indonesia to be a
schoolteacher. (The Mata Hari Founda-
tion/Fries Museum)

was a comfort to Rudolf, but he worried neurotically about her
health and moral character under the influence of her mother:

> *It is absolutely essential to remove her from the infectious influ-*
> *ence of the filthy nature of her mother, without whom she would*
> *lose nothing. . . . My little girl will become fatally ill if she*
> *stays another six months in the clutches of this woman. . . . If I*
> *were alone I could occupy myself with her education and if I*
> *lived long enough, I would be content, but always I am afraid to*
> *leave her alone [with Gretha] for a single day; then, God knows,*
> *she would be entirely in the hands of her mother, for then—*
> *kassian [an Indies expression meaning "alas" or "pity"] and a*
> *million times* kassian *for her and our name.*

Rudolf damned his wife over and over, labeling her "a scum of the lowest kind . . . a woman without heart, without love of anyone, who cares nothing for anything and who never thinks of my love of the little boy and doesn't speak of him ever."

As always, Gretha was interested in officers and they were interested in her. Jealousy was a potent weapon with which to punish her husband, who—she hinted in her letters—was sometimes impotent. MacLeod wrote that he caught her with a young second lieutenant named "J. v. D." The encounter provoked a violent scene, following which he forbade her to go to a ball in a low-cut gown. In fury, he even offered Gretha her freedom: a divorce. She refused, saying she would not give up her widow's pension when he died. She threatened to flaunt her lovers publicly and blacken his precious name. He admitted in his letter that he was so intensely jealous that he wanted to kill her.

He continued the letter with the mundane grievance that he had been transferred so many times he was going broke. He never accepted that the frequent transfers that marred his career might have been the consequence of his own actions or that the responsibility for his perpetual indebtedness, both before and after his marriage, was related to his extravagant living, drinking, and gambling. His tone ranged from bitter anger to near-suicidal despair.

> *One has nothing to look at but the mountains, and at night it is incredibly quiet, with only here and there a badly functioning lantern spreading an uncertain twilight at the crossroads. Someone who would have the pen to describe the situations in the nearby* kampongs *would give a picture of a "*bête humaine*" [human beast] that is totally different from the one [writer Émile] Zola has given us. Tonight we have another in-*

vasion of butterflies, plus flying ants and termites, and millions
of little insects that drive one crazy. . . .

    [Here there is] deathly monotony. . . . Sundays here are ab-
solutely miserable and people who have suicidal tendency could
easily put it into practice on a day like that.

In March of 1900 Gretha came down with typhoid and was
treated by the medical officer for that part of Preanger regency, Dr.
Roelfsema. Finally, he prescribed a retreat to the cooler tempera-
tures of a coffee plantation in the hills, where she could be nursed
and looked after. She probably went to Kemloko to convalesce.
Having some familiarity with the MacLeod family situation, Roelfsema may also have thought she would regain her strength more
rapidly away from Rudolf's hostility.

After the publication of Charles Heymans's 1936 *The Real Mata*
Hari: Courtesan and Spy, which was highly critical of Mata Hari,
Roelfsema wrote a letter to the prominent Dutch newspaper *General*
Trade Sheet (Algemeen Handelsblad) about the woman that he had
known in Java before she became Mata Hari.

    As a friend of the truth . . . I simply want to give the impres-
sion I have gotten as an impartial observer of this married couple
and also of their understanding during their marriage. . . . Dur-
ing this time I associated a great deal with the family Mac-
Leod and also visited them several times as physician and for
that reason I think I am able to judge the truth about who is re-
sponsible for the tragedy in this marriage. . . .

    During the year and a half I used to know the MacLeod
family, the conduct of Mrs. MacLeod was absolutely cor-
rect, notwithstanding the many rude insults she had to endure

in public from her husband. I often used to wonder whether
Margaretha Zelle might not have grown into a good wife and
mother if her husband had been a more equable and sensible
man. Her marriage to the uneven-tempered and excitable
MacLeod was doomed to failure.

I do not want to mention all the painful scenes, which were
provoked by the husband, for I would have to go into too many
details.

Rudolf's view of Gretha's typhoid, as expressed in a letter to his
cousin on May 31, was harsh and unsympathetic:

Two and a half months ago Griet got an attack of typhoid fever
and her condition got constantly worse. All the care for the
little girl fell on me, and the whole situation was one of endless
misery. Ten days ago Griet was finally able to travel and she is
now on the coffee plantation . . . near Ulingie to regain her
health. You can understand that her illness was an expensive
business when I tell you that we needed five bottles of milk a day
at 30 cents each . . . and now again that trip to Ulingie. I have
kept the little girl here. She is a lovely child, but she reminds me
constantly of my lost darling.

That Rudolf demanded sympathy for having to care for his
daughter—assisted of course by a full household staff, including a
babu and cook—reveals both the depth of his continued fear for
Non's health and the eternal vigilance that he felt was required to
stave off catastrophe. It is an ugly truth that Rudolf earned roughly
700 to 800 guilders a month and yet begrudged his deathly ill wife a
daily expenditure of 1.5 guilders for milk. His complaints reveal the
strength of his hatred for his wife and the extent of his indebtedness.

He continued his letter: "My dear cousin, the loss of that wonderful little boy has cracked something inside of me which will always remain there. The boy loved military music, especially the Monte Carlo march, and every time they play that here I get a pain in my eyes and my chest."

Their house in Banjoe Biroe was near Fort Willem I. Rudolf complained about the immoral atmosphere, with all the officers living nearby with their *nyais*. Perhaps he was too often reminded of his own faults.

On July 29 he wrote his sister that it was almost payday.

> *Merciful God, after tomorrow, payday, for I have not a cent; unhappily, as soon as the money comes in, it is necessary that I send it out [to repay debts] and* voilà! *so begins the whirlpool of another month. . . .*
>
> *With Multatuli [a well-known Dutch colonial writer who was in the civil service], I can cry out: "A little poetry, my God, that I do not perish from disgust because of all the disgusting things in my environment."*

At the end of July, Rudolf sent Gretha to Semarang to visit friends. He enjoyed being separated from her for two days and the unaccustomed peace and quiet, with no fighting or screaming at the servants. He wrote Louise: "After tomorrow, she returns here, to my great regret. . . . That good God should deliver me from this creature! I hope that with all my heart. Amen!"

But there was no deliverance from their desperation and wretchedness.

On October 2, 1900, Rudolf was granted a discharge from military service "because of the fulfilled period of service, [an] honorable [discharge], and with maintenance of the right of a pension."

On November 14 it was ruled that he was entitled to a pension of 2,800 guilders annually, a staggering decrease in income from the 8,400–9,600 guilders he had been earning. He may not have told Gretha the true amount of his pension. In at least one letter she wrote, she referred to it as 2,400 guilders, although the exact amount was of great concern to both of them.

They moved to the village of Sindanglaja, on the side of the volcano known as Gede, between Buitzenborg (now Bogor) and Bandung. A health resort had been set up in the village between 1850 and 1860 because of its mineral spring, altitude, and cooler climate. Living was inexpensive in Sindanglaja, and the scenery was beautiful. Like many ex-military men, Rudolf hoped to recover financial solvency by staying on in Java and living cheaply.

Gretha complained in letters to her father and stepmother that she was isolated from any sort of life, that there were few Europeans living nearby, and she was terribly unhappy. The state of the Mac-Leods' marriage was appalling, with open hostility and biting hatred on both sides. It was in Sindanglaja that Dr. Roelfsema, the family's physician, witnessed two revealing incidents.

In an interview with Sam Waagenaar in 1932, Roelfsema recounted being in the MacLeod home in Sindanglaja along with the top civil servant, the resident of the regency, and his wife. The conversation turned to Paris, perhaps because of the remarkable Paris Exposition of 1900, which attracted a great deal of press attention and, ultimately, more than fifty million visitors. To colonials isolated in a small village in the Dutch East Indies, the grand buildings, the amazing mechanical and technical exhibits, the glamorous Art Nouveau fashions and furnishings, must have seemed the epitome of chic and cosmopolitan taste. Perhaps the conversation recalled memories of the exposition in Amsterdam that Rudolf and

After Rudolf's retirement in 1900, he settled his family in this remote village. Margaretha wrote to her father that Rudolf "has me . . . 'packed away'—in Sindanglaja, a little town where there is not one European soul. Horrible! I never speak with anybody! It is like being dead! But in the name of God, where can I go and what can I do!" (Author's collection)

Gretha had attended in the year of their marriage—an exposition organized by Mr. Calisch, to whom they still owed three thousand guilders. As the conversation continued, Rudolf grew more and more agitated and finally shouted at Gretha, "What the hell! If you want that much to go to Paris, why don't you just go and leave me alone!" Their guests were shocked.

Dr. Roelfsema also overheard an exchange between Gretha and Rudolf at a large party given by the native governor of the district for all of the most important Europeans in the area. Gretha and her partner danced close to Rudolf, who was sitting and talking with friends. "Hello, darling," Gretha said, a seemingly innocent remark, yet one that insured Rudolf would notice she was dancing with another man. "You can go to hell, bitch," Rudolf replied. They had fallen so far that they were not even maintaining a pretense of civility in public.

Roelfsema also told Waagenaar that Rudolf used to stop at his house on the way to the post office so that he could open and read Gretha's outgoing letters, an act Roelfsema regarded as inexcusably dishonest and ungentlemanly.

The MacLeod marriage had gone from very bad to much worse.

Death of a Marriage

AFTER SEVEN MONTHS IN SINDANGLAJA, Gretha found her life and marriage no longer bearable. She wrote to her mother-in-law:

> *Ah, the Indies is a dirty country, I would much rather be in Holland. . . . Each night, before I go to bed, I pray to God that this could happen soon, because I will never have a life here. John, it is true, has been retired since September 1900, but for the last year they have held back his pension. If you want to know, he is a bad financial manager.*
>
> *What can I do? You understand, he could send me alone to Holland, for I have my passage paid. But where am I to go? My parents are dead, and I have nowhere to go. I find this terrible, but I have nothing. You understand it is difficult for me to seek a place as a lady's companion in order to go to Holland at any price [without shaming the whole family].*

Gretha's father was not yet dead, though she said he was. If her passage was indeed paid, this indicates that her marriage to Rudolf had been approved by the military, but this too may have been a convenient lie. In any case, Rudolf's mother did not pick up on the hint and offer living accommodations for her in the Netherlands. Rudolf's insolvency was not a new phenomenon and probably the entire family was tired of paying off his debts.

On May 27, 1901, Gretha wrote to her father, claiming that Rudolf was making her life a living hell. She said she feared for her life at his hands.

Adam Zelle was by nature litigious and always resentful of his son-in-law's high-handed ways; he sprang into action. As his daughter said in an interview with G. H. Priem many years later, "As far as I can remember, my father was always at odds with the whole world, on one side too good, on the other side too bad, someone who can't keep to the middle [has no moderation]. . . . This doesn't remove the fact that he remains my father and that, whatever in which objective way I judge him, I am grateful to him, because he was always ready to move heaven and earth, when I cried out in distress."

She counted on her father's response to her letters, and respond he did. He wrote a letter on June 28, 1901, and sent it to his daughter via the Office of Justice in Batavia, asking them to deliver the letter and to make sure his daughter was safe from her husband's violent rage. He now called her Gretha, not Griet as Rudolf did.

I have received your letter of 27 May—I have, being your father, taken immediate measures. To give you a certain security I have written to the Honorable Officer of Justice of Batavia who will, I trust, help you. You will have to ask for a separation subsidiair [a legal separation with financial support] from table and bed. An attorney will have to ask this of the court and then they will care for you and avoid offenses and mistreatments and your husband will be forced to provide for you, which [amount] possibly will be withheld from his pension. You will have to have two witnesses who can attest to the mistreatment and the offenses.

Please keep your courage strong; you see your father jumps in immediately to help you as no other will do. So dear Gretha, angel of my life, have courage, be wise and pious; always be careful that your life is irreproachable and then everything will go well; at the same time, be very wary and prudent; take care about everything so that no one can do wrong to you or your child. Then come as soon as possible back to your father.

This letter was put into a sealed envelope and enclosed with a letter to the officer of justice in Batavia, which read:

Honorable sir!

Enclosed is a letter dated 27 May which I have received from Margaretha Geertruida Zelle, married to the gentleman Rudolf MacLeod, a pensioned major of the infantry of the KNIL in Sindanglaja.

She has repeatedly complained of ill treatment by her husband and now I don't know anything better to do than to advise her to divorce or at least to ask for a separation. But if I send a letter to her address, her husband will receive it and destroy it or ill treat my daughter even more. I do not know what the results will be if he reads the letter.

Therefore, Honorable Sir, I direct myself as a last resort to you, begging that if possible one of your underlings could hand this letter personally to my daughter and also find a lawyer for her. At the same time I also beg you to take the

necessary steps to avoid any ill treatment by Major Mac-
Leod so my daughter will be protected against future abuse.

Gretha received the letter from her father after the usual time lag of a month, but in the meantime things had deteriorated rapidly. Rudolf had become very brutal and violent. He struck her more often with the cat-o'-nine-tails and threatened to shoot her, holding a loaded gun and taunting her by saying he could shoot her and no one would know. She was terribly alone and afraid. She believed some of the other Europeans were aware of his treatment of her but were too concerned with white status to speak out on her behalf. In those years, there was a real abhorrence of impoverished and badly behaved Europeans, which fed on a deep fear of the loss of European prestige and supremacy over the native population.

Gretha wrote again to her father on July 12, complaining about Rudolf's debts and his complete control over their money, which left her nothing for herself.

> And then I have to suffer every moment the observations
> about my family.... Father, I have bought his name and that
> rank with my happiness. And I am left absolutely without any
> more courage left.
> When I married him, I knew that I would get an old In-
> dies guest [a man with colonial attitudes and habits] and I ex-
> pected that I would be very happy. And so I have been happy,
> for one day! I am young, happy, beautiful, and still optimistic
> about life; and he is old and totally decrepit. I just hope that he
> will go to Holland and I can be a little bit better off, but he is
> old and jealous and doesn't want anyone to look at me. God
> above! As if they'd leave me alone on his account! The offi-
> cers here in the Indies, both old generals and second lieuten-

ants, have already come to me amorously and I already have had to reject them!

Yes, Father, the Indies is a very strange country. . . . But, oh God, could I come back [to the Netherlands]! I have so very many regrets and am so deeply unfortunate! What can I do! If I divorce him I will lose my part of the pension. He has spent all my money, so I will have nothing in the world! That is not a happy life! And I can't suffer this life any longer.

I wish I were in Amsterdam! [He] has me . . . "packed away"—in Sindanglaja, a little town where there is not one European soul. Horrible! I never speak with anybody! It is like being dead! But in the name of God, where can I go and what can I do! . . . I wish that I was with [Nonnie] in Holland; but MacLeod thinks: we are fine here; I don't have to give my wife clothes, nobody can look at her . . . fantastic!

But my nerves are shot and I just long for Holland. If I stay another year here, I think, I will be dead or mad. . . . As for MacLeod, I can never love him again. He has treated me far too badly. He is quick-tempered and sometimes he jumps at me with red, bloodshot eyes and spits on me. I just wish that one day I would become a widow—that would be the best solution, but . . . it is very ugly to desire somebody's death; it just came out of my pen before I knew it. I am always ill here; my nerves are bad and I also am very sick in my belly.

Gretha slipped into this letter a small admission that an old general—probably Rudolf's predecessor at the garrison in Medan, General Reisz—had been in love with her, though she claimed she had turned him down. This might be why Rudolf had decided Reisz would never again promote him. Gretha's theatricality, her deep need to be admired, her love of social life, shone out of her letters.

Much later, when she had reaped fame and fortune by performing as Mata Hari, she spoke of this time in her life to G. H. Priem.
She admitted that she "often gave [Rudolf] cause to be jealous."
Priem then asked what Rudolf's motivation was in taking her to a
remote place like Sindanglaja. She answered,

*Nothing else except the wish to find some rest at last. He under-
stood well that I wouldn't take up with Javanese boys. Looking back
at everything, he thought too highly of me. He supposed that, say,
without the chance to flirt with men, I would become calm, would
maybe repent, become a little housewife in every way. . . .*

   *But good heavens, he cheated himself! After everything that
had happened, how could he be such a donkey! Of course I had no
peace for a moment in that miserable hole. Even Dreyfus had it
better [as a prisoner] on Devil's Island. No, I wanted to leave and I
decided to make his life as unbearable as possible, so that he would
take upon himself all the trouble of arranging to leave.*

Priem interjected, "But you had a little child."
She replied,

*My doll! O yes, but I can't play with her the whole day! A human
being can't hold out. I snarled at him, he snarled back, I threatened him with walking away, he threatened to fetch me back.
Rightly, [my father] said in the "novel" [about me], that life was
a "real hell," but to tell the truth he should have said that I stirred
it up. I wanted to get away, at any price! I wanted to live, I did not
want to bury my youth in a grave like Sindanglaja, and I desired
to enjoy life.*

   *I wrote home again, hoping that they knew a way to get me out.
My father—who loves legal wrangling, who lodges a complaint to*

the Public Prosecutor after the slightest bagatelle, who in the past
was at loggerheads with half or the whole of the freemasonry [lodge]
and even brought up a complaint to the Grand Master—my father,
who later was at odds with the family and accused every member of
the family of unfair intentions, who overloaded justices of the peace,
lawyers etc. etc. with work, who always made a mountain out of a
molehill—meanwhile wrote a letter to the Office of Justice of
Batavia.

Three weeks later, on August 3, 1901, Gretha had not yet received word from her father and so wrote again. In this letter, she
made terrible accusations about her husband. Perhaps she thought
that if she blackened Rudolf's name thoroughly, her father would
never side with Rudolf over her. Probably, she was finally telling
long-hidden truths.

> *At the end of my tether I write you again and ask you for ad-*
> *vice and help. I am alone here in a foreign country without*
> *family and without anything and I can't fight against such a*
> *brutal man. It is as if when he took his officer's coat off [re-*
> *tired], the last bit of decency went away too. He treats me in a*
> *more than scandalous manner too vile to describe.*
>
> *If he is mad or if he has fits, I don't know, but it looks like*
> *that. He never treated me well in the six years of our marriage*
> *but what is happening now is abuse. Every second he threatens*
> *me with a loaded revolver; he hits me, spits on me, and says the*
> *worst things to me in his rage. He for example walks past me*
> *and without any reason hits me and says, "Hit me back if you*
> *dare!" Nobody hears or sees it and there is of course no wit-*
> *ness, so he can do what he wants.*
>
> *Now I still have to tell you the worst: Can you imagine,*

Dad, he has had the indecency to say to my face that all I have done is to bore him to death! He, with his old, decaying body, who according to doctors in Batavia is not fit to be married, is bored with a woman like me! Now he wants to have another young woman with him, but he understands that he can't get another woman without giving her his pension. He wants to force me to ask for a divorce so that I lose his pension and he can do what he wants.

Dad, I have never complained to anybody but you, but isn't this intensely dirty and vulgar from somebody with a name and a rank like his? "And if you don't do this," he says, "then you can die here!" I am ill and have been violently ill in the stomach for eight months. . . . But I don't want to die here with such a brute of a man. Oh Dad, his family doesn't know him. He writes beautiful letters and talks nicely and . . . Holland is so far away [that they can't see how he behaves]! But here in the Indies he is well known and he has no friends; here they know him better and he can't fool them.

Dad, I don't want to be treated like this anymore but I have no money and I do not want to go into the world without money just to please him. I have never dishonored the MacLeod name and they can't blame me for anything. But I don't want to die here, and if it goes on, then it is definitely the end of me!

My optimism is gone! I cannot live with a man who is so despicable. I eat and live apart and I prefer to die before he touches me again. My children caught a disease from their father, the monster, he gave them skin sores! And so have I [got sores]. I am under treatment from a doctor and I am luckily getting better. Shouldn't a man like that be deeply ashamed? A man with such a ruined body will always make a young woman unhappy!

She wrote, as she had to Rudolf's mother, that she had a free passage home, possibly because of the illness, but she didn't want to leave her child behind and would not divorce Rudolf just to get permission to go. Then her financial complaints resumed.

> *[Rudolf] has a pension of 200 guilders per month and gets another 100 from writing for a newspaper. He can easily pay 100 guilders per month for me and Nonnie in Holland. He could keep 200 for himself plus whatever more he can earn. But he has an enormous amount of debt that is really scandalous—debts from many years, still from Atjeh and before that.*
>
> *So please, Dad, help me, yes? But don't bring any strangers into this sad business—*Il faut laver son linge sale en famille—*think well on that! His family is high-born; he has changed into Indies habits, very nasty and cruel to his wife, especially when he is fed up with her.*
>
> *I am so beautiful; how is it possible that I bore a man, especially such an old one, who is so broken down? He says he only married me for my nice head, but now that he has seen it enough times, I can "bugger off" . . . as if I am a prostitute.*

What truly distressed Gretha more than anything else was the insult that she bored her husband. He did not find her sexually attractive anymore. Her vanity, pride, and fragile sense of self were deeply wounded. This statement was by far the most hurtful and dreadful thing Rudolf had ever done to her, in her own estimation.

In this letter Gretha was as blunt as possible about a deeply shocking matter. In the language of the day, she openly accused her husband of giving her and the children syphilis. The "disease" that "gave them skin sores" contracted from Rudolf, the "decrepit body," the shame he should feel for infecting them, and the statement that the doctors in Batavia declared him "not fit to be married" are point-blank accusations that Rudolf had syphilis and gave it to her and she to the children. All of these, especially the "not fit to be married," were standard Victorian euphemisms for referring to the transmission of syphilis to an innocent party by a guilty one. Even her remarks about Rudolf having fits of rage might be considered an oblique reference to the bouts of insanity that were a symptom of syphilis (Fournier in 1879 had demonstrated that general paralysis of the insane [GPI] was causally linked to the disease). By 1884, delusions and violent, manic fits or rages were listed among the classic symptoms of syphilis in a dictionary of medical sciences.

Previous researchers have failed to understand these accusations or else have failed to see how they confirm other evidence that syphilis lay at the heart of the MacLeods' tragic loss of their son and viciously unhappy marriage.

Were Gretha's accusations true, or was she slandering Rudolf in order to manipulate her father's emotions? There is no definitive documentary evidence of Rudolf's syphilis, but there is a good deal of circumstantial evidence, including Rudolf's medical problems, his unfaithfulness, this letter, and the peculiar circumstances of Norman's death.

Certainly Gretha was not above telling a falsehood when it suited her, and she displayed a keen sense (on most occasions) of what stories would advance her cause. But to accuse her husband of infecting her and the children with syphilis was a horrific claim in the nineteenth century. Such a claim was much more damning and humiliating than it would be today; it was considered much worse than wife beating or financial fraud, both of which Rudolf also indulged in. The range of incriminating clues, pointed remarks, and otherwise inexplicable behaviors on the part of both Rudolf and Gretha—and the power of this hypothesis to explain several puzzling aspects of their lives—makes a persuasive case that Rudolf was syphilitic when he married.

A day after writing the desperate August 3 letter, Mata Hari was visited by someone from the Office of Justice in Batavia who hand-carried the letter from her father. As soon as the official left, Rudolf's rage surfaced. He was disgraced by the official complaint and humiliated that someone was sent to check up on him.

According to Zelle, officials visited several times, which produced some reform in Rudolf's behavior but provoked an ever-deepening resentment, too. Zelle claims that Rudolf forced Gretha, with a cat-o'-nine-tails in his hand, to retract the accusations of abuse in writing. Conversely, Rudolf claimed that, upon being asked to swear to the truth of her accusations, Gretha could not—and went down on her knees in front of the official to beg his forgiveness for filing a false complaint. There is no way to know who is right, since no official records of the visit or visits can be found.

Rudolf claimed the story about his threatening her with a revolver was simply a malicious falsehood she had invented to blacken his name. Yet he wrote to his sister that he was tempted to make it into truth: "Think, to ruin my reputation and to serve for her some years in prison—no, not so bad [if I could get rid of her]! But then, the little one [would suffer]."

Gretha's sense that her life was being threatened was probably justified.

Once Zelle received Gretha's August 3 letter, he replied immediately:

> *With great sadness I received your letter—on September 3 1901—and I have understood that MacLeod is not a man of honor because he who hits or spits upon a woman is not worth the name of a man. Because of your letter I was at the end of*

my rope and being your father, I have been in touch with the Officer of Justice in Batavia again—this was 28 June but I haven't yet had your acknowledgment that anything has happened. So if it has had no result, get a lawyer to ask for a separation.

I have spoken to the sister of MacLeod and she knows of everything. Wouldn't one predict this? The first of August was to be—with her connivance—the day that you have to die? So now you know what kind of sister that is. Get a lawyer immediately because everything is not well. You know you can count on our help. More I cannot do at this moment. Try to get yourself through it and deal with it like an intelligent and courageous woman.

Rudolf told Gretha that if she insisted on returning to Amsterdam, they would again have to live with his sister, for reasons of economy. Gretha hated the idea.

She began trying to influence Rudolf's relatives. On March 1, 1902, she wrote to Madame A. Goodvriend, née Baroness Sweerts de Landas, a cousin of Rudolf's whom she found sympathetic and addressed as an aunt. She used her old nickname for Rudolf, John or Johnie. About Louise she wrote: "What woman cedes to her sister-in-law her place in her own house?" She felt that if they returned to Louise and her children, Louise would "very clearly annex" Rudolf's pension "for herself." It is an ugly letter, which continues:

Naturally [Louise] possesses nothing and will come with her children, who are dirty characters, to eat with us! . . .

I have no authority, myself. I cannot fight against her. Louise subjugates John entirely. She follows him like a dog to serve and help him to take off his underwear and his stockings as if

she is his valet; but all the time she jollies him and smiles always.
If John died, I would be free, but if this Louise dies, we would
all our lives have on our backs these dirty children [of hers who
are so] badly brought up and common, for she never teaches
them anything. . . . Certainly John physically is not robust but
when the puny ones like him are coddled and eat nothing but
eggs and meat, they can live a long time.

Later, in the same letter, she added:

I am persuaded that Louise feigns affection for her own profit,
but nothing has changed except John is naïve enough to believe
that this affection is addressed to his person. . . . Louise has none
but a very coarse conception of housekeeping, and the two chil-
dren are as greedy and gross as herself. And all this horde
come to eat silver with John [spend our money], to the detri-
ment of Nonnie and myself.

I can do nothing, my aunt, even when I wish to. I do not
have any fortune: all that I had, John has dissipated and here I
am! And I believe still that if he didn't have Louise, it would
be so different. . . . How is this then possible? She is not the least
a cultivated woman, au contraire; *her manners are decidedly*
lower class and rightly, John is so rigid on this point. Her chil-
dren are not well brought up. I would die with shame at launch-
ing them [in society]. Admiral MacLeod wrote that "their
education leaves much to be desired . . ."

But John is very susceptible to flattery. Louise jollies him
and obtains what she wants. . . . She is always sorry that I do
not grow ugly, for she cannot attack me on that score. She presses
me always to have more children but I cannot understand her
motive. . . . I have said to John "First you must change and

then I must take my [rightful] place in my house and after-
wards we will see [about having more children]," but for the
moment I do not think so.

In March, on their way out of the Indies, the family went to stay
briefly with Dr. Roelfsema and his wife. On the nineteenth the Mac-
Leods boarded the S.S. *Koningin Wilhelmina,* piloted by the master
captain P. Ouwehand, for home.

They could not maintain even a pretense of civility on shipboard.
They were greeted in Amsterdam by Tante Frida—Louise—and
taken to her apartment to live. Gretha was late for dinner every night,
probably to avoid Tante Frida and Rudolf. Her husband accused her
of flaunting herself in public.

Gretha and Louise managed to live in the same apartment for
barely two weeks before the MacLeod family moved out, going to
188 Van Breestraat. There Mr. Calisch, their onetime friend and
now anxious creditor, appeared asking for his three thousand guilders back. Some of Rudolf's other creditors brought lawsuits against
him, and Rudolf's temper deteriorated alarmingly. He became violent again and resumed heavy drinking. Gretha stayed out of the
house as much as possible and, when she was present, repaid his
temper with her own forms of mental torture.

On August 25, Nonnie was sick in bed, which brought back
frightening memories of the terrible time of Norman's death in
Medan. The next day Rudolf took Nonnie with him to the post office and didn't return. By evening, Gretha had called the police and
reported them missing. She surmised, rightly, that Rudolf had left
her and taken the child to Velp to live with friends. She got on a
train to Arnhem, seeking refuge and advice at the home of the
Goodvriends.

On August 27, Gretha filed for divorce in the court of Amsterdam, through the lawyer Edward Philips. The divorce petition read:

At the court of Amsterdam with notice that Margaretha Geertruida Zelle living in Amsterdam and for this as a domicile uses the office of lawyer Mr. Edward Philips. . . .

— *that she on 11 July 1895 married Rudolf MacLeod, a pensioned major of the Royal Dutch Indies Army, living in Amsterdam at 188 Van Breestraat;*
  that this gentleman has had intercourse with a woman other than his wife;
— *that during their marriage, especially in the last years, she was beaten almost daily and spat at in the face;*
— *that especially during the last week he offended her badly in different ways, for example he would address himself to the servants while she was present, calling her "that bitch of mine";*
— *that in June after a student flower show, while he was drunk, he shouted at her, "I will make your life so miserable that you will bugger off!";*
— *that during the last two months he often drank too much and he baited her and provoked her and insulted her and then sometimes didn't speak to her for an entire day;*
— *that in the presence of his lawyer Mr. D. W. van Gigch, at his house in June 1902, he spoke in such an undignified way to her that the lawyer said that he has never seen or heard a woman so insulted like that;*
— *that in June 1902 and July 1902, at her house, he gave her a beating with a walking stick so that the maidservant had to come between them;*

— *that in August 1902 he ran after her with his slipper to beat her so that one of the servants had to come between them with a broom and pan and that he then spit in her face;*

— *that in May 1902 at the home of his sister, Mrs. Wolsinck née MacLeod, in the Leidsekaade 69, he hit her so that she flew out of the room and fell into the corridor;*

— *that since a month ago, he has not given her any money for the household or given her any clothes and that he has a pension of 3000 guilders but left her completely without any means;*

— *that he sometimes gave a guilder to the servants for the household, he would say, "Bring the change and give it back to me or otherwise that bitch will keep it!";*

— *that he yesterday told Mrs. Lubeck who was there in court in the presence of her daughter: "That bitch of mine has poisoned my child with unripe pears";*

— *that he said to she who demands the divorce, in the presence of the servants, "you will stay no matter what; you want my money [pension]";*

— *that yesterday without giving notice to his wife, under the pretense of posting a letter, took their only child of 4 years old, who had been sick in bed the day before, named Louise Jeanne, with him to Velp;*

— *that the complainant, on the basis of all these events that happened during their marriage; adultery, insults, and excesses, committed by him toward her; and requests the Court to reach the conclusion, should it please the President of the Court, on the grounds aforemen-*

tioned, against her spouse, to grant a divorce, legal sepa-
ration from bed and board, with the provision:

1. *that the child Louise Jeanne should remain with the complainant;*
2. *the complainant would go and live with the Honorable Mr. and Mrs. Goodvriend-Sweerts de Landas in Arnhem, number 6 Amsterdamschen, without having to receive her husband there;*
3. *that he would give her a monthly payment of 100 guilders;*
4. *that support and items of daily living would be given to her.*

The next morning, Gretha's father received a letter from Louise. It read: "On request of my brother I have the honor to inform you, that he will visit you this morning at 9 o'clock. He has returned from Velp and is staying with me."

Zelle was surprised; he did not yet know that Rudolf had taken Nonnie, that Gretha had fled to Arnhem, or that she had filed for divorce. According to Zelle, during the meeting Rudolf offered not to contest the divorce, which would involve dragging Gretha's name and reputation "through the mud" and treating her "like scum," if Zelle gave him two thousand guilders. Zelle refused; almost certainly, he didn't have two thousand guilders to give away.

The alternative version of events given by Charles Heymans is that Rudolf decided not to contest the divorce, since it would be difficult and expensive to defend himself—and, of course, he also wanted to be rid of Gretha.

On August 29, Gretha was summoned to hear the judgment of

the court. On the basis of her petition, the court believed that reconciliation was impossible and granted the legal separation with the provisions she had requested on August 30.

Anxious to preserve his reputation among his Indies friends, Rudolf wrote a letter to the Balkstras in Java, telling them untruthfully that Gretha had left him. He pledged to see that she and Nonnie were always properly looked after—an ironic if not downright deceptive statement considering events that followed—and concluded: "I have no more debt, hunger, and suffering."

On the day the divorce was granted, Rudolf put a notice into the newspapers, including *The News of the Day* and the *Arnhem Daily:*

WARNING.
Do not furnish credit or merchandise to Mme. MacLeod, née Zelle, because the undersigned has resigned all responsibility for her.
R. MacLeod

The Goodvriends were embarrassed by the advertisement Rudolf had placed or by the notoriety of the accusations in the divorce petition, or perhaps they were simply tired of their guest. In any case, on September 2, Gretha and Nonnie moved to a boardinghouse in Worth-Rheden near Arnhem, depending upon the court-ordered support to pay the bills. At that time, Gretha had only three guilders and fifty cents—roughly thirty dollars in modern currency—to her name. She wrote to her father, thanking him for his last letter:

I have suffered terribly and hope that it is over with. But God knows, what a man like MacLeod will invent to take more from me and my child! Will you watch over me, for he is so base

and vulgar over nothing! Oh, the advertisement has injured me
deeply, for I never bought anything on his name [credit], never,
never! I have asked Mr. Philips if he wants to file a suit ask-
ing for a full apology, by name, in the papers; a different prose-
cution because of insult and calumny. Is he now able to do me
and Nonnie any further harm?

I have been here since yesterday, because I do not like to
impose too long on someone else's hospitality. It is pretty here
and quiet and I do not ask for more. Nonnie and I sit the
whole day in the woods or stay at home. May things remain
this way and [I pray] he does not make my life any more diffi-
cult! Surely my situation here has been made impossible by that
advertisement; I dare not put my name anywhere. It ran in big
letters also in the Arnhem Daily; *shame, shame!*

Oh, I am still so distressed and think it might be more ju-
dicious to go to Brussels or Wiesbaden to live. All of the
Netherlands knows my name and he has insulted me so!

She added a fervent postscript:

P.S. I am still in a terrible mess . . . I thank God that I have had
the courage to apply for the divorce, despite the consequences. . . . I
have placed a newspaper ad to do housekeeping for a lady who
lives on her own.

I don't find it shameful to work, and I must earn some-
thing honestly, I want to pay my lawyer respectably. I regard,
of course as given, that I keep Nonnie with me and plainly I
must not turn my nose up at anything. For rent I need 50
guilders [about $450 in today's currency]—then I have to pay
off the laundry, clothes, tuition fees and costs [for Nonnie];
well then, I do not [know] where that will come from. . . . In

reality I do not want to do housekeeping; I remain who I am, but want to settle my debts in an honest manner and not make a mess or a sharp bargain in the dark [cheat anyone]; you know that is not in my character.

But this way I look only like I am trying to live like a lady; with what I am owed [by Rudolf], then I will pay off my debts. The 100 guilder payment from MacLeod [that is coming] I will use for myself and what I save, I will take for Nonnie to the savings bank; then she will not stand without a penny in the world.

But Rudolf pleaded poverty to the court on September 10. He managed to get the amount reduced to fifty guilders, and even then he did not pay. The court ruled that his pension could not be garnished.

Gretha heard of this ruling and wrote hysterically to her father on September 12:

I am not well, I don't sleep and am very anxious. The Indies pension was paid on 2 September and was intended to last for the next three months [but it is already spent by Rudolf]. Therefore I must go three whole months before there is any more money! . . .

The court awarded me my child and 1200 guilders a year, and now he does not want to pay; help me, Father! Aunt Sweerts is a complete dear, but is not inclined to lend money, and how am I to live these three months? If nobody helps me, I must return [to him] out of poverty; I must live with my child somehow.

At the moment, I can do nothing more and cannot even get my washing because I have no money left. Yes, certainly, if I can find a rent-controlled room, I will come to live in Am-

sterdam, and as soon as I have money, I will come home one day with *Nonnie* to see you, perhaps next week; I will write you as this approaches, however. It is nevertheless too terrible that because of lack of money I should have to return to a coarse brute, who will not trouble himself to comply with the pronouncement of the court.

I am so nervous! my head spins. *MacLeod* does not pay and it is a cunning trick to recover his child; he will beat me, however, until I walk away and then the business is finished. . . .

My lawyer says that I should put a newspaper ad as follows: "Mrs. MacLeod Zelle explains that the advertisement, placed by her spouse in The News of the Day *of 3 August 1902, is a cowardly revenge because she brings a petition against him for divorce on the basis of abuse."* What do you think of this? I am ashamed myself of it, but write me at once what you think of it. I am entirely desperate; everything beats against my head; there was too much grief and when [I thought] *MacLeod* had to pay, everything was settled, but now I have no hope. I cannot go back to let him beat me and treat me in such an unworthy manner.

Aunt Sweerts wrote me a completely sweet letter but informed me I could not possibly stay with her [any longer]. She has taken *MacLeod's* side! These three months I shall receive nothing! It is such madness! *MacLeod* is obliged to take care of us! I am so deeply unfortunate. Can't you lend me something? Someone must help me; I will shoot myself rather than return to *MacLeod.*

After receiving Gretha's letter of September 12, Zelle managed to send her twenty-five guilders, which, although it would not pay all her bills, was something. Neither she nor Nonnie had proper warm clothes or shoes for the winter in the Netherlands.

Rudolf was having second thoughts about the divorce, or perhaps his strategy of depriving his wife of money so she would come back to him was not working as well as he expected. On October 13, he wrote to Zelle: "I have thought long and hard and I have decided that you are the person who I need to sort things out, because you know about everything and I want to make immediate peace, I want it to be as if everything that has happened could be forgotten as if it had not happened. If you know something, can you please contact me at once."

Zelle met with Rudolf and chastised him but also tried to negotiate an arrangement. Nonnie could live with Captain van Mourik, a pensioned military friend of Rudolf's in Velp, so that both Rudolf and Gretha could see her. Zelle also asked Rudolf for fifty guilders for Gretha, but Rudolf replied that he cared nothing for the ruling of the court and that he could not pay, as he had no money.

Instead, writing through Captain van Mourik, Rudolf proposed a reconciliation. Gretha had no money and mounting bills. She had already entertained some gentlemen in *maisons de rendez-vous*— houses for intimate, discreet meetings of a sexual nature, and was perilously close to becoming a full-time prostitute. Although she knew Rudolf had taken up with another woman, Gretha's only options were prostitution or returning to her husband.

She wrote back to Rudolf in a pleasant tone, using the nickname Gretha, which he liked. She apologized for calling him a cad, a tyrant, and a drunkard. She closed her letter with "The idea that all is arranged [for our reunion] makes me happy and content, with a big kiss always, your Gretha."

Rudolf sent her some money and she replied, thanking him but pointing out she had no winter clothes. Her strategy worked; Rudolf sent more money. On November 1, she wrote him again: "What a surprise this afternoon [to receive the money] . . . it is so kind of you; I am happy and almost confused. Tuesday we return [to our life together]. I am very very happy and you know, I will thank you well." Though she signed her letter affectionately "with big kisses from Gretha to John," her previous letters suggest this affection was simply a ploy. Being nice to men was the only way she knew to obtain money.

In early November of 1902, she returned to Amsterdam to live with Nonnie and Rudolf in a small apartment on the Ruyterkade near the café Czaar Peter. The reunion was predictably short-lived and unhappy. Somewhere during this unsettled period, it was agreed that Rudolf would keep Non with him and Gretha would never see her again. He had longed for years to free his daughter of Gretha's influence, and Gretha was now desperate enough to agree.

Her marriage and her motherhood were finished.

The Birth of Mata Hari

GRETHA WAS A LOST SOUL without direction during this period of conflict and unhappiness. She was no longer daughter, mother, or wife. The variety of names by which she identified herself up to this point reflected the labile nature of her identity; she tried on new personas as if they were dresses, hoping to find a more flattering one. She was at heart a shape-shifter who became what those around her wanted her to be. It was her greatest charm and her most dangerous trait.

She had lightened her responsibilities by giving up her daughter, but she had not improved her circumstances materially. She had no home, no income, no husband, and no future. The situation seemed so hopeless that she went to stay briefly and miserably with Tante Frida, who encouraged her to work as a mannequin, modeling clothes. Gretha hoped instead to pursue an acting career, though women who pursued this path were considered to have loose morals. She left Tante Frida's to stay with her aunt and uncle in The Hague, but she found no honorable work there either. Everything she tried reinforced

the message that her body, appearance, and sexual favors were her only
useful assets.

She decided to leave for Paris, the
place of chic fashion and cosmopolitan life that she had longed for while
trapped in Sindanglaja. "Why Paris?"
a journalist asked her years later.

"I don't know. I thought all women
who ran away from their husbands
went to Paris," she replied with a
charming naïveté.

She arrived in Paris early in 1903
with very little money and no connections. She looked for work posing
for artists but, according to Charles
Heymans, was told she looked better
with her clothes on—which seems
improbable considering her later acclaim as a performer who was nearly
naked onstage. She claimed to be a
widow of a Dutch Indies soldier who

In 1902, the MacLeods legally separated. Changing her name to
Lady Gresha MacLeod, Margaretha
fled to Paris. "I thought all women
who ran away from their husbands
went to Paris," she later told a journalist. (Author's collection)

was trying to support herself and her two children, but sympathy got
her few jobs. She tried acting and may have toyed with dancing, but
the only dependable source of income available to her was pleasing
men for money. Rudolf threatened to have the police bring her back
or to place another ad in a prominent newspaper that would ruin her
socially. He was still her husband, despite their legal separation, and
it is unclear on what grounds he could have had her arrested. One
source suggests that he threatened to have her extradited and committed to a state institution for "incorrigibles." This probably meant

that, in the view of society at large, she had demonstrably lost her mind because she was a respectably married woman and yet had taken to a life of prostitution. If she had, then she was merely a sex worker and not yet a high-priced, fashionable demimondaine.

After months in Paris with little work, Gretha was desperate again and wrote to Rudolf's cousin General Edward MacLeod, in Nijmegen, begging for help. She returned to the Netherlands, feeling beaten and defeated, and went to stay with the general and his wife in their rural home. In January of 1904, she wrote in a letter:

> *Behold me, then, condemned to remain here [in Nijmegen], here where there exists only the shadow of a gray and humid hearth in which only the copper pots have the right to shine in the pale sunlight. Where there exists the silent, the grave, the hostile street, in which an alien footstep calls the anxious housewives to windows shrouded in lace curtains. Here, where a little tulip garden shudders in the winter winds. Here where the fog, the soft fog, veils everything and blankets to a silvery chime to strokes of the municipal carillon. Here there is the incessant overseeing of beldames [mothers-in-law] and matrons who have vaguely heard reports of a flight to Paris and dances in theaters. Here, in fact, is shame and nostalgia.*

Her complaints of Rudolf's behavior finally moved the general to write to reprimand his nephew, who promptly told the general his version of the truth. Gretha was turned out of the MacLeod house. She left again for Paris in the spring of 1904. With no money in her pocket but a lot of bravado, she arrived and checked into a very good hotel, intending to pay her bills in whatever way she could.

Gretha obtained a job with the equestrian circus and riding school in the rue Bénouville. Ernst Molier had set up his circus in

1880, hiring attractive and skilled performers to do trick riding for audiences comprising mostly Paris society. Though Gretha was a fine horsewoman and striking in appearance, Molier advised her that she might do better with dancing than riding and helped her make contact with society ladies who might provide entrée to the right circles.

With a superb sense of what would succeed, she developed a series of "sacred dances" that she ostensibly learned in the Indies and began to create a mythology about herself. Her style was utterly novel; her ability to create a mood was strong; and her costumes were extremely revealing. As she explained later to friend and painter Piet van der Hem about this time in her life, "I never could dance well. People came to see me because I was the first who dared to show myself naked to the public."

Her genius lay not in what she did but in how she presented herself. She adopted the name Lady Gresha MacLeod, claiming to be the widow of a Scottish officer who had been stationed in the Indies, where she had learned the secrets of Oriental dance. Cancan girls at the Moulin Rouge and even less respectable theaters showed their naked legs and bosoms. She distinguished herself from them by claiming hers were sacred, holy dances—a form of worship, part of a fusion of sexuality and religion. It was a brilliant move.

Her first few performances were private, starting in the home of Madame Kiréevsky, a society hostess who favored new artists. Francis Keyzer, a correspondent from London for the society magazine *The King*, got himself invited to the exclusive performance at Madame Kiréevsky's and wrote a lengthy article on February 4, 1905. He was entranced by what he saw:

Vague rumors had reached me of a woman from the Far East, a native of Java, wife of an officer, who had come to Europe, laden with perfumes and jewels, to introduce some of the richness of the

Oriental color and life into the satiated society of European cities; of veils encircling and discarded, of the development of passion as the fruits of the soil, of a burst of fresh, free life, of Nature in all its strength untrammeled by civilization. . . .

The door opened. A tall dark figure glided in. Her arms were folded upon her breast beneath a mass of flowers. For a few seconds she stood motionless, her eyes fixed upon a statue of Siva at the end of the room.

Her olive skin blended with the curious jewels in the dead gold setting. A casque of worked gold upon her dark hair—an authentic Eastern head-dress; a breastplate of similar workmanship beneath the arms. Above a transparent white robe, a quaint clasp held a scarf around the hips, the ends falling to the feet in front. She was enshrouded in various veils of delicate hues, symbolizing beauty, youth, love, chastity, voluptuousness and passion.

The first notes of a plaintive weird melody were sounded and with slow, undulating, tiger-like movements she advanced towards the God. It was an appeal to the spirit of evil, an invocation to help her avenge a wrong. Her eyes shone with the fire of revenge when she began, but after a while a softer light crept into them as she strove to win the favor of the Deity. Then the movements became more and more intense, more feverish, more eager. She first threw flowers and then divested herself, one by one, of the veils, implying that, as a sacrifice, she gave beauty, youth, love, etc.; and finally worked to a state of frenzy, unclasped her belt and fell in a swoon at Siva's feet.

Siva is the Hindu god of destruction and of transformation, symbolizing the new creation that follows annihilation. The choice of Siva as the focus of Gresha's first dance was singularly apt.

Whether Gresha explained the symbolism of her dance to Keyzer or not, his words vividly evoke the enormous impact her performance had upon spectators. Perhaps unwittingly, the dance held stunning parallels to her own life: the appeal for help in avenging a great wrong, followed by the sacrifice of first her beauty, then her youth, and virtue after virtue in mounting desperation; then, symbolically, the giving of her entire sexual being to the god of destruction in order to triumph.

Touches like the motionless pause after she entered, the slow unveiling of her body, and the increasing frenzy of her passionate movements were calculated to capture her audience. Neither traditional ballet nor Isadora Duncan's "classical" dances were her models. Her steps, poses, and movements made little reference to those forms of dance; what she did was entirely new. She offered spectacle, emotion, and the mystery of the Orient, which was just beginning to be fashionable. Keyzer concluded, "Lady MacLeod is Venus."

Her costumes, recorded in contemporary photographs, owed much to the costumes of traditional court dancers in Java. Something of the Javanese style can be seen in some of her postures, the undulating movements of the arms and the sweeping use of loosely draped cloths or veils. There are hints of the Javanese style of dance, said to be derived from marionettes, in the angulation of her wrists and elbows, but she was certainly not accurately reproducing dances she had learned in Java. Her dances were her own.

She created a sensation. After her performance at Madame Kiréevsky's, she was invited to dance at the Musée Guimet, a museum of Oriental art assembled by the prosperous Émile Guimet, an industrialist from Lyon who had traveled and collected extensively in the East. His Paris museum had opened in 1889. Having a much-sought-after new dancer perform the fascinating sacred dances of the Orient in his museum was just the event to draw a crowd of Paris's elite, aristocratic, and wealthy art lovers. Her debut was scheduled for March 13, with a second performance the following

Two young Wayang dancers demonstrate the traditional movements and costumes of this Javanese form of the dance. Mata Hari must have seen similar performances in the Dutch East Indies. (Author's collection)

night. It is said that Guimet made a valuable suggestion: rather than dancing as Lady Gresha MacLeod, she should adopt a stage name that was suitably enigmatic and evocative.

She chose to become Mata Hari. Guimet is sometimes credited with inventing the name, but that is most unlikely. The Malay phrase *mata hari* was often used in the Dutch East Indies to mean "sunrise," or, more literally, "the eye of the day." One of her childhood friends in Leeuwarden recalled reading a letter in 1897 or 1898—the first year or two of the MacLeods' residence in the Dutch East Indies— in which she spoke of becoming a dancer and using the name Mata Hari. In Padang, Sumatra, there was a Masonic lodge known as the Loge Mata Hari. Rudolf MacLeod may have visited the Loge Mata Hari because the brother of his old friend de Balbian Verster was a member.

There was more to becoming Mata Hari than simply changing her name; Gresha had to re-create herself in a new persona. She later told G. H. Priem:

In the beginning, [my career was] less in the artistic domain, but from the moment that I introduced my Javanese dances my fate was quickly decided. I liked life there, I received protection of the richest strangers and I did not lack the skill to profit from that.

At the time that I appeared onstage in Paris, I chose an Indian name for the theater and in daily life I used the name of my husband. People who thought that I was English or Scottish, I left them under that impression. . . .

At this moment, I enjoy my passion for theater with full rein. More than I could ever think, I see now, that all success depends on attendant circumstances. I was pretty—why may I not say it now also one time?—and the people, the men, they love a pretty woman. They like to see much of a pretty woman until the border of the indiscreet. I have never been afraid to catch a cold, remember my décolletés, which my husband tried to forbid. Well then, I started to use décolletés, and to use décolletés more and more. With every veil I threw off, my success rose. Pretending to consider my dances very artistic and full of character, thus praising my art, they came to see nudity, and that is still the case.

Later, she continued: "I act as thousands do; I speculate on sensuality; I behave coquettishly, and flirt now and again with a full house, that comes easily to me, that came always easily to me."

Here, Priem reported that Mata Hari laughed. "The artistic cachet to which I connect everything, that protects me against banality."

The artistic cachet, in any case, protected her against charges of indecency.

Guimet invited a carefully selected six hundred of Paris's most chic and fashionable to attend Mata Hari's debut at his museum on March 13, 1905. There were artists, musicians, writers, aristocrats, intellectuals, officers, diplomats, ministers, and bankers—hundreds of powerful men with their well-dressed wives or bejeweled mistresses on their arms, all crowding into the museum to see this extraordinary new dancer of whom everyone was speaking. Those who had already seen her at Madame Kiréevsky's were anxious to establish their credentials as among the first to have seen her; those who had not yet experienced one of her performances were eager to know if she was as mesmerizing and beautiful as gossip claimed.

Guimet had transformed the domed library into a semblance of an Indian temple, with flowers and vines wrapped around the stately columns that supported the dome. The room was dimly lit by dozens of candles that provided enough illumination for the audience to see a rare eleventh-century bronze of a dancing Siva, his four arms extended in strange and sinuous postures, with a circle of flames surrounding his body like a bizarre halo. A hidden orchestra played music with an Asian flavor, said to be inspired by melodies from Java and India. Monsieur Guimet gave a brief introduction, and then the performance began.

Mata Hari entered the spotlight wearing a costume of the type that would become her signature: an elaborate, golden, jeweled headdress of vaguely Javanese design; a beaded metallic bra; a set of diaphanous lengths of cloth, or *slendangs*, that were wrapped around her shoulders, torso, and waist, with others that hung to the floor. She wore large, dangling earrings, a necklace, bracelets of exotic design, and armlets that clasped around her upper arms. Her feet were bare and her flimsy garments did little to conceal her naked body. Her dances were emotional, voluptuous, erotic, and utterly novel. The symbolism was obvious enough for the audience to un-

Margaretha's first performance as Mata Hari took place at the Musée Guimet, a museum of Oriental art in Paris. A journalist wrote, "Wearing a casque on her head like a peacock's, the mark of a god, the sharp sword in her fist, the *kris* between her teeth, she coils around her waist an opaque and gleaming belt, throws around her hips transparent material marked with the emblem of the divine bird. . . . She cries for vengeance. . . ." (Réunion des Musées Nationaux/Art Resources NY—Musée Guimet des Arts Asiatiques-Guimet, Paris, France)

derstand, subtle enough to support her claim that these were ancient, sacred dances of the Orient. Above all, she was a consummate
and captivating performer.

One source reported that Mata Hari gave a brief explanation—
repeated in French, English, Dutch, German, and Malay—between
dances:

> My dance is a sacred poem in which each movement is a word and
> whose every word is underlined by music.
>
> The temple in which I dance can be vague or faithfully repro-
> duced, as here today. For I am the temple.
>
> All true temple dances are religious in nature and all explain,
> in gestures and poses, the rules of the sacred texts.
>
> One must always translate the three stages which correspond to
> the divine attributes of Brahma, Vishnu, and Siva—creation, fe-
> cundity, destruction. . . . By means of destruction toward creation
> through incarnation, that is what I am dancing—that is what my
> dance is about.

If this account is correct, the simple exposition was a brilliant
element in Mata Hari's performance, designed to demonstrate her
refinement and to evoke the mysteries of Eastern religions.

The day after her debut at the *musée,* newspaper reporters and
attendees vied to find lavish enough praise for what they had seen.
For an audience who had been used to the set pieces of formal ballet,
or even Isadora Duncan's looser interpretations of classical themes,
Mata Hari's type of dance was thrilling, daring, and exotic.

The Gallic thanked Monsieur Guimet for bringing such a talent
to the public, praising Mata Hari as "so feline, extremely feminine,
majestically tragic, the thousand curves and movements of her body
trembling in a thousand rhythms . . . far from the conventional

entrechats of our classic dancers." *Parisian Life* wrote coyly about "Lady MacLeod, that is to say Mata Hari, the Indian dancer, voluptuous and tragic, who dances naked in the latest salons. She wears the costume of the *bayadère* [female Javanese court dancer], as much simplified as possible, and toward the end, she simplifies it even a little more."

The Flash referred to the evening's performance as "an exotic spectacle yet deeply austere"; the latter adjective hardly sounds like a realistic description of a dance performed in a set dressed with vegetation and hung lavishly with flowers, performed by a dancer clothed in colorful, diaphanous garments to the strains of haunting music. Of Mata Hari herself, the reviewer wrote: "She is tall and slender and supple like the sacred serpents balanced erect by snake charmers; her flexible body takes the shape of the undulations of the flames, and then suddenly she freezes in her contortions, like the wavy edge of a kris."

The Press's reviewer, Henri Ferrare, gives an account of a passionate performance that shows why Mata Hari was so immediately successful:

Mata Hari does not perform only with her feet, her eyes, her arms, her mouth, her red lips; Mata Hari . . . dances with her muscles, with her entire body, thus surpassing ordinary methods. Wearing a casque on her head like a peacock's, the mark of a god, the sharp sword in her fist, the kris between her teeth, she coils around her waist an opaque and gleaming belt, throws around her hips transparent material marked with the emblem of the divine bird. This time she penetrates alone into the sanctuary, she goes to implore Soubramayen, god of the stars, to deliver an unfaithful lover; she cries for vengeance, asks how to grasp the traitor; slowly, skillfully, she poisons the two blades, then she watches, like a spy, perceives her victim. . . . Then the purple belt unrolls, slowly, imitating the flowing blood, the weapon trembles until the hand of the priestess plunges it at last into the heart of the cursed lover. Savagely, she brandishes her victorious blade.

Although several newspapers mention that she was assisted by four young women dressed in black as *nautch* girls—erotic Indian dancers—their main function was to chant when required or to cover her nearly naked body with veils when she collapsed at the close of the first dance.

Without doubt, it was Mata Hari's unparalleled ability to dramatize herself and to convey emotion in a convincing fashion that earned her success. As she had been since childhood, the woman who now faced the world as Mata Hari was exotic, hyperbolic, emotional, and fascinating: a star. Her frequent changes of identity were over; she had found the one that fit. She would never again be anyone except Mata Hari.

The Toast of Europe

MATA HARI'S PERFORMANCES were hugely popular. During 1905, she danced more than thirty times in theaters like the Trocadéro and in exclusive salons at the homes of those such as the banker Baron Henri de Rothschild, the chocolate king Gaston de Menier, the actress Cecil Sorel, and soprano Emma Calvé of the Metropolitan Opera in New York. From the performance at Menier's came a series of photographs that show her dancing completely nude in his conservatory, which was filled with tropical plants, and a letter from her smitten host extolling the "Oriental dream" she had created and praising "the lines of your beautiful body."

The French novelist Colette was present at the performance at Menier's and remarked cattily, after Mata Hari was dead, "She did not actually dance, but with graceful movements shed her clothes. She arrived fairly naked at her recitals, danced 'vaguely' with downcast eyes, and would disappear enveloped in her veils."

Colette may not have regarded Mata Hari's performances

as dance or art, but a wide and enraptured audience did. Even Colette's cutting criticisms did not prevent her friend Natalie Barney from having Mata Hari dance not once but three times at her notorious lesbian garden parties in Neuilly. Once Mata Hari made her entrance as Lady Godiva naked on a white horse.

Mata Hari kept a scrapbook and pasted into it every newspaper review, every photograph, and many letters, and she kept notes about the size of the audiences. She was in her element and elated by her success. There were many reporters anxious to interview her, and she told them varied and clever stories of her past, none of which corresponded closely with the truth. She was

Another journalist described her dance: "Her movements became more and more intense, more feverish, more eager. She first threw flowers and then divested herself, one by one, of the veils, implying that, as a sacrifice, she gave beauty, youth, love, etc.; and finally worked to a state of frenzy, unclasped her belt and fell in a swoon at Siva's feet." (The Mata Hari Museum/Fries Museum)

the daughter of a temple dancer in India, or perhaps the Indies, who had died giving birth to her . . . she was taken as a child to become a sacred temple dancer . . . she had been rescued by a Scottish lord, George MacLeod, who married her and then tragically died . . . he was a colonel, not a lord . . . she was European but born in Java . . . she was half-caste . . . she was purely Indian . . . The point was not to tell the truth about her ancestry but to tell a story that helped create the public persona of Mata Hari. Her life became an unending performance, both onstage and off.

Despite or perhaps because of the smokescreen of stories about her origins in the Dutch East Indies, Mata Hari soon became a subject of interest in Holland. Might she be Dutch? On April 19, *The News of the Day* repeated portions of some of the French reviews of her dancing and posed the apt question: "Who can Mata Hari be?"

The answer, given in an article in the monthly publication *Today's Woman,* was this:

Mata Hari's real name is Mrs. MacLeod. She was born on Java and married an English officer. Being a passionate lover of the dance, she studied its movements with never ending patience. Through a cunning ruse which, had it been detected, might have cost her her life, she managed to be admitted to the secret temples of India, where far beyond the reach of profane eyes the bayadères, nautches *and* vadashis *dance before the altar of Vishnu. Her sense of postures and poses was so amazingly innate that even the fanatical priests who guard the golden altar regarded her as a holy dancer.*

Both the question and the answer echo faithfully the stories that Mata Hari had spun for eager journalists, raising the issue of whether or not she somehow contrived both the original article and the letter to the editor.

Another Dutch journalist followed up on the sensational story, writing in the *New Rotterdam Daily* on May 31:

Mata Hari! Strange, well-modulated name, which suddenly resounded throughout Paris, through the smart and political Paris— a name that floats on the lips of the common man like something secret, unbelievable, far out of reach.

Priestess, dancer, lady? People ask—and guess. It is said that

four ministers of State invited her to supper and that in the intimacy
of their dining room she regaled them with her art.

On a visit to Mata Hari's hotel room, the writer found her "a tall
and slender, chic young woman, beautiful, with dark complexion,
gay, dressed in a smart suit, straw hat with dark-red flowers, who
smiles, talks, who moves gracefully and with ease through the
room—Mata Hari! Yes, she says, she is Dutch, she is Mrs. MacLeod."

As the journalist questioned her, she alluded vaguely—cleverly—to her deep knowledge of Oriental dance and art, and to a
most unpleasant and difficult time when she first arrived in Paris
and was forced into modeling and circus riding. In the midst of a
sentimental and novelistic account, the journalist abruptly perceived
and revealed the essence of Mata Hari's story:

Suddenly she is no longer the plain young woman, suddenly she
becomes a strange, energetic, proud human being—proud indeed,
too proud to accept defeat, too proud to be ugly, or small or helpless,
too proud to be without talent. She laughs about herself and talks
about a thousand things, about all the people she has met so sud-
denly in the very center of that high society, among the fabulously
glittering crowd that constitutes Parisian life.

This newspaper publicity was invaluable for building the mys-
tique that surrounded the name of Mata Hari. She was fast becoming an icon, a symbol of all that was deeply female, mysterious,
exotic, and wildly erotic.

Unfortunately, the publicity also drew Rudolf MacLeod's attention to his estranged wife's successes and caused him real embarrassment. Who would want to be the man who had been deserted by
a sex symbol like Mata Hari? In rural, conservative Velp, Rudolf

struggled to hold on to his own respectability by blackening Mata Hari's reputation. He was afraid he would hear cruel whispers about the Dutch woman from Java who danced nude in Paris, the woman who was once married to the retired major with the dark-haired daughter, Non.

The biggest problem was that in 1906 Rudolf wished to marry again. His intended was Elisabetha Martina Christina van der Mast, a woman twenty-eight years his junior. He could no longer deny his connection to Mata

A photograph of Mata Hari wearing her striking headdress was featured on the cover of the magazine *Monsieur et Madame* in October 1905. (The Mata Hari Foundation/Fries Museum)

Hari, and so he chose the only option left to him, seeking to divorce her, citing as grounds her immoral behavior, indecency, and adultery. His attorney went to Paris to persuade Mata Hari not to fight for custody of her daughter. She deferred the matter for weeks, with charm, with diversions, and with claims that she so enjoyed speaking Dutch again that it was a pity to discuss unpleasant matters. At last he produced a photograph of her dancing nude and threatened to produce the photo in court if she contested the divorce or fought for custody. Both he and she knew full well that any Dutch judge would regard her as depraved if this item was entered as evidence. With supporting testimony from the retired general MacLeod in Nijmegen, "Aunt Sweerts," and Vice Admiral MacLeod, Rudolf was readily awarded custody of Nonnie, despite protests from Adam Zelle on his daughter's behalf. The divorce was granted on April 26, 1906.

The grounds for the divorce were

—that she had carnal knowledge of other men and by consequence rendered herself a culpable adulteress, which is the motive for divorce;

—that the defendant who lives actually in Paris produces in the aforesaid city in the cafés, concerts, and the circuses and there executes the so-called brahmanique dances and presents herself almost entirely nude;

—that she also posed entirely nude as a model for a sculptor and this work of sculpture was offered to public view;

—that these facts must qualify as indecent extravagances. . . .

The claim of adultery was judged to be supported by this evidence.

In the meantime, Mata Hari had achieved a new level of professional success. Working through a civil lawyer, Edouard Clunet, who was many years her senior and besotted with her, Mata Hari acquired a manager-cum-agent, Gabriel Astruc. Astruc was a top impresario who handled great artists such as the singer Chaliapin, Diaghilev's Ballets Russes, the dancer Nijinsky, the composer Igor Stravinsky, and many others; he later founded the Théâtre de Champs-Elysées in Paris to provide a venue for more innovative and daring musical performances. Astruc booked her into the Olympia Theater in Paris—a high-class music hall—for a performance of "Le Rêve" (The Dream), with music by George Bing, in the autumn of 1905. For the first time, a large audience could watch Mata Hari perform, and the public was eager to do so. She gave an advance performance on August 18 and opened on August 20, earning the magnificent sum of 10,000 francs, which had a buying power equivalent to about $42,000 in today's currency.

Once again, the reviewers struggled to find superlative adjectives with which to describe Mata Hari's dancing. The reviewer for *The*

Mata Hari was such a popular performer that a series of postcards showing her dancing was issued in 1905–1906. Her costume resembled that of true Wayang dancers but was much more transparent—a move calculated to appeal to her audience. (Author's collection)

Journal wrote glowingly: "Mata Hari personifies all the poetry of India, its mysticism, its voluptuousness, its languor, its hypnotizing charm. To see Mata Hari in a rhythm and with attitudes that are poems of wild voluptuous grace is an unforgettable spectacle, a really paradise-like dream." The review in *The Press* sounds rather like a love letter, exclaiming, "One would need special words, new words to explain the

I longed to live as a colorful butterfly in the sun. . . ." Mata Hari
to journalist G. H. Priem. (Hulton
Archive/Getty Images)

tender and charming art of Mata Hari!
Maybe one could simply say that this
woman is *rhythm,* thus to indicate, as
closely as possible, the poetry which
emanates from this magnificently
supple and beautiful body."

Other newspapers and magazines
were similarly entranced with Mata
Hari, and the performances at the
Olympia continued to fill the house.

On October 8, 1905, Mata Hari
wrote to her father again, telling him
of her joy in her success at the Olympia Theater, and adding:

*You ask me, Dad, if I want to know
what is happening in Holland. No,
Dad, I don't want to know anything. It would hurt me and make
me sad. I have overcome everything. At the moment I have my
own carriage and within a month I go to Russia where I can enjoy
myself. I am still very beautiful, healthy, and full of life. I don't fall
in love with anyone and I like this kind of life. Never ever will I
go back to the brute MacLeod—and I don't have to depend on
the hospitality of his family [any longer]. I thank God that I took
the train to Paris. Now I am compensating for all the abuse I
suffered from MacLeod and I am happy. I know MacLeod
and his sister live in Velp; that [Non] of course has no clothes
and will be polluted by a woman like [Tante Frida], who doesn't
ever clean herself, but my dear God, I cannot do anything about it!
I know that nobody gave me anything when I was poor and I know
that everybody is wonderful when I have money.*

In the meantime, typically, Mata Hari was spending more than her generous income. In October she was sued by a Paris jeweler to whom she owed 12,000 francs—about $57,000 in today's currency—and who agreed, after the effective intervention of Edouard Clunet, to allow her to keep her jewels if she paid him 2,000 francs a month. The debts were of little concern to her; success continued to follow success.

On November 1, Astruc arranged for her to sign a contract to dance in the opera *Le Roi de Lahore* (The King of Lahore), the premiere of which had established Jules Massenet as the most popular composer of the day. A new production was being mounted in Monte Carlo in February 1906. Obtaining a role in a serious and much-

After her enormous theatrical success, Mata Hari was considered the most desirable woman in Paris. She was photographed at social events and fashionable spas. (The Mata Hari Foundation/Fries Museum)

loved opera signaled Mata Hari's acceptance as a professional artist.

Before she left for the opera engagement, she danced for two weeks in Madrid, where her dances were pronounced "discreetly voluptuous" by reviewers. Not only did she enchant her Spanish audiences, but she also began a romantic relationship with Jules Cambon, the French ambassador in Madrid. Cambon was an important diplomat, who had been ambassador to the United States and negotiated the settlement of the Spanish-American War. Enamored of his new mistress, Cambon hosted a reception for her at which he pronounced her "a true ambassadress of France." Another prominent romantic conquest was the diplomat Henri de Marguérie. Both Cambon and de Marguérie figured importantly during Mata Hari's espionage trial.

Her next engagement after Madrid was Monte Carlo, where the new production of Massenet's opera opened to considerable acclaim. Both Massenet and Giacomo Puccini were in the audience and sent her notes of admiration afterward. Massenet was enamored of the much younger dancer, and after visiting her in Berlin, where her next performances were, he wrote her a passionate note: "How happy I have been to see you again! Mata, Mata,—I am leaving for Paris within a few minutes! Thank you, thank you—and my fervent admiration."

She left a trail of smitten admirers behind her wherever she went in Europe.

In Berlin, she captured the German imagination and became the mistress of Lieutenant Alfred Kiepert of the Eleventh Westphalian Hussars, Crefeld. Like many other celebrated beauties in the theater, she found no conflict in being both a well-known performer and a much-admired courtesan. Kiepert established her in an apartment in the western part of Berlin, on the Nachodstrasse, to keep her well away from his beautiful and jealous Hungarian wife. Having a mistress was hardly shocking in those times, and Kiepert made no particular attempt to keep Mata Hari out of sight, only to keep her away from his wife. Mata Hari tried to forget the unpleasantness of Rudolf's suit for divorce in the luxury of being loved and kept by a powerful man. According to Mata Hari's own later testimony, "I remained three years with him. He set me up in Berlin, we traveled a great deal and because he was very rich, he kept me sumptuously. In December 1906 and January 1907, I danced in Vienna where he accompanied me."

Mata Hari's appearance in Vienna provoked what was later called the "war of tights" as she competed with two other well-known dancers who performed in scanty costumes: Isadora Duncan and Maud Allan. Duncan had shocked the world by dancing corsetless, with naked legs, in loosely draped garments that vaguely resembled togas, but was well established as a dancer years before Mata Hari made her debut in Paris. Maud Allan was a rising young dancer who was achieving considerable fame for playing the seductive Salome, who demanded the head of John the Baptist on a platter. She wore breastplates, jewelry, and a headdress not unlike the one worn by Mata Hari, who regarded her as little more than a cheap imitator. Underplaying Allan's talents, Mata Hari referred to her as one of a group of "ladies who style themselves 'Eastern dancers' [who] have sprung out of the ground and honor me with imitation." She scorned the dancers who now crowded the music halls, dancing in pseudo-Eastern costumes and performing with snakes, remarking, "Born in Java, in the midst of tropical vegetation, I have been taught from my earliest childhood the deep meaning of these dances which constitute a cult, a religion. Only those born and bred there become impregnated with their religious significance, and can impart to them that solemn note to which they can lay claim."

Such pronouncements are astonishing in the extent that they boldly contradict the truth of Mata Hari's life. That she could and did, repeatedly, express such sentiments with heartfelt seriousness shows her remarkable ability to convince herself of new versions of reality. She believed her own lies, which was the key to her sincerity.

Mata Hari apparently won the rivalry with Isadora Duncan, with Maud Allan coming in a poor third. The *New Vienna Journal* shouted, "Isadora Duncan is dead! Long live Mata Hari!" Her fluency in the German language, not matched by either Allan or Duncan, was a major advantage. Critics and reviewers who were native German-speakers commented on both her charm—an attribute that does not always come across when a translator is at work—and beauty. An interviewer for *Foreign News* described her as "slender and tall, with the flexible grace of a wild animal and blue-black hair . . . a small face that makes a strange foreign impression. Forehead and nose are of classical shape—as if copied from antiquity. Black long lashes throw a shadow on her eyes, and the eyebrows are so finely and so gracefully bent that it seems as if they were drawn by an artist."

She enchanted interviewer after interviewer, telling each a slightly new version of her life story and ancestry; to one she claimed her Friesian grandmother was the daughter of a Javanese prince.

She appeared, at least briefly, onstage completely nude in the Secession Hall after dropping the proverbial seven veils. At the Apollo Theater, she continued to persuade audiences that her dances were art, not pornography. The theater was packed every night, even if a few critics suggested her dances might not be authentically Indian. The public adored her.

Vienna was not a complete triumph for Mata Hari. Kiepert's wife and family, tired of his spending large amounts of money on such a notorious woman, issued an ultimatum, and he was forced to break off with her. As Mata Hari later explained the situation, "His family having given him an order to abandon me under penalty of a judiciary council, he separated from me and gave me 300,000 marks." It was an enormous sum of money, equivalent to well over one million dollars in today's currency.

Adam Zelle was proud of his daughter's success and—being as ever short of money—thought he might profit from her fame. He contacted a publisher with some material for a potential biography of his daughter, but when the publisher consulted Rudolf MacLeod and learned more of the truth, he withdrew from the deal. Undaunted, Zelle was able to publish his work, which was highly critical of Rudolf and blamed most of the marital problems on him, with C. J. G. Veldt. Revealingly, the book was called *The Novel of Mata Hari, Mrs. M. G. MacLeod Zelle: The Biography of My Daughter and My Grievances Against Her Former Husband.*

The second word of the title in the original Dutch, *roman,* can be translated into English as either "romance" or "novel." It was apparently a concession to those who might object to a few loose interpretations of the truth. The book was supposedly written by Mata Hari herself on a ship en route to America and contained numerous highly sentimental internal dialogues and musings on her feelings and fate that Zelle invented entirely. Mata Hari never went to America and wrote nothing

Mata Hari performed in Vienna in 1906–1907, vanquishing her dance rivals, Isadora Duncan and Maud Allan. Her German lover at the time, Alfred Kiepert, provided a parting gift of 300,000 marks, the equivalent of more than $1,000,000 in today's currency. (The Mata Hari Foundation/Fries Museum)

in the book save a premarital letter to Rudolf and a series of letters to her father from the Indies, which Zelle presented in their entirety. Zelle's intent in writing the book, other than making money, was to air his grievances against MacLeod especially because he had attacked Mata Hari's reputation during the divorce proceedings. Zelle's version of Mata Hari's life was blatantly slanted, designed to emphasize her youth and innocence when they married and his gambling, jealousy, and violent temper. The Mata Hari of Zelle's book was a thoroughly romanticized and sentimental young woman treated badly by a dreadful older husband.

It was not long before a lawyer, G. H. Priem, undertook to investigate the truth of Zelle's claims for himself. He wrote up his interviews with Mata Hari, which contradicted some of the "facts" Zelle had presented. His seventy-two-page book was entitled *The Naked Truth about Mata Hari.*

Despite his initial bias against her, Mata Hari managed to disarm Priem with her candor and charisma. They spoke in Dutch, but he recorded their conversation as being sprinkled with French and German words, writing:

> *A charming woman, indeed; slender, pretty, in the eyes something cool, beautiful eyes. . . . She had spirit, she was truly a woman to turn somebody's head, especially now as she fell at the sofa at full length and took a cigarette out of the case that lay before her on a small table. She said "It doesn't annoy you, if I smoke?" With the nonchalance of an amusing friend she offered me the case: "Please!"*
>
> *I followed her example and we spiraled the blue smoke upward for a moment, without saying anything. "And may I now know?" she asked then. I took out of my inside pocket* The Novel of Mata-Hari, *"that you were so kind to send to me directly." "Je sais!" [I know!] She laughed. "What a joke, eh? Exquisite! Did you read it? But of course. How can I ask something like that? And what do you say of it?'*
>
> *"Pardon, Madam, but I thought, that I came for an interview and not* you!*"*
>
> *"That is true!" she laughed. "Please yourself!"*
>
> *"What do you say about this book?"*
>
> *"I? I do not say anything about it! Do you think that they make money out of it?"*
>
> *"I think so."*

"Well, that is the Hauptsache *[main point]! What do I care, what they say about me in Holland! I am happy that I am out of it and I do not wish to go back."*

"But why do you ask if I think that they make money out of it?"

"Well, everything started of course in the first place because of that!"

"And your father says that he does this for the honor of his daughter. . . ."

She burst out laughing. "I read it too! Heavenly! Heavenly!"

"You read it too? But of course, you have written the book your-self?"

"I? Writing a book? For God's sake! With my legs, yes!"

In his interviews, Priem obtained greater frankness from Mata Hari and a clearer perspective on her character than almost anyone else.

She spoke so calmly, so pleasantly, that I got the idea that her brains were excellent and that she even possessed a somewhat philo-sophical talent. Apparently, she had thought a lot about her own life in connection with the world as she lived it, and she possessed an honesty and open-heartedness which one finds more often in such natures, but in this case carried by a great measure of wise insight.

The next day he returned for an additional interview. He asked about the failure of her marriage to Rudolf. Again, Priem recorded their dialogue.

"Look," she began, "I shouldn't have married. I was not the kind of girl to marry."

"Many say that. Regret comes after sin."

"Exactly! From the time that I was a child I loved men: a strongly built male brought me to a state of ecstasy. I say this sans gêne *[without pretense], because a journalist appears to me as a kind of doctor, to whom I could say calmly: so many centimeters above my knee I feel this or that . . ."* We both smiled. [Priem thought]: What an everlasting lovely type! *"Thus, I loved, as I said before, robust men. . . ."* She smiled again when she looked at me. [Priem wondered:] Why am I such a small poor creature?

She spoke to him frankly of her early marriage, their money problems, the conflicts with Tante Frida—and took a large part of the blame upon herself, a trait Priem found endearing. She admitted to her infidelities and Rudolf's jealousy as well. "Now I understand fully, that I was in the past not the person that I should have been; a man who marries a woman has the right to expect from that woman what has already been dictated by the law, in the first place: faithfulness. And in every respect I have not been faithful; this knowledge made him—yet naturally quick-tempered—a furious bull. Blame him, if you can!"

For Zelle's book she had little enthusiasm. She suggested her father and stepmother wrote it together, and complained,

This beautiful "novel" is no compliment. With all their good intentions—I am even willing to overlook the financial motive for a moment—they didn't do me a service. They spoilt my whole image; the artistic side [of me] is completely absent. They made a tearful wifey out of me, one that gnashes her teeth, that scolds, that scratches, like a woman from a back street who works with her pins. I am not like that, truly not, I am not like that. I have a tally [of lovers] and there is almost no room for [another] notch, but I am not ashamed of that, I confess this frankly. A woman like me, as I am,

is quite unmanageable within a marriage; it may work for a mo-
ment, in the long run this calm life of little household duties,
kitchen-glittering and living-room-glory is boring.

Priem also quizzed her about her career and her current life, and
she replied candidly: "Certainly, this life suits me. I can satisfy all
my caprices; to-night I dine with Count A and tomorrow with
Duke B. If I don't have to dance, I make a trip with Marquis C. I
avoid serious liaisons."

Priem's final conclusion about the guilt and responsibility for the
breakdown of the MacLeod marriage is surprisingly favorable to
Mata Hari, considering that his initial motivation was to counter
Zelle's book.

I will absolutely not claim, that Mr. M[ac] L[eod] is a little saint,
where two quarrel both are guilty, but I am convinced that the guilt
of Mr. M——L—— is out of all proportion [in Zelle's book]
compared with that of his ex-wife and therefore I consider it very
low to try to . . . portray him as a monster, when really he did noth-
ing else than that what thousands of men would have done in such
circumstances. . . .

I asked Mr. ML if he wanted to [respond to Zelle's charges]
himself, his answer to me was: "No! I consider the whole caboodle
that agitates against me not worth an answer!"

I grant that he is completely right.

Priem closes with these majesterial words: "My only intention is:
to stigmatize the novel of Mata Hari as a dirty, dissolute disgraceful
lampoon."

He damned the novel, not the woman.

Living Like a Butterfly in the Sun

MATA HARI WAS DECLARED "a Star of Dance" in 1908. Such recognition was pleasing, but it was another thing altogether to sustain her success and keep drawing the audiences, especially since "Oriental dancers" in flimsy costumes were suddenly all too common on the music-hall stages of Europe. Mata Hari was over thirty, and everyone who was anyone had already seen her dance at least once.

She needed to offer something new. In 1907 she had taken a break from performing to travel to Egypt after her lover Alfred Kiepert returned to his wife. According to journalist René Puaux, he discovered her among the passengers on the S.S. *Schleswig* sailing to Khartoum, to his surprise. It is almost beyond belief that his meeting the famous dancer on the ship was an accident; the encounter was far more likely to have been stage-managed by Mata Hari, who knew full well that she needed to stay in the public eye especially if she was not performing. Besides, she needed to promote her career; she had lost her lover and a major part of her income, despite his generous settlement. Puaux's article read in part:

> *Saturday—Just today, on leaving Naples, did we get a chance to see the full list of passengers. But at Marseille certain Parisians on board had recognized a celebrity: Mata Hari, the famous Hindu dancer, the exponent of the sacred dances of the East. She is going to Egypt for the purpose of discovering new [dances]. . . . She has renounced Siva and her cult. She has become Berlinoise and speaks German with an accent that is as un-Oriental as possible.*

She had told Puaux that she was also renouncing her stage career, but gave her reason for going on the trip as looking for new techniques or new dances. The contradiction did not bother Mata Hari, and in his thoroughly charmed state, Puaux was apparently not bothered by it either. The trip itself was extremely brief, much too short a time to see or learn Egyptian dances in any but the most cursory sense. Mata Hari was traveling because she liked it, because she wanted to, because she needed to figure out how to continue to live in the style to which she was by then thoroughly accustomed.

She had only two alternative means of supporting herself, and she preferred to use them simultaneously: men and dance. She also preferred that each pay handsomely.

By the end of March 1907 Mata Hari was back in Paris writing to her agent, Gabriel Astruc, that she wanted to dance the part of Salome in Richard Strauss's soon-to-be-produced opera of the same name. She campaigned vigorously for the role, writing to Strauss as well and suggesting he contact her paramour Massenet who would vouch for her talents. Part of her longing for the role was undoubtedly its firm association with her rival Maud Allan, who had danced

Salome in the scandalous production by Oscar Wilde; doubtless Mata Hari wished to prove she could dance a more emotionally compelling Salome than Maud Allan. She never succeeded in landing the role.

While she lived in a first-class hotel (this time the Hotel Meurice), Mata Hari was telling tales to the press about her "two years" spent traveling in India and Egypt, and promoting her upcoming performance with three new dances. She previewed the dances at some elite, private parties, including a benefit performance at the Trocadéro. She soon found another rich lover: well-to-do, handsome, and married stockbroker Xavier Rousseau. During most of 1908 and 1909 she appeared rarely, dancing several benefits, and attending horse races (and being eagerly photographed) at the track. Rousseau first installed her in a hotel and then rented a country château in Esvres, near Tours, where she lived until late 1911 as Madame Rousseau. He even told his business partners he had remarried, which must have infuriated his wife. Rousseau visited Mata Hari there on weekends and provided four fine horses for her to ride, a coach, luxurious furniture, and a staff, which, in addition to her faithful Dutch maid, Anna Lintjens, included another maid, Pauline Bessey, a groom, a coachman, a cook, and a gardener. Pauline found "Madame" to be "a beautiful woman" who was "very nice" and got along very well with Rousseau: "There was never any quarrel, and they used to go riding together a lot."

Neither Rousseau's wife nor his mother was able to persuade him to give Mata Hari up. His mother paid a lengthy visit to the château, but somehow Mata Hari managed to charm even this formidable lady. According to Pauline, "she did not have a chance [of convincing him to return to his wife]. The moment she saw Mata Hari she began to feel very friendly toward her, and remained with us for six months off and on. When she left, Mata Hari stayed on."

In January 1910 Mata Hari danced the role of Cleopatra in Monte Carlo in the opera *Antar*. When the opera moved to the Odéon in Paris, she was again contracted to dance for the full fifteen performances at 200 francs a performance (for a total of about $115,000 in modern currency). But the director, André Antoine, found she was putting on weight and was difficult during rehearsals; among other problems, she refused to practice in front of the mistress of ballet at the Paris Comic Opera. Mata Hari claimed it was to protect herself from having her "interpretation" of the dance stolen; others suspected she might be afraid to have her dancing judged by such a professional. Antoine fired her and she sued for breach of contract, winning her case two years later.

In 1911, she and Rousseau moved to a charming Normandy-style mansion at 11 rue Windsor, Neuilly-sur-Seine, bringing the horses and carriages from Esvres. Mata Hari was sometimes seen riding in the Bois de Boulogne in the mornings, in a stylish riding habit. One magazine gushed, "Those who see her pass by daily on one of her magnificent horses, and who are impressed by the grace, nobleness and beauty of this aristocratic *cavalière*, would certainly not imagine that this admirable amazon is none but Mata Hari, the holy dancer!"

All seemed well, but trouble was brewing. Rousseau was nearly bankrupt. The annual rent on the house in Neuilly was a hefty sum, 5,500 francs (almost $22,000 today), and the lavish furniture was apparently never paid for. Eventually a bill for the furniture came to his wife, who had no intention whatsoever of paying for her husband's mistress's furniture. She characterized her husband as "a skirt-chaser and very good-looking." Unfortunately, he had not such a good head for business and his bad investments swallowed up Mata Hari's parting gift from Kiepert as well as the money of many of his clients. His business went bankrupt. "When at long last he came back to me," his wife claimed bitterly, "he was ruined." Of course, his wife blamed Mata Hari for his financial ruin, and when she later came under suspicion of espionage, the accusation that Rousseau had been Mata Hari's "victim" resurfaced.

Mata Hari's version of the affair was more pragmatic: "My lover squandered my private fortune losing up to 200,000 marks. I separated from him, sold everything, and resumed my life in the theater in 1912."

Late in 1911, Mata Hari's confidence was restored by a two-month engagement at La Scala in Milan, dancing "The Princess and the Magic Flower" in Gluck's opera *Armide*. She danced again at La Scala, early in 1912, as Venus in Marenco's ballet *Bacco e Gambrinus*. Reporters and critics were enthusiastic, one proclaiming, "The part of Venus will suit her magnificently." And it did, though a few critics were taken aback by the difference between her style of dancing and traditional ballet. The conductor, Tullio Serafin, considered Mata Hari "an adorable creature," who was "very cultured . . . with an innate artistic disposition, who gave the impression of being a simple member of the aristocracy." She earned 3,000 francs (almost $12,000 in today's dollars) monthly and restored her fame as a premier dancer, albeit, as ever, an original one.

Unable to win the role she longed for, Salome, Mata Hari undertook to dance Salome at a private performance for the Prince di San Faustino, using Strauss's music and basing her role on Oscar Wilde's *Salomé*. The prince was so moved by her performance—and probably by her person—that he had a portrait painted of her as Salome, nearly nude, gloating seductively over the head of John the Baptist. But when she returned to Paris in February, Rousseau was bankrupt and had left her, and she was again in need of money to refurbish her wardrobe and finance her luxurious lifestyle. She needed either bookings or a rich patron to keep her. She wrote an extraordinary letter to her agent, Astruc:

> *I wonder whether you know anyone who would be interested in the protection of artists, like a capitalist who would like to make an investment? I find myself in rather difficult circumstances and need immediately about 30,000 francs [about $116,000 today] to pull me out of this unpleasant situation, and to give me the tranquillity of mind which is so necessary to my art. It would really be a pity to cut such a future short. As a guarantee for this loan I offer everything I have in my home, including horses and carriages.*

Mata Hari pasted this photo of herself as Venus in the opera *Baccho e Gambrinus* in her scrapbook. Conductor Tullio Serafin pronounced her *"una creatura adorabile"*—an adorable creature. (The Mata Hari Foundation/Fries Museum)

She promised that the money would be paid back out of her theatrical fees within a few years. It was a ridiculous scheme that came too close to asking Astruc to act as her pimp to be proper—but Mata Hari was never much concerned with other people's ideas of morality. She was a woman who lived as she liked and took whatever lovers she liked. As she had said to Priem six years earlier, she wanted to live like a butterfly in the sun, and so she did.

There is no documentary evidence that Astruc found a benefactor for Mata Hari, but neither did she appear to be short of cash. She was still photographed, exquisitely and fashionably dressed, at the most important horse races in Paris or riding one of her horses in the Bois de Boulogne, which was also a way to meet wealthy men. She made a brief trip to Monte Carlo to meet with Diaghilev about possibly performing with his Ballets Russes; the trip was fruitless because Léon Bakst, the sensational costume designer for the troupe, found her figure a bit too matronly when he examined her nude.

Hurt and in need of reassurance, Mata Hari decided to reclaim her daughter, Non. She tried in vain to see Non or to get the Dutch government to restore custody of the child to her. Her action may have been provoked by the fact that Rudolf had separated from his second wife, Elisabetha van der Mast, after five years of marriage, so Non had no mother substitute. Mata Hari even sent her maidservant Anna to try to kidnap Non as she left school one day, but Rudolf was there to meet his daughter and dismissed Anna with a curt word or two. After that, Mata Hari apparently gave up the idea of resuming her motherly role for a while. Her career resumed its importance in her life. She wrote to her former lover Jules Cambon, by then France's ambassador in Berlin, to ask if he could help her obtain a booking to dance at the Berlin Opera; he promised to try but nothing resulted.

Determined to keep herself in the spotlight, Mata Hari gave garden parties for various influential friends, sometimes with press photographers in attendance. She was accompanied by Inayat Khan's Indian orchestra, playing traditional instruments. Inayat Khan, a highly respected musician in the Indian tradition, was engaged in a tour to bring Indian music to the Western world, so the pairing with Mata Hari—self-proclaimed as the one who brought Oriental dance to the Western world—seemed natural. Photographs of one such event were published in a British society magazine in 1913. The title was "Lady MacLeod Dances in the Light of the Moon to Her

Mata Hari danced in the garden of her house at Neuilly-sur-Seine and at the Université des Annales in Paris, accompanied by an Indian orchestra led by Sufi holy man and master musician Inayat Khan. (The Mata Hari Museum/Fries Museum)

Friends," and it was an effective piece of advertising, reminding readers of her supposed aristocracy, her use of transparent veils and skimpy costumes, and her ability to adopt striking poses, fluidly shifting from one to another.

These parties, at which she acted as hostess and entertainment, were probably part of her many schemes to earn money. In May of 1917, when Mata Hari was under investigation for espionage, Henri Liévin, a stockbroker, testified about the garden parties at Neuilly:

At a time that I cannot pin down precisely, but before the war, I had some vague connections with Mata Hari and I saw her at the theater sometimes. She lived then in a small mansion at Neuilly, and when she found herself short of money, she rented it for soirées and

dinners. When I say she rented it out, the expression is not quite
right. In reality, she gave parties at which certain friends (of the
Bank of Paris, notably) and I paid the expenses.

    At one of these parties, Mata Hari danced with some Brahmin
[musicians] with whom she made tours.

On December 14, Mata Hari and Inayat Khan performed before
an audience at the Université des Annales in Paris, to illustrate a
lecture by music critic Paul Olivier. Olivier referred to Mata Hari as
a lady of noble birth born along the Ganges and as a *bayadère*—a
female Javanese court dancer—thus implying his acceptance of the
authenticity of her work and life story. Shortly before the performance was to begin, the director of the university, Madame Brisson-
Sarcey, decided that Mata Hari's costume might be altogether too
revealing for the more staid members of the audience, especially if
she dropped her veils as she usually did. She insisted on draping
Mata Hari's lower abdomen and genitals with the only thing on
hand—a piece of red flannel—which must have given a bizarre
touch to her costume. Olivier, like so many men, was completely
captivated by Mata Hari, and wrote her afterward that she

    was an unforgettably radiant and living centerpiece of this all too
short festival, a festival of exquisite and unique art, which to all of
us, and in particular to your lecturer, will remain a scintillating
souvenir. . . .

    I put at your feet, Madam, my most fervent and grateful hom-
age, and beg of you to consider me sufficiently worthy to accept the
certitude of my profound and absolute devotion.

Whether Mata Hari and Olivier became lovers before or after
the performance is not recorded, but the love-struck tone of his let-

ter is unmistakable. Olivier was neither the first nor the last man to be enraptured after brief acquaintance with Mata Hari. She was very good at charming men.

The year 1913 saw Mata Hari desperate enough to dance for relatively low pay at private parties and in musical comedy in Paris. She also played to sold-out audiences at the Folies Bergère, where she performed a Spanish piece based on a Goya painting, and in a much lower-class theater in Palermo in Sicily, on a music-hall-type program that included a trained-dog act. She earned lavish praise for some performances and more criticisms and catty remarks for others. She must have been frantic for money. It was during this period that it was reported again that she sometimes went to *maisons de rendez-vous*—houses one step above brothels—with men. Curbing her expenditures or extravagant lifestyle was not, in her mind, a viable option. She returned to Paris and was interviewed and photographed for a highly flattering article in the acclaimed fashion magazine *Vogue*. The magazine printed additional photos of her dancing in her garden at Neuilly that must have been taken at one of her parties.

Early in 1914 she decided to prepare a new dance, based on ancient Egyptian culture. Whether to research her dance at the outstanding German museums, which had unparalleled collections of Egyptian antiquities, or for financial and romantic reasons, she returned to Berlin. Although she was the mistress of Constant Bazet, director of a prominent banking firm, she also took up again with Alfred Kiepert. A gossip columnist noticed the couple "talking animatedly and confidentially in a booth in one of the most fashionable restaurants in town" and concluded, coyly, that France (Mata Hari) had vanquished Austro-Hungary (Kiepert's wife was Hungarian). The writer wondered if she had returned because she had spent the "several hundred thousand [marks] which she had received from Mr. K. as a farewell present"—apparently this arrangement was publicly known—or whether she had returned out of affection. The use of the pseudonym, Mr. K., spawned a rumor that her lover was in fact the Crown Prince Wilhelm—the *Kronprinz*, in German—himself. In May, Mata Hari signed a contract to dance for six months at the Metropol in Berlin, starting in September of 1914 with a very respectable salary of 48,000 marks (nearly $220,000 in modern currency).

In Berlin, Mata Hari began to feel more acutely the change that was coming over Europe. The Belle Époque—golden era of art, science, and culture in France that began in about 1890 and lasted until the beginning of the First World War—was an era of lavish spending and open luxury; successful men had beautiful mistresses who were paraded openly and received in society, sometimes even holding intellectual salons. In 1914 a darker, more puritanical mood was sweeping across Europe and the days of exuberant living were drawing to a close. When she told Kiepert of her upcoming engagement at the Metropol in the autumn, he remarked cryptically, "You will be there before then and so will I." Another lover, Captain Lieutenant Runtze, who was chief of the seaplane station at Pützig, made similar vague but ominous predictions. Something great was happening that would transform the world in a process that would be anything but pleasant.

In late July, shortly after the invasion of Serbia by the Austrians, Mata Hari was dining one evening in a private room—the sort reserved by wealthy men for intimate adventures—of a fashionable restaurant with one of her lovers, a chief of police, Herr Griebel.

We heard the noise of a great disturbance. This demonstration was certainly spontaneous and Griebel, who had not any warning of it, took me in his car to the place where it was held. I saw an enormous mob that was giving way to a frenetic demonstration in front of the Emperor's palace and shouting, "Deutschland über Alles!" [Germany over all!] Several days later war was declared. At that time, the police were treating foreigners like animals. Several times, I was stopped in the street and transported to the station, because they were absolutely convinced I was Russian.

She was anxious to return to Paris and her lovely house at Neuilly, lest it and her possessions be seized—she was not a French citizen. She attempted to break her contract at the theater, arguing that war was an act of God. Her costumier, who had not yet been paid, seized her furs and her jewelry and refused to hand them over without payment. Her German agent held on to her money and the bank froze her accounts, as she was a longtime resident of France and Germany was at war with France.

On August 6, with hardly any money, she boarded a train for Switzerland but the German guards would not let her past the border without a passport certifying her neutral Dutch citizenship, especially as she made the mistake of telling them she was headed for France, Germany's enemy in the war. She was put off the train without her extensive luggage. She had to return to Berlin, now deprived of both money and a change of clothes. She called Griebel, but he could not risk being seen to help a foreigner. Suspicion of foreigners and open hostility toward them was growing daily as patriotic fervor reached a jingoistic frenzy.

Friendless and short on cash, Mata Hari fell back on her greatest talent. Before very many days had passed, she had charmed a Dutch businessman who listened to her tale of unfair treatment and worry. She would not have anything left after settling her hotel bill, she told him. He agreed to pay her fare back to Amsterdam. He left Berlin immediately but bought a ticket for her to use a few days later, after she had traveled to Frankfurt to obtain a Dutch passport.

In handwritten ink, the passport gave her age correctly as thirty-eight, but at some point someone (probably Mata Hari herself) wrote over the 8 with a 0, to produce a more flattering age of thirty. The change was made without changing the date of birth, so that anyone could calculate her true age. She was described as five feet eleven inches tall, with a big nose, brown eyes, and blond hair. A blond Mata Hari is difficult to imagine. If she was a bleached blonde, it was purely temporary.

A remarkable anecdote suggests that what was needed at the time of her leaving Berlin was the attention of a skilled hairdresser to help conceal her age. Mata Hari eventually took the train from Berlin to Amsterdam. After descending from the train in Amsterdam, she unexpectedly saw a familiar face. It was Maurice van Staen, her former hairdresser from Paris, in uniform. Van Staen had made a good career in Paris out of his secret technique for putting henna in women's hair.

Astonished and delighted to see him, she called out across the crowded platform, "Maurice! You must immediately do my hair!" She asked him to come to the Hotel Victoria and added, "And I did not even know that you were an officer in your own land!"

Van Staen must have cringed at the attention she was drawing to him. Mere weeks before, he had enlisted in the Belgian army to fight the Germans; then, as the Germans invaded Belgium in August of 1914, he had fled across the border into Holland as a military refugee. He had been interned in a camp in Harderwijk, which he had found so distasteful that he had decided to break out. He had stolen an officer's uniform and escaped—an act he himself described as "reckless youthfulness"—reasoning that people in a neutral country would be less likely to question an officer than they would a simple enlisted man. His plan had worked remarkably well until, to his "inexpressible stupefaction," he was hailed by Mata Hari in Amsterdam. He assumed officials were looking for him; drawing attention to himself was the last thing he wanted to do. But Mata Hari drew attention wherever she went, whatever she did.

He took her aside and explained his precarious situation to her, while she listened carefully. He did, of course, come to the hotel and do her hair not long afterward. When he wrote about his experiences many years later, he expressed the opinion that she had used her connections to prevent a serious search being made for him and had thus saved his life.

After settling in at the hotel, Mata Hari again made contact with the generous businessman who had paid her train fare to Amsterdam. When she met his wife, Mata Hari reassured her that her husband's kind gesture had not been based on a sexual relationship. Asked by the curious wife why she had not attempted to seduce him, Mata Hari replied frankly, "Because I had only one chemise left, as everything else had been taken away from me—and really, I didn't feel clean enough." She was promiscuous, but she had her inviolable standards nonetheless.

Once again Mata Hari used her talents to survive. For a month or two, she entertained a Dutch banker who laughably mistook her for a Russian lady and proudly showed his exotic "foreign" mistress around Holland. By the time someone recognized Mata Hari in his company, and enlightened him as to his embarrassing mistake, Mata Hari had lived well for a month, refurbished her wardrobe at his expense, and resettled herself in Holland. She wrote to Rudolf asking to see her daughter but was of course refused.

Two months after returning to Holland, Mata Hari had reestablished relations with a former lover, Baron Edouard Willem van der Capellan. He was more than ten years her senior, wealthy, married, and a colonel in the Dutch cavalry. He was only too happy to welcome back his mistress. He visited her when he could and took care of her bills, including the salary of her maidservant, Anna.

She rented a house in The Hague, at 16 Nieuwe Uitleg, and ordered extensive and expensive renovations and redecoration. She persuaded the contractor to give her two years from the day she moved in to pay; he also agreed that she might make payments of whatever amount she chose. Soon he was tired of trying to meet Mata Hari's exacting standards; she threw temper tantrums and once pushed an armoire down the stairs when he told her it would not fit through a doorway. He wanted to end the job and get his pay immediately. After a visit or letter from Mata Hari's attorney, the job was finished; she moved in on August 11, 1915. Despite van der Capellan's support, she had not paid her hotel bill and was hounded for some time by her creditors.

She was soon bored with life in a quiet house on a quiet canal in The Hague while she waited for van der Capellan to visit. Life in Holland during the war was restricted and a little grim, even though the country remained neutral. The very atmosphere filled Mata Hari with ennui. Since the war, life everywhere seemed to be dull and gray and penny-pinching; there was no life, no glamour anymore.

Then in the autumn of 1915 she was visited by Karl Kroemer, the honorary German consul in Amsterdam, whose name has been misspelled as Craemer, Cremer, Kramer, and Krämer in various contemporary accounts.

Kroemer recruited espionage agents for Germany, and he hoped to convince her to join his organization. He offered her 20,000 francs—a very substantial sum roughly equivalent to $61,000 today—but she demurred, saying it was not enough. He indicated that this was a test or trial period and if she was successful, she could earn more for later assignments. Kroemer asked her to write him in invisible ink and gave her three bottles. She disliked the very idea of invisible ink—it seemed complicated and incriminating and undignified—and she did not want to sign her name. He instructed her to sign her communications with a code name, H21.

The H of H21 indicated her communications were to be handled by Captain Hoffman; all his agents had the prefix H. The numbers following the H were assigned sequentially; later analysis has shown she must have been recruited in the autumn of 1915, not in May 1916 as she later remembered.

What Mata Hari remembered perfectly accurately was that, at the time Kroemer approached her, she was living in The Hague and bored because van der Capellan was rarely with her. She was suffering from wartime shortages of food and coal, not to mention luxury and amusement. Her furs and monies would have been very welcome, but instead they had been unfairly seized by the Germans after the war broke out. She felt distinctly resentful against the Germans. As she later said, "My 20,000 francs in my pocket, I bowed Kroemer out the door, but I assure you that I never wrote him anything during my time in Paris. I add that once I was on the canal between Amsterdam and the sea, I threw away my three bottles [of invisible ink] after emptying them."

As she never had the slightest intention of spying for Germany, she felt no guilt or obligation to do anything for the twenty thousand francs she had accepted. She always had taken money from men because she needed money and they had it; she always felt she deserved it. The matter was over and done with as soon as she got the money, at least as far as she was concerned.

In early December, she had an engagement with a troupe known as the French Opéra at the Royal Theater. To music by François Couperin, she portrayed through her dance a series of eight moods, including virginity, passion, chastity, and fidelity. The Hague newspapers were complimentary, although she did not drop her veils as she had previously, and the show moved to Arnhem. Though Arnhem was very close to where they lived, neither Rudolf nor Non attended.

Later in December she could not bear The Hague any longer and returned to Paris. Her stated intent was to collect her household belongings from Neuilly and to sell those she did not wish to keep. But she could not resist the allure of Paris and stayed longer to enjoy herself and perform. She renewed her love affair with Henri de Marguérie, then the second secretary to the French legation in The Hague. He later testified:

> A certain time after the declaration of war, I encountered her near the Opera, she was staying then at the Grand Hotel, I invited her to dinner, and during the meal she began to tell me that she was in Paris with a residence permit, that she had come to look for furniture and that she found herself indecisive about a return to Holland.
>
> During those days, I saw her again several times, she was always undecided, but appeared to me to long for her life in Paris. One beautiful day she was leaving for Spain and I accompanied her to the station.

She also wrote to her agent, Astruc, from the Grand Hotel in Paris on December 24, suggesting that her new and strange dances might fit nicely into Diaghilev's Ballets Russes performances, but he was unable to arrange anything. She was still very beautiful, though nearing forty. On March 13, exactly ten years after her debut performance at the Musée Guimet, Mata Hari appeared on the cover of a Dutch magazine. She was no longer in her first youth, but she was breathtakingly beautiful. She was shown in a scandalously low-cut white dress, a large picture hat decorated with plumes, and a string of pearls. Ten years was a long run for a dancer, especially one who made her fame through novelty and nudity. It is the last photograph pasted in Mata Hari's scrapbooks.

When she departed from Paris with her ten crates of silver, linens, and furniture, she was headed home to the baron, traveling via Spain and Portugal. She left behind an enamored Belgian officer, the marquis de Beaufort, with whom she had begun a relationship while she was at the Grand Hotel.

The last photograph in Mata Hari's scrapbook was this stunning portrait, published March 13, 1915, ten years after her debut at the Musée Guimet. (The Mata Hari Foundation/Fries Museum)

She had left behind something else, something that was to prove far more indelible than another lover, however exciting: a record of her travels was made by the British counterintelligence and espionage unit. On her way to Paris, she had stopped at the port of Folkestone, England, where officials questioned her along with the other passengers. The notation from December 4, 1915, read in part: "I beg to report that Madame Marguerite Gertrude Zelle, age 39, a Dancer and a Dutch subject, arrived here by the Dieppe boat-train at 11.15 am yesterday."

She told the police that she was en route to Paris in order to sell her effects from the house at Neuilly and to sign some contracts for performances. When questioned further by Captain Dillon of MO5 (the organization that was the precursor of MI5), she told a slightly different story, emphasizing that she was moving from Neuilly to The Hague, where her lover Baron van der Capellan, the colonel commandant, Second Regiment of Hussars, Eindhoven, of the Dutch Army, could visit her more conveniently. The notes on her questioning continued: "Although she was thoroughly searched and nothing incriminating found, she is regarded by Police and Military to be not above suspicion, and her subsequent movements should be watched."

The report was signed by Frank Bickers, PC sergeant, and P. Quinn, superintendent. A copy of the report was duly sent to Paris, the French being British allies. A notice was also sent to all the British ports informing them that Madame Zelle MacLeod seemed "most unsatisfactory and should be refused permission to return to the U.K."

"Not above suspicion," "most unsatisfactory," and "should be refused permission to return to the U.K." proved to be damning phrases. On what was this harsh assessment based? She was searched and questioned without anything incriminating being found. One possibility is the minor discrepancies in her account of why she was going to Paris, though surely such inconsistencies are typical of those questioned by the police. Another entry in her British security file—information obtained from Folkestone—hints at another problem:

Summary and description "Height 5 feet 5 ins [sic]—build, medium stout; hair, black; face, oval; complexion, olive; forehead low; eyes, grey brown; eyebrows, dark; nose, straight; mouth small; teeth good; chin, pointed; hands, well kept; feet small; age, 39. Speaks French, English, Italian, Dutch, and probably German. Handsome, bold type of woman. Well and fashionably dressed in brown costume with raccoon fur trimming and hat to match."

The real problem was probably not what Mata Hari said but who she was. She was a woman, traveling alone, obviously wealthy and obviously an excellent linguist—too educated and too foreign to make a British officer comfortable. Worse yet, she was a "handsome, bold type of woman," one who admitted to having a lover. Women like that were immoral and not to be trusted. This was wartime and women were expected to be dutiful, brave, home-loving, and patriotic. Nothing about Mata Hari ever convinced anyone she had those traits. She was, indeed, to be suspected.

In Time of War

IN EARLY 1916, Mata Hari returned to The Hague via Portugal and Spain, where she left satisfied lovers behind her as usual, including the Spanish senator Emilio Junoy. Unfortunately, life in The Hague was no more amusing in 1916 than it had been in 1915. A few months after getting back to the Netherlands, she was longing to return to Paris again. Traveling through Europe was made more difficult and cumbersome by the war, but it was by no means impossible.

She was completely unaware that she was being investigated by the British counterespionage unit, which in a few months' time would be renamed MI5. On February 3 a report was filed by Richard Tinsley, a British intelligence agent working in Holland, that contained information from an unnamed source about Mata Hari. The most crucial notation was that, although she was said to be in financial difficulty, there were rumors that she had received "15,000 francs [about $45,700 in today's currency] from the German Embassy via a certain Hans Sagace (?)."

Hans Sagace is a name that never again figured in any document about Mata Hari, nor can he be traced. This alleged transaction vaguely resembled her dealing with Karl Kroemer, from whom she had received 20,000 francs. The report also remarked that it was suspicious that she received letters under the name of MacLeo [*sic*] and that she appeared to have two addresses in The Hague (one being where Colonel van der Capellan and his wife lived). Without any further evidence, the writer of the report concluded: "One suspects her of having gone to France on an important mission that will profit the Germans."

Code-named T, Tinsley was not always a reliable agent. Ivone Kirkpatrick, a future permanent undersecretary at the British Foreign Office, found T "a liar and a first-class intriguer with few scruples."

Two weeks later, another British report said that she had apparently succeeded in her mission and would now go to collect the money that the Germans had deposited for her in a bank. It also expressed concern that the story of Mata Hari's life had been written in a book published by her father through the Veldt press, which was thought suspicious.

On February 22, 1916, a circular was sent by the British secret service to the French saying simply that if Mata Hari entered Great Britain, she was to be arrested and sent to Scotland Yard.

In May she received a new passport from the Dutch government. The French consulate issued her a visa; she hoped to stop in Britain on the way to France, but the British consulate would not issue her a visa. She went to the Foreign Office in The Hague for assistance, as she knew of no good reason the British should refuse her entry, and they sent a telegram to the Dutch ambassador in London, de Marees van Swinderen:

WELL-KNOWN DUTCH ARTIST MATA HARI, DUTCH
SUBJECT WHOSE REAL NAME IS MACLEOD ZELLE,
WANTS TO GO FOR PERSONAL REASONS TO PARIS
WHERE SHE HAS LIVED BEFORE THE WAR. BRITISH
CONSULATE ROTTERDAM DECLINES TO PUT VISA TO
PASSPORT THOUGH FRENCH CONSUL HAS DONE SO.
PLEASE BEG BRITISH GOVERNMENT TO GIVE ORDERS
CONSUL ROTTERDAM THAT VISA MAY BE GRANTED.
WIRE.

After consulting the Home Office, van Swinderen replied that the British had reason to consider the entry of Mata Hari into Britain "undesirable." The notations in her security file from her previous questioning in Folkestone made her entry into Britain impossible. The Foreign Office decided not to reveal the contents of this reply to Mata Hari and apparently advised her to take another route.

She chose to sail on the S.S. *Zeelandia,* which left from Amsterdam. Her plan was to disembark at Vigo in Spain, for which she obtained a visa without difficulty, and then proceed to Madrid, where she could take a train to Paris.

Her trip was troubled by a bizarre occurrence involving a fellow passenger on the *Zeelandia* with the Dutch name of Hoedemaker. He was a salesman and was said to be a Jew—a highly derogatory term in those days—who regularly denounced German sympathizers to the British, so he claimed. Mata Hari was warned by a fellow passenger that Hoedemaker was claiming to have been in her cabin, implying he had had sex with her. Mata Hari demanded a confrontation. In front of all the passengers, she asked him if he had been in her cabin and he denied it but admitted to spreading a rumor to that effect. She slapped him, hard enough to draw blood, and she thought the matter was finished. But the consul of Uruguay, who was also on the ship, warned her that Hoedemaker was threatening to avenge himself for this humiliation. According to Mata Hari, she then said, "I shall wait for it. If he wishes, I will place a slap of the sort he has already received on the other cheek." The consul suggested that Hoedemaker would speak against her to authorities and she would have difficulty at the border crossing. More immediately, he followed her after she disembarked from the ship and she asked two gentlemen to accompany her to Madrid, for protection. Though she obtained a visa from France without difficulty, as the consul had predicted, she was stopped and interrogated at the border at Hendaye. When she went to the consul of Holland, she found he was a Spanish wine merchant who could offer her little assistance.

Mata Hari wrote an indignant letter about this affair to the Dutch consul in Madrid, van Royen. His inquiries revealed that she was on a list of suspects in Britain and thus she had been refused entry into France. A letter of explanation was written to Mata Hari by van Royen's assistant, telling her that "not even the intervention of the Minister could avail anything; neither [could] the declarations that your sympathies are pro-Ally." She also wrote a letter to her lover Jules Cambon, who had been promoted to secretary-general of the French Ministry of Foreign Affairs. When she returned to Hendaye the next day, apparently her self-assurance and threats to take matters to her lover intimidated the border guards, who decided not to challenge her further.

But who was Hoedemaker? And what was his role in Mata Hari's increasingly frequent difficulties with French and British security? The name is not listed in the indices of the Public Records Office in London for this period. Of course, if he were indeed a spy or spy-catcher working for British counterespionage, he might have had numerous aliases. The British files on Mata Hari now kept by MI5 do not include anything that would suggest Hoedemaker was working for them or indeed that he was anything more than an ill-mannered blowhard. One source traced the fate of a Henry Hoedemaker, presumably the man on the *Zeelandia* in 1916, who told relatives he had been responsible for Mata Hari's arrest and conviction. He committed suicide in 1921. Were his boasts and threats on that voyage simply indicative of the tenor of the times, of the way people perceived a woman like Mata Hari in 1916? Or was he something more sinister? These questions remain unanswered.

Once she arrived back in Paris on June 16, Mata Hari resumed as glamorous a life as was possible in wartime there. Early in 1916, Paris had been bombed by zeppelins, but the damage was comparatively minor. She lived at the Grand Hotel, still an excellent and luxurious establishment for those with money to spare. There were plenty of handsome men in Paris in the summer of 1916, and many of them were high-ranking officers. Mata Hari expected to have a good time.

Mata Hari must have known that the ferocious Battle of Verdun—which would become the longest in World War I—was being fought fewer than two hundred miles from Paris. All of the newspapers were full of battle stories. It was at Verdun that General Erich von Falkenhayn, chief of staff of the German army, had pledged to "bleed the French army white" with a massive attack. In response, the commander charged with holding Verdun, Henri-Philippe Pétain, vowed, "They shall not pass." When the fighting at Verdun began, a valiant 200,000 Frenchmen expected to defeat 1 million Germans. Before the grueling battle ended in December 1916, both sides had fulfilled their grim goals. About 550,000 French and 434,000 German casualties were reported, of which about half died. The enormous death toll devastated French morale. Before the war, the French generals had sincerely believed that the spirit of the French soldier would make him more than a match for a much greater force of Germans. Deaths necessitated reinforcements, which rapidly increased the number of French involved until eventually 259 of the existing 330 French infantry regiments fought at Verdun. The diversion of an enormous number of farmers into the military caused food shortages and further depressed morale.

Yet there was still food and luxury for those who could afford it. The main effect of the war on Mata Hari was to increase the number of uniformed officers in Paris.

So used was she to having men look at her and follow her that it was a few days before she noticed that the same two men were following her everywhere she went. They were a pair of Paris inspectors, Tarlet and Monier. As soon as she noticed them, she complained to the bellboy of the hotel on June 21 that she was being followed. They noticed her noticing them but nonetheless resumed surveillance on June 24. The situation would have been an amusing French farce were the ultimate consequences not so serious. Tarlet and Monier followed her nearly continuously from morning until the lights went off in her room, from June 18, 1916, until January 13, 1917. For their pains, the inspectors received an unexpected education in the best hotels, restaurants, dressmakers, furriers, and jewelers of Paris. They steamed open her mail, questioned porters, waitresses, and hairdressers, and collected abundant evidence of her love life but not of espionage.

Tarlet and Monier were clearly out of their depth tailing Mata Hari. They remarked in an early report that she was *"très élégante"* and described her clothes and hat in some detail. Occasionally she managed to give them the slip, which they felt was deliberate. Sometimes she hailed taxis or carriages that made abrupt turns, so she could pass them going in the opposite direction and stare at them triumphantly. Tarlet and Monier filed stiff, formal reports detailing where she went, what she bought, whom she saw, whom she spoke to on the telephone, where she ate lunch and dinner and with whom, day after day.

The general pattern of her days was to go down to breakfast in the hotel at about 10 A.M., return upstairs afterward, and go out at about 11:00 or 11:30. Sometimes she stayed at the hotel, writing letters or performing invisible (to Tarlet and Monier) actions in her room until after she had her midday meal. In the afternoons, she shopped or visited boot- and shoemakers, dressmakers, hatmakers, furriers, florists, jewelers, parfumiers, hairdressers, manicurists, pharmacies, banks, bakeries, and purveyors of fine luggage, gloves, handkerchiefs, chocolates, paper, lingerie, or handbags. She took a great many taxis, which posed a problem for her policemen.

On July 11, she reserved a room next door to hers for her lover Fernand, the marquis de Beaufort, at the Grand Hotel. The marquis was a Belgian officer, forty-two years old, who was the commandant of the Fourth Belgian Lancers, Division of the Cavalry of the Army of the Yser. He was expected to arrive in a few days' time. Yet that same evening she was seen in the company of a second lieutenant of the Eighth Chasseurs d'Afrique (African Hunters), a light cavalry regiment.

The next day, their report states that she had lunch with a military man in khaki, an unidentified adjutant or second lieutenant. She also visited the home of Madame Dangeville, a retired actress who entertained officers in her salon. The language of the inspectors' report was plain but nonetheless conveyed their raised eyebrows. If she was waiting for her lover de Beaufort, why was she seeing these other men? Tarlet and Monier had not yet taken the measure of Mata Hari and had not become used to the constant parade of admirers who passed through her life.

When de Beaufort arrived, he and Mata Hari sequestered themselves in her room for a blissful twenty-four hours, having food and drink sent up to them. Over the next few days, they spent a great deal of time together. According to their reports, Tarlet and Monier somehow learned that Mata Hari wanted to go to Vittel, a fashionable spa town, to pass the season. They wrote drily in their report: "Suffering from pains, it is said. But one must be very skeptical about the point of the voyage. She has foreseen the difficulties that she will have to surmount to obtain a safe-conduct [pass] for this part of the war zone."

This entry is interesting because there is no apparent reason why Mata Hari would want to go to Vittel unless it was simply her usual wanderlust. There is also no indication of how the inspectors obtained this vague information.

To the policemen's evident disapproval, after de Beaufort left on the morning train on July 19, Mata Hari had dinner with another man, whom she also saw on the subsequent day: a purveyor of fine liquors, Bernard Antoine, who was traveling through Paris. After identifying him, they wrote: "We do not know on what terms the aforementioned [Mata Hari and Antoine] were together, because this encounter appears to be nothing more than a flirtation."

During this time in Paris, Mata Hari met many men, but three would assume enormous importance in her life. Two were lovers, one a spymaster. Among them, they spun a web in which Mata Hari became fatally entrapped.

The first lover was Second Lieutenant Jean Hallaure, whom the inspectors did not name outright in their reports out of discretion but who was well known to them. After being wounded in battle, Hallaure had been moved to the Deuxième Bureau of the Ministry of War. He had met Mata Hari many years before, when she performed at Molier's circus. In 1917 he was twenty-six years old, tall, handsome in his cavalry uniform, and wealthy. He saw her at the Grand Hotel and recognized her, despite—so he said—her having dyed her hair blond again. He sent her his card and an invitation to meet for coffee; Mata Hari was delighted to resume their acquaintance. They were observed together on July 21, 22, and 25.

Hallaure was infatuated with Mata Hari, although an ominous event occurred. "Around this time, my friend Capt. Christian de Mouchy . . . said to me one day, 'My boy, in your place, I would not go around so often with this woman. You belong to the army, where the most unfortunate rumors circulate about her. She is an alien, she was [involved] with a German before the war, and I believe she is a suspect.' "

On July 27, Hallaure sent her a *pneumatique,* using a citywide system that delivered messages within Paris via pneumatic tubes. According to later testimony by Hallaure, the content of the *pneumatique* concerned Mata Hari's request for the name of a physician who would attest to her poor health and her need to go to Vittel to take the waters, but this cannot be accurate. Mata Hari could not have known until July 31, when she applied at the Police Commissariat for a safe-conduct to go to Calais and Vittel in August, that such a request would be delayed or refused because both cities were in the war zone. Only after being refused would she need to seek advice from her lover in the Ministry of War, Hallaure. She did not know that her friendship with him was about to lead her into serious danger. Quite possibly, having been warned by his friend Captain de Mouchy, Hallaure himself was planning to entrap Mata Hari.

Mata Hari asked Hallaure what she must do to get a permit to go to Vittel; he apparently told her that perhaps a physician's certificate attesting to her need to take the waters in Vittel would do. As Hallaure later recounted the story:

Abruptly, without my observing any change in her, Mata Hari told me she was suffering and had an urgent need to go to Vittel. She

asked me how she might do it. At that time, it was essential in order
to go into the armed zone, in which this station was, to go to the
Military Bureau for Foreigners, 282, boulevard Saint-Germain.

That office referred her to the Deuxième Bureau [the French
intelligence unit], which is directly upstairs from it. . . . I gave
Mata Hari the address and I spoke of her to a little second lieuten-
ant that I knew vaguely and that I knew was in the military
bureau. . . . Then she left Paris without warning [me].

If their relationship was as casual as he says, there is no reason
why Mata Hari would warn Hallaure that she was leaving Paris.
Thus his testimony seems a blatant attempt to deny responsibility or
intimacy with Mata Hari. Too, the reports of Tarlet and Monier reveal that he continued to see her frequently. He testified:

In the days which preceded her departure for Vittel, she was more
and more distant with me. I went to see her at her hotel, but I found
her less friendly, she saw all the world at the Grand Hotel, notably
numerous officials from other countries. On the evening before her
departure, she broke with politeness and, forgetting I had invited
her to dinner, she dined with an English officer with whom I saw
her in deep conversation.

I was supposed to accompany her to the station where she can-
celed on me under the pretext that her departure was delayed. She
promised to meet with me on another date, but she did nothing and
I heard nothing more from her.

In fact, Hallaure had seen Mata Hari more often than he wished
to admit. He saw her on July 21, 22, 25, and 27 and on August 1; he
called unsuccessfully to see her on August 2, corresponded with her
that day and the next, visited her again on August 9 and 17, when he

appeared to be "very animated," and corresponded again on the eighteenth. On August 19, he took her around to look at apartments; they found one she liked, but according to Hallaure, "the proprietor refused her because in his opinion, she had on too much makeup and was too bleached blond." Hallaure saw her again on August 30 and expected to dine with her the next night but found to his dismay that she was with another officer.

Most of their meetings followed a pattern: he would arrive at her hotel and stay for an hour or two in the early afternoon about once a week. This suggests a regular sexual encounter at a time of day when he was not required to be in his office. By the time he was officially questioned about his relations with Mata Hari, he probably wished to distance himself from association with her. Although she fell truly and deeply in love in the summer of 1916, the blossoming of this affair did not prevent Mata Hari from seeing many other men, so it is unlikely that it caused her to become aloof with Hallaure.

The second lover to influence the rest of Mata Hari's life was Vladimir de Massloff, a Russian officer whom she had met at Madame Dangeville's salon probably on July 29; they were introduced by de Massloff's colleague, Second Lieutenant Nicholas Casfield. De Massloff was even younger than Hallaure—twenty-one to Mata Hari's thirty-nine years—and a captain in the Special Imperial Russian Regiment of the First Brigade. By all accounts, it was a fervent affair. She called him "Vadime"; he called her "Marina"—a pet name to mark another important stage in her life.

On July 30, Vadime and Mata Hari struck up a conversation in the Grand Hotel and then went for a promenade in the Bois de Boulogne. After that, they dined at the very chic Pavillon d'Armenonville, where she had been taken by de Beaufort. The restaurant was within the Bois in a romantic setting. After another lengthy stroll, they returned to the Grand Hotel.

It was the very next day, July 31, after spending the night with Vadime, that Mata Hari first went to the Police Commissariat on the rue Taitbout to apply for permission to go on August 7 to Calais and Vittel, vaguely near Mailly, where Vadime was stationed at the western front. She was told that her permit was refused because both Calais and Vittel were in the war zone. After all, Vittel was not far from the front line. It was hardly a time to allow civilians— much less a woman of foreign nationality—to visit the area. Nonetheless, she determinedly went to the

In 1916, Mata Hari fell deeply in love with a Russian captain eighteen years her junior, Vladimir de Massloff. She called him "Vadime" and he called her "Marina."

prefecture of police to request a copy of her French registration paper to append to her permit application.

She also sent a note to Hallaure, probably to arrange their meeting the next day, and another to her couturier, asking if he would be so kind as to look after a trunk of hers while she took a brief trip to Vittel.

She returned to the prefecture of police on August 1, to pick up the copy of her registration paper. After an hour-and-a-half interlude with Hallaure during the middle of the day, she went to 282, boulevard Saint-Germain for the first time, apparently at Hallaure's suggestion. The two government offices housed at that address were the Military Bureau for Foreigners and the headquarters of the Deuxième Bureau.

All accounts except that of Hallaure himself concur that Hallaure deliberately sent Mata Hari directly to the third man who shaped her life: Captain Georges Ladoux, the head of the Deuxième Bureau, or French intelligence. It was Ladoux who had ordered Tarlet and Monier to tail Mata Hari; it was he who received the warning from the British that Mata Hari was under suspicion. And it was he who determined to bring Mata Hari down.

The Tangled Web

WHAT MATA HARI DID in the summer of 1916, and why, is difficult to unravel. There is much testimony and documentation about her activities, nearly all of it tainted by personal interest. The final truth is elusive, as is so much about her life.

Georges Ladoux, the man Mata Hari met at 282, boulevard Saint-Germain, was in a peculiar position. He had graduated from a prestigious military academy, Saint-Cyr, and was a friend of General Joseph-Jacques-Césaire Joffre, chief of staff of the French army. With his background, Ladoux might have expected by the age of forty-two to be in an important and powerful position. On August 4, 1914, Joffre had appointed Ladoux to be the head of the Deuxième Bureau of the Army Headquarters.

The agency formerly in charge of intelligence operations, the Intelligence Service, had been discredited because of its involvement in the wrongful conviction of Alfred Dreyfus. The taint lingered over the Deuxième Bureau, so Ladoux's appointment was not the triumph that might have been expected.

Spying was generally regarded as a dirty, underhanded endeavor carried out by the scum of society. It was seen as opportunistic, mercenary, and ill planned, of little true importance.

Ladoux's outlook toward espionage was a bold departure from previous attitudes. He thought the threat of enemy espionage much greater than his predecessors did and envisioned a vast network of well-trained spies who moved at the highest levels of society, detecting secrets or simply undermining morale and military efforts. Ladoux took it as a personal challenge to make the military aware of the great danger of such spies.

In a letter to the minister of war and the minister of the interior on September 10, 1915, Ladoux had written: "Counterespionage is not today a simple task for the interior police [the Sûreté]. The enemy does not limit himself to spying the details of our military operations: he searches also to dissolve all our national defense forces. His action attacks establishments working for the State, in an attempt to destroy them, or tries to debauch the personnel. He tries to injure our credit or to drain our gold."

Ladoux had his sights set on counterespionage as well as intelligence collection, though the Deuxième Bureau was technically responsible only for the latter. Counterespionage was the charge of the Sûreté. Like most of his peers, Ladoux made a clear connection between lax morals—debauchery—and spying, but his real aim was to obtain the power to run his unit in his own way. In his memoirs he remembers this power struggle lasting for eighteen months, until the end of 1915. From then on, he boasted, things had changed.

In 1916, when Ladoux encountered Mata Hari, he had won his administrative battles and was on a spy hunt. Having staked his reputation on capturing more of the foreign spies that he claimed were on every street corner, he needed to produce the proof. It was he who, acting on the vague communications from the British, ordered Mata Hari's night-and-day tailing. Such a glamorous and notoriously immoral woman, who seemed to have an endless supply of money and military lovers from every nationality, was a juicy target.

Ladoux needed an attention-grabbing case; he wanted to capture a spy as a major victory. His need to succeed was strongly influenced by the war, which was going very badly for French troops. The slaughter at Verdun had begun in February of 1916 and showed no signs of letting up. The Battle of the Somme, intended to distract German attention and draw troops away from Verdun, had begun July 1 and was proving to be just as brutal. It would be heroic for Ladoux to catch a spy who could be blamed for the misery and death that bombarded the French population daily.

In fact, later developments would suggest that Ladoux may have had an even more sinister motive. He may well have been working as a double agent for Germany. If so, he needed a scapegoat to divert attention and suspicion from his own activities even more than he needed someone to blame for the French suffering.

Ladoux described his first meeting with Mata Hari:

It was in August 1916 that I first encountered Mata Hari, and I see her still as if it were yesterday, dressed, despite the summer, in a suit of somber color and sporting a straw hat with a large brim above which floated a gray plume. She entered into my office with the easy gait of an artist, habituated to walk into a scene, but she had in addition a graceful swing of the hips of a dancer.

There is no doubt her physical presence impressed him, as it did numerous other men. She was a beautiful woman with excellent taste, fashionably dressed.

As for Ladoux himself, he was far less impressive. Mata Hari described him as "a fat man with very black beard and very black hair, and spectacles. . . . He was tall and fat. Fatter than a man of 50 years. . . . He smokes all the time. He always has a little cigarette in his lips."

As their relationship progressed, Mata Hari found Ladoux to be small-minded and coarse, a man of no imagination or grand vision. He regarded her as little better than a prostitute, money-grubbing and manipulative. Though she had a great need for money, Mata Hari had a grace and elegance combined with a charm and sophistication that either eluded Ladoux or that so disturbed him he had no option but to cover up his admiration by expressing scorn for her.

According to Ladoux, that fateful first interview proceeded along surprising lines. He wrote in his memoirs:

When I was slow to ask her to sit down, she approached a chair at my worktable and installed herself familiarly, as if she were already at home. "What do you wish of me?" she said to me in a French troubled only occasionally by a certain guttural inflection typical of her Oriental type.

"I don't wish anything of you, but I hear from one of our mutual acquaintances that you intend to take the waters at Vittel, and as the spa is in the military zone, you must have a laissez-passer *[permit] to go there. Now, it is I who gives them out and I am ready to oblige you."*

"Therefore, would you like to do a great service, which is to say to the gentlemen of the police who are downstairs and who don't leave me any more than my shadow does, as it is very warm, will you authorize them to drink my health at the bistro across the street?"

"I have no authority to do so, Mata-Hari. But you are now under surveillance?"

"Yes, stupidly, and for several months, day and night. Every-

*where I go, they follow me . . . and they use my absence from the
hotel to search my luggage. . . . When I return, everything is upside-
down . . . and you know that I have not the means to pay a ladies'
maid."*

*The ice is broken, but not the charm, and I ask myself, at seeing
my visitor's tranquil assurance and self-control, if the English service which pesters me with notes about Mata-Hari, for more than a
year, is not deceiving itself in telling us, without any proof, that she
was a German agent.*

Ladoux's account is remarkable in several ways. The Mata Hari
he portrays is audacious, cunning and bold in her acknowledgment
of her surveillance and the searches of her rooms, and yet so foolish
as to almost dare him to suspect her. His words deliberately emphasize Mata Hari's foreignness.

He also deviated from the truth. He had received two communi-
qués from the British about Mata Hari, which hardly amounts to
pestering. A report from the British was sent to France in December 1915; its most damning words were "Although she was thoroughly searched and nothing incriminating found, she is regarded
by Police and Military to be not above suspicion, and her subsequent movements should be watched."

The second circular, issued February 22, 1916, said that if Mata
Hari entered Britain, she was to be arrested and sent to Scotland
Yard—a plain statement of suspicion but not a direct accusation of
being a German spy.

Ladoux wrote his memoir to justify and dramatize his actions.
He wanted to insure that his readers believed his plan was all along
to entrap a known German spy rather than appearing to be an in-
competent who tried to recruit a woman to spy for France who was
already suspected of being a German spy. Ladoux wrote that he

hinted he had tried to draw her to his office, using their mutual acquaintance Lieutenant Hallaure. He told her:

"We have often spoken of you with him and always good, I assure you. H[allaure] . . . does not believe that which our English friends say about you . . . that is to say, that you are—"

"A spy," she interrupted. *"But upon what do they base this accusation? Someone has followed me since I arrived. Has someone revealed something against me?"*

"Absolutely nothing, it is why I will authorize you to go to Vittel."

"Then, this stupid game needs to stop. Either I am dangerous, and then you will expel me, or I am nothing but a pretty little woman who, having danced all winter, wishes very much, now that the summer has come . . . to be left in peace."

According to Ladoux's memoir, he agreed to sign her permit to Vittel on the spot and did so. He expected her to come back to see him upon her return and asked only that she refrain from seducing pilots from the airfield near Vittel, at Contrexéville. "With fliers," Ladoux claimed he said, cleverly, "you never know what can fall upon you from the sky."

But Mata Hari told him she was in love and that she would not be seeing other men. Ladoux asked if it was Malsoff, a garbling of "de Massloff," and from this Mata Hari deduced that it was Ladoux or his agents who had searched her room. Ladoux promised to stop such behavior, though of course he did not. Ladoux's version of this incident closes with another assertion of his intuition that she was a German spy, though little in his behavior confirms that:

And the strange creature left with an even more supple allure than that with which she entered.

"Tate, the dossier of Mata-Hari!" I cried. And a few instants later, my faithful secretary, who was at the listening post in the bathroom where he transcribed night and day the most secret information, brought to me the collection of reports from the English police and French, a voluminous and useless packet where, during several months, we had been piling up the communications from the "Intelligence Service" and the reports of the surveillance by our agents.

I glanced through all the pieces once more. I reread the intercepted letters; most, moreover, were those exchanged by the dancer with her Russian captain at the front for several months; all had been submitted to a most minute examination and were cleared by all the chemical tests of our laboratory. There was nothing, absolutely nothing, which permitted another interpretation except a vague feeling!

For her part, Mata Hari described her first encounter with La-doux somewhat differently, saying that Hallaure had advised her to go to 282, boulevard Saint-Germain:

There, I was received with more respect than the other visitors. An officer in uniform came to look for me on the ground floor and, taking my papers, led me to the second in an office where a gentleman in civilian clothes asked me to sit down facing him and received me very amiably. She, too, recounted the dialogue between herself and Ladoux:

Him: *I see, madam, that you have asked to go to Vittel, but do you know it is in the military zone?*

Me: *It is a resort where I have gone before. I have even a note from a doctor.*

Him: *It is very difficult for foreigners to go there.*

Me: *If it is as difficult as that, I could go near Rome, to Fiuggi, where the waters are of the same nature.*

Him: *We need not refuse you, but it is necessary [first] to respond to certain questions, because you have been pointed out to us as a suspect.*

After further questioning, Ladoux got down to important issues. He asked about her feelings for France.

Him: *If you love all of France, you could render us a great service. Have you thought of it?*

Me: *Yes and no, but this is not the sort of thing for which one offers oneself.*

Him: *Would you do it?*

Me: *I have never thought it through.*

Him: *You would have to be very expensive.*

Me: *That, yes!*

Him: *According to you, what would it be worth?*

Me: *All or nothing. If one rendered you services as grand as you expect? Then that is worth a great deal; if one fails, that is worth nothing.*

Him: *Reflect upon it, see if you could do something for us. I will give you your pass for Vittel, only promise me that you will not seduce any French officers.*

Me: *There is no danger of it. I know a Russian [there] with whom I am much in love.*

Him: *I have seen you having lunch with him at Ambassadors. In any case, when you have reached a decision on the subject about which I have spoken to you, come back to see me.*

Thus Ladoux enlisted Mata Hari as a spy for France.

The entire encounter with Ladoux was bizarre. If Mata Hari was indeed already a German spy at the time, as Ladoux claimed in his memoirs and at her trial, then he was most foolhardy to grant her a permit to enter the war zone.

If she was not a German agent, then she was a most peculiar choice to be a French one. Mata Hari was known by sight to thousands throughout Europe. Despite wartime austerity, her comings and goings, her rendezvous with important men, and her fashionable costumes were noticed and reported in the gossip columns and newspapers. Even those who did not recognize her as Mata Hari were magnetically drawn to her. Wherever she went, she was likely to be the center of attention. It is difficult to imagine a woman less likely to be able to go unnoticed or to be able to engage in clandestine activities than Mata Hari. She was a star, a celebrity in the modern sense of the word. While she was certainly seductive, which might be viewed as useful for a spy, she was never on any occasion invisible.

Exactly when this meeting between Ladoux and Mata Hari occurred has been a point of confusion. They both suggested it was near the end of August 1916, but the reports from Monier and Tarlet show that her first visit to 282, boulevard Saint-Germain occurred on August 1, at which time Ladoux began intercepting her mail.

After the extraordinary meeting with Ladoux, Mata Hari continued her life much as usual. Vadime was still in Paris. On August 2, Hallaure called again to see her, perhaps hoping to hear about her meeting with Ladoux. She preferred to spend her time with Vadime and asked the hotel to tell Hallaure she was resting and could not see him.

On August 3 her activities grew increasingly frenzied. Either Mata Hari did not trust Ladoux's assurance that she would get her permit for Vittel, or else she was hesitant to become associated with the business of espionage. In either case, on August 3 she went first to the Prefecture of Police, Bureau of Aliens. She hoped they would grant her a permit to travel despite the first refusal from the Commissariat of Police on the rue Taitbout. Then she visited the commissariat twice, taking the copy of her registration paper to further her reapplication for the permit, despite its initial refusal.

Later that day, she and Nicholas Casfield went to meet Vadime at the Pavillon d'Armenonville in the Bois de Boulogne. After about an hour, Casfield tactfully left them alone. The couple later returned to the Grand Hotel, where they dined and spent the night together. The next morning Mata Hari accompanied Vadime to the station, where he boarded the train back to the front. She promised to come to Vittel as soon as she could. After Vadime's departure, she asked anxiously at the hotel every day for any letters; she had received none from the time of her first visit to the Deuxième Bureau because Ladoux was having them intercepted. The letter from Vadime that arrived at the hotel on August 9 was similarly diverted to Ladoux.

For the rest of August she carried out her usual daily round of visiting hairdressers and manicurists and shopping for luxuries. She often went to the jewelry store Walewyk, which is probably where she bought a "gift of silver"—perhaps a cigarette case, photograph frame, or flask—for Vadime. She also visited several photographers, presumably to have the portraits taken that she gave to Vadime, and called several times at pharmacies. She did not cease meeting with and presumably having affairs with officers during this time.

She relentlessly pestered the police and various government offices about her permit to go to Vittel. She visited 282, boulevard Saint-Germain repeatedly (August 3, 5 twice, 7 twice, 8, 11, and 21) and sometimes stayed for several hours. There is no indication why

she went so often to that address. Was she meeting further with Ladoux? Were the conversations that Ladoux and Mata Hari reported
as being held at their first meeting conducted over a series of visits?
And if Ladoux had signed her permit to go to Vittel on their first
meeting—a point that is not supported by the date on the permit—
why did she continue to make the rounds of the various other offices
where she might be granted the permit? It seems that she continued
to apply at both the Police Commissariat and the Prefecture of Police in hopes that one of them would produce a permit for Vittel.

On the eighteenth, she went twice to see her old friend Henri de
Marguérie, secretary of the Ministry of Foreign Affairs, at his office, to ask for advice about Ladoux and about spying for France.
De Marguérie warned her that accepting an espionage mission from
Ladoux was very dangerous but told her that if anyone could render
services to his country, it was she. He picked Mata Hari up at her
hotel at about 7 P.M. in a taxi. They promptly lost the inspectors—
or perhaps the inspectors decided it was more discreet to become
lost when the secretary of foreign affairs went out with Mata Hari.
The couple had not returned by 11 P.M. when the inspectors called
off the surveillance for the night, after intercepting two letters addressed to Vadime and an expedited *pneumatique* to Hallaure.

The next day, August 19, she told the hotel that she would be
moving out after she returned from Vittel. The implication that de
Marguérie exercised some influence on her behalf, after spending a
romantic night with her on August 18, is supported by his later testimony. She also went with Hallaure to look at apartments to rent
after she returned from Vittel, and signed a lease for number 33,
avenue Henri-Martin.

A few days later, August 21, she went to the Ministry of Foreign
Affairs to see de Marguérie, and then went back to the Commissariat of Police on rue Taitbout. Late in the afternoon, she went to the

Deuxième Bureau. On this occasion, her last visit before leaving for Vittel, she told Ladoux, "Captain, in principle, I accept." Her terms were that she would go first to Vittel for her cure and that she would come to see him when she returned. She also asked if it was possible to send "an expedited telegram to the front to a Russian officer." Apparently refused this service, she went to the post office and sent the telegram to Vadime. She had not heard from him, and she was growing very worried. When no word came, she stopped at both the Russian embassy and the Russian mission on August 24, inquiring about Vadime's well-being. On the twenty-ninth, she picked her permit up at the Police Commissariat. On the thirty-first, Hallaure called to see her and was insulted to find her occupied with a British officer.

She left by train for Vittel the next morning, September 1, and arrived there in the late afternoon, followed by the inevitable duo, Tarlet and Monier. The doctor who was to attend her "cure" had been called up, and she did not consult with another for over a week. She checked into the Grand Hotel of the Baths, booking the room adjacent for Vadime, for propriety's sake. On September 3, her beloved Vadime arrived and they were reunited. She saw, to her horror, that he had been injured and wore a bandage covering his left eye. Mata Hari talked about her stay in Vittel during her interrogation.

> [Vadime] had been gravely injured by the asphyxiating gas, had completely lost the vision in his left eye and was in danger of going blind. One night, he said to me: "If this terrible thing comes to pass, what will you do?"
>
> "I will never leave you," I responded to him, "and I would be to you always the same woman."
>
> "Would you marry me?" he asked me.

I responded affirmatively, then I began to reflect: Here my life is well laid out, I said to myself, I must ask Captain Ladoux for enough money that I never have to deceive Vadime de Massloff with other men. I will let go of the marquis of Beaufort, I will let go of the Colonel Baron [van der Capellan], I will go to Belgium to do what the captain asks, I will reclaim my furniture and my precious objects in Holland. I will go to Paris and live in the apartment that I have rented; Captain Ladoux will pay me, I will marry my lover and I will be the happiest woman on earth.

Georges Ladoux was the head of the Deuxième Bureau, the espionage unit in Paris. He recruited Mata Hari to spy for the French but may have been a double agent himself. (Collection Roget-Viollet)

Not every woman during World War I remained faithful to a fiancé or husband who came home seriously wounded; often the psychological wounds and the realities of their disabilities were too much to be borne. Mata Hari was very much in love with Vadime and ready to settle down. She was perhaps tired of her constant work to earn enough money to live in the style she felt necessary. Besides, Vadime was much younger than she and from an aristocratic family who were likely to regard her with horror as a potential daughter-in-law. But if he went blind, they might not be so dismissive of a potential wife with money, even if she had a notorious reputation. And if he went blind, she may have thought, he would always remember her as beautiful and would not see her aging.

Of course, the effects of phosgene gas were only beginning to be known; it had been introduced by the Germans into battle use at

Verdun in early July. The terrible mixture turned into hydrochloric acid when it was inhaled into the moist atmosphere of the lungs, producing immediate coughing, searing pain, and permanent lung damage that made a vigorous life difficult. When a soldier's eyes were exposed to the gas because his gas mask leaked or was not put on fast enough, his eyeballs were burned by the acid too. Permanent blindness, disability, and disfigurement were common aftermaths.

This lovers' portrait of Marina and Vadime was probably taken in Paris in 1916. After Vadime was blinded in his left eye by phosgene gas, Mata Hari drew the patch on this photo.

None of this seemed to spoil the romance of the brief interlude they spent together. Vadime and Mata Hari strolled in the park, took the waters, had their picture taken, dined together, and spent a great deal of time in their hotel. It was a wonderful lovers' holiday. On the back of one of the photos they had taken of themselves, Mata Hari inscribed: "Vittel, 1916—In memory of some of the most beautiful days of my life, spent with my Vadime whom I love above everything." She drew an eye patch on that particular photograph perhaps covering a wound. Vadime was wearing a St. George's Cross and two other medals, which may have been the Croix de Guerre and the Knight of the Legion of Honor. One photograph he had given her showed himself with one of his horses and was signed "To my dear little Marina—your Vadime."

She and Vadime made some acquaintances among the other hotel guests, including Brigadier General Jules Le Loup de Sancy de Rolland. According to the inspectors, Mata Hari was trying to ingratiate herself with other guests and enter into their social circles. She was at all times an intensely social creature. A few days after making his acquaintance, Mata Hari asked the brigadier general to introduce her to Madame Pauline de Fleurian, wife of the French ambassador in London. He asked; de Fleurian declined. While in Vittel, Tarlet and Monier questioned the brigadier general and Madame de Fleurian about Mata Hari and warned them against her. The burgeoning friendship turned to social snubs.

Later, when the brigadier general was questioned formally about Mata Hari, he expressed extreme doubts about her character, but what his attitude might have been without the intervention of the police is unknown. De Sancy said:

> *I was at Vittel [in 1916] for the season, when in the room of the restaurant of the hotel, I remarked upon a Russian officer in uniform who, knowing without a question my rank, gave me a military salute. We immediately entered into conversation, I questioned the officer on the military situation, as he was assigned to the French front, and wished him well for the grave eye wound which he had received in the service of France. I knew immediately that I was in the presence of one of those brave young Russian officers, as was indicated by his decorations.*
>
> *We were conversing when a tall woman came to sit at the table with the officer, a woman whom he presented to me as his fiancée. The person gave the impression of being too old for him and I smelled right away an adventuress and I distanced myself from the false fiancée, showing the greatest reserve. What I saw next did nothing but confirm my assessment.*
>
> *For six years I was the premier military attaché at the embassy*

of France in Berlin. I was in the habit of judging women of this type for I saw the enemy used them for the worst and I could tell you that the companion of the Russian officer had to me so clearly the bearing of a spy that I notified the Special Commissionaire at the station when I left Vittel.

Everything about her indicated that she wished to make the Russian officer her dupe in all regards. I knew then that she was trying to satisfy an indiscreet curiosity. It is thus that she made herself very lively and asked to visit hospitals, as I told Madame de Fleurian. It is Madame de Fleurian who unmasked her by recognizing that she was a former dancer of the Folies Bergère. The former dancer did not approach me on subjects of a military character. I always kept myself on my guard.

Ironically, de Sancy's testimony shows that *he* asked indiscreet questions of the Russian officer about military matters but Mata Hari did not.

De Fleurian also gave formal testimony after Mata Hari had been arrested. She was a society matron well past her years of youth and beauty and perhaps jealous of one still beautiful but no longer young. De Fleurian was class-conscious, pompous, and scandalized by the presumption of a dancer passing as a respectable person. Like de Sancy's, de Fleurian's view of Mata Hari was doubtless prejudiced by the warning they were given by Tarlet and Monier.

When questioned later, de Fleurian said:

My doctor, Dr. Boulommier, was the first to alert me that a very beautiful woman was staying at the same hotel as I and asked me with a certain enthusiasm if I had seen her. I said no. A few days later, I was taking tea in the park with . . . the doctor and his wife, when the person in question passed.

I found her to be of the gaudy type which showed me her social background. I became aware that this person had inflamed the masculine element at the hotel. Most of the men found this woman elegant and pretty.

Me, I was of a little different opinion, I noticed that she was of a certain age and that she had the air of a person who used morphine or cocaine. Her style throughout (I do not criticize otherwise her lack of propriety) rarely pleased me. For example, she said to the maid that she was a Dutch princess and I knew that this sort of title did not exist. [The Dutch royal family would be surprised to learn this "fact."]

For the other part, she held strange conversations with a nun, in front of several people, saying for example that she had a château in Touraine and that she had danced in Russia. I finally understood when, one evening, I found myself entering by accident into the salon of the hotel where she was finishing singing; she made a great bow as if she were in the theater. Then a name was pronounced, that of Mata Hari, and a memory came to me of a dancer spoken of by the young people, perhaps my nephews.

This woman was most often with a young Russian officer.

When I was leaving Vittel, one morning Brigadier General de Sancy introduced to me an officer of the gendarmerie. . . . We spoke of Mata Hari and he told me that this woman was under suspicion. As far as I was concerned, I had no suspicion of espionage, I had taken her for a schemer, one of the cosmopolitan women that one saw in the spa towns before the war.

De Fleurian and de Sancy made a point of telling others in the hotel that she was a woman of "dubious morality," and the hotel maids gossiped about her and her fiancé sharing a room. Despite all the social disapproval, even a nun who was in the hotel accompanying an invalid could not help but admire her beauty and attire. A year later, Sister Delphine Perrod remembered Mata Hari in the hotel salon, wearing "a costume all of lace and a superb hat."

Before Vadime left Vittel on September 7, Tarlet and Monier reported that Mata Hari gave him "a jewel of some value." Whether this was part of or in addition to the gift of silver Monier later reported is not clear.

Mata Hari's idyll with her lover was over.

cMaelstrom

FROM SEPTEMBER 7, 1916, the day that Vadime left Vittel to return to the front, until the day of her death on October 15, 1917, Mata Hari was caught up in a maelstrom of events. She was manipulated, betrayed, and lied to. Admittedly, she was never one to stick close to the truth when telling an invented story suited her purposes better, but she did not lie with malicious intent, only for convenience. She was sadly ignorant of the extent of the conspiracy working to entrap and condemn her.

After Vadime's departure, Mata Hari remained in Vittel for several uncharacteristically solitary days, dining alone, walking alone, and spending much time on her correspondence. The summer was drawing to a close, and the hotels were soon to shut down for the season. She sometimes spoke of Vadime to others, calling him her fiancé or, sometimes, her "nephew"—this was a euphemism of the day, parallel to the phrase used by mature gentlemen who checked into hotels with young mistresses who were referred to as their "nieces." She regarded herself as legitimately affianced, and all her plans and dreams were of life with Vadime. She consulted with her physician, presumably the Dr. Boulommier who had so enthusiastically commented upon her beauty to de Fleurian. A few times she went for promenades and dined with a couple staying at the hotel, Monsieur and Madame Roux. She retrieved the photographs that had been taken of her and Vadime, then departed for Paris, arriving on September 17.

For mysterious reasons that have never been explained, Ladoux suspended the surveillance on Mata Hari from September 13 until October 13. The most probable rationale for this bizarre decision was that he had decided she was not an enemy spy. Alternatively, he believed she was a spy but wanted to prevent Tarlet and Monier from recording in their reports something he knew Mata Hari would be doing. This gap in the surveillance reports links up with other peculiar omissions, such as the persistent substitution of "Lieutenant X" for the name of Lieutenant Hallaure and the tactful "losing" of Mata Hari on nights she spent with important dignitaries such as Henri de Marguérie.

As soon as she was back in Paris, Mata Hari was reminded of her precarious financial situation. Van der Capellan still sent her money, though she had been away from The Hague for months, but he never sent as much as it took for her to live as she did. She had earned no money in Vittel and in fact spent a good deal on herself and Vadime. She went promptly to visit Ladoux, hoping to arrange a lucrative deal that would enable her to retire and live quietly with Vadime.

The fullest account that exists of this meeting between Ladoux and Mata Hari is from Ladoux's memoirs, which are in ways demonstrably inaccurate. He wrote:

She had been the most docile and calm of sick persons [in Vittel] and never even seemed to notice the presence in her hotel of a special valet de chambre *for the occasion, nor the attentions of a handsome lieutenant aviator who had never flown. . . .*

It was in this mood that she found me when she returned to see me again, as she had promised, two days after she returned to Paris. She wore the same costume, but her beautiful face seemed to me more pale and drawn. I made a discreet remark, asking if the slightly rough treatment of the cure had not made her too tired. "It is not the treatment," *she responded. . . .* "I am enervated and wish to see my lover again."

"You love him so much as that?"

"He is perhaps the only love of my life!"

"Then, you must marry Malzov [sic]!"

"He wants nothing of me [but myself]. [However] he is from an aristocratic family and his father the Admiral forbids this mismatch." *A sigh, then a long silence, then:* "Ah! If I only had money."

We shall see about that, *I thought; now I would like to know something . . .* "How much do you need?"

"You could not pay so much . . . a million!"

Ladoux was appalled at her audacity and told her that to earn such a sum, she must penetrate German military headquarters and learn many important secrets from someone knowledgeable but not too high up in the hierarchy, such as an ordnance officer. According to Ladoux, Mata Hari offered as an alternative plan that she might become the mistress of the crown prince.

"I have already been the mistress of the Crown Prince and I can do with him what I will. . . .

"Listen to me and try to understand: The Germans adore me and I was treated like a queen among them, whereas among you [French] I am nothing but a tart. . . .

"Ah! if you had been at the orgy nights in Berlin! . . . When they were groveling on the ground at my naked feet, I unchained them and searched for their bestial desires. All obeyed me. I still maintain my influence over them. I am certain. . . . Would you permit me only to try?" She was upright . . . shuddering . . . a marvelous artist, who created her role and played it at the moment that the ideas came to her, upon them she modeled her attitudes and even the tone of her voice.

Her attentive regard followed mine which didn't know where to look, for I was afraid that a word would slip out, just one word which would betray me . . . me and not her . . . for the only weapon that she knew with which she could finally strike me down . . . my love for my country and the passion for my profession. And the word came at last, because choking back for one last time my curiosity, I played my part well. "No one, Mata-Hari, could obtain what you will seek . . . and then . . . return to France."

"Yes, one man could, and he was also my lover; he is one of the biggest suppliers of the German army and could come and go as he liked at the grand headquarters."

"You tell me so. . . . And what is his name?"

"Craemer [sic]!"

Ladoux's account is dramatic and self-serving but hardly accurate. Craemer was presumably Karl Kroemer, the honorary German consul in Amsterdam, who had already tried to recruit Mata Hari for Germany. Kroemer was Ladoux's counterpart. If Ladoux already knew Kroemer had recruited Mata Hari, then his relaxing surveillance on her is truly incomprehensible. In this account, Ladoux paints Mata Hari as lascivious, immoral, and cunning, but his prejudice is too obvious. There is no evidence that Mata Hari was ever the mistress of Crown Prince Wilhelm or Karl Kroemer—and she never shied away from admitting the identities of her important lovers. And although there were cabarets in Berlin devoted to hedonistic pleasures and at which famous dancers performed, these flourished in the postwar Weimar period, not before the war. Thus, Ladoux's description of Mata Hari's participation in "orgy nights" in Berlin seems anachronistic and designed to emphasize her moral guilt.

When she returned from Vittel, Mata Hari went to see Ladoux because her financial situation was dire. The Hotel Meurice, where she had stayed in 1913, was hounding her for 1,300 francs (almost $4,000 in modern currency) that she still owed them. She owed money to many of her favorite shops and had not settled her bill with the Grand Hotel, either. She also needed to furnish the flat at 33, avenue Henri-Martin, where she hoped to live with Vadime.

According to Ladoux, his plan was unfolding perfectly. In his memoirs he wrote:

From the beginning of June 1916 . . . the Sûreté and the Prefecture of Police were advised and a surveillance was organized which shadowed her in Spain and followed her to Paris, where it did not cease until the end of August.

This surveillance has revealed numerous signs of the indiscreet curiosity of Mata Hari, but no proof that she was in the service of the German intelligence agency. To get this, it was necessary to gain her confidence and to propose to her a mission on behalf of France. The interviews which she had with me had no objective except to diminish her fear that all the shadowing of her had given her, at precisely the same time that she was in contact with German [intelligence].

Astonishingly, Ladoux admitted that constant surveillance of her meetings, telephone calls, mail, and telegrams for two months yielded no evidence that she was working for German intelligence— the surveillance had not uncovered even a vaguely suspicious contact—and yet he remained convinced that Mata Hari was working as a German agent "at precisely the same time" that she was being watched. Even more peculiar is the fact that he had called off her surveillance for a month. Why?

At their meeting, Ladoux made an explicit offer to Mata Hari of a great deal of money if she would spy for France. Ladoux remembered that he said to her:

> "*Be serious. You really wish to enter into our service? Take care; the profession is dangerous.*"
>
> "*I don't doubt it.*"
>
> "*And next, that is not all. . . . Let's say that you succeed. But when you have your information, what will you do? It is necessary that we receive it in our turn.*"
>
> "*Oh! You must have a means of doing that. An agent . . . in Amsterdam . . . for example?*"
>
> "*But no, alas! We have no one in Holland and it is for that reason that you would be precious to us. You do not know how to use invisible inks?*"
>
> "*No, but I will learn. . . . They have a pretty name [in French they are known as "sympathetic inks"].*"
>
> "*Yes, but if one is pinched, it is the end.*"
>
> "*Nobody pinches Mata Hari, she knows how to protect herself.*"
>
> "*So we have observed!*"
>
> "*What! Always these vile suspicions?*"

At this juncture, according to Ladoux, he got up and looked her in the eye, saying:

"Listen well, I am certain, absolutely certain, that you are an agent in the service of Germany. But I will overlook that at this moment, because you have come to make me this proposition which will put you in such a situation, if I accept, that you will proceed to betray either Germany or us.

"You are a gambler, Mata Hari, and you must play. Rouge et noir. . . . *Red, it is us, over the line that you see there, that of the front, where the blood flows night and day, for two years already. Black, it is your German friends.*

"I warn you, red wins, black loses. Reflect well before placing your bet. Tomorrow it will be too late. I will leave you this night to think it over."

"I have thought it over. I will play red. I am a gambler, but I am superstitious also, and I am sure, in coming to you, that it would bring me happiness!"

The dialogue is melodramatic and inaccurate. Even the small details, such as her alleged willingness to use invisible ink, ring false. She refused to use invisible ink to communicate with Kroemer, though she had no intention of communicating with him anyway. She objected to it as a matter of style. And she testified that she refused to use invisible ink for Ladoux as well. What's more, it would have been ludicrous for Ladoux to tell her he thought she was a German agent—how could he trap her then?—and stupid of her to agree to work for him to spy for France in light of that accusation.

Mata Hari's version of the meeting is significantly different. She said that Ladoux asked her if she had thought about spying for

France and how she intended to operate. She replied, "Do I go to Germany or to Belgium?"

She did not want to go to Germany, for fear that German intelligence would capture her and ask what she had done with their twenty thousand francs.

Ladoux told her she'd go to Belgium. She remembered an important contact she knew there, a rich Belgian banker and importer, Monsieur Wurfbain, who worked very closely with the German occupiers of Belgium. Wurfbain had indicated his interest in Mata Hari and invited her to his mansion in Brussels, but she had disliked him and declined. However, she knew he was close to the military general of occupied Belgium, Ferdinand von Bissing, and would provide a useful entrée. She improvised:

> "Here is my plan: From my house in The Hague, I will write a little note to Wurfbain to offer him a cup of tea. I will go to Brussels dressed in wonderful clothes, I will frequent the headquarters and I will not say more than that. My character is a little outspoken and very spontaneous. I don't intend to laze around there for several months picking up tidbits of small information. I will make a grand coup, one only, then I will quit."
>
> The captain was enthusiastic. He asked me right away why I wanted to serve France, adding that he asked always this question of those he employed.
>
> "I have no other interest," I told him, "except that of becoming able to marry my lover and be independent."
>
> "The reward will be worth the trouble," he observed. "And the question of money? Have you thought of it?"
>
> "I ask a million francs," I said, "but you can pay me afterward when you have recognized the value of my services."
>
> "Oh! Oh! That is a great deal of money," remarked the captain,

"but if you truly render us a service that we ask of you, then we will pay it. Once we gave someone two and a half million."

Ladoux began questioning her about Antwerp, asking if she had been there and claiming he had a photograph to prove it, which he did not. Antwerp was the location where, it was rumored, a mysterious blonde, a German Ph.D. known as Fräulein Doktor Schragmüller, ran a spy-training school. It was said that her agents were given code names using the initial A for Antwerp, the place of their training, and a second initial for the country in which they operated—in this case F for France—followed by a number. Apparently Ladoux believed that Mata Hari was both a German agent known as H21 and one known as AF44. There is little evidence that such a spy school existed and none that Mata Hari ever attended it. During the period in which she was supposed to have been training in Antwerp, she was actually living in The Hague.

After she left Ladoux's office, Mata Hari began to think of the practicalities of spying for France as only a woman of her nature would. She was far less concerned with a means of communicating with her spymaster than she was with the true essentials of her task: a wardrobe suitable for seduction.

Once again, Mata Hari's life took on the aura of a French farce. Her approach to the problem was delightful and most unclandestine. Two days after meeting with Ladoux, she sent him an uncoded letter through the regular mail, informing him that she must have an advance on her payment to buy new clothes, explaining she could hardly expect to seduce the military general of Belgium or any other man of taste and power without a stylish wardrobe.

She waited two days for an answer from Ladoux and, when he failed to reply, went to his office again on September 20. She asked if he had received her letter, and he admitted that he had. She urged him to hurry, then, as it took time to make up an expensive wardrobe and there were only two ships per month going to Holland, where she was to start following her plan.

Ladoux, astonishingly, did not reprimand her for doing something so stupid as sending him an incriminating letter *en clair* that anyone might have intercepted and read. Instead, he told her that his superior, André Goubet, had decided she was not to be given an advance.

She reminded him that she could not expect van der Capellan to pay for everything and that if he suspected anything, he would drop her and she would have no income, no safe haven in Holland. Reluctantly she agreed to delayed payment, no doubt confident that she would find some man to pay for her.

Ladoux asked her to use invisible ink, and again she refused: "No. That sort of trickery goes against my nature." In that case, he instructed her, she must await further instructions from a person who would come to her in The Hague. She would recognize his agent by the number AF44. He asked if she did not recognize the number, as it was "hers."

Mata Hari was flatly annoyed by Ladoux's crude game playing. She exclaimed, "Captain, I beg you once more, drop these insinuations that irritate me, with the information from your little agents and all these dirty tricks, this will only harden my character, there will come a moment when I will no longer want to do anything [for you]."

She refused to denounce other spies—a practice she regarded as disgusting—but only to pass along military or diplomatic information. Mata Hari might be a woman who lived off men, and a spy, but she had standards that she would not betray. At Ladoux's direction, she went to the office of Henri Maunoury at the Prefecture of Police, where she obtained a visa to return to Holland via Spain.

On October 14 the Hotel Meurice got a court order to seize some of her trunks in payment of her debt to them. She paid the hotel two hundred francs and then, irritated, went to plead with the manager to relinquish her possessions. Eventually she paid another three hundred francs—and then hid her trunks in the avenue Henri-Martin apartment to prevent their seizure yet again. She also wrote to the Dutch consul in Paris, Otto Bunge, asking him to write Anna Lintjens, her longtime servant, and ask her to communicate to Baron van der Capellan that she urgently needed six thousand francs (about eighteen hundred dollars today). She never wrote to the baron directly, because he was married, so this roundabout means of communication was normal.

She visited Ladoux and sent him a *pneumatique* on October 17; this pattern of visit and *pneumatique* was repeated on October 19. She moved into cheaper rooms at the Grand Hotel and began seeing more men, doubtless to make money. In late October, she made frequent visits to her bank, in hopes that money from van der Capellan had arrived.

Before embarking on her first mission as a spy, Mata Hari longed to see Vadime again. He had a brief leave and came to Paris on October 23. She took him first to view their new home at 33, avenue Henri-Martin, and then they began a round of dining out, strolling in parks, and spending time alone together. On October 26 he left on the train. Two days later Mata Hari sent Vadime three letters by express mail; these were intercepted and sent to Ladoux.

She met with Ladoux again on October 31 and begged fruitlessly for an advance. Fortunately, van der Capellan had sent her money, which arrived on November 4. She collected it and sent Vadime a money order for five hundred francs. Vadime is the only man known to have received money from Mata Hari rather than vice versa. If any proof of her complete devotion to Vadime were needed, this was it.

On November 5, 1916, Mata Hari left Paris on the night train for Madrid. Ladoux's men at the Deuxième Bureau sent telegrams warning of her arrival to border towns and secret service agencies. Ladoux's new spy would be spied upon every step of the way—and given every opportunity to incriminate herself.

Stepping into the Trap

As Ladoux had ordered, Mata Hari proceeded to Vigo, where on November 9 she boarded the S.S. *Hollandia* bound for the Netherlands. On November 14 the *Hollandia* docked at Falmouth to be checked by British authorities, a usual procedure even for a ship from a neutral nation. Mata Hari explained:

Upon our arrival in this English port, the boat was invaded by marine officers, police, soldiers, and suffragettes, the last charged with searching the women. Two suffragettes searched my trunks and my cabin with an unheard-of thoroughness. They were unfastening the mirror from the walls and looking under my bed with an electric lamp. Then an officer submitted me to a formal interrogation. He asked me if I indeed carried the names written in my passport and if I never traveled under another identity. Then, he stared at me fixedly for at least two minutes. Seeing that I did not lower my eyes, he took from his pocket an amateur photograph, representing a woman dressed in Spanish style, with a white mantilla, having a fan in her right hand and her left hand on her hip. The portrait resembled me a bit. Overall, the woman was a bit too small and more strongly built than I. I laughed, but my protestations did not convince the officer. He told me that the photo was taken in Malaga where I swore I had never been. The captain of the boat and certain Dutch passengers were kind in attesting to my identity, but nothing doing. The officer made me disembark and sent me to London with my baggage.

The officer was George Grant. Grant and his wife, Janet, were special agents of MI5, stationed at Falmouth. Although in 1915 the British had issued a circular stating that Mata Hari (Margaretha Zelle-MacLeod) was to be arrested if she set foot in the United Kingdom again, neither of them recognized her name. She was instead mistaken for Clara Benedix, about whom a notice had been circulated in May 1916 with a photograph attached. Benedix, like Mata Hari, was to be arrested and brought to Scotland Yard if she appeared in Britain.

A couple from the ship was also seen as suspicious and taken in for questioning.

Grant remembered the occasion vividly in 1964, when he was interviewed by Sam Waagenaar. "She was one of the most charming specimens of female humanity I had ever set eyes on," Grant enthused, and spoke of her "commanding carriage." Janet Grant strip-searched Mata Hari while Grant and his men tore her cabin apart. "We found absolutely nothing incriminating in her luggage," Grant remembered. Grant sent a message to London saying that among the passengers who arrived from Vigo was

MARGARETHA ZELLE MacLEOD, traveling on Dutch passport No 2603, issued at The Hague, 12-5-16. . . . It is believed

that she is the woman "CLARA BENEDIX," a German agent,
circulated by MI5 E and DID.

"MI5" was the British secret service unit and "DID" was the
Department of Interior Defense. Grant mentioned that she claimed
to have been living in Paris and was engaged to a Russian officer.
She denied being Clara Benedix but admitted she had met her once
on a train. Grant's report concluded: "As Madame MacLeod's story
seems altogether very strange, it was decided to remove her and
to send her to London for further examination. She is being sent to
C.O. tonight under escort."

He and his wife took her by train to London that night. Mata Hari
was terrified, weeping and refusing to eat. She asked repeatedly,
"What do you want from me?" Despite her fear, her legendary
charm was still effective. By the time the Grants took her to Scotland
Yard and turned her over to Chief Inspector Edward Parker, she and
Janet Grant had become very friendly. She had given Janet Grant
her visiting card, some photographs of herself, and a small glass or
crystal dog. The Grants had also permitted her to go to a hotel so she
could bathe and change clothes before her interrogation.

At that time, Sir Basil Thomson was assistant commissioner of police and head of the Special Branch (Scotland Yard). He was impeccably upper-crust and had held a number of impressive civil service jobs.
Nonetheless, neither his reports at the time nor his reminiscences are
notable for their accuracy. Though he knew that Margaretha Zelle-
MacLeod was Mata Hari—and knew she was an exotic dancer like
Clara Benedix—he wrote in one report that her passport was French,
not Dutch, and spelled her name variously as MacLeod and McLeod.

Mata Hari immediately asked to communicate with the Dutch
legation and was given pen and paper. She wrote a letter dated
November 13, 1916:

*May I beg Your Excellency politely and urgently to do every-
thing possible to help me. A terrible accident has happened to
me. I am the divorced Mrs. Mac-Leod [sic], born Zelle. I
am traveling from Spain to Holland with my very own passport. The English police claim that it is false, that I am not
Mrs. Zelle.*

*I am at my wits' end; am imprisoned here since this morning
at Scotland-Yard and I pray you, come and help me. I live in
The Hague at 16 Nieuwe Uitleg, and am well known there as
well as in Paris, where I have lived for years.*

*I am all alone here and I swear that everything is abso-
lutely in order. It is a misunderstanding, but I pray you, help me.*
Sincerely,
M.G. Zelle McLeod [sic]

As ever, Mata Hari's handwriting on this document is bold,
large, and stylish; her mistaken date (it was November 14), her em-
phatic underlinings, and her different spellings of "MacLeod"
reveal her anxiety. Thomson held on to her letter until he had
questioned her for two days, not notifying the Dutch authorities
until November 16.

Her interrogation was begun in Dutch, but this soon proved unsatisfactory. Mata Hari intensely disliked her translator. She remembered: "For four days, three men in uniform interrogated me. They
questioned me in Dutch through a Belgian who had a visible horror
of the people of my country. He spoke my language like a dirty Fla-
mand and he had the audacity to say to the three men that I had a
German accent. Then he asked me insidious questions about Dutch
cities where I had lived, trying to catch me out."

At some point, the language switched to French, which Thomson almost certainly spoke. Two other men were present, Captain

Reginald Hall and his assistant, Lord Herschell, both of whom worked for DID and, as well-educated Englishmen of the day, would have known French. The man transcribing the interrogation, whoever he was, did not know French and struggled mightily with the spelling of non-English names and places.

Thomson accused her of altering her passport and of being Clara Benedix, both of which she consistently denied. He asked her about her parents, her childhood, her marriage, interspersing critical questions with more routine ones in hopes of provoking a lie. As she was wont to, she told a few small lies—saying she had been in Italy when war broke out, not Germany, and that Norman had died in India—but on the whole, she told the truth. She said her father had been dead since 1913 and that she hadn't seen her daughter, Non, in ten years. She admitted her father had written a book about her and that she was embarrassed by it.

Finally the questions circled back around to the photograph. Most of the questions were asked by the assistant chief constable, whose part in the dialogue with Mata Hari is indicated by ACC; hers is indicated as MZM.

ACC: Did you ever have an inflammation of the left eye?

MZM: No, I have never had anything the matter with my eyes.

ACC: You know that one of your eyes is more closed than the other?

MZM: Yes it has always been so.

ACC: This photograph [Clara Benedix] has this peculiarity.

MZM: It is possible, but that is not me.

Later, the assistant chief constable resumed the line of questioning about her identity:

ACC: Where did these pearls come from?

MZM: From Paris.

ACC: It is a very rare thing that two people should have a droop in the left eye and the peculiarity in the left eyebrow is exactly identical, as they are in the photograph and yourself.

MZM: That is not my photograph, sir.

ACC: Then you are the victim of circumstances. There is another circumstance in which you are the victim. There is handwriting under the photograph in this passport, and if it is forged it is a very clumsy forgery.

MZM: It is not a forgery. Can I be visited by the Dutch ambassador?

ACC: You can communicate with the consul. I am going to write to the Dutch Embassy as we have grave doubts [believing] you to be Clara Benedix, a German.

The next day, the team resumed questioning her and focused on monetary transactions.

ACC: Just before you went to Paris, did you receive the sum of 15,000 francs from anybody?

MZM: No.

ACC: That was in Holland.

MZM: No, but I took my 15,000 francs from a bank and gave it to another bank. I have two banks in The Hague.

ACC: What was the bank you took it from?

MZM: Londres, and I have another bank Sch [sic].

ACC: Londres bank is the bank of the German Embassy. . . .

We have information that Mata Hari received 15,000 francs from the German Embassy.

MZM: That was the amount I took to go to Paris.

Probably the fifteen thousand francs in question originally came from Kroemer, the German consul. How the British knew about it is unclear.

The British also questioned Mata Hari about a lady—or two—who was calling herself Mrs. MacLeod in Antwerp and also in Liverpool. Mata Hari steadfastly denied being in these places, suggested misidentification was at fault, and told them of receiving a letter at the Grand Hotel in Paris meant for a Mrs. MacLeod at the Grand Hotel in London.

Later that same day, Mata Hari suddenly decided to confess that she was a French agent.

MZM: Now I have something to tell you that will surprise you. I thought it was too big a secret. This captain, Captain Ladoux, asked me to go into his service, and I promised to do something for him. I was to meet [his agent] in my home at The Hague. . . .

ACC: You ought to have mentioned this to me yesterday. Where did you meet Captain Ladoux?

MZM: That is old history. In my lawyer's office [which was next door to 282, boulevard Saint-Germain].

She recounted a dialogue that combined her meetings and recruitment by Ladoux before and after her trip to Vittel. She ended her tale with "He said 'Go to Holland, and you will receive my instructions.' . . . So I went to await his instructions in my home."

She also told them that the French consul from the Dutch legation also tried to recruit her as a spy, hinting, "You love a Russian
officer" and asking her to "do something for the Russians."

The British officers must have worked hard to conceal their surprise and amazement at the remarkable tale Mata Hari unfolded. As
she offered names and information about various people—several
prominent men who were her lovers, plus Ladoux, Maunoury of the
French police, the physician who delivered her first child, and her
lawyers—the assistant chief constable could not resist remarking
drily, "It would be awkward to have a levee of all the belligerent
countries in your room."

They had already begun to doubt that she was Clara Benedix;
before questioning her on November 16, Thomson had sent a message to the Netherlands minister in London. It read:

> *I have the honor to inform you that a woman carrying a French
> [sic] passport bearing the name of Margaretha Zelle MacLeod,
> No. 2603 issued at The Hague on the 12th of May 1916, has been
> detained here on suspicion that she is a German agent of German
> nationality named Clara Benedix of Hamburg. She denies her
> identity with this woman, and steps are being taken to establish
> it. The passport bears signs of having been tampered with. She has
> applied to be allowed to write to your Excellency, and materials for
> the letter have been furnished to her.*

After questioning Mata Hari that day, Thomson sent a second
letter to the Dutch minister, which differs in interesting ways from
the first.

> *We have the honor to inform you that a lady bearing a Dutch pass-
> port, named Madame Zelle McLeod, has been removed from the*

Dutch ship Hollandia *on her arrival at Falmouth, there being grave suspicion of un-neutral acts against her. She has asked me to forward to you the enclosed letter.*

Inquiries are being made as quickly as possible by cable, and she will not be detained longer than necessary. If, however, she proves to be a person suspected of un-neutral acts, it may be necessary to take further action against her.

Thomson promptly initiated inquiries as to Mata Hari's identity. He claimed later in his memoirs that the Britons had been persuaded she had been working for the Germans since 1915, but if so, they had not plainly informed their allies of this conviction. He sent a telegram in cipher to Ladoux, asking if he employed Margaretha Zelle-MacLeod.

In the meantime, the interrogation of Mata Hari continued. She made a strong impression on Thomson, who described her as being

tall and sinuous, with glowing black eyes and a dusky complexion, vivacious in manner, intelligent and quick in repartee . . . a severely practical person who was prepared to answer any question with a kind of reserved courtesy, who felt so sure of herself and her innocence that all that remained in her was a desire to help her interrogators. The only thing graceful about her was her walk and the carriage of her head. . . . Time had a little dimmed the charms of which we had heard so much, for at this time the lady must have been at least 40.

In hindsight, Thomson felt that Mata Hari thought she had triumphed in their interviews, but remembered that he was not persuaded of her innocence. "We were convinced now that she was acting for the Germans, and that she was then on her way to Germany with information which she had committed to memory." Thomson also claimed that he warned Mata Hari, in a fatherly way, to "give up what you are doing" and that she promised to, like a dutiful daughter.

These remarks would be more convincing if he had accurately remembered her arrest and questioning as occurring in November 1916 instead of "early in 1916" as he wrote. The next observation in his memoir—that Mata Hari was arrested with "compromising documents" a month after he released her—was entirely untrue and suggests that his hindsight might have been clouded by a desire to demonstrate his own prescience about Mata Hari.

While they waited for responses to their cables of inquiry, the men at MI5 catalogued and searched Mata Hari's "very large professional wardrobe." This consisted of:

Box with gilt clock.

Hat box containing 6 hats, 3 hat pins, feather boas, one veil, 2 fur stoles, 3 hat decorations, one imitation peach [presumably to decorate a hat], *1 dressing gown.*

Trunk with 1 pair gent's boots, 1 brush, 1 bundle washing, 1 pair putties [strips of cloth used by the cavalry, who wound them around their lower legs from ankle to knee for protection], *1 pair spurs, 3 pairs shoes, 3 chemises, 1 napkin, 1 pair leggings, 3 veils, 1 box ribbons, 3 bra shells, 2 belts, 2 underskirts, 3 skirts, 1 dress, 4 pairs gloves, 1 umbrella, 3 sunshades, 1 douche, 1 pair stockings, 1 blouse, 3 scarfs, 1 night dress case, 1 coat, 1 costume* [matching jacket and skirt], *1 bag of dirty linen, 1 bundle sanitary towels.*

1 box containing 4 hair ornaments, 1 hat pin and false hair, 3 fur necklets, 1 bottle Vernis Mordore Dore, 1 box powder, 1 bottle white fluid

Boot trunk containing 6 pairs slippers, 1 box face cream, 3 pairs boots, 2 pairs shoes, 1 pair stockings

Trunk containing 2 pairs corsets, 30 pairs stockings, 1 lavender packet [sachet], *1 veil, 8 under bodices, 1 handkerchief, 1 underskirt, 1 shawl, 10 pairs knickers, 3 princess petticoats, 3 combs, 2 dressing jackets, 11 chemises, 1 dressing gown, towel, 1 garter, 2 coats, 5 blouses, 4 dresses, 1 petticoat, 1 scarf, 2 pairs gloves, a collar, 2 powder puffs.*

Trunk containing 1 handbag with mirror inside, 1 hair comb, 3 coats, 1 box containing comb, 1 dress, 1 ornament, 2 pairs shoes, 2 fancy boxes, 1 box containing copper plate and visiting card in the name of Vadime de Massloff, Capitaine, 1ere Regiment Speciale Imperial, Russe, 1 pair gloves, 1 blouse, 7 dresses, 2 princess robes, 1 petticoat, 1 belt, wooden box with 2 brushes and china tea service.

Gladstone bag containing 3 pairs shoes, nail polishers, box of powder, pair of stockings, 2 boxes containing cigarettes, 8 hair nets, box visiting cards, box soap, pair gloves, 2 powder puffs, 1 under bodice, 2 nightdresses, handkerchief sachet containing 21 handkerchiefs, 1 dressing gown, 1 empty cash box, bunch of keys, pearl necklet in case, monocle in case, 2 earrings in box, 2 pearls in a case, green stone ring in case, green stone necklet and 2 earrings in a case, 3 fans, 2 cloth purses, one containing 1 £ treasury note, 5 or 6 pounds in silver, 1d copper, 14 silver coins and 5 bronze coins, holdall of cotton, needles etc., handbag containing cigarette case (photos inside), powder puff and rouge stick on chain.

Boat tickets, visiting card stamp, treasury note case (empty), bank note case containing four 100 franc notes, two 1000 franc notes, one 60 guilder note, one 40 guilder note, one 50 pesetas note, one 400? [sic, presumably ruble] Russian note, 2 pieces music, bundle of photographs and French dictionary, check book, crayon drawing, pocket wallet containing papers etc.

One traveling rug.

One fitted ladies dressing case.

Letters etc.

This listing gives a deliciously vivid image of Mata Hari's lifestyle while traveling. It is fascinating that she had some of Vadime's clothes, possibly intending to have them laundered and sent back to him at the front.

Most significant of all the responses Thomson received to his cables of inquiry was one from Ladoux himself. In his memoirs, Ladoux says that he replied to the coded message, coldly, "Understand nothing. Send Mata Hari back to Spain." What is recorded in the British files as the translated and decrypted response from Ladoux is somewhat different. "Ref. our telegram No. MA 22939 of Nov 16 [1916] instant to Captain Ladoux—he replies 'He has suspected her for some time and pretended to employ her, in order, if possible, to obtain definitive proof that she is working for the Germans. He would be glad to hear that her guilt has been clearly established.'" In the margins a British lieutenant colonel with an illegible signature has scrawled, "I'll BET he would!"

Ladoux abandoned and betrayed his own agent, claiming his hiring of her was a ruse to entrap her, and reinforced the British suspicions of her. But the British had no evidence upon which to hold her. Neither her questioning nor the searching of her possessions had turned up anything suspicious. When the cables came through from Baron van der Capellan; the marquis of Beaufort; the Dutch consul in Paris, Otto Bunge; and others, Thomson decided to release her.

On the fourth day of Mata Hari's detention, the British told her that they no longer believed she was Clara Benedix and had decided to release her. Whether at Ladoux's instigation or their own, they decided to forbid her to travel onward to Holland, her home country, and insisted she had to go back to Spain—an extraordinary decision.

In addition to denying hiring Mata Hari as an agent, Ladoux took it upon himself to write to the Dutch authorities, alerting them to his suspicions. Ladoux was apparently very anxious to deflect blame from himself now that his new spy seemed to be arousing awkward questions. Though everyone recoiled in alarm, no one had the least bit of evidence against her.

Mata Hari spent some time at the Savoy Hotel in London recovering from her frightening ordeal. She applied for a permit to go to The Hague, with the object of her journey being "to marry Captain Vadime de Massloff," which in her mind it was. The Permit Office consulted Thomson, who told them she was believed to be an agent of the Deutsche Bank—a new suspicion the significance of which is not clear—and she was not to be given a permit for Holland. When she visited him begging for permission to take a ship to Rotterdam leaving on November 25, Thomson denied her again, insisting she might only return to Spain.

On December 1 she left to catch the S.S. *Arguaya* back to Vigo, Spain. The same day, the Dutch minister of foreign affairs in The Hague wrote to the Dutch envoy in Madrid, warning him of her impending arrival and spreading the rumors and suspicions further.

The compatriot had originally been stopped because one thought her passport was a fake and it was suspected her real nationality was German and that she was a certain Clara Benedix from Hamburg. However, these suspicions were soon proved unfounded but official messages from Paris gave reason to believe that Mrs. MacLeod had indeed been carrying out activities in ways that the [French] police look on unfavorably. . . . She said that the allies in Paris trusted her to convey messages and she had to do this in Holland. The police were suspicious about these communications and this was confirmed from information gained from Paris from which it became clear that the orders had not gone out from the allies but the enemy. . . . She declared she was willing to return to Spain of her own free will . . . I detect she wants to avoid anything which could spread rumors about this "adventure" (I quote) of hers.

Arriving back in Spain on December 11, Mata Hari did not quite know what to do. She spent a few days at the Hotel Continental in Vigo, renewing her acquaintance with Martial Cazeaux, a French-man who was the Dutch consul in Vigo. Cazeaux expressed his surprise and concern that she had been mistaken for Clara Benedix: "What, they took you for Clara Benedix [?] . . . You'd have to be English to make such an idiotic mistake." Restored to confidence by Cazeaux's admiration and support, Mata Hari confided to him that on the *Hollandia* had been a Belgian husband and wife by the name of Allard, and the husband spied for England while the wife spied for Germany; the captain had told her so. Perhaps she felt passing this piece of information on to an English ally would demonstrate her good intentions to the French.

Astonishingly, Cazeaux's response was to invite Mata Hari to spy for the Russians. In fewer than eighteen months, Mata Hari had been asked to spy for Germany by Kroemer, France by Ladoux, and now Russia by Cazeaux. The question is, why?

No one questioned in connection with Mata Hari ever suggested that she was politically alert or motivated. None of her lovers or acquaintances recalled her asking about military secrets or informa-tion. The closest approach to such curiosity was when she asked after Vadime's health and whereabouts when she did not hear from him regularly. In fact, she was so unaware of the day-to-day progress of the war that she had only the vaguest notion where her lover's regiment was fighting. Strong political convictions cannot possibly be painted as the reason Mata Hari was repeatedly asked to function as a spy.

As a famous performer and striking beauty, Mata Hari attracted attention wherever she went. It was part of her personality to seek the spotlight, and she was very, very good at it. This made Mata Hari a ridiculous candidate for a job that required clandestine behavior. Even when she was in company with Vadime (or, for that matter, Rudolf MacLeod), and her flirtatious manner might be expected to be curbed, Mata Hari drew the eyes and admiration of men wherever she went. True, she was intelligent and an excellent linguist—useful attributes for a spy. But the attribute that she possessed that was the reason so many asked her to spy for them was her willingness to do things normally judged immoral for money. Because she was visibly a woman of the demimonde—a high-class prostitute, in ugly terms—men assumed she would also stoop to espionage, which had a very negative connotation at the time. Thus she was incriminated, recruited, and suspected for her readiness to sleep with men for money rather than anything else. She was considered a spy, or a likely spy, because she was Mata Hari—the epitome of beauty, seductiveness, and sexuality.

Neither accepting nor declining Cazeaux's offer, Mata Hari traveled to the Ritz Hotel in Madrid. She had written to Anna Lintjens from Vigo, asking her to explain to van der Capellan why she had not arrived in Holland as planned and asking, once again, for money. From Madrid, she telegraphed the baron directly, as discreetly as possible. She was very short of funds, being down to her last 2,300 francs (roughly $7,000 today).

She also wrote to Ladoux *en clair* asking how she should proceed, since she had been prevented from reaching The Hague. She did not suspect that it was Ladoux's manipulations that had blocked her travel or that he had a great investment in proving she was a German spy. Ladoux was no longer her protector or employer but instead her worst enemy and the last person she should have asked for advice.

Secrets and Betrayal

AFTER MANIPULATING EVENTS so that Mata Hari would return to Spain, Ladoux took one more decisive step in preparing his trap for her. He ordered that all messages intercepted by the Eiffel Tower radio station that involved communications between Berlin and Madrid should be monitored and sent to him. The French had broken the German encryption code some time earlier, so why this procedure of recording messages to or from Berlin had not been put in place earlier is more than puzzling; it is almost impossible to believe. Why Ladoux had not ordered these messages to be monitored as soon as the code was broken is unexplained.

Could Ladoux have arranged for messages incriminating Mata Hari as a German agent to be sent? He could indeed, if he was a double agent.

While waiting for money from the baron to arrive, Mata Hari also attempted to contact a Diego de Léon, who had promised her a commission for acting as his broker in the sale of some paintings in Paris. She was told he was in Tortoza on the coast; how convenient for de Léon to be out of town when a creditor came calling.

Days passed and Mata Hari had no word from Ladoux and no money from van der Capellan or de Léon. Needing money urgently, she telegraphed Cazeaux, asking where the Russian was who wanted her to spy for him; he had been supposed to meet her in her hotel. She was told to keep waiting, that the Russian was in Switzerland.

Mata Hari still believed that Ladoux was in Paris awaiting her big coup, with a million francs to pay for it. She decided to improvise, which was much more to her taste than careful planning anyway. She could not get to General von Bissing or the crown prince, since she was stranded in Madrid, so she would have to obtain military secrets from the Germans at her disposal in Madrid. Who were they? She took up the diplomatic list helpfully provided by the hotel and searched for a high-ranking German whom she might contact. She selected an army attaché listed as captain and wrote asking for an appointment to meet him. She slipped into the envelope one of her visiting cards, which referred to her as *Vrouwe* Zelle-MacLeod—an aristocratic title—and which had an embossed crown on it. In later testimony, she consistently referred to Kalle as *von* Kalle, awarding him (as she had herself) an aristocratic title to which he had no right.

Kalle gave her an appointment to meet him at home on Saturday, December 23, at 3 P.M. Mata Hari's account of their meeting and conversation shows that she used a clever ploy, pretending she had come to demand why she was arrested for being Clara Benedix. By asking such a question, she implied that she knew he was connected with German intelligence, as indeed he was. He at first took her for an intelligence agent but pointed out that such a person would not address him as *captain*, as she had, because his enemies knew very well of his promotion to major. She had written to him in French, the diplomatic language, but finding that she spoke fluent German, Kalle used that language. Mata Hari's account sounds like a script for the stage:

Him *(in German): Why do you come to see me?*

Me *(in German): I was held 4 days in England; I was stopped and taken for German during the voyage, it would appear, with a false Dutch passport. They wished very much that I was Clara Benedix, what is the full story?*

Him *(without responding directly): How well you speak German! How is that?*

Me: *I lived 3 years in Berlin!*

Him: *You must know some officers [there].*

Me: *Yes, many.*

Him: *Give me some names.*

Me: *I give him some and I add: I was the mistress of Alfred de Kiepert.*

Him *(smiling): Now I know who you are. You are the woman of whom Alfred was so jealous. That reminds me. I saw you at dinner with him at the Carlton Hotel. You had come from the Silesian maneuvers.*

Me: *It is easier for you to recognize me than for me to recognize you.*

Him: *I will tell you. What happened to you on your trip was not my concern. I am not occupied with such things since the king personally asked me to abstain [from espionage affairs]. What was done was ordered at Barcelona, but I went immediately to ask for the explanations from the Baron du Roland.*

Becoming more and more intimate, Kalle offered me cigarettes and the conversation turned to life in Madrid. I made myself very attractive. I played with my feet. I did that which a woman may do in such circumstances when she wished to make a conquest of a man and I knew that von Kalle was mine. At one moment, he said to me, as I lay on the chaise, "I am tired. I concern myself for the moment with the disembarkation of a submarine of German officers and Turks and munitions on the coast of Morocco, in the French zone. That takes all my time and my brain."

I did not judge that it was appropriate to pursue any further during this first interview and, after several instants of conversation on miscellaneous topics, I left von Kalle after conquering him.

That night Mata Hari triumphantly wrote to Ladoux, telling him she had made contact with a high-placed German official, who had told her that there had been a submarine landing in Morocco and had identified Baron de Roland as the head of German intelligence in Barcelona. Either of these, she thought, was a significant piece of information that ought to earn her a substantial reward. Because she believed Kalle to be completely infatuated with her—"I can do what I wish with my informant"—she asked for further instructions from Ladoux.

The next Sunday she dined at the Palace Hotel with one of the attachés from the Dutch legation, Mr. G. de Wirth. De Wirth presented her to Colonel Joseph Denvignes, an attaché of the French embassy in Madrid, a most distinguished man, with a slight limp and the Legion of Honor decoration. Denvignes was much taken with her beauty and grace, seeking her out the next evening at a gala ball at the Ritz Hotel, which she attended on the arm of yet another attaché. "Madam," she remembered him saying, "I have never seen anything more breathtaking than your entrance yesterday at the

Palace Hotel." He so monopolized her company that Mata Hari was slightly embarrassed.

Under the warmth of Denvignes's attention, Mata Hari recounted the remarkable tale of her travels, the arrest and questioning in England, and her return to Spain. He grew a little agitated and asked her what the point of her visit to Madrid was. Realizing his anxiety was caused by the whiff of espionage in her story, Mata Hari tried to reassure him, saying with a smile and a naïve degree of trust:

> *"My colonel, calm down, I am one of yours." He took my hand. I added: "If I had known you one day earlier, I would not have had to go to the trouble of sending my information to Paris, I could give you the letter yourself and that would have been quicker."*
>
> *"What information?" he questioned. In a moment, I gave him all the details, including the name of von Kalle. I added that I had found the last a little unwell, but sweet as a lamb.*

Denvignes was intrigued, both by the woman and by the information. With her remarkable simplicity, Mata Hari did not consider that it might be unwise to confide her espionage secrets to a man she had just met, on the strength of his being with the French embassy.

The next day she lunched with de Léon and then found the colonel waiting for her in a jealous fit in the hotel reading room. He demanded to know with whom she had been dining and what their connection was. He also urged her to obtain more specific information about the landing place in Morocco; where was it? Thinking this would not be too difficult a point to pin down, she went again to see Kalle. Her pretext was that she was planning on returning to Holland via Switzerland and Germany but knew things were very difficult at the border. Could Kalle not facilitate that part of her journey, as a favor to her? He regretted he could not assist her but again offered her cigarettes.

She accepted, seeing that Kalle was nerve-wracked and exhausted. She said sympathetically:

> [Me:] *Well, always tired, always ill, always the thoughts in your head?*
>
> [Him:] *Do not speak to me of them . . . I cannot be relaxed when you do.*
>
> Me: *But it must be so very difficult to disembark troops from a submarine on the coast of Morocco. Where do you have to bring off this coup?*
>
> Him: *Beautiful women must not ask too much.*

She wisely decided to let the matter drop for the time being.

When Denvignes came to see her at the hotel late that afternoon, she told him he had forced her to make a false step and arouse Kalle's suspicions. She indicated she preferred to operate on her intuition in the future, rather than following directives. She had apparently completely adopted Denvignes as both her spymaster and admirer. For his part, he was deeply enamored. He took her to lunch and dinner the next day, pursuing her very publicly. The day after that, he came again to see her and to tell her that he regrettably must go to Paris. He asked for a bouquet of violets she wore on her bodice and her handkerchief as romantic souvenirs. He also asked if he could do something for her while he was in Paris.

She asked him to go to see Ladoux—who had still not answered her letters—and his superior, Colonel Goubet. "Tell them," she instructed, "what sort of woman they are dealing with [how well I

have done] and ask them to treat me more nicely and more openly."
Denvignes advised her to write a letter containing all her new information and leave it with his replacement, the marquis de Paladines,
at the embassy. Denvignes would see that it reached the minister of
war. This may have been as much a warning not to trust Ladoux as
Denvignes's attempt to commandeer any important secrets she discovered for his own credit.

Amusingly, as soon as Denvignes left, Kalle immediately invited
Mata Hari to come see him. Her account of their meeting provides a
fascinating insight into the way she seduced so many men. At first
Kalle made some peculiar remarks that she did not understand, and
then he grew angry. She supposed he was jealous—a common occurrence in her life.

> Him: *Come here into the light. You have certainly repeated*
> *what I told you, for the French send their radio mes-*
> *sages everywhere asking where the officers will alight*
> *[in Morocco].*
>
> Me: *They might easily know from another source than me.*
> *And then, the radio messages! How do you know*
> *what they are telegraphing?*
>
> Him: *We have the key [cipher] to their radio!*
>
> Me: *Ah, that is something else! How clever you are.*

> *Seeing Kalle was beginning to soften, I redoubled my sweetness*
> *with him.*
>
> *The conversation continued:*

> Him: *With a beautiful woman [such as you] all is forgiven,*
> *but if they knew it was me who told you, it would cost*
> *me a great deal in Berlin.*

Seeing him become again submissive, I precipitated things: "My word, never mind," I said to myself. "Let's go!" And I let him do what he wanted.

His gushing over, he began again to speak to me in these terms: "This war will perhaps lead elsewhere. There are among us some officers who are brutes." He spoke sincerely, wishing to confess to me? I don't know, but I never reply directly to him. I have even said to him that he must not denigrate his army. Germany has the most handsome men, and I insist that this army has many very brave men.

Him: *But the French do also. The aviators notably. They have one right now who flies over our lines and deposits among us a passenger that we must search for. But we are informed and one of these days we will see him. We know everything; we have agents in France who are very well informed.*

Me: *How do they warn you?*

Him: *There are many means.*

Me: *Well, that astonishes me very much. I have traveled a good deal during this war and judging by the inspections to which I have been subjected, I ask myself how one could pass the frontiers with secret things. One cannot even pass with a hatpin. In England, they checked the ribbons on my chemises.*

Him *(caressing me): But it is surely not with women like you that one transports such things. That would be the biggest stupidity in the world. We use people who are a little dirty, those whom one doesn't notice. They carry ink formed into little white balls under their fingernails and in their ears.*

Me *(totally naturally): My God, what inventions!*

Like a dutiful spy, Mata Hari wrote all this new information down in a twelve-page letter to Denvignes that evening: the aviator who had dropped a spy, the secret ink, and above all, the breaking of the French radio code. She did not mention that Kalle had given her 3,500 francs, the equivalent of about $11,000 today. She regarded this as the usual "gift" her gentlemen friends gave her. She went to the French embassy but, not finding the marquis de Paladines as instructed, left her letter with another attaché of her acquaintance, asking him to see that it reached Colonel Denvignes.

The situation with encoded messages had grown complex. According to Ladoux, the French had broken the German cipher and were intercepting German messages at the Eiffel Tower. He hoped—or planned—to find evidence that Mata Hari was a German spy thereby. But as Mata Hari had learned from Kalle, the Germans had in their turn broken the French code: the Germans knew that the French could read intercepted German messages. Thus the Germans could send messages in the broken code, which would seem to be genuine secret messages but which would be planted disinformation. Probably both Ladoux and Kalle appreciated that false messages from Berlin offered a clever way of implicating Mata Hari and taking pressure and suspicion off of others. Both regarded her as expendable—even a loose cannon—with her demands for money, her not-so-subtle questions, her habit of drawing attention to herself, and her naïve trust in anyone French.

Feeling she had completed her spying mission, Mata Hari prepared to return to Paris to collect her reward. A few days before leaving on January 3, she received a timely warning from Senator Emilio Junoy. Junoy had been a lover of Mata Hari's, as is shown by the coy and sexual content of a letter he wrote her later, on March 1, 1917. The letter warned her that he had been visited by a French secret agent who had questioned him about his relations with her. The agent described her as "a person known to be hostile to the Allies." Outraged, Mata Hari went to the French embassy to demand an explanation; finding it closed, she went to the home of the marquis de Paladines. The marquis, not surprisingly, disavowed both responsibility for and knowledge of this questioning.

Mata Hari did not understand that Ladoux was working against her. She had not heard from him at all since arriving in Spain and of course did not know that he had denied she was his agent to the English. She was annoyed with Ladoux, but assumed that Denvignes had taken matters over Ladoux's head since (in her view) Ladoux was a "little man" incapable of understanding the sort of funding and cooperation she needed to carry out her mission, even though she was meeting with great success.

As soon as she reached Paris on January 3, she settled into the Hotel Plaza Athénée and then went to have her hair tinted, to cover up the gray. She also wrote a letter to Vadime, asking the hotel how long it would take to reach Verdun; she did not realize his regiment was not at Verdun. Since Vadime's safety was a major worry, Mata Hari's ignorance of the whereabouts of his regiment shows how little the war concerned her. The First Special Imperial Russian Regiment—like all of the Russian units on the western front—was in the department (similar to a county) of Champagne, not Vosges, more than one hundred miles from Verdun. Besides, the battle of Verdun had ended on December 19, 1916, some weeks earlier.

Her first priority was to meet with Denvignes, who had been besotted with her to the point of pestering her just a short time before. She was certain he had been very impressed with her espionage coup and would have everything arranged for her triumphal reception. But when she telephoned the hotel where Denvignes had told her he would be staying—the hotel where he had promised to meet her and had given every indication of expecting to have sex with her—the hotel denied knowing him. She telephoned the Ministry of War and received the same answer: Denvignes was unknown. This was not possible. She addressed a letter to him at the Ministry of War but, dissatisfied, made another attempt to locate him. She went to the Deuxième Bureau at 282, boulevard Saint-Germain and was turned away again. Finally, an officer who was leaving the Deuxième Bureau took pity on her and said, "Ah, yes, the military attaché, but he leaves this evening for Madrid."

The subsequent events are best told by Mata Hari herself:

Wishing desperately to see the colonel, I took myself at 9 P.M. to Orsay station. The ticket collector forbade me access to the platforms. I went then to the office of the conductors of the wagon-lits company and I wrote a little note to the colonel in which I said that I wanted urgently to see him and I begged him to stand at the door of the carriage at Austerlitz where I would go. An employee, whom I tipped, gave the porter my letter and I, I left in a taxi for the station of Austerlitz where I could pass onto the platform with a suburban ticket. The train entered the station, but the colonel was not at the door. I called a conductor and begged him to ask the military attaché of France to come speak to me. Colonel Denvignes appeared then at the door of a carriage. He had a very embarrassed air. I saw another man than the one who had made so many advances to me in Madrid.

> Me: *And so this is the way you leave, my colonel, without warning me. And our business! Have you seen Captain Ladoux?*
>
> Him *(in a very small voice): I have seen him very little, but I have seen his chief, Colonel Goubet. He told me that your information, especially the first, interested*

> *him very much and that you are an intelligent*
> *woman.*

Me: *That's all?*

Him: *He asked me also if my relationship with you was cur-*
rent and I told him no.

Me: *Why have you lied?*

Him (*in a plaintive voice*): *My little one! My little one!*

That was all, the train left and the employees asked me to take
myself off. I remained dumbfounded on the platform.

Mata Hari had been betrayed by Denvignes. Possibly never before had a lover treated her so badly. Usually her lovers and former lovers helped her and did favors for her; it was how she managed her world. A man rarely parted from Mata Hari without a smile on his face; most remembered her with great fondness, admiration, and affection. And yet, Denvignes had let her down over a matter of great importance. Despite the hints and warnings—the lack of response from Ladoux, the lack of money, the breakdown of the message transmission through the marquis de Paladines, the letter from Junoy—she never expected such treatment.

After Mata Hari's own conviction, Denvignes was arrested on espionage charges. After some months of imprisonment and interrogation, he was acquitted, but he was also demoted, suggesting that he was not completely cleared of the charge. Was he actually a double agent, trying to divert suspicion from himself to Mata Hari? This is yet another unanswerable question.

For Mata Hari, the trap had been set, but she had not yet felt the snap of its teeth.

Caught in a Trap

THINGS RAPIDLY DETERIORATED.

The next morning she went to the Dutch consulate, where she sent a telegram to van der Capellan saying she had arrived in Paris and asking him to notify Anna. Later she wrote postcards to Anna and Vadime, the latter reading, "4 January. My dear, will I soon hear from you? Could you come [to Paris]? Kisses from your Marina."

She also went again to 282, boulevard Saint-Germain. Whether accidentally or intentionally, the police who had resumed shadowing Mata Hari as soon as she returned to Paris had lost her; they did not record her second visit to the Deuxième Bureau. There, she produced the pass Ladoux had given her so she could see him upon her return. After a wait, the pass was returned to her with the word "Absent" written on it. This was an appalling, unbelievable reception for a spy successfully returned from a dangerous mission, having gathered valuable information.

She went back the next day and waited for an hour, only to

be told to try again the subsequent day at 6 P.M. When she finally saw Ladoux, he was acting "bizarrely." He said that Denvignes had seen him only briefly and had conveyed no information from her. She told him about the letter from Junoy and asked who had authorized Junoy's questioning, which smacked of blackmail. Ladoux denied knowing anything about it. He had in fact abandoned her altogether, and said:

In any case, you must never forget that you do not know me and I do not know you. It is certainly not we who have sent someone to the senator, and if an agent did this stupid thing, he will be sent to the front.

Me: *It is all the same to me, but I suppose that you have no interest in spoiling my work by the intervention of little secret agents. If a real French secret agent sees something that he does not understand, he runs to the embassy of France and not to the house of a Spanish senator. What's more, I was astonished by the reception you gave me. Where are the thanks for the services I have rendered you?*

Him: *What services? That about the Baron du Roland and the submarine?*

Me: *You forget that about the radios, the aviator and the secret ink.*

Him: *That is the first news of it I have heard!*

Me: *What, the colonel told you nothing!*

Him: *I repeat to you that he did nothing except pass through here. What! You say that they have the code for our radios. The military attaché is pulling your leg.*

Me: *Is there not one chance in a hundred that his informa-*

tion is correct and that this would repay the pain of
verifying it?

Him: *Evidently, but I am open-mouthed in astonishment*
[at the thought of it].

Me: *Me too.*

Ladoux, appalled at the information she had uncovered, improvised madly and asked her to remain in Paris until he could check out her story. However, he made no move to verify her report.

The German cipher had first been broken by English cryptographers in 1914, but the Germans did not realize this until 1916, at which point they switched to a new code. Although the French radio listeners on the Eiffel Tower intercepted the messages in the new code and passed them on to the cryptographers, no one could read them until later that year when Dr. Edmond Locard managed to break the second code. Locard was the founder and director of the first scientific criminology laboratory. Known as the Sherlock Holmes of France, he had a formidable reputation. He had volunteered for duty as a cryptographer and was an excellent one. When he broke the second code, it gave the Allies a distinct advantage.

Then, at the end of 1916, something very peculiar happened: messages intercepted at the Eiffel Tower having to do with Mata Hari began coming in, written in the old, broken code. If, as Mata Hari claimed, the Germans knew the French could read messages in this old code, why would they revert to it? Was it inconceivable carelessness? Or were the Germans using the broken code to feed false information to the French? Was Ladoux using the German messages to manufacture evidence against Mata Hari?

Though he did not tell anyone for months, Ladoux later claimed he had been receiving messages intercepted at the Eiffel Tower—messages signed by Mata Hari's former lover, Major Arnold Kalle, addressed to the headquarters in Berlin—since December 13, 1916, in the broken code. These intercepted messages referred explicitly to a new agent, H21. Whether this agent was male or female was unclear, because "he" and "she" are not distinguished in German. The first message, sent while Mata Hari was in Spain trying to pry information out of Kalle, contained nothing more than common gossip about Princess George of Greece, the general dislike of the French prime minister Briand, and a vague warning about a British offensive to occur in the spring. More messages about H21 followed, including one from Berlin on Christmas Day, instructing Kalle to give agent H21 3,000 francs (about $9,000 today). Kalle replied he had given H21 3,500 pesetas (roughly $12,500 today) and that the agent would request that additional funds be made available to his/her staff in Roermond (where Mata Hari's servant, Anna Lintjens, lived). On December 28, Kalle sent a message that H21 would arrive in Paris "tomorrow" and would ask that 5,000 francs (approximately $15,000 in modern currency) be sent to her at once, naming Anna Lintjens and the Dutch consul in Paris, Bunge, as intermediaries. On December 29, Kalle sent another message confirming that H21 had left Madrid for Paris.

Here was what Ladoux had been seeking: the solid proof that Mata Hari was actually a double agent working for Germany and known as H21. Or was it? Though Mata Hari had a servant named Anna Lintjens, who lived in Roermond, she did not leave Madrid for Paris until January 3, not prior to December 29 as the telegram of December 29 indicated. All of these incriminating messages were sent in the broken cipher, as if they were intended to be read by the French. Why would such specific information about the whereabouts of H21—not to mention the name of her servant and the town in which that servant lived—be disclosed in a telegram at all?

If Ladoux believed these telegrams to be genuine, why hadn't he ordered Mata Hari's arrest immediately upon receiving them in decoded, translated form? Since the code was already broken, decoding and translating the messages would have taken very little time. Since Mata Hari had paid several visits to 282, boulevard Saint-Germain soon after her arrival in Paris, finding her to make an arrest would not have been difficult. Why had Ladoux avoided her rather than seizing her? And why had he not at least passed the information gleaned from the telegrams on to the army magistrate, in preparation for arrest? Ladoux's behavior is puzzling at best, self-incriminating at worst.

Frustrated by her interview with Ladoux, Mata Hari returned to the Hotel Plaza Athénée. Again she was followed on her usual round of shopping and visits to the hairdresser, the dressmaker, the manicurist, the jeweler, the dentist, and the pharmacy; again her telephone conversations were listened in on; again her mail was steamed open and sometimes withheld from her. She complained to Maunoury, who told her there was nothing to worry about.

She expected to see Vadime on January 8, writing him a letter on the seventh that read: "Tomorrow evening—My God, it is your [Russian Orthodox] Christmas today. I hold you for a long time. See you soon, Your Marina." But the next day, he did not appear and she was terribly worried. When no messages of explanation arrived from Vadime, she wrote to the Russian attaché Count Ignatieff begging for news of her lover. She visited a fortune-teller, hoping for promises of good news and happiness. She was seen weeping over her dinner in the hotel, sick with worry about Vadime.

She wrote Vadime loving cards and letters almost daily and corresponded with Anna often, as she was once again in desperate need of money from the baron. She was also very anxious about her situation, for she was beginning to realize that things had started to go very wrong after she agreed to spy for Ladoux. Those who had once been so eager to see her and recruit her into spying now shunned her, denying knowledge of or responsibility for events that they must have known about, and offering no support or financial reward.

On January 12 she went to the Dutch consulate and asked for advice and protection; she was received immediately, even though the consul Bunge was out with an illness. She complained that she was very worried about being tailed and spied upon. The attaché tried to reassure her and promised to come to the hotel to take tea with her soon, doubtless thinking she was a most attractive but silly woman. Mata Hari was much cleverer than many people realized. She sensed that some scheme against her was unfolding.

At about this time, her shadows complained that she was taking many precautions, changing her routes and doubling back, crossing the street abruptly to take a taxi, and looking suspiciously around to see if someone was following her. She retired to her room early and sometimes had her meals sent there. The concierge handed over to the inspectors an incoming letter from Vadime on January 14, which she never received. On the fifteenth, she started out of the hotel but then returned precipitously. She complained to the concierge, pointing out a man who she thought was following her. She did not go out again that morning.

According to Locard's 1954 memoirs of the Mata Hari case, it was on or about January 15 that one of his colleagues brought to Ladoux's attention the fact that the Germans had been using the original, broken code for the Mata Hari messages. It seems unlikely that such an important point would have gone unremarked for a month, but perhaps it is true. Possibly Ladoux was ignorant of this fact and its significance until mid-January. Possibly he knew about the broken code but did not want to acknowledge that the Germans might be planting disinformation through these messages. Finally, he may have been in fact the mastermind who planned the broken-code stratagem in order to divert suspicion from real spies to Mata Hari.

Mata Hari decided it was time to demand answers to her questions. She wrote a letter to Ladoux, which she showed first to her lawyer and old friend, Edouard Clunet. As she recalled, the letter said: "What do you want of me? I am disposed to do all that you ask. I do not ask you your secrets and I do not wish to know your agents. I am an international woman. Do not discuss my methods, do not ruin my work with secret agents who cannot understand me. That I desire to be paid is legitimate, but I wish to go [leave Paris]."

Clunet found her letter a little blunt and was shocked by her demanding payment, which sounded mercenary, almost indecent. Naïvely, he had never realized how often she had accepted money from men. She told him, "If I am not ashamed to accept money, then I must not be ashamed to say so." She mailed the letter herself, rather than entrusting it to the concierge at the hotel. She was in terrible need of money. She had already moved from the Hotel Plaza Athénée to the Hotel Castiglione, which was cheaper. Then she moved again, to the Elysée Palace Hotel, which was cheaper still. According to Ladoux's men, she was spending 500 francs a week—the equivalent of $1,610 today—though her hotel cost only 210 francs a week ($720). She had unpaid debts all over Paris.

Finally, she received a letter from van der Capellan saying he had sent her 3,000 francs (about $8,000 today) through the Dutch consulate. She promptly picked it up. In the same letter, ominously, the baron told her he could not continue to keep up the house in The Hague if she was not going to return to it. Her long-suffering baron was finally fed up with paying for a mistress whom he never saw. As he had been the mainstay of her financial existence, this was indeed a serious threat. That, added to her uneasiness about the surveillance and Ladoux's evasive manner, persuaded her she must leave Paris soon.

Despite her own precarious situation, she sent Vadime 1,000 francs of the 3,000 she had just received.

There is another inexplicable gap in the surveillance reports on Mata Hari from January 15, 1917, until her arrest on February 13. Ladoux had apparently called off Tarlet and Monier at about the time Locard informed him that the broken code was being used. In his book about Mata Hari, Léon Schirmann disputes this point, noting that both Police Commissioner Albert Priolet, in a report dated April 18, 1917, and Henri Maunoury, in his *Police of the War* (1937), asserted that she was tailed until the time of her arrest. If she was under surveillance during the last month before her arrest, what has become of the daily police reports? They are not in her file, which suggests their deliberate removal. What could the inspectors have seen that was more scandalous than the nights they had observed her going off with prominent French politicians?

If their recollections are incorrect, and her surveillance was halted, the dubious decision to let a strongly suspected spy operate freely in Paris demands explanation. Perhaps Ladoux was disheartened to learn that the incriminating messages upon which he had hung so many of his accusations had been written in a broken cipher. Perhaps he was being pressured by his superiors to stop the expensive surveillance. Certainly the months of manpower and time had been a complete waste, yielding no evidence whatsoever of espionage and abundant evidence of the life of a courtesan in wartime Paris.

Mata Hari never lacked for male admirers, even though she was nearing forty years old and even though she was in love with Vadime. From her perspective, she needed money and money meant lovers. From that of the officers she entertained, she was enchanting.

An officer leaving the horrors of the battlefield and the dreadful responsibility of command to spend a few days or a week in Paris with Mata Hari entered a dream world. The life expectancy of those fighting on the western front could be measured in weeks, not years, and they knew it. To enjoy the attentions of a beautiful woman who was fashionably dressed, to take her to fine restaurants, and to make love to her with passionate abandon were the surest escapes from the realities that haunted these men. No wonder so many sought her company and savored every moment of it, knowing that the battlefield, that blood, death, and hardship, would be temporarily held at bay.

Many of the men Mata Hari loved told very similar stories of their meetings. They encountered her in a garden, a tearoom, or some other public place. Drawn by her beauty, the men struck up a conversation with her, took her to tea or arranged to meet with her again. Sometimes these encounters were merely transient and pleasant; sometimes they led to a brief affair. A typical story was told by Paul Bourgeois, a military nurse, who recalled:

The 6th or 7th of February, I cannot be precise about which of the two days, having permission, I went to Paris and in midafternoon found myself on the rue de Castiglione. I entered into the garden of the Tuileries to take photos of the snow. It was then that I saw, walking before me, a pretty young woman, extremely elegant, about thirty-two years old. I approached her and asked if she would pose for my photos to animate the scene. We fell into conversation and finally, we went together to take tea in a house in rue Caumartin, near the place de l'Opéra at the left, and going toward this street. I do not know the name of the place because I had never been there before. If I remember correctly, the facade is painted blue. My new friend, she seemed to know the house and it was she who chose it and we were directed to a table on the right that she seemed particularly fond of.

There, we continued to chat about everything but not military matters. This woman posed not a single indiscreet question of that type, she never asked me where I was [stationed]. The conversation was very gay and mostly superficial. I wanted to see this young woman again and asked her if she would be my marrine *[a female pen-pal or sweetheart] and naturally she accepted. . . . In leaving, I arranged a rendezvous with her for the next day.*

Mata Hari continued to entertain many soldiers and brought joy to their leave, but in the meantime she was growing frantic for word of Vadime. She knew that she might have to return to The Hague soon and would be unable to see him perhaps for months. She wrote letter after letter—sometimes several a day—and longed for his replies. She renewed her acquaintance with Adam Wieniawski, with whom she had worked on some of her theatrical performances. He was delegated to the Russian Red Cross, and she thought he might be able to get her information about Vadime. Wieniawski later testified:

She showed me various photos [of herself] with this officer with extremely amorous dedications. Of all her questions, the only one that shocked me was when she asked, "Was Massloff grievously wounded at Verdun?" However, the Russian troops were never in that sector. I told her that her friend, as far as I knew, was simply bruised. And at her demand I gave my word to inform her if something serious happened to Massloff. I had promised also to recommend to his boss, General Netchvofodoff, to give him permission for a convalescent leave if he needed it. I had soon thereafter to telephone the general several times; he responded to me: "She is a tall, brown [skinned] woman, an exotic type? In that case, I counsel you to have nothing to do with her, I have had very bad reports of her. . . ."

At about this time, Madame Zelle found a way of telegraphing

*me at Chalons [his base]. I do not know how she had my address, I
believe that she asked me for news of Massloff. I did not respond
and have not heard further from her.*

Wieniawski's remarks reveal two important points. First, Vadime's superiors knew of his intense affair with Mata Hari and disapproved. Second, and more surprising, Wieniawski's words reveal a vital facet of Mata Hari's personality. Despite her devotion to Vadime and her ever-mounting anxiety about his well-being, she followed the war's progress in such a cursory fashion that she did not know what battles his regiment was in, nor did she apparently know that the fighting at Verdun had ended some weeks earlier, in December of 1916. Since the newspapers reported daily on the war and the battles being fought by different military units, Mata Hari must have been totally disinterested in the war itself to be so ignorant.

In mid-January—just after Mata Hari's surveillance had ceased—Vadime finally obtained leave to go to Paris. He showed her a letter written by his colonel's military attaché, forbidding him to marry her or even to have any further contact with her. The problem was that the colonel had received a report from Count Ignatieff at the Russian embassy in Paris, who in turn had been informed by an unnamed French officer that she was a "dangerous adventuress": a "gold digger" in modern slang. Vadime had been warned not to associate with Mata Hari, and the strongly worded caution was reiterated shortly before he began his leave. But he had no intention of staying away from her, despite his commanding officer's wishes, and instead showed her the letter against her.

Who was working to ruin her reputation? She thought at the time that Ladoux was sabotaging her romance for some reason, but later she believed it was Colonel Denvignes. Denvignes had already proven himself a ridiculously jealous man when he had met her in Madrid. He monopolized her attention and after a few days' acquaintance thought he had the right to question her sharply about whom she saw and where she went. He demanded to know the name of the officer with whom she was in love: de Massloff. Later, Denvignes had turned against her and failed to pass the information she had entrusted to him along to Ladoux.

Too soon, Vadime had to return to his unit and Mata Hari was again alone. When she failed to receive any instructions from Ladoux, her impatience took hold again. She went to Maunoury at the Prefecture of Police, asking for a travel permit to go to Holland via Switzerland. Maunoury told her Ladoux was on the Riviera for at least three weeks and no one could give her a travel permit without his approval.

As she had done when trying to get to Vittel, Mata Hari simply went to another office to apply for a travel permit. This time, because the Prefecture of Police had refused to give her a permit, she went to the Ministry of Foreign Affairs.

On February 10, 1917, a request for a warrant to arrest Mata Hari was written by the minister of war on the letterhead of the War Ministry, Army Headquarters, Cinquième Bureau, Section of the Centralization of Information number 3455—SCR 10. It was stamped SECRET and addressed to the General of the Division, Military Governor of Paris, Office of Military Justice. It read:

I WISH TO MAKE KNOWN that the here-named Zelle, divorced spouse of MacLeod, a.k.a. Mata Hari, dancer, Dutch subject, *strongly suspected of being* an agent in the service of Germany. [The italicized phrase is inserted between the original typed lines.]

This information came from a very reliable secret source

and the following indications have become known to the counterespionage service of the Army Headquarters:

1) Zelle MacLeod belongs to the Cologne intelligence service where she is known by the designation H21.
2) She has been twice in France since the onset of hostilities, undoubtedly to receive intelligence for Germany.
3) During her second voyage, she offered her services to French intelligence, when in fact, as she showed later, she would share whatever she learned with German intelligence.
4) Arrested by the English on her attempted return to Holland, she was returned by them to Spain where she entered into relations with the German military attaché at Madrid, at the same time she offered to the French military attaché to pass on information about the activities of German intelligence in Spain.
5) She confessed the points mentioned in the above paragraph to the German military attaché, as is established by a secret document coming from her, and further that she had received 5,000 francs from the German intelligence service at the beginning of November in Paris.
6) She has, further, remitted to the German military attaché a series of intelligence reports about military and diplomatic orders which were then transmitted by the headquarters to Berlin.
7) She finally agreed to return to France where a sum of 5,000 francs was sent to her by successive transmissions from the German ambassador in Holland at the general consulate of Holland in Paris. This sum effectively reached Zelle on January 16, 1917, and then she had made a photo of the receipt

signed M. Bunge, consul of Holland, whose exact role in this affair could not be established except by questioning.

I COMMUNICATE TO YOU THE information which will permit you to appreciate the opportunity that is offered by issuing an order of denunciation against Zelle MacLeod, on the strength of which two dossiers of information have been constituted, one by the Army Headquarters and the other by the Prefecture of Police, dossiers which they could use for investigation.

There are several interesting points about these charges. Item 4—embarking on an affair with Major Kalle and offering to pass information gathered from him through Denvignes to the French government—sounds damning but was exactly what Ladoux had asked her to do: to seduce a high-ranking officer and then to gather information for the French. Though the code name "H21" is mentioned, the telegrams that identified Mata Hari as H21 are not. When Ladoux had recruited Mata Hari, Ladoux had accused her of being enemy agent AF44, trained in Antwerp. She denied it and the matter was seemingly dropped. Now she had become H21, but again no evidence was offered.

Not knowing she was on the verge of arrest, Mata Hari returned to the Ministry of Foreign Affairs on February 12 to inquire about her permit to travel. She was told her papers had not arrived. She returned to her hotel, hoping, as always, for a letter from Vadime.

The warrant for Mata Hari's arrest was issued the same day, citing the crimes of attempted espionage, complicity, and passing intelligence to the enemy. The warrant was stamped for execution on February 12. Captain Pierre Bouchardon, an investigative magistrate of the Third Council of War (the military court that tried espionage crimes) instructed Police Commissioner Albert Priolet to carry out the arrest and a detailed search, seizing letters, other documents, messages, and bank information. He was also charged to intercept her ongoing correspondence.

On the morning of February 13 a knock came at the door of Mata Hari's room, number 131 of the Elysée Palace Hotel. When the door was opened, Priolet led in five inspectors to find Mata Hari eating breakfast, probably dressed in an exquisite, lace-trimmed dressing gown of the sort she loved to wear. Contrary to rumors that circulated later, Mata Hari did not appear naked in front of the men who had come to arrest her. Priolet read her the warrant for her arrest. While Mata Hari dressed, his men began their search of her room and possessions. They itemized the various objects and documents they thought might be suspicious, placing them under seal.

Seal Number One. 1) A French visa issued at The Hague on the 27 of November 1915 to Madame Zelle (Register 312), issued for Paris for the last time the 4 January 1916 for the Low Countries via Spain and Portugal.

2) A travel permit issued under the number 1498 E to Madame Zelle for a trip to Vittel.

3) A residence permit in the name of Madame Zelle, issued in Paris the 13 December 1915.

4) An extract from the registry of enrollment for aliens in the name of Zelle. (Registry 41.13, volume 32).

5) An addendum to the visa number 312 issued in London the 2nd of December 1915, to go to Hendaye 11 January 1916.

6) A visa issued in The Hague the 12 of May 1916 in the name of Madame Zelle (Dutch passport).
Seal Number Two (wrapped). One lot of correspondence.
Seal Number Three (wrapped). Different receipts, bills, and diverse papers.

Seal Number Four. Ten papers dealing with the sending of money, the rental of a safety deposit box, bank matters, the rental of an apartment at 33, avenue Henri-Martin.

Seal Number Five. A checkbook for Credit Lyonnais, account number 147045, in the name of MacLeod, Mata Hari.

Seal Number Six. Fifty-three diverse addresses.

Seal Number Seven. Thirty photographs.

Seal Number Eight (wrapped). A valise containing books, brochures, programs, and various objects.

Seal Number Nine (wrapped). A box containing a pendulum clock and addressed as a gift from Mme. Zelle.

Seal Number Ten (wrapped). A box containing various objects that Mme. Zelle intended to take to Holland, as gifts to her servants.

Seal Number Eleven (wrapped). A traveling bag containing toilet products being submitted for examination by the judicial identification service.

Seal Number 12. An envelope containing six bank notes in the value of 100 francs, numbers 79885324–79885326–06968003–28148089–58349558–67750343; a bill for 60 florins, number AA094887; a bill of 40 florins, number UB2363; a Russian bill, number 609466. (Separate from this, a sum of 100 francs was left with the aforenamed Zelle.)

After ransacking her belongings, Priolet and his men took Mata Hari for her first interview with the investigator, Pierre Bouchardon. He would become her nemesis.

Grinding Her to Dust

MATA HARI ENTERED Pierre Bouchardon's office at the Palace of Justice at eleven o'clock on the morning of February 13, 1917. The office was so small that Bouchardon referred to it as his cupboard; with two small tables and three chairs, one for Bouchardon, one for the accused, and one for his clerk, the room must have been uncomfortably crowded. As investigating magistrate, Bouchardon should have been fully informed of any information gathered by any source, but he had not. For his own reasons, Ladoux had not yet confided to Bouchardon any information about the coded telegrams. As for the surveillance reports, Bouchardon scoffed that they were little more than a list of addresses for couturiers and teahouses.

Bouchardon was a small man, forty-six years old, the son of a family in which law and medicine were the favored professions. He had worked as a substitute judge and an attorney before he obtained the post of assistant director of criminal law in the Ministry of Justice. When the Third Council of War was created, he was proud to be appointed its sole investigative

On the day of Mata Hari's arrest, her interrogator, Pierre Bouchardon, wrote: "Was she, had she been pretty? Without a doubt. . . . Feline, supple, and artificial, used to gambling everything and anything without scruple, without pity, always ready to devour fortunes, leaving her ruined lovers to blow their brains out, she was a *born spy*. . . ." (The Mata Hari Foundation/Fries Museum)

magistrate. He liked to quote a passage from Robespierre: "Justice must know neither friend, nor parents. She grinds in front of her all those who are guilty."

By nature, Bouchardon was tense; he smoked, chewed his fingernails, and paced across his office. He was obsessive about his cases; he wished to know everything, every detail. His colleagues knew him to be a relentless investigator and nicknamed him "the Grand Inquisitor." As a contemporary of his remarked, his name—Pierre, meaning "stone," and Bouchardon, derived from *bouchard*, or sculptor's hammer—was especially apt. Like a stony hammer, he pounded away at the accused and at unsolved enigmas until he shattered them. And he proceeded to use this approach to the fullest with Mata Hari. Even if he had little or no evidence against her, he was sure he could break her mentally and physically and get her to confess.

The first meeting between Bouchardon and Mata Hari was of the utmost importance. It was witnessed only by Sergeant Emmanuel Baudouin, who took notes in shorthand that were later transcribed in full. Following standard procedure, Bouchardon first asked Mata Hari if she had read the warrant against her; she said she had. He informed her that she had the right to call a lawyer; Baudouin recorded that she replied she did not need one. He wrote down her statement, which she signed as accurate:

"I am innocent. Someone is playing with me—French counter-espionage, since I am in its service, and I have only acted on instructions!"

She maintained that she needed no lawyer. This was a very foolish decision. She formally waived the right to have her attorney present at her first and last questioning and so received little legal advice. She did not yet understand the gravity of her situation.

Of course, Mata Hari denied all accusations and at the end of the interview rose to go, thinking it was over. It would be, she may have thought, like that foolishness when she was arrested in Falmouth and mistaken for Clara Benedix. Instead, Bouchardon grimly informed her, she was to be committed to prison. He seemed to take a certain glee in her panic-stricken response. He wrote a description of her in his notes after the interview: "I saw a tall woman with thick lips, dark skin, and imitation pearls in her ears, who somewhat resembled a savage. . . . [When I told her she was to stay in Saint-Lazare prison], she turned to me, a haggard look came into her eyes, which were dumb with fear; bits of dyed hair stuck out at her temples."

Philippe Collas, Bouchardon's great-grandson, speculated that Bouchardon was especially merciless with Mata Hari because of her immorality. Bouchardon had recently discovered that his own wife had taken a lover. His personal notes indicate that he had decided upon Mata Hari's guilt from their very first meeting, if not beforehand. He later wrote: "From the first interview, I had the intuition that I was in the presence of a person in the pay of our enemies. From that time, I had but one thought: to unmask her." Not only was she guilty because she was an immoral wicked woman—like Madame Bouchardon—but she was guilty because she had been arrested,

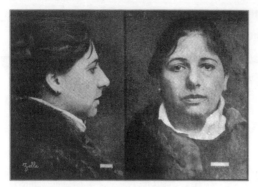

Bouchardon gloated that he had frightened Mata Hari when he told her she must stay in Saint-Lazare prison. "I saw a tall woman with thick lips, dark skin, and imitation pearls in her ears, who somewhat resembled a savage. . . . She turned to me, a haggard look came into her eyes, which were dumb with fear; bits of dyed hair stuck out at her temples." (The Mata Hari Foundation/Fries Museum)

because the war was going badly for the French and she was accused of passing secrets to the enemy, because the French troops were starting to mutiny. Bouchardon and the French government needed someone to be guilty, and Mata Hari was perfect for the role.

One of Bouchardon's most effective tactics was to isolate and disorient the prisoner. Another was to put her into the worst conditions possible, and Saint-Lazare was perfect for that purpose.

Bouchardon ordered her to be confined in the most horrific nightmare of a prison that Paris had to offer, the notorious Saint-Lazare. The first night she spent in a padded cell, a normal provision for newcomers. A suicide watch was kept on her, using a small hatch in the door. Her filthy, flea-infested straw pallet lay on the cold floor. She was assigned number 721 44625.

Saint-Lazare had originally been a prison hospital treating streetwalkers with venereal disease. In the early twentieth century it housed female criminals, usually from the lowest class and convicted of the most heinous crimes. The prisoners were attended to, minimally, by nuns of the order of Marie-Joseph. From February 13 until July 24 of 1917, Mata Hari lived in almost complete isolation. Two elderly nuns, Sister Léonide and Sister Marie, were assigned to her. Their company, a few meetings with her attorney, some exami-

nations by the prison doctor, and interrogations by Bouchardon were all
that broke the monotony.

Saint-Lazare was dark, damp,
filthy, rat-infested, unheated, and
furnished primitively. The prisoners
had no privacy, and their food was
scanty and appalling. The elegant
demimondaine who had dined in the
finest restaurants of Europe faced
thin soup and bad coffee for breakfast, bread and boiled vegetables for
her second meal, with a thin slice of
poor-quality meat once a week—
and she was forced to pay for these
meals. The fastidious woman who
had insisted on a private bathroom in
every hotel was restricted to a small

The cells at Saint-Lazare were stark, filthy, and rat-infested. Mata Hari pleaded with her captors: "I cried from fear in the night and no one could hear me. . . . I think I am going mad. I beg you not to leave me locked up in this cell." (Collection Roget-Viollet)

bowl of cold water in the morning for her ablutions. The glamorous dancer who favored silken costumes decorated with jewels
now received a clean, coarse chemise once a week. The Amazon
who rode horses beautifully and danced with strength and grace
was permitted fifteen minutes of exercise a day if she caused no
trouble.

Even for poor streetwalkers, conditions at Saint-Lazare were
brutal; sometimes the prisoners actually revolted in protest. For
Mata Hari, it was the crushing destruction of the world of luxury,
comfort, and admiration she had built with such effort. The even-
tual result of her prolonged imprisonment was the nearly complete
obliteration of the identity of Mata Hari.

Léon Bizard, the senior prison doctor, remembered that he visited

Mata Hari on her first night at Saint-Lazare, but there is no document describing such a visit in her dossier. He recalled that he asked her if she needed anything and she answered vigorously, "Yes! A telephone and a bath." The prison had no bath and certainly did not supply telephones to prisoners. She did not yet comprehend the full horror of her situation.

Bouchardon gave Mata Hari a day to experience the realities of prison life and then called her in for an interview on February 15. He was mentally set for a duel with a woman he felt was evil. After their first meeting, he had written a description of Mata Hari that bears little resemblance to descriptions offered by any other acquaintance of hers:

> *Was she, had she been pretty? Without a doubt, if one consulted the portrait taken in her youth which was the one in her passport. But the woman who was led to me in my office at the Third Council of War had suffered much at the hands of time. Her eyes large as eggs, bulbous, yellow and disfigured with red veins, the snub nose, the skin showing the application of too much rouge, the mouth stretching almost to her ears, lips like the fat rolls of a Negro, large teeth like paddles with a space between the incisors, hair graying at the temples where the dye had not lasted as long; in the pallid light that infiltrated the courtyard of the jail, she did not resemble at all the dancer who had bewitched so many men. But she had kept the harmony of her figure, the slenderness and a certain swing of the hips that was not devoid of grace, a little like the undulations of a tigress in the jungle.*
>
> *Feline, supple, and artificial, used to gambling everything and anything without scruple, without pity, always ready to devour fortunes, leaving her ruined lovers to blow their brains out, she was a born spy. . . . She squandered money with such frenzy that she*

was often reduced to penury. Then she frequented the houses of as-
signation. Dr. Léon Bizard, doctor of the prefecture of police, en-
countered her in the course of his visits [to check prostitutes for
syphilis], in an establishment in the quarter of l'Etoile. In addi-
tion, she had prohibitive rates, fifty louis for a "passing fancy" [a
slang phrase meaning a quick and crude sexual encounter].

At irregular intervals from February 15 onward, Bouchardon
called Mata Hari in for questioning. She had begun to appreciate
that the charges against her were very serious, yet she could not
believe that she would be convicted, since she was innocent. At this
interview, she again renounced legal help, signing a statement that
read: "I expressly renounce, for the present interrogation, all of the
formalities of the law which concern the assistance of legal counsel
and the benefit of procedures at his disposition."

Prodded by Bouchardon, she began to recount the story of her
life during the interview, piece by piece. Typically, she changed
some of the details to cast herself in a better light. For example, she
said Rudolf divorced her not because of adultery and her immoral
life—the real charges—but because she had "abandoned the conjugal home." She made some of her relationships of longer duration
than was true, skipping over periods when she was earning a living
by much shorter affairs or borderline prostitution. She bragged of
the large fees she received as a dancer at the top theaters of Europe.
She was very vague about dates. She also mentioned her lover, Colonel van der Capellan, who maintained for her use a charming house
in The Hague, thinking it would make her sound respectable.

At the end of the interview, she said:

I wish, for the rest of the questioning, that Maître Clunet, who
is already occupied with my affairs, should be designated as my

attorney. As for the rest, I ask you to permit me to have my linen dressing gown, which is indispensable to me. Finally, I am in Saint-Lazare under conditions that I cannot withstand and I ask that you have me examined from the point of view of health. I am suffering greatly and I need special care.

Bouchardon recorded grudgingly that "she had taken hold of herself again, and put up a good fight." But he knew, as she perhaps did not yet, that this would be a fight to the finish. He was determined to win.

Accordingly, Mata Hari was examined by one of the prison doctors—Jules Socquet—two days after her arrest. He reported that she was

aged 40 years, tall, well-formed and seemingly vigorous. Because of the emotions caused by her arrest, she says, and the rules to which she was subjected since that day, she vomited blood that night. This frightening state is heightened by the fact that she finds herself in a cell that is dark and airless.

The cell where we visited her is spacious; the walls are padded, but it is aerated by only a single circular window with a grill measuring about 25 centimeters [less than 10 inches] in diameter, in the middle of which is an electric lamp.

At the time of our examination, we were able to verify that she was menstruating. The accused had no fever; her tongue was clean and not coated.

She was very emotional and nervous. Asculation of her chest revealed no unusual sounds; it was the same with the sounds of the heart.

CONCLUSION: The accused Zelle is not actually suffering from any organic disease or complaint or fever. She can without any

serious inconvenience withstand a regime of preventative detention.
As soon as possible, as a measure of humanity, we suggest it would
be necessary to change this cell for a lighter and more airy one.

On February 19 she was briefly admitted to the infirmary—a
point that contradicts Socquet's cheerful assessment of her health—
and then moved from her first cell to a marginally better one. The
latter can be imagined from the name of that section of the prison:
La Ménagerie. Desperate women, rats, fleas, and lice were the inhabitants of this dreadful zoo.

She was left to sit in her cell until February 21, when she was
called in for more questioning. Maître Clunct was present but not
very effectual. Bouchardon later described him as "an old and somewhat naïve admirer of the dancer. . . . He carries out his defense of
his client with an ardor of a neophyte and he has a tenderness toward her that I cannot explain to myself, for he knows that at the
outbreak of war, the accused was in Berlin itself, the mistress of two
officers and *of the chief of police*. It was Madame Zelle herself who
told him this."

Bouchardon made a considerable error in this statement, describing Griebel as "the" chief of police rather than "a" chief of
police. But errors aside, his real point was valid: Clunet had never
handled a client accused of espionage before and had little idea how
to proceed.

In this interview, she described returning to Paris from The
Hague to collect her personal belongings from her house at Neuilly
that had been put into storage early in the war. She needed certain
toilette articles, she explained, that were not available in the Netherlands. For the first time, her love affair with Vadime came into the
official record. They met in July of 1916 and "it was a grand love on
both sides," she confided to the cold-eyed Bouchardon.

Bouchardon never believed that Mata Hari was in love with Vadime or anyone else, except herself and her sensuous pleasures. He wrote:

> Already the official mistress of Colonel van der Capellan, of the Dutch army, she was also the mistress of the Belgian commandant the marquis de Beaufort and of the Russian Captain de Massloff, who presented her as his fiancée and for whom she played the comedy of great love. This triple liaison did not stop her from having fleeting relations with one Montegrin officer, one Italian, two Irish, three or four English and five French officers. Far from being ashamed, she flattered herself about it. "I love officers," she declared; "I have loved them all my life. I would rather be the mistress of a poor officer than a rich banker. My greatest pleasure is to go to bed with them without thinking of money, and then, I like to make comparisons among the different nationalities."

In Bouchardon's view, Mata Hari was not only a whore but, worse yet, an unashamed whore. He viewed with great skepticism her claim that she applied for a permit to visit Vittel because of her love for Vadime. It was that application that had ensnared her in the tangle of espionage because it took her to 282, boulevard Saint-Germain: the home of the Deuxième Bureau and Georges Ladoux. It was Ladoux who suggested she spy for France, she told Bouchard, reciting their conversation, and it was he who gave her the permit to go to Vittel. Everything was Ladoux's fault.

Convinced she had almost talked her way out of the charge of espionage, Mata Hari returned to her cell. Shortly she wrote a letter to Bouchardon that is surprising and pathetically amusing in its naïveté.

I again ask for my provisional liberty from the military governor of Paris. I beg you, please help me to obtain it. You see that neither my trunks nor my letters contain anything improper and never, never, have I done the slightest thing like espionage against you. I suffer too much. Until I am freed, I beg you for the following:

1. *My couturier Madame Chartier, 5, rue Delambre, has at her shop a cloak of white cloth, decorated with black fox. I have 25 or 30 francs yet to pay her for a small repair to it. Could you get this garment and pay her 50 francs?*

2. *The chambermaid of the first floor of the Elysée Palace Hotel must have received my lingerie back from the laundress. There are 5 or 6 francs to pay. Would you please go look for this?*

3. *Would you ask the agents who searched my rooms what they have done with my toilet articles and my gold earrings, the large Portuguese rings, which were found in the drawer to the right of my dressing table.*

4. *Madame Dalodier, milliner, 14, rue Duphot, for my boa with white plumes. There are 15 francs left to pay.*

Would you like to arrange all this. I would be grateful.

And then there is something close to my heart. It is the permission to go see my fiancé Captain de Massloff. I cannot find words to ask you for more.

I have never—never—done anything bad toward you.

Give me my freedom.

This may have been the only time in history that an accused spy asked her interrogator to collect and pay for her laundry and personal possessions. These requests clearly display Mata Hari's implicit assumption that she was innocent and that a man would do almost anything for her. Doubtless she felt it entirely reasonable to ask Bouchardon to perform these errands, if he insisted on imprisoning her. Astonishingly, Bouchardon ordered a police inspector, Curnier, to carry out her demeaning requests and pay these bills. Curnier even put in for reimbursement for the taxi he took while on these errands.

At Bouchardon's request, the police continued to intercept Mata Hari's mail. By February 23, they had collected three postcards and two letters from Vadime to Mata Hari. February 12 Vadime wrote to tell her he was in the hospital at Epernay for an operation on his throat—the aftermath of being gassed—and begging her to come visit him. On the thirteenth, he wrote again.

> Dearest Marina,
>
> For five days I have been in hospital at Epernay (Hospital Marguerite). You would not believe how this life brings me down. I need so much to have you close to me to whisper words of love in my ear until my heart is full. Alas the distance that separates us obliges me to do nothing except think of you. I visit you in dreams that are so strong that I forget it is only a dream and I am seized by a sudden foolish thought that I wish to embrace you, I open my arms and suddenly the vision disappears leaving me saddened. In these painful moments your photograph, which never leaves me even on the day of battle, is a sweet consolation.
>
> I have already expedited a letter to ask you if it is possible for you to visit me. What would it take for you to do it? Please upon receipt of this, telegraph me your response. Epernay is a small city where you will not need to bring all of your trunks, because you could come only for three or four days.

My kisses and thoughts. I cover your splendid body with kisses.

The next letter, undated, says that he has been evacuated to a hospital in Paris. On the eighteenth, Vadime wrote again "completely astonished by your silence." He awaited her visit impatiently, not knowing she had been arrested. These letters and cards leave no doubt that Vadime was still deeply in love with Mata Hari in February, despite the warning and admonitions of his commander. She never received his letters, of course, because Bouchardon would not allow her to see them.

In addition to his surgery, Vadime also contracted diphtheria and spent most of February and March in the hospital. He was desperate to see his lover again. In March, he was well enough to be granted three days' leave in Paris, but he could not find Mata Hari at the last hotel where she stayed. No one told him what had happened to her. What he must have thought of her disappearance can only be imagined.

Months later, after Mata Hari's arrest had become public knowledge, Vadime was questioned in the hospital in Rennes. Then he testified that he had intended to end their relationship during the visit in March, though his ardent letters in February suggest quite the opposite. The statement seems an attempt to distance himself from her. At least he had the courage to say that she never asked him about anything military. He had been astonished to hear of her arrest. Vadime swore, "She asked me simply what part of the front I found myself on, so that she might follow in the newspapers where the Russian troops, of which I was a part, were being tested. . . . In the course of my relations with her, I never saw anything that was suspect from that [espionage] point of view. I had a lengthy correspondence with her, she never asked me for any military information." Vadime turned their intimate correspondence over to the officers who had come to question him. He did not testify at her trial.

On February 23, Bouchardon received reports that nothing incriminating had been found among Mata Hari's possessions that had been seized and placed under seal. The jewels and money from her safety deposit box were turned over to the court clerk, whom Mata Hari had to beg for small sums of money for incidentals such as postage or cigarettes. Bouchardon ordered an analysis of the substances—soaps, creams, makeup, perfumes, and the like—in her traveling bag, hoping one would be revealed as invisible ink. Inquiries sent to banks all over Paris kept coming back with negative results: not one had an account or safety deposit box in Mata Hari's name with a suspiciously large quantity of money in it.

Frustrated, Bouchardon called Mata Hari in for interrogation again on February 24. He focused on the period immediately following her invitation to spy from Ladoux. Mata Hari told Bouchardon that, even as Ladoux was trying to persuade her to enlist as a spy for France, he strangely accused her of being German spy AF44—yet he sent her on a mission for France. She recounted her bizarre arrest at Falmouth, England, where she was mistaken for Clara Benedix; this had happened only about six months earlier. She did not know Ladoux had denied knowledge of her to the British, but Ladoux's manipulations were visible at every crucial step in her case. The flimsy web constructed of unproven guilt somehow grew thicker.

On February 26 the petition to give Mata Hari provisional liberty, as there was no solid evidence of espionage, had been denied; written in bold hand across it was "REJET"—reject.

On February 28 Bouchardon questioned Mata Hari again, and she described her affair with Kalle, the German major whom she seduced in Madrid trying to fulfill her mission for Ladoux. Being

Mata Hari and impressed by titles, she referred to him as *von* Kalle to indicate aristocracy. No one in France ever seemed to notice this inflation. Her account offered interesting insight into her wiles but little solid information. Kalle suspected that Mata Hari was a spy; she suspected that he might be; each tried to get information out of the other. It was from Kalle that Mata Hari learned that the Germans could read the French ciphers and could decode all their messages. When she gleaned useful information—and broken codes were of great importance—she had no means of communicating with Ladoux. This would be a fatal difficulty for any espionage agent and simply shows how ludicrous her entire "mission" was. Instead, she gave the information to Colonel Denvignes of the French embassy in Madrid. Denvignes was smitten with Mata Hari and, she foolishly thought, was placed highly enough that he could surely serve as a safe conduit for her secret information.

She was questioned again on March 1 and continued her story of naïveté and entrapment. She explained that Denvignes apparently satisfied his lust and then found it too embarrassing to be associated with Mata Hari.

By early March, Clunet had received several letters from Mata Hari pleading with him to help her. She found conditions in Saint-Lazare intolerable; she had written: "Please I beg you, ask Lieutenant Mornet, commissioner of the government: Why does he refuse me clean chemises from my lingerie for which I have asked him *two times* in *fifteen days*. I need them. Why oblige me to live in filth? What is the point of that?"

The tone of her letters was increasingly hysterical. Clunet was beginning to fear for her sanity. He wrote a very reasoned and almost genteel letter to Bouchardon asking for her to be given provisional liberty or, failing that, to be transferred to the prison hospital. His request had no effect, so he wrote a very similar letter on

March 7, citing her high fever, chest complaint, and throat problems. This moved Bouchardon to request that Socquet assess her health once again.

Socquet's report on March 10 was another masterpiece of pleasing Bouchardon. He noted that Mata Hari was in a better cell, better lit and more spacious than her previous cell, with a stove for heating.

> *At the time of the examination, we found the accused in bed complaining of a headache in the occipital region, a respiratory complaint, and a sore throat. She was in a very extreme state of nervousness and never stopped crying.*
>
> *Upon examination, we found nothing in particular: the patient had no fever, no temperature, and ascultation of her chest revealed nothing abnormal; her tongue was clean and had no coating. In fact she was being treated by the physician of Saint-Laẓare.*
>
> *CONCLUSIONS: The woman Zelle, of a very nervous temperament, preoccupied with her situation as a defendant, is not currently suffering from anything serious.*
>
> *The prolongation of her detention at Saint-Laẓare, under the current conditions, is not likely to present any serious inconveniences.*

Apparently the onset of a nervous breakdown was not considered "serious" by Socquet, in keeping with the general lack of recognition of mental illnesses at the time.

The treatment started by the prison doctor Bizard, mentioned incidentally in this report, is of interest. In his writings, Bouchardon openly accused Mata Hari of having syphilis, a point that some previous biographers have regarded purely as a reflection of his disdain for her immoral life. But when the report on the substances in her traveling bag came in, one of them was a cream she had obtained on prescription in Madrid. It contained oxycyanide of mercury.

Mata Hari unblushingly claimed it was a douche to prevent pregnancy. She had among her belongings another therapeutic lotion, obtained in Paris, that contained mercury bi-iodine and potassium iodine that she also claimed was spermicidal. Both potions were standard prescriptions for treating syphilitic sores at the time and were much used by prostitutes. Bizard also believed that she had syphilis, a diagnosis at which he was undoubtedly highly skilled because of his experience inspecting prostitutes.

These indications put Socquet's assertions of Mata Hari's health in a new light. Quite possibly, given the nature of the population imprisoned in Saint-Lazare, Socquet did not consider her having syphilis to be extraordinary, nor would it necessitate special treatment. He performed a pelvic examination of her shortly after her arrival, when she was menstruating. If her case was in remission, a common occurrence with syphilis, he may not have observed syphilitic sores or lesions upon her body.

Alternatively, Socquet may simply have glossed over Mata Hari's symptoms because Bouchardon made it abundantly clear that he did not want her to be released on bail or imprisoned in a hospital room. The chemist Edouard Bayle, who analyzed the potions from her luggage (as well as her makeup, cold cream, perfumes, and other toiletries) declared that she might well have legitimate medical needs for these potions, which had been obtained by prescription. However, in his conclusion he observed that both potions could be diluted to make invisible ink. Of course, more common substances, including milk and lemon juice, can also be used as invisible ink. Bayle was clearly trying to produce an answer that would be useful in Mata Hari's conviction.

Between March 9 and 12, Mata Hari sent an undated note to Bouchardon, asking to postpone her questioning until Monday, as she was too ill to get out of bed. On the twelfth, in the presence of

Mata Hari, Bouchardon examined the contents of various sealed packages taken from her hotel room. There was little of interest, save a large number of calling cards belonging to various officers, letters from various lovers, others from Vadime, Anna, and van der Capellan, clothing, and some jewelry. Bouchardon asked her if she had returned to Germany during the war, and Mata Hari answered firmly: "No, I absolutely did not."

Bouchardon sent police to undertake questioning of the fifty-three men whose cards or letters were found in Mata Hari's possession. They agreed universally that Mata Hari was a charming and lovely companion, that they had initiated the contact with her and not vice versa, and that she had never asked them about anything that could be construed as military information. Many were embarrassed at being questioned by the police, because they were married, and begged that their name be kept out of the court proceedings.

On March 16, Clunet again wrote a respectful letter to Bouchardon, regretting that his own poor health had not permitted him to visit his client or her interrogator. He continued, mildly, "I receive pitiful letters from Mata-Hari. She is in a pathological state of anxiety; she coughs up blood and feels her life is in danger. Excuse me for insisting, but it would be a minor inconvenience to grant a hospital room to this sick one who poses no risk of flight. It would be common humanity to arrange this."

Coughing up blood is a classic sign of tuberculosis, which was probably rampant in Saint-Lazare. Though this symptom had been mentioned in various reports and letters, no one seemed to take this alarming development seriously.

Isolated by then for more than a month in her dirty, dank cell, Mata Hari wrote again to Bouchardon, saying pathetically, "I cried from fear in the night and no one could hear me. Take pity on me.

The shock has upset me so much that I no longer feel myself. I think I am going mad. I beg you not to leave me locked up in this cell."

The military governor of Paris rejected a plea for provisional liberty for Mata Hari again on March 16. Under the impression that a request for hospitalization (not provisional liberty) had been refused, Clunet wrote Bouchardon again on the twenty-first, asking for a second medical opinion. Mata Hari was spitting up blood, coughing, and wasting away; she was "physiologically depressed," and, Clunet noted, such problems could ruin her constitution bit by bit.

Mata Hari wrote a pleading letter to the military governor of Paris on March 23, repeating her request for provisional liberty and asserting that she had never spied against France. Clunet petitioned through Bouchardon once again, pointing out that her already long imprisonment and investigation had not established any point of her guilt. His letter had no effect.

The terse second opinion as to the state of Mata Hari's health, signed March 26, pronounced it "satisfactory."

Bouchardon carried on questioning the men whose calling cards he found in her belongings—fruitlessly—hoping one would admit to some action on her part that smelled of espionage. He also took a formal deposition from Georges Ladoux, the man who enticed Mata Hari into agreeing to become a spy in the first place.

Ladoux's testimony was openly self-serving. His battle for control over the Deuxième Bureau (within the larger Cinquième Bureau) and his fights to make espionage its special purview and himself its supreme chief were for nothing if he did not bend the facts to his advantage. One tactic he employed was using the passive voice in his deposition, so that nothing that had happened appeared to have been his idea or action.

His testimony emphasized that Mata Hari had had many affairs with officers, "without regard to their rank, from all armies, of all ages and nationalities," as if her sexual behavior were direct evidence of espionage. He stated that in June 1916, his agents in Spain notified the Sûreté and the Prefecture of Police of Mata Hari's intended return, so a surveillance operation "was organized" that tailed her in Spain and followed her to Paris. The most he could truthfully claim for the surveillance was that it continued until the end of August. He exaggerated considerably when he said that it revealed a "number of indications of her indiscreet curiosity, but no proof that she worked for the German intelligence service." He continued:

> It was very shortly evident that MacLeod was in the service of our enemies, but it was necessary to prove it, and for this it was necessary that MacLeod spent a long time in Spain where our intelligence service is particularly well organized.
>
> After the voyage to England and Holland was interrupted, she acted like a good agent and went to place herself at the disposition of the German military attaché in Madrid. This put the proofs of MacLeod's guilt into the hands of the head of the army and he could place her under arrest a few days after her return to Paris.
>
> . . . In case it should seem to you that the documents of a particularly secret nature to which these proofs refer are indispensable to your interrogation, you would have to ask for permission from the Minister of War who alone could authorize their release.

Ladoux's performance was masterfully persuasive. He produced not one piece of solid, verifiable evidence of Mata Hari's guilt; he did not even allude to any particular information or event. He referred vaguely to information in unseen, highly secret documents. Without taking either credit or blame, Ladoux mentioned his questionable tactic of recruiting a widely recognized celebrity, who was suspected of being an enemy agent, to spy for France—and made this action appear to be a masterstroke of counterespionage.

Like Bouchardon, Ladoux believed firmly that Mata Hari was guilty because she slept with many men and traveled widely in wartime. Such a woman *must* be a spy. And, from his perspective, someone—someone he had been seen to catch—*needed* to be a spy.

Frustrated by the lack of incriminating evidence, Bouchardon continued searching. He did not call Mata Hari into his tiny office for questioning again until April 12. She was left to go mad in her cell. Bouchardon felt his plan was working.

Mata Hari was deteriorating daily from the harsh conditions of her imprisonment, from his relentless pursuit of evidence against her, from his merciless grinding of her world and her celebrity into dust.

Suffering

CLUNET MAY HAVE BEEN INEFFECTUAL and Mata Hari highly distressed, but she was still intelligent. She could not send letters to anyone she chose because Bouchardon intercepted and monitored them closely, but she tried to notify her consulate. The French were in an awkward diplomatic situation, as they were holding a citizen of a neutral county in prison on suspicion of a serious charge and they had yet to notify her embassy. They had also forbidden Clunet to notify the Dutch embassy, arguing it was a matter of state security.

Six weeks after Mata Hari's arrest, on March 26, she wrote a letter to Count Limberg-Styrum, the secretary of the Dutch legation in Paris, and to Dutch consul Bunge telling them of her arrest and begging them for help. She also asked that they notify her servant, Anna, so she might in turn notify Baron van der Capellan. Bouchardon pondered what to do with the letter and sought advice from others, including the minister of war and Jules Cambon, one of Mata Hari's former lovers who was then the secretary-general of the Ministry of Foreign Affairs. Far from having a sympathetic view of her plight, Cambon was concerned chiefly with preventing scandal or interference: "After studying the question, I believe we cannot prevent the accused from addressing an appeal to a representative of her country. [If we did that], when the situation of the Dutch woman is finally known, we would have exposed ourselves to claims by the legation of the Netherlands and from the Dutch government."

Cambon proposed two possible solutions to the dilemma. First, they might send the letter to the Dutch minister, Ridder van Stuers, letting him know verbally that Mata Hari was guilty of espionage. Van Stuers was not the appropriate person to handle such an affair, but he might be able to exert a subtle and helpful influence in persuading the Dutch to do nothing on her behalf. Alternatively, they might suggest to Mata Hari that she address the minister instead of the Dutch consul, thus ensuring a delay while the information was forwarded. Cambon also cunningly suggested sending the letter by regular post, not diplomatic courier. In the end, they decided to misdirect the letter rather than send it to Bunge, whom Bouchardon suspected of somehow being involved with Mata Hari's unproven espionage. It did not arrive on Bunge's desk until April 22, almost a month after it had been written.

Mata Hari knew nothing of these discussions. On April 6 she wrote again to Bouchardon:

> *I beg you, stop making me suffer in this prison. I am so weakened by this system and [confinement to] the cell is driving me mad. I have never carried out any espionage in France and I have nothing bad in my luggage, neither in my bottles nor in my safety deposit box. Give me provisional liberty, then you can search [for evidence], but do not torture me here. I am a dancer,*

you cannot expect that I think and laugh calmly as before. Stop,
I entreat you. I will not abuse [your kindness].

Another appeal for provisional liberty for Mata Hari was rejected on April 10. By April 11, van der Capellan had become seriously worried about his "little kitten," asking the Dutch foreign
minister, Loudon, to have inquiries made. Loudon sent a telegram
to Consul Bunge in Paris and received a leisurely reply saying that
they had been notified that Mata Hari had been arrested on a charge
of espionage and was in Saint-Lazare.

When interrogation began again on April 12, Mata Hari was
in worse psychological shape than ever. Bouchardon no longer
listened quietly while she told him stories of her life; he questioned aggressively. He began by asking her if she had not already been a German spy when she presented herself at 282,
boulevard Saint-Germain, offering to become a French spy. As if
he had genuinely misunderstood her previous testimony, she simply corrected him, saying that she went to the office to obtain her
permit for Vittel.

Bouchardon challenged her sternly: "Our question should not
surprise you. Have you not told us yourself that you were an international woman and haven't you acknowledged that there was a
time before the war when you were in Berlin and had intimate relations with Lieutenant Alfred Kiepert of the 11th Hussars of Crefeld,
with Captain Lieutenant Kuntze, chief of the seaplane station, and
with the chief of police Griebel?"

The phrase "an international woman" had an implication at that
time that it does not today. An international woman was a worldly
woman, a cosmopolitan woman, and by extension, a woman of
loose morals. In Bouchardon's eyes, Mata Hari's labeling herself an
international woman only reinforced his low opinion of her.

Mata Hari saw things rather differently. "The fact that I had re-lations with these people does not imply at all that I committed es-pionage. I never did anything for Germany nor for any country except France. In my profession as a dancer, I could easily have rela-tions with the important men of Berlin, without any mental reserva-tions that you would later suspect something. Besides, it is I who gave you their names."

By providing the names of her important lovers, Mata Hari felt she was being cooperative and open—unlike a spy. Bouchardon saw her "cooperation" as a further sign of her moral depravity.

He pressed her on the subject of her funds, and she explained that the baron had sent her five thousand francs through the Dutch con-sul in Paris, so she would have money for her trip. This was not pay-ment for espionage. "I assure you," she said innocently and doubtless truthfully, "that I had nothing in my safety deposit box in Paris. I had eaten up all that I had." She offered to authorize Bouchardon to open her box, not knowing that he had already taken steps to do so. He also quizzed her about the potions and lotions in her traveling bag, not yet having received the chemist's report on them.

After the interrogation was finished, she wrote him another let-ter, begging to have her toilet articles returned to her because, as he could verify, there was nothing suspect in them.

> *I am very astonished and saddened that you have refused my provisional liberty.*
>
> *I am not abused, but the conditions under which I must live here are . . . so dirty that I do not know how I can bear them. Realize that I am quite a different sort of woman than those around me and yet I am treated like them. I beg of you, review this decision and permit me to live outside of prison. It is not very difficult and I will make no trouble.*

> *Also I beg you in the name of humanity, send the letter I have written to Captain de Massloff. Do not leave him in uncertainty. Do not make him suffer needlessly.*

Her toilet articles, including her medicines, were inventoried and placed in the warehouse. Alone in her cell, increasingly desperate, ill, and disoriented, Mata Hari began to write to Bouchardon frequently. Unlike the purported transcripts of her testimony, which frequently sound stilted, these letters are full of personality, emotion, and urgency. It was as if she was having a mental conversation with Bouchardon, arguing her points, emphasizing her innocence over and over, and perhaps explaining too much. On April 13 she wrote, emphasizing that it was not her choice to go to Spain after her arrest in England, that she had taken up with Kalle to fulfill her mission, and that she had written to Ladoux about the information she had gleaned immediately and soon also passed the information to Denvignes. Having sensed Bouchardon's disapproval of her various liaisons, she added,

> *As for the three officers about whom you spoke to me yesterday Kiepert, Kuntze, and Griebel. Do you understand that I knew them in* February *or* March *of 1914, well before the war? when I was in Berlin to prepare for my engagement at the Metropol Theater where I had signed for six months?*
>
> *Never did I hear from them again. What wrong is there in that? Have I told you that, after war was declared (my engagement at the theater was canceled), I filed a lawsuit against a couturier in Berlin? and that I had lost the suit in two instances by default [failure to appear]? The proofs of this suit can be found in the Ministry of Foreign Affairs at The Hague and in the office of my attorney, Maître Hijmans (in The Hague)....*

Also, in Berlin they seized my magnificent furs which were worth from sixty to eighty thousand francs [approximately $250,000 in modern currency]! Perhaps I will never be able to buy their like again. You see, my captain, that my relations with Germany were not very happy and the only way I could save . . . my jewels and my money was by the intervention of my government and an attorney. Because the appeals were not yet lost, I did not know in which bank my possessions were held. This judgment [against me] could not be enforced outside of Germany but if I traveled there, I risked my trunks being seized and it was for this reason *that I did not follow the advice or the wish of Captain Ladoux who wanted me to go to Holland in November by Switzerland and Germany.*

Later the same day, she wrote to him again, repeating her points.

Like a moth throwing itself against a lighted window, Mata Hari continued to beat herself against the unyielding, unresponsive Bouchardon. She wrote letter after letter, furiously explaining her motives and actions, trying to break through to some core of humanity within him. But there was no mercy for her, no pity.

Clunet also forwarded a letter to Bouchardon from Mata Hari, an undated one marked only "Sunday": "I have asked you to let me have a little bit of money and you have given me nothing. You know here I am refused necessary items and even stamps for letters to Maître Clunet. Please do not leave me like this, I beg you. It has been already four days." Bouchardon dutifully allowed her to have one hundred francs of her own money but gave her no written answer. He simply left her brooding frenzy to grow.

Clunet forwarded to Bouchardon another letter from Mata Hari, written on April 17, which repeated the same points as her earlier letters. Then she wrote another note detailing some dates and places of residence she felt she had forgotten to mention. Soon there was yet another letter with more details, ending with another pitiful entreaty:

> I am very grateful that you let me have a few underclothes, but I have neither toothpaste nor mouthwash.
>
> I beg you again to let me have my freedom. I will give you all the explanations as well in freedom as in this horrible prison, where I am so uselessly humiliated.

Mata Hari was losing her pride and begging for any scrap of improvement in her dire situation. Bouchardon redoubled his efforts to prove her guilty as her breakdown proceeded; frustratingly, he had yet to find any solid evidence.

On April 23, Clunet, who was a mild and gentlemanly character, wrote Bouchardon a very stern letter demanding Mata Hari's release.

> I must insist most energetically of you that the questioning of my client must come to an end. It has been two months since she was imprisoned in Saint-Lazare under suspicion of espionage.
>
> No proof has been furnished against her that supports this indictment. It is not possible any longer to maintain such a state of things against this unhappy woman, or at least it is necessary to give her provisional liberty. The accusation came from the Minister of War, so it is this department which is obliged to produce some proof immediately. It would be unjust and cruel to prolong this situation.

All Clunet's letter accomplished was to increase the pressure on Bouchardon.

At about this time, the Dutch consul in Paris, Bunge, learned of Mata Hari's arrest and imprisonment, as did her longtime lover, Baron van der Capellan, and her servant, Anna Lintjens. Both Lintjens and van der Capellan could have verified much of Mata Hari's testimony about travel dates and finances, but they were never contacted by Bouchardon, nor could they write to Mata Hari directly.

By the end of April, Mata Hari was terribly nervous, often weeping uncontrollably. Bouchardon told her that he intended to question Vadime, with whom Mata Hari had been forbidden to communicate and whose letters, intercepted by the police, had not been given to her. The thought of his feelings increased her anxiety. She wrote:

> *I thank you very much for the information about Captain de Massloff [that he had been hurt and was in the hospital] but I do not understand. Captain de Massloff has nothing to do with the Third Council of War. Does he even know that I have been arrested? Because you have forbidden me to write to him, he thinks I have left [Paris, without telling him]. Wouldn't you let me write to him now?*
>
> *Captain de Massloff was my lover. He knows nothing of my life or my projects. He knows nothing of my visits to Captain Ladoux. I have never spoken to him of that. We amused ourselves together and that was all. I beg you likewise never to ask him to appear before the council of war. He is a very brave officer, who has before him too beautiful a career to let it be the least bit damaged by this.*
>
> *But I desire absolutely and I beg you again to permit me to let him know what has happened to me by a word from me. I do not want him to think of me things that are not true. He could*

think I have left Paris without saying anything to him. He does
not deserve to suffer because of me in any way.

Though she honorably tried to spare her lover embarrassment, he did not reciprocate by coming to her assistance. In testimony, Vadime downplayed the importance of their affair. He did not appear at her trial. In his defense it must be said that the First Regiment of the First Brigade, in which he served, was in open and dangerous mutiny against its officers at the time of her trial. Disheartened by enormous losses on the western front and confused by the abdication of Czar Nicholas II in March 1917, the common soldiers of the First Brigade rioted, refused to obey orders, and demanded to be returned to Russia. Even if Vadime had wanted to attend Mata Hari's trial, he may not have been able to do so.

Telegrams and Secrets

THE INVESTIGATION WAS STALLED, so Ladoux decided to assist Bouchardon by producing some evidence. That the evidence he produced was manufactured or at the very least enhanced by him is quite possible. On April 21 he sent a report to Lieutenant General Dubail, the military governor of Paris who had been routinely rejecting requests for Mata Hari's provisional liberty, informing him of the existence of a series of intercepted and decoded telegrams from Kalle addressed to Berlin. These secret telegrams were instrumental in Mata Hari's conviction.

Ostensibly, the first telegrams in the series had been intercepted in December of 1916, but even allowing for bureaucratic inefficiency, word of their content should have reached Dubail and Bouchardon months earlier. It was not until late April that either Dubail or Bouchardon or anyone associated with the investigation heard about the telegrams. The delay is flatly inexplicable unless Ladoux, the only man who seemed to know much about these telegrams, was manipulating the situation to his advantage.

In his report to Dubail, Ladoux offered information about fourteen incriminating telegrams. However, he sent transcripts of only nine, as if this were the entire series, to Bouchardon. Today Mata Hari's dossier contains only twelve copies and no originals. Ladoux never told Bouchardon that the telegrams were written in a broken code that the Germans knew the French were able to decipher, raising questions about their authenticity. Neither Bouchardon nor anyone associated with Mata Hari's trial ever examined either the original encrypted telegrams or the unencrypted versions of those telegrams in the original German. No originals of these telegrams, in any form, are in the archives in Paris. Further, some of the unencrypted, translated telegrams are missing—if they ever existed.

According to Ladoux's report, the first telegram was sent on December 31, 1916, from Kalle to the Berlin headquarters. Since the first two telegrams (decoded and translated) are dated December 13, his writing "31" instead of "13" may have been an ordinary transcription error. But this is only one of numerous peculiar and rather suspicious errors and inconsistencies in the telegrams, as noted by Russell Howe in his book.

The first telegram notified Berlin that

AGENT H21 FROM THE INTELLIGENCE OFFICE IN COLOGNE, SENT IN MARCH FOR THE SECOND TIME TO FRANCE, HAS ARRIVED HERE. SHE HAS PRETENDED TO ACCEPT OFFERS OF SERVICE FOR FRENCH INTELLIGENCE AND TO CARRY OUT TRIPS TO BELGIUM FOR THE HEAD OF THE SERVICE.

The telegram then recapitulated her voyage on the *Hollandia*, her arrest in Falmouth, and her intention to proceed to Holland via Paris and Switzerland. H21 was allegedly sent back to Spain by the British, not by Ladoux's orders, which the French knew to be the case. Kalle promised to forward her "very complete" reports by letter or telegram. Though H21 had been paid 5,000 francs (roughly $15,000 today) in Paris, she asked for an additional 10,000 (about $30,000), the telegram said; Kalle asked for instructions.

The story of the Falmouth arrest would seem to positively identify H21 as Mata Hari. The agent's request for an additional large sum of money lent a nice touch of verisimilitude to the telegram for anyone who knew Mata Hari.

Other telegrams furnished more and more damning details: information (inconsequential) that Mata Hari had allegedly furnished to Kalle; a demand for 3,000 francs that corresponded loosely to the 3,000 francs sent to Mata Hari by van der Capellan; a purported payment of 3,500 pesetas to H21 by Kalle that Mata Hari explained as a payment for her "services" from a lover; instructions to send funds via Consul Kroemer in Amsterdam; a reference to H21's servant, Anna Lintjens, in Roermond; a statement indicating the exact date upon which H21 left Madrid for Paris (which was incorrect). Who else could this H21 be except Mata Hari?

And yet, how could such incriminating pieces of evidence against Mata Hari have gone unnoticed until mid-April? The first had been sent and intercepted the previous December, four months earlier, and the last sent March 8, 1917. Decoding them was hardly difficult, since the French had already broken the code. And, once decoded and translated, even the first telegram was more convincing evidence of Mata Hari's espionage than anything else that Ladoux or Bouchardon had been able to turn up. Some of them—such as the one that mentioned Anna Lintjens—were undeniably persuasive.

If Ladoux had access to these telegrams as they were deciphered, why did his men expend so much time and energy in early

1917 tailing Mata Hari night and day and finding nothing suspicious? Surely the telegrams alone were sufficient to warrant her arrest months earlier.

Similarly, from the time of Mata Hari's arrest in February, Bouchardon had struggled manfully to uncover some solid evidence against her, having many witnesses questioned, dispatching inquiries all over France, analyzing the contents of her hotel room at the time of arrest, studying the reports of the surveillance, and trying to break down Mata Hari's defenses. In his memoirs, Bouchardon declares that these telegrams broke the case wide open, when it was going nowhere. Why was all of his effort necessary when these telegrams were so incriminating?

The argument that the information contained in them was secret and had therefore been withheld from Bouchardon is inadequate. There is nothing of military importance in the telegrams, except the fact that the Germans knew the French had broken their code. One possible answer is that these telegrams did not exist—or did not exist with the alleged contents—until shortly before they were turned over to Bouchardon in April.

Some or all of these telegrams may have been deliberate disinformation, falsehoods intended to distract French attention from investigating genuine double agents working for Germany. The most likely author of that disinformation—the most probable individual to have inserted false telegrams into the series or altered words in the transcripts—was Ladoux. It was Ladoux who "authenticated" these telegrams, Ladoux who failed to mention that the telegrams were written in an old code the Germans knew was broken, Ladoux who denied and ignored Mata Hari's information about the codes, Ladoux who inexplicably canceled surveillance on Mata Hari several times, and Ladoux who would look like a terrible fool for hiring Mata Hari in the first place if she were a double agent.

While Bouchardon studied the telegrams and planned his attack on Mata Hari, she continued to write detailed, almost frenzied letters. On April 29 she wrote demanding that Bouchardon question Lieutenant Hallaure and Colonel Denvignes, certain that Hallaure would verify her claim that he directed her to 282, boulevard Saint-Germain and that Denvignes would affirm that she had reported the information she had gleaned from Kalle to him. She had not yet realized how quickly and definitively most of her former lovers would abandon her, even if they had to lie in order to do so.

When Mata Hari was hauled into Bouchardon's office again on May 1, he felt he had the upper hand in their duel. He questioned her mercilessly about her contacts with Kalle and her identification as agent AF44 from Antwerp, or perhaps as H21. He accused her of playing "the most audacious comedy" of counterespionage and boasted that he had material proof of this. He taunted her with the contents of the telegrams that so blatantly pointed to her identity as H21. Mata Hari steadfastly dismissed these accusations.

Von Kalle can say what he likes [in his telegrams]. It could well be that . . . he knew about the exchanges between my domestic in Holland and me. When I telegraph, I give the paper to the porter at the hotel without going myself to the post office. In any case, I am not agent H21, von Kalle did not give me one sou *and the 5,000 francs I received in November, like that which I received in January 1917, came to me from my lover the Baron van der Capellan.*

Ladoux's men were keeping track of her telegraph messages by obtaining handwritten copies from the porter at the hotel; Kalle's men might have been doing the same.

Bouchardon challenged her to respond to the contents of various intercepted—and probably doctored—telegrams, but she maintained her dignified denial of any involvement in espionage. Bouchardon accused her of offering her services to spy for France, and she repeated, wearily, her emphasis that it was *Ladoux* who asked *her* to spy, not vice versa. She insisted she had had no contact with German intelligence before seducing Kalle and then only as proof of her loyalty to France.

Mata Hari scored one significant point during the interrogation by mentioning that there had been a couple on the *Hollandia* with her who were also arrested in Falmouth; perhaps one of them was H21. Bouchardon, taken aback by this possibility of which he knew nothing, initiated inquiries on May 3. At the end of May he received confirmation of the arrest of Lisa or Elise Blume, a German, who was interned as a spy in England.

A few days later Clunet embarked on a different tactic to try to save Mata Hari. He wrote a densely reasoned legal argument to Bouchardon. He cited a 1916 law concerning the functioning of military tribunals, which stated that the counsel of an accused *must* be present at the first and last questioning or else the entire case was nullified. But, he observed, this law did not mean that a counsel could *not* be present at *every* questioning, a right that was guaranteed under a previous law passed in 1899. He reasoned that, since military procedure imposed more severe penalties than common law, then the accused was surely entitled to greater guarantees that his or her defense was adequate. He also pointed out that he had a right to see her entire dossier and it could not be denied to him for reasons of security. Clunet sent similar letters to Commandant Schedlin, chief of the Bureau of Military Justice of the Military Government of Paris.

His letter was a serious threat to Bouchardon's case. Bouchardon immediately wrote a confidential memo to Major Jullien, the chief military prosecutor, enclosing Clunet's letter. Bouchardon felt that the 1916 law completely superseded the 1899 law and that he was justified in interpreting it strictly. Further, he said he dared not let Clunet attend every questioning because Clunet—enamored of Mata Hari as he was—was blinded to the gravity of the case and could not be trusted to maintain proper discretion about the intercepted telegrams. Some facts could not be disclosed without endangering France.

The same excuse—state security—was offered as the rationale for withholding the contents of the telegrams from Clunet, as it had been for withholding their contents from Bouchardon. But nothing in the telegrams was of any military value whatsoever; no secrets were revealed, no military plans or operations confided. There was only chitchat about H21, her travels, and her payments in addition to gossip that could be found in any newspaper. Jullien responded with more legal discussion, siding with Bouchardon. He agreed that the wisest course was not to permit Clunet to attend questionings.

In early May, Mata Hari sent another undated message, via Clunet, to Bouchardon, begging him to allow her to use some of her own money to take a taxi to his office. She continued:

> *The frightful women in this place make such remarks about me*
> *and in front of me, I have suffered a great deal. I ask you to let*
> *me have my money quickly. I am very unhappy. I am ill.*
>
> *I understand perfectly the game that Captain Ladoux has*
> *played in his profession, but he has strayed too far with his*
> *promises and his words. I believed he was sincere. An officer*
> *does not lie and I was so persuaded that my life had nothing*
> *suspect [in it], because I did not concern myself with espionage,*

that I could not even imagine that you would consider someone who had done nothing to be as guilty as one who had done something.

It never entered my head. I swear to you again that I never carried out any espionage and I never wrote a letter [with secret information in it]. Me, I am not guilty. I am Dutch. Obviously I know some Germans. I am a dancer and after the war, I will be obliged, perhaps, to take some engagements in the theater in Berlin and Vienna, as in Paris.

I am not married. I am a woman who travels and amuses herself a great deal. I can be excused for sometimes forgetting about money. Sometimes I win, sometimes I lose. And the money concerned is nothing but a win, as I will again.

The loss of my furs grieves me. I lost them because I was engaged in the theater in Germany. The war thus caused all these bad things and I think that [the Germans] should reimburse me, at least in part. I recall also the conversation that I had with my visitors, after my return to Paris. I will tell you about it. I beg you, my captain, to be less hard with me. I am not guilty of espionage or even attempted espionage. And now that my love for Massloff has become the sentiment that rules my life, because he is the man for whom I would do anything, and for whom I would lose everything, Captain Ladoux can calm himself.

There are appearances, it is true, but not any serious actions. I swear to you. If Captain Ladoux gives me freedom I will still keep my word. He will want and need it. I always told him true information about the Germans. Never did he wish to believe me. There are little agents who can provide little information. And since he wanted for great information, it is only the great women who can get them. There is no need

for revenge because I have done nothing against his country
and never even intended to.

While Mata Hari's defenses grew more urgent and repetitive, Bouchardon's evidence accrued very slowly. He asked the police to try to trace Mata Hari's money, to show that she must have had a source of income beyond what the baron sent her. Clunet passed on Mata Hari's demand to confront Ladoux, Denvignes, and Hallaure. In extreme agitation, Mata Hari wrote again to Bouchardon.

> *This is what I will ask of Captain Ladoux, when I see him. He arranged for me to come to his office at the Ministry of War. He asked me if I wanted to enter his espionage service. He gave me the idea to be of service to France and Germany at the same time [to become a double agent] in order to do great things. He promised me, if I succeeded on the mission completely, one million [francs] as payment. He knew that I frequented the German headquarters. He was up to date on my visit to Spain. He was not opposed to my passage across France, when I was asking for my passport at the French consulate in Madrid. He refused three times to see me when I went to the Ministry of War in Paris, in order to explain to him all that I had written. He seeks to avoid a confrontation now?*
>
> *Then, my captain, it smells very much as if he has acted against me and I beg you to give me my liberty, as he has done nothing other than assure me passage across two enemy countries, that which was impossible.*

There was no answer from Bouchardon. The silence and isolation were effective tools at breaking Mata Hari down.

On May 15 she wrote again.

For three months I am imprisoned in this cell. Morally and physically, you have done me such harm that I beg you to end it. I cannot support any longer the filth, the lack of care for my body, and the disgusting food to which I am not used.

You cannot degrade a woman, day after day, as you have ordered. I am here because of a misunderstanding. I beseech you: stop making me suffer. I cannot take any more, truly, truly.

Whether the confrontation that I asked for is the cause of the waiting. Whether this wounds the vanity or another sentiment of Captain Ladoux. Beg him to give me my liberty. I will speak to no one about what has happened to me here in Paris, but let me leave this terrible prison Saint-Lazare. I cannot stand any longer this wretched life to which you have condemned me.

Stop, I beg you.

Unable to escape, unable to bear her situation, Mata Hari wrote Bouchardon again later the same day, pleading, "It has been three months that I suffer, imprisoned in this cell. I am going mad in here. I swear to you I cannot live this horrible life any longer."

She repeated her questions about Ladoux and why he refused to see her when she returned from Spain. She repeated again that the whole mission was his idea. Her words were a meaningless prayer to a sort of god who could not or would not hear her.

I beg you, my captain. I have always been an honest woman and well received everywhere. Do not make me suffer in Saint-Lazare, it is frightful.

I am losing my sanity here. I told you what I believed on the

*first day. I say it again. A candid interview with Captain
Ladoux will be enough.*

*What is the point of driving me insane in this cell where I
lose my head and my word? I cannot bear it. I have done nothing that merits this and I beg you again, speak with Captain
Ladoux, give me my liberty. I will go and never speak of what
has happened here.*

Tell him, I beg you.

She added under her signature:

*Captain Ladoux was wrong to mistrust me. He wanted me to
bring off something great, he wanted to rise high. If he wanted
me to tell him all my plans at the beginning, he would have had
to pay me in advance, as I asked.*

*Time would not have been wasted, and I swear to you that I
alone would have given him such services that no other person
ever will.*

*I was so in love with my lover, and this made me work with
the illusion of being able to win what would be my only happiness, and that I believe still.*

Mata Hari wrote a similar but more hysterically pitiful letter to
Clunet on May 15. She alluded to blemishes or spots on her body.

*The brusque change, the horrible food and the lack of cleanli-
ness, these are the cause of the blemishes on my body. I grow
more and more unhappy. I cannot stand this life. I would rather
hang myself from the bars on my window than to live like this.
I beg you, please speak to the investigating magistrate and tell*

him that he cannot degrade a woman used to cleanliness and
care, from one day until the next, until she lives in dirty misery.
    Where will it end?
    Does he wish to kill me?
    Must he kill me?
    Or give me my liberty?
    One day it will be too late, there will be nothing left to do. It
is horrible, horrible. If you could see how I am forced to live
here! It is shameful, shameful. Have pity on me, I beseech you.

Within a few days, she wrote another letter to Bouchardon. "That which I have feared for several days arrived last night. I have a fever in my head. You have made me suffer too much in this cell. I am completely mad. Do you wish to end it all? I am a woman, I cannot bear more than my strength."

She was, at last, broken.

Bouchardon ordered Socquet to examine her once again. He pronounced that she was not actually suffering from any "serious physical affliction" but had "an extremely nervous temperament." He added, in a matter-of-fact statement: "One does not observe in the Zelle woman any appreciable stigmata on the different parts of the body permitting a current diagnosis of progressive syphilis. She says she never had any vulvar lesion, eruptions on her body, nor plaques on her lips. Since her incarceration at Saint-Lazare, she has been following a treatment for syphilis."

Socquet's conclusion: no change in her condition since her last examination. She had syphilis, currently in remission, and was having a nervous breakdown, in modern terms, but she was not really ill.

Bouchardon had succeeded. Mata Hari was shattered in spirit, mind, and body. He interrogated her again on May 21. She opened the session with a statement: "I have decided today to tell you the truth. If I have not told everything before, it was because of certain doubts which I will explain."

What she had been hiding from Bouchardon was that she had been visited by the honorary German consul, Karl Kroemer, in autumn of 1915, at her home in The Hague. Since Mata Hari had applied for a visa for France, he knew she was planning a trip there and asked if she might "render them a service" by gathering useful information in France, for which he would pay her 20,000 francs (roughly $61,000 today) in advance. With the extraordinary logic that made no sense to Bouchardon, Mata Hari explained that it was honest to accept this money and do nothing. It was, she felt, repayment for the valuable furs that the Germans had unfairly seized from her.

She had never mentioned this encounter to Ladoux, she told Bouchardon, because she had never done anything for Kroemer and astutely judged it wiser not to bring the matter up. Unfortunately, Ladoux was a less tractable spymaster than Kroemer and refused to give her any advance. When she was arrested in Falmouth, Ladoux did not come to her aid, nor did he respond to her letters. She was in Spain, with mounting bills and very few pesetas left, and Ladoux had abandoned her, so she turned to Kalle. She told Kalle that the French had tried to recruit her and offered him some useless information cobbled together from newspaper reports and gossip. She asked for ten thousand francs in payment and Kalle dutifully telegraphed Berlin for permission to pay H21. Berlin refused.

After a few more meetings, and some "great intimacies" performed in his office, he gave her 3,500 pesetas. She interpreted this as being a lover's gift, like so many she had received from men previously. As for the payments received in Paris through the Dutch consulate, she was not sure from whom those had come. She had instructed Anna to ask the baron for money but, if that was impossible, to ask Kroemer.

Bouchardon seized the advantage, questioning her ferociously. "Whom have you served? Whom have you betrayed? France or Germany?" Her response, that she wanted to help France and hurt Germany, and had succeeded in both, barely registered on Bouchardon. He had at last cornered his quarry and brought her down. It remained only to complete the triumph.

At this interrogation, Bouchardon told Mata Hari that he had indeed questioned her old friend and lover Jean Hallaure, and that Hallaure had not supported her version of events. Like so many other former lovers, Hallaure had been at pains to downplay his affair with Mata Hari, remarking disdainfully that she "flirted not at all badly" and admitting that he had been her casual lover some years previously. He conceded that "Mata Hari never asked me questions about military matters."

Hallaure had said he was surprised when she asked for his advice on getting a permit for Vittel because she seemed perfectly well to him. His remarks imply much but say nothing specific. Her request for advice occurred shortly after she had met Vadime and fallen in love—a turn of events unknown to Hallaure, who was annoyed at being put off when he called to see her. In fact, Hallaure reversed the story, saying he had broken off with her after being warned by a friend that being associated with her would hurt his career. During Hallaure's second questioning on May 19, he emphasized that she had not seemed sick when she wanted to go to Vittel and that he had not sent her to 282, boulevard Saint-Germain, nor had the trip to Vittel been his idea.

Her response to the details of his testimony was to correct certain points—for example, she had never said he sent her to *Vittel* but only to 282, boulevard Saint-Germain. She could not refrain from adding that it was not gentlemanly of him to criticize her so cruelly considering their former relationship.

Making no effort to conceal his disgust, Bouchardon recited to her a list of the officers she had been with in Paris, with names and dates, accusing her of gathering much information from them that must have been of great interest to the Germans. Astonished that he so ill understood her nature, she replied frankly that she had a great fondness for officers and liked to have sex with them, confirming the worst Bouchardon had thought of her.

Mata Hari was doomed from this point on. Even with Ladoux's doctored telegrams, Bouchardon did not have a strong case against her. The telegrams said that she was a German spy but did not even hint at any information she passed, and they contained peculiar inconsistencies. But with her confession of accepting money from the Germans, her conviction was assured.

The Lowest Circle of Hell

BOUCHARDON QUESTIONED MATA HARI again the next day, May 22, pressing her on details and hoping for still greater revelations. He opened by saying, "We have recorded your confession yesterday, but you can hardly expect us to believe that Kroemer gave you 20,000 francs point-blank, without demanding any proofs from you. The Germans give nothing for nothing, and the sums that Germany gives to its agents for travel expenses are very far from that much."

Mata Hari's response was to point out the obvious: "You cannot simply send a woman like me, who has a house and lovers in Holland, without giving her anything." However, that was precisely what Ladoux had done: sent her off without a franc in her pocket or a new dress on her back. The implied criticism of Ladoux's shortsighted, penny-pinching ways became more pointed when Bouchardon brought Captain Ladoux into the office to help in the questioning.

Ladoux reaffirmed his earlier deposition and denied that Mata Hari had ever been "engaged" by him. As proof, he offered the assertion that she had never been assigned a number or been given money and a means of communication.

Mata Hari made a simple statement: "Captain Ladoux promised me, if I succeeded, one million [francs] as payment." Ladoux denied this, saying he had only remarked that, if she could penetrate the German general headquarters and bring back information on the plans and operations of the German army, such information would be worth one million francs.

"The captain was more affirmative than that," Mata Hari responded tartly.

The interrogation proceeded with this sort of twisting of facts, first one way and then the other. Mata Hari maintained that she was spying for France; Ladoux insisted it was all rather hypothetical, especially as he already suspected she was a German spy. Why had she not mentioned this relevant fact during their meetings? "I didn't dare," she replied. "Besides, I never considered myself a German agent with a number, because I never did anything for them."

Ladoux countered, "One cannot give a mission to an agent unless one is certain of him. MacLeod was always suspect to me." He added that he had asked her repeatedly to tell him everything she knew about German intelligence, but she had offered nothing.

"I said nothing to you because you didn't want to pay me and because I didn't feel obliged to give you my great secret." Mata Hari's annoyance with Ladoux's petty concerns was palpable.

Confronting Ladoux gave Mata Hari none of the satisfaction she longed for. He altered every fact, every utterance in their interviews to present himself in a better light and her in a worse one. Nothing factual or new was established during the interrogation except that the differences in philosophical outlook between Mata Hari and Ladoux were underlined.

The most sinister and prophetic remark of the interview was made by Bouchardon: "We must make clear that, from our point of view, maintaining contact with the enemy is considered legally to be a crime equivalent to actually furnishing information to the enemy."

And so it would prove.

In the remaining month of investigation and interrogation, Bouchardon never managed to identify the smallest shred of intelligence that Mata Hari had passed to the Germans. The overwhelmingly probable reason for this failure was that she had passed none. "The case was perfectly clear," Bouchardon wrote in his memoirs. Having "broken" the case on May 21 by breaking the spirit and health of the accused, Bouchardon moved on with renewed vigor.

During the interrogation of May 23, he read her Denvignes's deposition. Denvignes had been questioned about his relationship with Mata Hari and, in particular, whether she tried to pass information through him to Ladoux. As a married man and a colonel, Denvignes was anxious to protect himself for the sake of his marriage and his career. After giving a sanitized version of their meeting and his infatuation with her, he admitted that she had told him she was a spy for France and had poured out some information he found embarrassing and garbled. But he admitted he had urged her to return to Kalle's embraces to gather more detailed information that would be of greater value to France. He said that when he reported her information, it was dismissed as being "already known," though this reaction differed markedly from Ladoux's astonishment when Mata Hari told him the same information.

Concluding this self-serving account of his relations with Mata Hari, Denvignes declared: "My absolute conviction is that MacLeod was in the service of German intelligence. Because of the surveillance of which she was the subject in Madrid, she could not hide her visits to Kalle from Captain Ladoux . . . she had to pretend that she was going to the German military attaché for us. Otherwise, she needed to give us the illusion of great zeal in order to avoid arrest when she returned to France."

Since he had admitted that he told her to return to Kalle to gain more information, accusing her of pretending to go to Kalle for France was particularly hypocritical. This unsupported assertion that she was indeed a German spy was a heartless accusation coming from a man who had been embarrassingly besotted with Mata Hari in Madrid.

Mata Hari's response, when Bouchardon read her Denvignes's statement, was simply:

A man of Colonel Denvignes's rank should not throw stones at a woman in trouble. All the more since he asked me to become his mistress, to which I responded that my heart was taken by a Russian captain who wanted to marry me. Nonetheless, he invited me to dine with him in Paris, gave me his address at the Hotel d'Orsay [so I could visit him there].

On the subject of his suppositions that I was part of German intelligence, I respond thus: it is completely ridiculous, if he had believed this idea, he would never have displayed himself in public with me in Madrid as he did. He kept a bouquet of violets and a ribbon of mine [as souvenirs].

Mata Hari was truly frightened at this point. She had confessed to accepting money from the Germans, offering the entirely plausible (to her) explanation that she viewed the money as nothing more than compensation for the seizure of her furs. She insisted that she had had no intention of spying for them. And yet, instead of recognizing her innocence and giving her freedom, Bouchardon treated her more than ever as a convicted spy. She began writing to him frantically again, explaining, excusing, trying to make him see the truth as she saw it. It was an impossible task.

On May 24, she wrote Ladoux one letter and Bouchardon two. She begged Ladoux to see her and vowed again that she had never acted against France. To Bouchardon, she wrote that she was now convinced it was Denvignes, not Ladoux, who had spoken to the commander of Vadime's regiment about her, saying she was a dangerous adventuress. She wanted this mark of Denvignes's jealousy noted in the file. She also repeated the story of Denvignes's pursuit of her, his encouraging her to go again to Kalle to uncover more information, and his strange refusal to meet with her in Paris. She implied that Denvignes had betrayed and lied about her because she was in love with Vadime, not him. To her mind, this interpretation of events completely refuted his deposition. To Bouchardon's way of thinking, she had underscored, yet again, her lack of morals.

In hindsight, Mata Hari's sense that Denvignes was working against her might have been accurate. Three months after her execution, Denvignes was arrested for treason and imprisoned for four months of interrogation. He was acquitted in April 1918, but the acquittal was accompanied by a demotion, suggesting a lack of evidence rather than an affirmation of innocence. The arrest left a permanent stain on his career.

Hoping for more concrete evidence against Mata Hari, Bouchardon sent policemen to various shops that she frequented, to see if they were points at which she might have dropped off intelligence. He met with no success except for a list of her expensive purchases.

Bouchardon had Mata Hari brought in for questioning on May 30. She repeated many of the same accounts of her relationship with Denvignes, emphasizing his bitter jealousy. Cruelly, Bouchardon then produced Vadime's deposition and allowed her to read his denial of their love. Shocked and bereft by this ultimate betrayal, Mata Hari answered simply: "I have nothing to say." A moment later she added, "I am not guilty of the death of even one of our soldiers."

She had nothing left. All of her lovers had abandoned her and lied about her, even Vadime. There was no future to look forward to, no vision of a happy life with her lover after she was acquitted. And she was beginning to believe, with an awful, deep-seated dread, that she would never be cleared of the charges against her.

Later that day, Ladoux met with Mata Hari, but she made no dent in his ironclad belief in her guilt and forthcoming conviction. He told her she would be shot as a spy, unless she agreed to name her accomplices. She was terrified.

On May 31 she sent a letter to Bouchardon about her meeting with Ladoux and his threats. She had no accomplices and refused to invent one.

> *Captain Ladoux . . . understands nothing of my character. . . .*
>
> *Me, because of my travels, my foreign acquaintances, my manner of living, I see grand events and grand methods. For him, it is the opposite. He sees everything as petty and small. . . . He did not know how to use me. It was his fault, not mine. . . .*
>
> *Today, all around me, everything is collapsing, everyone renounces me, even he for whom I would have gone through fire. Never would I have believed in such human cowardice. I will defend myself and if I fall, it will be with a smile of profound contempt.*

Desperate to clear herself and earn her freedom, she wrote Bouchardon a second letter on May 31, offering to tell him the details of German intelligence in France. Of course, she could not learn their current secrets as long as she remained in a cell at Saint-Lazare. If Ladoux gave her immediate liberty, she would provide the information he desired within a month. "You can menace me and make me suffer, but I cannot tell you what I do not know."

Her grip on reality was loosening to a dangerous degree. Her long and hard imprisonment, her isolation, and the betrayal by Vadime had shattered her sense of who she was. Did she really believe there was any chance that Bouchardon and Ladoux would free her so that she could gather information about German intelligence for them? In her confused existence, in which lies became truths, and truths lies, this far-fetched possibility seemed as likely as anything else.

She continued to write to Bouchardon, repeating and repeating her points: she was innocent; Ladoux had suggested espionage to her, not she to him; France could have refused her reentry but did not, thereby indicating official approval of what she had been doing. Over and over she thrashed helplessly against the network of lies and misinterpretations that bound her as guilty.

Clunet sent another pro forma letter to Bouchardon on June 3, asking for her provisional liberty, and yet another on June 8.

On June 5, Mata Hari wrote the most revealing letter yet. She was certainly in the throes of a nervous breakdown: disoriented, obsessed, terrified, and then strangely optimistic for brief periods. Yet her intelligence still functioned; she could perceive clearly the horror of what was happening to her.

> *There is still something which I beg you to take into consideration, it is that Mata Hari and Madame Zelle MacLeod are two completely different women.*
>
> *Today, because of the war, I am obliged to live under the name of Zelle, and sign it, but this is a woman unknown to most people.*
>
> *As for me, I consider myself to be Mata Hari. For twelve years, I have lived under this name. I am known in all the countries and I have friends everywhere.*

That which is permitted to Mata Hari—dancer—is certainly not permitted to Madame Zelle MacLeod. That which happens to Mata Hari, these are events that do not happen to Madame Zelle. Those who address one do not address the other. In their actions and their manner of living Mata Hari and Madame Zelle cannot be the same. For this reason, my captain, do not be astonished at that which has befallen me. . . .

Mata Hari is obliged to defend herself. I learned this to my downfall. Everywhere that I dance, I am celebrated, I love my jewels, furs. I am everywhere pursued by the vendors who work at the theaters. The lawsuits are numerous, the seizures are immediate, and to avoid this, it is I or a lover who "pays" or else I leave my coveted possessions in the hands of others.

I know that there is nothing to do about it. It is the life of the famous, of all *women of the theater. These are things of which one does not speak.*

But, one makes up the loss when the occasion presents itself. And that is what happened to me, with my furs in Berlin when the war broke out. I assure you, my captain, at eight o'clock in the morning, when the Berlin police went to every hotel, knocked on every door to see who lived there, that morning of the declaration of war, the bank seized the deposits and valuables of foreigners. All the vendors presented their notes and since no one could pay, they seized the trunks, the stored furs. That is what happened to me, and happened to others. And since they pretended that I had lived more than ten years in France, and that I had lost my Dutch nationality, I was treated harshly. . . . And so, when Mata Hari had the occasion to take a little reimbursement [from the Germans], she did it.

All this letter is to point out to you that everything has happened to Mata Hari—and not to Madame Zelle.

It was Mata Hari who was obliged to go to Paris to protect her interests.

Madame Zelle had nothing to do there. I beg you, my captain, take this into consideration and do not be so hard on me. Realize that I have lived all my adult life as Mata Hari, that I think and I act as her. I have lost the notion of travel, of distances, of dangers, nothing exists for me now. Even the difference between races [has vanished]. Everywhere, I encounter rascals and brave people. I lose—I win—I defend myself when I am attacked—I take—sometimes I am taken. But I beg you to believe me that I never did a single act of espionage against France. Never, never.

And I beg you, my captain, I have suffered enough. Let me leave Saint-Lazare. It is not just to keep me locked up. I have never carried out any espionage.

Arguing that she was two different people, which she was in a real sense, did nothing to influence Bouchardon. Indeed, he took it as evidence of her insincerity, almost as playacting. He later recalled this time, saying:

To forget that she was a woman and beautiful, I had to remember all the evil that her treasons had inflicted on our heroic soldiers. In the course of our interrogation, Mata Hari played all the great emotions of the theater: the tears, the smile, the disdain, the coquetry, the anger, the feminine dignity. . . . By turns, she was familiar and pathetic, always nervous, she spoke surprising words. . . . I have never known a woman more cultivated nor a linguist more astonishing.

He left her growing sicker and more desperately anxious in her cell. She wrote Bouchardon letter after letter, grasping at tiny details, trying to conjure up a vision of innocence and misunderstanding that Bouchardon could embrace, but he never would. Bouchardon questioned her again on June 12 but discovered no new information.

On June 9, Clunet's appeal for provisional liberty for Mata Hari was again denied.

Inspector Curnier compiled a report on Mata Hari's expenditures, amounting to an astounding 13,000 francs in a few months, the equivalent of about $1,000 a week. Not surprisingly, he also uncovered unpaid bills all over Paris; she may have spent nearly $35,000, but she certainly did not pay it out.

In fact, on June 27 she received in prison a communication forwarded by her Dutch lawyers to the consulate in Paris, who sent it on to her in prison. The subject was a large bill (3,211 guilders and 80 cents, the equivalent of about $25,000 today) that had been outstanding at a couturier in The Hague since 1915. The couturier was threatening to seize and sell the furnishings of her house in The Hague in lieu of payment. Despite her dire circumstances, Mata Hari sent off a feisty letter through the consulate, asking that her Dutch attorney, Mr. Hijmans, be informed of what had happened to her. The letter has all the dash and style of Mata Hari before her imprisonment.

> *I have the impression they do not know in Holland [what has happened to me]. . . . They think I am in Paris to amuse myself and that I do not intend to come back. . . . I suppose nothing serious can happen to me, the more so because I have a charming house in The Hague and have no other debts than this one with the couturier, which happens to every woman. The couturier has to wait. I cannot accept a bill which is five hundred guilders*

too high, and on which seven hundred guilders have already been paid, without first checking the various bills which I have from them, and on which most likely some other items have also been paid already. The couturier does not have to worry. He will receive the money I owe him, with interest, if necessary, but I am in prison on account of a war accident.... It is impossible for me to handle my affairs at this moment....

What has happened to me is terrible, but I am innocent, so it will all be cleared up.

On June 21, Bouchardon questioned Mata Hari for the last time, in the presence of Clunet, as required by law. He told her it was "a case of *en flagrant délit*," for she had been caught in the act like an adulterous lover. She responded with a pretty speech about her plans for carrying off a great espionage coup for France so she could marry Vadime. She had intended to reestablish contact with a former lover, the duke of Cumberland, who had renounced the throne of Hanover but whom she hoped to convince to try to reclaim it. She was foiled by her arrest in England and being sent back to Spain, but she still tried to gather proofs for Ladoux. What she learned, she gave to Denvignes, who betrayed her. Summing up the circumstances, she commented acidly: "As the situation is now, he gets all the honor, and I am in prison."

The long process of interrogation and investigation was over. There remained only the waiting, the trial, and the execution.

The Kangaroo Court

ON JULY 24, Bouchardon completed his official report on his investigation of Mata Hari. It was an extraordinary document that spelled out his formal conclusions and unwittingly revealed his deep prejudices against any woman as openly sexual as Mata Hari. Indeed, her sexuality and her guilt were inseparably intertwined in his mind. In the very first paragraph, Bouchardon wrote that she "descended on the Grand Hotel where she really set her snares. Ignoring the other inhabitants of the hotel, no matter how rich they were, she selected as her victims a certain number of officers of the Allied armies, one by one as they came along."

He was convinced that she was a predatory woman, deliberately tricking men.

He accepted Ladoux's version of events, that she presented herself at his office at 282, boulevard Saint-Germain offering to become a spy, and endorsed Ladoux's claim that his acute intuition told him from the first that Mata Hari was already an enemy agent. The mission Ladoux suggested for France was not an actual mission but only a means of entrapment. Much was made, too, of the check Mata Hari received for five thousand francs through the Dutch consulate in November of 1916. Bouchardon assumed that this money had been pay from German intelligence, but no one ever carried out the simple and obvious step of contacting Bunge or Baron van der Capellan to ascertain the source of those funds—for reasons of security, it was said.

Bouchardon mentioned that Mata Hari went to Kalle, "a formidable adversary [of France] in espionage matters," in Madrid. Only a few days later, "after freshening up from her coquetries, she entered . . . into relations with our military attaché Colonel Denvignes, telling him she was in our service and brought to him certain intelligence that she had so skillfully, she pretended, obtained from Kalle."

To be a coquette and indulge in coquetries had a far more sexual connotation in 1917 than it does today; the slang term for a prostitute, *cocotte*, was probably derived from *coquette*. His phrases make it sound as if she hopped immediately from Kalle's bed to Denvignes's. Bouchardon's disapproval of Mata Hari's free-loving ways was obvious. During questioning, he wrote:

> Her long stories left us skeptical. This woman set herself up as a sort of Messalina [the sexually voracious wife of Claudius I], dragging a throng of adorers behind her chariot, on the triumphant road of the theatrical success. . . . She appears to be as one of these international women—the word is her own—who have become so dangerous since the outbreak of hostilities. The ease with which she expresses herself in several languages, in French especially, her innumerable affairs, the flexibility of her finances, her style, her remarkable intelligence, her immorality, born or acquired, all contributed to make her suspect. It was not possible that the enemy,

who searched the five parts of the world to find agents, would leave untouched one with these exceptional qualities and when, after two years of war, the woman Zelle entered into the office of Captain Ladoux, it was certain that she was no virgin in espionage matters.

Though Bouchardon's opinion was strongly stated in this report, his evidence was very thin. Aside from her intelligence, linguistic skills, immorality, sexual rapacity, and style—none of which indicated that she was a spy—there were only three types of evidence against her. One was the contents of the intercepted telegrams about agent H21; a second was her receipt of monies through the Dutch consulate, the source of which had not been traced; the third was her admission that she had taken money from Kroemer, the German consul, who wanted her to spy for Germany. There was no frequenting of suspicious places, no excessive interest in military matters during her liaisons with officers, no invisible ink, no evidence of particular plans or secrets that had been leaked to the Germans, no demonstrated access to such secrets.

The telegrams were the strongest evidence against her. Considered objectively, if they were real, they were surprisingly rich in unimportant detail and amazingly poor in actual intelligence. With the exception of assertions that H21 was an agent, nothing in the telegrams indicated that she was.

That Mata Hari received money from sources outside of France was very weak evidence because there was no identification of those sources. Many foreign nationals traveling in France during the war had money sent to them from their homeland via their embassy. This was in no way a crime.

As for the twenty thousand francs Mata Hari accepted from Kroemer, her explanation is perfectly in line with her character and her eccentric views about debts and money, to which Bouchardon had had abundant exposure. Moreover, neither Bouchardon nor anyone else could point to a single piece of information that had been given to the Germans to earn the twenty thousand francs. Considering the gross hyperbole that the prosecution later used during Mata Hari's trial—she was blamed for the deaths of fifty thousand Frenchmen—it is especially revealing that no one ever identified any specific defeat or leak of information that could be blamed on her.

Had Mata Hari been able to withstand the pressures of questioning, isolation, and imprisonment—had she not confessed to taking money from Kroemer—Bouchardon would probably never have discovered that she accepted money from the Germans. Even with modern methods of investigation and intelligence, spies can rarely be convicted unless they break down and confess.

Bouchardon had been convinced of her guilt before he questioned her for the first time, and close exposure to the story of Mata Hari's life had only hardened his feelings against her. Toward the end of his report, his moral prejudices again became dominant. His wholesale condemnation of Mata Hari drew upon his notes during her interrogation.

> One can see that a woman such as Mata Hari, with her successive liaisons, could play a useful role in obtaining the half-secrets that fit together. It is in vain that her partners tried to keep up their guard. In the battle of the sexes, men, so skilled in other things that they are usually the victors, are always defeated.
>
> This dangerous creature is even more so because her primary education permitted her, when she wished, to speak and hold herself correctly in order to create an illusion. Speaking several languages, having lovers in all the capitals of Europe, spread across all the

world, there finding discreet collaborations, she flatters herself that
she is, in her own words, an "international woman."

He recommended remanding her for a trial on the charges that she

1. *Entered the entrenched camp [war zone] of Paris in*
   December of 1915, in any case within the statute of limi-
   tations, in order to obtain documents or information in
   the interest of Germany, an enemy power.

2. *In Holland, . . . notably during the first half of 1916,*
   procured for Germany, an enemy power, notably in the
   person of Consul Kroemer, documents or information
   susceptible to damaging the operations of the army or of
   compromising the security of places, posts, or other mili-
   tary establishments.

3. *In Holland, in May 1916 . . . maintained contact with*
   Germany, an enemy power, in the person of the afore-
   mentioned Kroemer, in order to facilitate the enterprises
   of the enemy.

4. *Entered the entrenched camp of war in Paris in June*
   1916 . . . in order to secure there documents or informa-
   tion in the interests of Germany. . . .

5. *In Paris, since May 1916 . . . maintained contact with*
   Germany, with the aim of assisting the enterprises of the
   aforementioned enemy. . . .

6. *In Madrid, in December 1916 . . . maintained contact*
   with Germany . . . in the person of military attaché
   Kalle, with the aim of assisting the enterprises of the
   enemy.

7. *In the same circumstances of time and place . . . delivered*

> to Germany . . . in the person of military attaché Kalle,
> documents susceptible to damaging the operations of the
> army or of endangering the security of places, posts, or
> other military establishments, said documents or infor-
> mation dealing in particular with interior politics, the
> spring offensive, the discovery by the French of the secret
> of German invisible ink, and the disclosure of the name
> of an agent in the service of England.
>
> 8. In Paris, in January 1917 . . . maintained contact with
> Germany . . . with the aim of assisting the enterprises of
> the aforementioned enemy.

There is something strongly religious, almost catechismal, about the litany of "sins of intentionality" allegedly committed by Mata Hari. There are no secrets specified to have been passed, no military operations compromised, no concrete assistance given to the enemy: only intentions and presence in "entrenched camps" such as the city of Paris. Although the charges seem remarkably vague to modern eyes, the military governor of Paris agreed with Bouchardon's conclusion. He forwarded Mata Hari's case and charges to the Third Council of War for action.

In the meantime, Mata Hari must have sensed that she was headed for trial, but she still managed to generate occasional bursts of hope. She switched her attention from Bouchardon to Lieutenant André Mornet, her prosecutor, who seemed to have power over her at this point. On June 25 she asked, in a brief sentimental note, if she might be allowed a photograph of Vadime—"*one* . . . just one for me?"—out of the many in her possession at the time of her arrest. She also begged him not to call Vadime to testify in court, because she could not see him without weeping.

Over the weeks that passed until her trial, she wrote Mornet asking for clean lingerie, for copies of documents for Clunet, for money so she might marginally improve her life in Saint-Lazare, and for permission to communicate with the outside world, all of which were refused. She also wanted to have additional funds sent from the Netherlands, to help pay her legal costs, arguing: "It is shocking, my lieutenant, how you behave toward me. . . . If 200 francs is needed to pay the copyist [so that Clunet can have access to documents], take my gold cigarette case which is worth 400 francs. But *leave me my lawyer* and do not prevent me from defending myself."

She complained to Mornet, bitterly and frequently, about the filthy conditions and the appalling food, which had not improved:

I am scandalously malnourished . . . they dare to give us rice water to eat that is so dirty that dogs would refuse it. Each day the quantity of bread grows smaller and smaller. . . . I cry at this moment from shame that one dares to give me such squalid rations.

The women who are here can again cry out or revolt but I can only weep. The beds are full of vermin. Hunger every day.

I cannot take any more. . . . Why, my lieutenant, make me suffer this great misery? You can interrogate me but I am always a woman.

On June 30, at long last, the Dutch government expressed some interest in and concern about their long-interred citizen. Only then did the secretary-general of the Ministry of Foreign Affairs contact Clunet, asking to be kept closely informed of developments and remarking that there had been a number of articles about Mata Hari in Dutch newspapers. Seemingly no diplomatic pressure was brought to bear on the French government for arresting a Dutch citizen without notifying them or for keeping her in prison under horrendous conditions for five months.

On July 16, Clunet sent a request to the commissioner of the government, asking that Mata Hari might be given her blouses, lingerie, and other clothing that were seized upon her arrest. Three days later, two blouses, two corsets, a matching skirt and jacket, a pair of slippers, a pair of ankle boots, and a buttonhook were delivered to Saint-Lazare for Mata Hari. Though it does not appear on the itemized list, several reports said that on her way into the court she was wearing a jaunty tricornered hat that matched her jacket and skirt. They also commented that her blouse was rather low-cut. Since these clothes were chosen for her to wear and were not ones she had specifically requested, the symbolism of the military-style hat combined with an indelicately low-cut blouse was undoubtedly deliberate. These clothes conveyed a deeper message: Mata Hari was no better than a prostitute, and one who took neither war nor the loss of soldiers' lives seriously.

On July 20, Mata Hari was finally freed from Saint-Lazare, only to be moved to the Concièrgerie, to be nearer the trial venue; she was accompanied by Sister Léonide from Saint-Lazare.

The trial began on July 24 at 1:00 P.M. at the Palace of Justice. Clunet notified the Dutch government of the trial on the very day it began; he was expecting no help from them, and he received none.

To get to the courtroom, in the company of a guard, Mata Hari crossed the courtyards of the Palace of Justice and entered the central building, where she climbed the impressive spiral staircase to the second floor. She was no longer glamorous and beautiful. Her hair was dirty and ill-dressed; she wore no makeup on her tired face; she had lost an unflattering amount of weight. Yet she still walked like a dancer, supply and fluidly, and held her head high and her back straight with the noble carriage that had been admired by so many men.

Mata Hari herself would have known little of the recent progress of the war at the time of her trial. She had never concerned herself with its details, except insofar as they might have affected Vadime, and she certainly received no war news in Saint-Lazare. She was probably aware that it was a very dangerous moment in history to be suspected of espionage. "Spy fever" had broken out all over Europe, and people were encouraged to look for, and report, any potentially suspicious actions. Casual remarks and such trivialities as the rearrangements of laundry on the clothesline were suspected of being evidence of sympathy with or signals to foreign powers. Foreigners were often arrested—her own experiences told her this—and questioned or imprisoned without courtesy. Travel was much more difficult, permits were always essential, and even with proper papers, foreigners were generally viewed with distrust.

The first three years of the war had gone badly for the Allied forces, and shortages caused hardships at home as well as among the troops. Wounded, crippled men, missing limbs or coughing and wheezing from gas, were becoming a sad and familiar sight in the streets of Europe. Many families had lost a son, a brother, a father, an uncle, or a cousin. Most lived in terror that the next report from the war would include heavy casualties in whatever sector their loved ones were stationed.

In Russia, conditions were so bad that Czar Nicholas II had been forced to resign in March of 1917—an unthinkable revolution. An interim government was formed, but the Russian troops, which had diverted many German soldiers to the eastern front, became disorganized and unstable. They might withdraw, collapse, mutiny, or simply run. Without the vast Russian army in the war, the other Allies feared that all of the German troops would soon be concentrated on the western front in France.

The French troops themselves were weary, weakened, and demoralized, having endured prolonged fighting and heavy losses during 1916 at Verdun. They were not confident of their ability to beat the Germans, especially if the troops now on the eastern front moved to the western front. In April and May of 1917 the French commander-in-chief, Robert-Georges Nivelle, had confidently predicted that a brilliant attack on the German line at Chemin des Dames—"the Road of the Women"—could break through in a single day and end the war.

Instead, the Chemin des Dames had been a prolonged disaster. On the first day, April 16, there had been an appalling slaughter of thousands of French and Russian troops in the Aisne Valley. Crossing the ground, they had met with a network of barbed wire that had forced them into clumps. They were mowed down by German machine guns entrenched on the plateau above the valley. Vadime was among the wounded. Hospital services had been unable to handle the numbers of wounded; some had been loaded onto trains heading to hospitals as far away as Paris. Despite his own statements earlier that the attack must be brief, Nivelle had continued to hurl troops into the battle day after day.

By the time in May that an end to the battle had been called, roughly 187,000 French lives had been lost, along with numerous tanks and guns, which were much needed for any further offensives. Instead of an end to the war, all that had been gained at Chemin des Dames was a few hundred meters of ground. The defeat had been so costly that half of the divisions of the French army had mutinied and refused to fight. Infantrymen had refused to go up to the front for an offensive, though they had vowed to defend themselves if attacked; protest demonstrations had been held, red flags had been flown, and stones had been thrown at military transports; railroad lines had been sabotaged; and, occasionally, unpopular officers had been attacked. The Russian troops also mutinied, refusing to obey orders, because of their massive losses—about half of the First Brigade had been wounded in the Chemin des Dames—and their poor food and medical treatment.

On May 15, Nivelle had been replaced as commander-in-chief by Philippe-Henri Pétain, who had ruthlessly identified fifty-four men as ringleaders of the mutiny and summarily tried and executed them at the front line. Three hundred French mutineers were dispatched in disgrace to the prison on Devil's Island, off the coast of French Guiana. This suppressed the mutiny but left morale dangerously low. Pétain had decided not to commit French troops to offensive actions for a while; he gave soldiers more leave and their families more generous allowances and tried to improve the food for front-line soldiers. The French demanded that the Russians restore order in their brigades. When initial attempts failed, the First and then the Third Brigades were confined to a camp in La Courtine. Instead of solving the problem, the two brigades fell to fighting each other and the mutiny grew even worse.

In the summer of 1917 the entire French military establishment lived in a volatile milieu of anxiety, shame, terror, courage, despair, and optimism. Attempts to capture and convict spies were stepped up as the war turned worse, in the same way that Pétain had executed soldiers identified as "traitors" because they had not wished to join in hopeless martyrdom on the battlefield. The Allied commanders, especially the French, needed someone to blame, to punish—to defeat, as they were being defeated by the Germans.

And there she came, on July 24, the perfect scapegoat: a tall dark woman in a low-cut blouse and a hat that mocked the military establishment. She was an immoral foreigner with a sensuous walk who had shamelessly seduced men from all armies. She had not only killed Frenchmen, she had stolen them from their wives and families while they were still alive. She had lived flamboyantly and expensively—the quality of her clothes and boots was evident to any observer at the trial—at a time when ordinary people could not get enough bread to eat.

The day of the trial was close and warm, eighty-two degrees F. Mata Hari faced seven men, all from the military: Lieutenant Colonel Albert-Ernest Semprou, president of the tribunal; and the six other judges, Major Ferdinand Joubert, Captain Lionel de Cayla, Captain Jean Chatin, Lieutenant Henri Deguesseau, Second Lieutenant Joseph de Mercier de Malval, and Sergeant Major Berthommé. Most of these men were in their fifties or sixties and had had distinguished military careers. The prosecutor intent on convicting Mata Hari was Lieutenant André Mornet, a tall man with a full beard showing streaks of gray. The clerk was Sergeant Major Rivière. The only friendly face in the courtroom was that of her attorney and former lover, Clunet, whose inefficacy she had surely begun to suspect. He was not nearly as familiar with the peculiarities of military law—embodied in the leather-bound tomes of the Military Code of Justice, the Code of Criminal Instruction, and the Ordinary Penal Code, which were required to be in the courtroom— as her prosecutor or the members of the tribunal.

The room was crowded with spectators and reporters, for word of the trial had leaked out. Something as titillating as the espionage trial of the notorious Mata Hari, whose dancing had thrilled so many, was not to be missed. Many of the reporters and spectators had seen her dance; all knew of her many triumphs; most would consider her a glamorous sex symbol, the epitome of seductiveness.

Semprou asked the accused to state her full name, date and place

of birth, civil status, profession, and address. Mata Hari did so, with
dignity. The court was then officially convened. The first action
was taken by Mornet, who requested that the courtroom be cleared
of spectators for reasons of security, since it was anticipated that
state secrets would be discussed. He also asked that publication of
the trial record be prohibited. After some discussion among the tribunal members, these motions were granted. Guards removed everyone from the room save the accused, the tribunal, the attorneys,
and other necessary officials, and kept spectators ten meters from
the doors, so they could not overhear the proceedings. Major Émile
Massard, in his memoirs, claimed he was also present as the representative of Governor Dubail, but his presence is not mentioned in
documents. Bouchardon also claimed to have witnessed the trial,
but his presence is not recorded.

The only available accounts of the trial are the official judgment
(now declassified), which does not detail the lines of questioning; a
letter about the trial written after the fact by Captain Jean Chatin,
one of the judges; and eyewitness accounts written years later by
Bouchardon and Massard, who may not have been present at the
trial. Massard and Bouchardon report exchanges with Mornet that
are sometimes identical to or at least closely parallel to those during
Mata Hari's interrogation. Either Mornet followed Bouchardon's
questions very closely, and Mata Hari's responses were sometimes
word-for-word repetitions, or those "eyewitness accounts" are
based on the interrogations and not the trial itself.

Captain Chatin's letter about the trial was reproduced by Massard in his memoirs. Chatin's words reveal the impression of Mata
Hari that was given to the tribunal judges during the trial. First he
congratulated Massard on facing up to someone who suggested that
Mata Hari had been unjustly convicted.

On what is this person [basing his conclusion]? . . . Well, me, I relied on the proofs that I had in my hands, and on the confessions of this vile spy, to affirm that she caused to be killed about 50,000 of our children, not counting those who found themselves on board vessels torpedoed in the Mediterranean upon the information given by H21 no doubt.

Moreover, it must be remembered that H21 was in Germany, in July 1914, the mistress of a German prince, and that after she was justly condemned to death, no recourse or pardon was to be given, so evil was her cause.

No evidence could have been presented about how Mata Hari caused the death of fifty thousand children, or the torpedoing of ships, because Bouchardon had uncovered none. As for the German prince whose mistress Mata Hari allegedly was in July 1914, he was the policeman Griebel—hardly a prince.

Bouchardon's report on the questioning of Mata Hari was presented to the court by the prosecution, including his conclusion that she was a "born spy." Mornet's subsequent questioning must have been designed to bring out precisely those points that Bouchardon had emphasized in his report: that Mata Hari was immoral and highly sexual; that she spent a great deal of time with officers from various armies; that she traveled during wartime; and that she accepted money from men, some of whom were involved in espionage.

Mornet called five witnesses.

The first was Inspector Monier, one of the two who had tailed Mata Hari all over Paris for so many months. He certainly testified about her extravagant ways and the many influential men she was seen with, but he could not supply any damning evidence of espionage because he had been able to uncover none. Police Commissioner

Alfred Priolet testified about her arrest and the items seized from her hotel room, none of which constituted evidence of espionage.

Then Captain Ladoux and his superior, Colonel Goubet, presented their view of Mata Hari and her enrollment as a spy for France as a clever means of unmasking her as a German spy. In Goubet's words, she was "one of the most dangerous that counter-espionage ever captured." Mornet almost certainly asked Mata Hari why she had not confessed to Ladoux that she had already accepted money from Kroemer to spy for Germany when Ladoux asked her to spy for France. She repeated that she had done nothing for Kroemer or the Germans—that she regarded the twenty thousand francs as reimbursement for her seized furs—and that it would have been foolish of her to tell Ladoux about this. She wanted Ladoux to trust her and give her a big mission for France, both to help the French and, more important, to give her sufficient funds to support Vadime for the rest of their lives together.

Ladoux must also have testified extensively about the H21 telegrams, since he was the main expert on this subject. Much more plainly than anything else, these telegrams, *if* they were genuine, identified Mata Hari as a German agent. Further, if his testimony followed his depositions, Ladoux would have denied that he ever recruited Mata Hari as a spy for France or gave her a mission, falsehoods that destroyed the credibility of her version of events. If the head of the Deuxième Bureau swore that Mata Hari had never been a spy for France, then her activities as a double agent were reduced to simply being a single agent, for Germany. Ladoux's testimony constituted the primary evidence that Mata Hari was engaged in espionage for Germany.

Two witnesses that Mornet wished to call, Vadime de Massloff and Lieutenant Hallaure, were unable to attend the tribunal. Mata Hari must have been relieved not to have to face Vadime and hear him deny loving her. The trial proceeded without them, but their depositions were read aloud.

Mornet closed his summation with a theatrical pronouncement that would have played well on the stage: "The evil that this woman has done is unbelievable. This is perhaps the greatest woman spy of the century."

The tribunal was adjourned at 7:00 P.M. Accompanied by a guard, Mata Hari made her way back to the Concièrgerie and Sister Léonide. On July 25 the tribunal was convened again at 8:00 A.M.

Clunet was invited to present his defense and called various influential men as witnesses.

Jules Cambon of the Ministry of Foreign Affairs, Mata Hari's former lover who had helpfully thought up the stratagem to delay the Dutch government from learning about her imprisonment, testified that she never asked him about military or diplomatic affairs.

Another potential witness was Alfred Messimy, who had been minister of war when war was declared. He had spent some idyllic days and nights in Mata Hari's company. Though summoned to court, Messimy did not appear. His wife—who signed herself boldly "Andrée Messimy, née Bonaparte"—sent a letter to Semprou stating that her husband was ill with rheumatism and had never met Mata Hari in any case. It seemed that marital considerations prohibited Messimy's testifying on Mata Hari's behalf. Messimy's name was not mentioned in court; he was only identified as M——y, a cabinet minister, when some of his letters to Mata Hari were read out in court. Messimy's categorical denial of an affair with Mata Hari led to the widespread presumption that the lover in question was Louis Malvy, the minister of the interior, whose subsequent political career was damaged as a result.

Henri de Marguérie, a lover since the time of Mata Hari's debut in Paris, courageously came to court to testify for her. During his first wartime visit to Paris in 1915, he recalled, "Madam did not ask me a single question" about politics or military matters. "You well know she is not a spy!" he reproached Mornet, according to one account. Mornet feigned incredulity that he had spent three days in Mata Hari's company in 1915 and yet never once discussed the war, the obsession of the day. "We spoke of art, Indian art," de Marguérie insisted. "Nothing had ever spoiled my good opinion of this lady."

His assertion tallied well with the depositions from Hallaure and Vadime—and, though they were not presented, with depositions from dozens of other men. In addition to her beauty, part of Mata Hari's appeal to the war-weary men she entertained was precisely that: she did not speak of war, she spoke of music, art, theater, books, anything to help them forget the horrors they had endured and had yet to endure. Men on leave from the front did not want to discuss the hell from which they had come; they wanted peace, magic, pretty women, and music. Men in positions of importance who were charged with ordering soldiers to their deaths, or calculating how long a regiment might hold an impossible position, felt the same, no doubt.

Clunet's quiet reasoning as he pointed up the flaws and inconsistencies in the prosecution's case was certainly heard. Doubtless he argued for Mata Hari's rather different interpretation of numerous events. But his impassioned words made little impact on the members of the tribunal compared with the lurid accusations hurled at Mata Hari by the prosecution.

By the end of July 25 the evidence had been presented and the arguments heard. Massard reported that, during Clunet's summation, he watched Mata Hari transform herself, as an actress does, from a mere woman to "a siren with strangely compelling charm." She smiled brilliantly at the judges, and Colonel Semprou asked if she had any closing words with which to defend herself. "My defense is to speak the truth. *I am not French*. I have the right to have friends in other countries, even those at war with France. I remain neutral. I count on the good hearts of French officers."

She seemed confident, though this attitude was probably mere performance. Where was the evidence that she had harmed France? Where were the secrets she was supposed to have passed? Why should the officers of France turn against her, when so many French officers had loved her?

Semprou declared the hearings closed, and the judges retired to consider their verdict. According to Massard, they deliberated for only forty-five minutes. Massard also claimed to have heard a Commander C— (not a member of the tribunal) remark while the judges were out of the room: "It is frightful to send to death a creature so seductive with such intelligence. . . . But she has caused such disasters that I would condemn her twelve times if I could!"

They had eight charges to consider, the eight that Bouchardon had recommended for prosecution in his report.

Had she entered the entrenched camp of Paris in December 1915? Yes. This point was uncontested. Since all of Paris was considered an "entrenched camp," Mata Hari did enter the entrenched camp of Paris in December 1915—on a government-approved visa. The tribunal agreed unanimously. She was guilty.

Had she given documents and information to Consul Kroemer while she was in The Hague, during the first six months of 1916? Six men voted yes although no evidence was produced that Mata Hari gave any documents or information to Kroemer. She was again guilty; one voted no.

Had Mata Hari maintained contact or talked with Kroemer in May 1916? The judges—and Mata Hari in her testimony—concurred that she had indeed met with Kroemer in May of 1916.

(Actually, she met with him in the autumn of 1915, though her memory was faulty on this point.) To demonstrate the breadth of this charge, contact was probably also maintained with Kroemer during May of 1916 by his butcher, baker, cook, and many other people wholly innocent of espionage. Mata Hari was again pronounced guilty.

Had she returned to Paris in June of 1916 with the intention of obtaining information to aid the German cause? Again, each judge voted yes, as she clearly did return to Paris in June 1916. No evidence of Mata Hari's *intention* was produced, but the charge was framed in such a way that the judges could not agree to the statement of fact (that she was in Paris in June of 1916) and disagree with the statement of intention. She was guilty again.

Had she maintained contact with Germans while she was in Paris in 1916? Again, most voted yes, but one man still answered no, since the prosecution had produced no evidence of meetings, telegrams, or letters passing between Mata Hari and the Germans.

Had she maintained contact with Germans, in the person of Kalle, while she was in Madrid in December of 1916 with the intention of furthering the aims of Germany? She admitted that she had been in Madrid in December and had met with Kalle. The second part of the charge was not separately supported by any evidence, and Mata Hari testified that her meetings were in the service of France. Nonetheless, she was considered guilty by unanimous vote.

Had she passed "documents susceptible to damaging the operations of the army or of endangering the security of places, posts or other military establishments, said documents or information dealing in particular with interior politics, the spring offensive, the discovery by the French of the secret of German invisible ink, and the disclosure of the name of an agent in the service of England"? This was a complex charge.

Yes, she gossiped with Kalle about Princess George of Greece, about political maneuverings in Paris, and about rumors of a spring offensive. Any of these topics were in the daily newspapers, and even Bouchardon and Mornet, who were totally convinced of Mata Hari's evil intentions, could not support the accusation that she had passed vital details along on any of these matters. What precisely was meant by the part of the charge that dealt with invisible ink is mysterious; Mata Hari had reported to Denvignes information *from* Kalle that German agents carried invisible ink in crystals under their fingernails, but this hardly constituted passing information *to* Kalle. Ladoux claimed he had told her that the French had discovered how to reveal all invisible inks used by the Germans, but this discovery occurred after she had left Spain, so she cannot have passed Kalle that information. The last part of the charge implies that Mata Hari revealed the identity of an Allied agent to the Germans. On her voyage on the *Hollandia,* she had been told by the captain that a Belgian couple on the ship named Allard were spies. He worked for England, she for Germany, was the shipboard gossip. She repeated this story to an Allied agent in Madrid and to Kalle. And so, on this charge also, she was judged to be guilty by six members of the tribunal, innocent by one.

The final charge was that in January 1917 Mata Hari had maintained contact with Germans in Paris. No meetings were observed during her extensive surveillance, nor were there letters, phone calls, or telegrams. Nonetheless, the tribunal voted unanimously that she was guilty of this charge.

Pronounced guilty on all charges, Mata Hari needed to be sentenced. Semprou asked the tribunal to vote that she should be shot, and they concurred.

The tribunal returned to the courtroom. With much pomp and circumstance, the verdict and sentence were read.

IN THE NAME OF THE PEOPLE OF FRANCE,

The Third Permanent Council of War of the military government of Paris has rendered the following judgment:

Today, *the twenty-fifth of July 1917*, the Third Permanent Council of War in Paris, heard by the Commissioner of the Government in the requisitions and conclusion, has declared

the named ZELLE, Marguerite, Gertrude, called Mata-Hari,

divorcée of Mr. Mac Leod,

guilty of espionage and intelligence with the enemy with the end of assisting his enterprises.

In consequence, the aforementioned Council condemns her to pain of death, by application of articles 205 paragraph 2, 206 paragraphs 1 and 2, 64, 69, 269, 139, 187 of the Code of Military Justice and 7 of the Criminal Code.

And, by the articles 139 of the Code of Military Justice and 9 of the Law of 22 July 1867, the Council condemns the aforesaid ZELLE

to reimburse, by the gifts of her property and by sale, to the Public Treasury, the costs of the trial.

It was not enough that she was sentenced to death, but her possessions were to be sold to pay the French state for the cost of prosecuting and convicting her. The total amount called for was 335.65 francs. The greatest single expense (299 francs), ironically, was the fees to be paid to the medical men who examined her and attested to her ability to withstand the rigors of her imprisonment.

Paris newspapers gleefully reported that Mata Hari, sitting next to Clunet, heard this appalling verdict and whispered, "It's impossible! It's impossible!" Another described her as "a sinister Salomé, who played with the heads of our soldiers in front of the German Herod." The evocation of a biblical seductress who killed heartlessly only heightened public feeling against Mata Hari. She was condemned twice over, once for her sexuality—which was undisputed—and once for her dubiously proven espionage.

Waiting

BACK IN SAINT-LAZARE, Mata Hari was moved to cell number 12, where those condemned to death waited. There were two beds in addition to her own, occupied by other prisoners who had earned a position of trust by their good behavior. The task assigned her companions was to keep her from suicide. Sisters Marie and Léonide also kept a close eye on her. Out of kindness, Sister Léonide brought her a cup of coffee early every morning.

Within a few days, Mata Hari resumed her letter-writing campaign while she awaited the appeal: a review of her trial to determine whether correct procedure had been followed. She wrote to Dr. Bizard, asking for permission to walk for a few minutes in the prison courtyard every day, a privilege that had been given her before the trial but that had been revoked because she was under sentence of death. "I cannot stand it any longer," she wrote. "I need some air and exercise. This will not prevent them from killing me if they absolutely want to, but it is useless to make me suffer, closed in as I am. It is too much to bear."

She received no visitors during this period, no letters except those from Clunet. She attempted to write to Anna Lintjens, each missive asking her to carry out a list of commissions for her, such as paying for a very pretty portrait of her in pastels that she felt either Baron van der Capellan or Anna herself would want to own. She also wrote to her Dutch solicitor Hijmans, in hopes of straightening out the long-unpaid bills with the couturier. She attempted to send letters to the Dutch legation in Paris, though all her letters were read before posting and some were returned to her because of the unflattering description of French justice contained in them. She asked for a list of the objects seized from her and their whereabouts, but this was refused until after her appeal was heard.

On July 28 the Dutch ambassador to Paris was asked to try to have Mata Hari's punishment reduced to a prison sentence, if the appeal was unsuccessful. Mata Hari passed her forty-first birthday on August 7, in Saint-Lazare. On August 17 her appeal was denied.

In September, she became more frantic and wrote more urgently. She wrote to Consul Bunge, in Paris—the man Bouchardon suspected of participating in her espionage activities—begging for assistance in obtaining additional funds from the Netherlands. She also asked what the Dutch government was doing to help her, adding truly: "Here, I am without defense."

Though in prison, Mata Hari was still viewed as potentially dangerous. The request by Maître Milhaud, the solicitor appointed by the court to wind up her affairs, to meet with her was debated, lest she somehow smuggle out vital information. Milhaud's letters to Mata Hari were scrutinized, but he was reluctantly given permission to visit her in prison.

On September 12 a Dutch publisher from Sneek, A. J. Kooij,

wrote what must be one of the most outrageous letters of the entire affair. Knowing Mata Hari was in prison and condemned to execution—and almost certainly acquainted with her now humiliated and embarrassed relatives in Sneek—Kooij wrote asking for the rights to publish her memoirs, which he hoped she was working on. He addressed the letter to her "à Vincennes" (at Vincennes, the execution ground). The letter was forwarded to the Military Government of Paris on September 29, but there is no indication whether she received it. She did not reply. She did, however, have a soldier clerk make four copies of a memoir, for which her account was charged 5.50 francs. However, the chief of the Bureau of Military Justice found it "repugnant" for a soldier to receive money from Mata Hari and denied the payment. The memoir disappeared.

On September 22 she wrote to the Dutch legatee in Paris, van Stuers, to intervene on her behalf and beg for a presidential pardon for her. Since her first appeal had been turned down, her next hope lay with the Supreme Court of Appeals. They too refused to overturn Mata Hari's conviction. Van Stuers and Clunet consulted, and the latter wrote to the Dutch envoy. A request for clemency from The Hague was sent via van Stuers to the French foreign minister, to be forwarded in turn to President Raymond Poincaré. The basis of the request was "for reasons of humanity."

Poincaré never granted such appeals during his tenure and would certainly not commute the sentence of death for one such as Mata Hari. He was dealing with mutinies in both the French and Russian armies. He was so strongly anti-German that he was personally blamed by some for the outbreak of war. His conviction that traitors deserved no leniency was strongly supported by Georges Clemenceau, former prime minister and a rising political power in 1917. Though the two men disliked each other intensely, on November 16 Poincaré suppressed his loathing of Clemenceau and asked him to form a government as prime minister. Clemenceau immediately purged the country of leaders whom he thought weak or traitorous, including Minister of the Interior Louis Malvy, who was wrongly thought to have been a lover of Mata Hari, and Joseph Denvignes, who had indeed been her lover. Poincaré's rejection of the appeal for pardon was sent to Clunet's office on October 13.

On Sunday, October 14, in a last attempt to save his client, Clunet wrote to the commandant, hoping to use a technicality in the law to postpone the execution.

> In the theater world, where everyone is naturally interested in the fate of Mata Hari, the rumor is that she is pregnant. If that is so, and if the pardon is rejected, the execution by the Third Council of War will naturally be suspended. My concern is to beg you to order that a medical expert be consulted to determine the physiological state of the condemned?
>
> ... P.S. My compatriot and friend, the eminent general Marchand, reported as missing in a recent combat, was not killed but imprisoned by the Germans. Why not impose on our enemies the restitution of this general, in exchange for Mata Hari, deprived by us of all value, and the capital punishment commuted to exile?

Clunet's clever appeal did not work. Considering the conditions of her imprisonment and her isolation from all men except the physicians Socquet and Bizard, her remorseless interrogator Bouchardon, and Clunet himself, a recent pregnancy was most unlikely. Even if she had been pregnant, this provision for postponement in such cases was a matter of civil, not military, law. However, the dramatic possibilities of such a last-minute claim appealed to Massard, who wrote a scene in his memoirs claiming that, on the morning of her execution, Clunet all but begged Mata Hari to say she was pregnant by him.

The news of Mata Hari's impending execution had reached Holland in September, but there was little solid information. Neither the Dutch newspapers nor even the Dutch minister of foreign affairs could get a copy of the charges upon which Mata Hari had been sentenced to death. Clunet did not pass on the news of the French president's refusal to pardon Mata Hari to the Dutch envoy immediately, because he did not wish to disturb such an important man on the weekend. When the envoy received the information on the morning of Monday, October 15, Mata Hari was already dead.

The order for her execution was signed on October 14. All her appeals had been exhausted. Clunet was to be taken as a witness to the execution grounds at Vincennes at six-fifteen the following morning. In attendance would be Captain Thibaut, the chief scribe, or recorder, for the Third Council of War (who had not been present at the trial); Lieutenant Colonel Semprou, president of the tribunal; and Lieutenant Choulot, a tribunal judge who had not been present at Mata Hari's trial. The execution would be carried out by firing squad provided by the Fourth Regiment of the Zouaves. The coup de grâce would be delivered by Sergeant Major Petoy of the Twenty-third Regiment of Dragoons. A military physician, Robillard, would be present to declare her dead. Pastor Arboux and Sisters Marie and Léonide from the prison would also attend.

A tender story of dubious accuracy involves Bizard, the resident physician at Saint-Lazare, who learned on October 14 that Mata Hari was to die the next morning. Mata Hari had had great difficulty sleeping since her trial. She worried all night, each night, because she never knew when the sentence would be carried out.

Bizard wrote that he visited her cell on the evening of October 14 and deliberately turned the subject to dancing. He and Sister Léonide asked Mata Hari to show them one of her dances, so she arose and performed for a few minutes. While she was preoccupied, Bizard slipped a dose of chloral hydrate, a sleeping potion, into her water. She would have a good sleep on her last night on earth.

Dying Well

THE CROWD OF MEN woke her in the darkness just before 5 A.M.

Her hated interrogator, Bouchardon, was there along with Jean Estachy, the prison director; Bizard, the prison doctor; Captain Émile Massard, the chief of military staff in Paris; and her dear old attorney, Clunet. The prison pastor, Jules Arboux, was waiting with Captain Thibaut, the chief military recorder of the Third Council of War.

Her time had come. She may have been fuzzy-headed from the chloral hydrate Bizard had slipped into her drinking water the night before. She quickly realized that he had known what would happen on this morning even if she had not. And she understood why the doctor and Sister Léonide had asked her to dance a little for them the night before. They had wanted to see Mata Hari, the true Mata Hari, once before she died. She had shown them as best she could, though her long and wretched months in the dismal prison had stolen most of her grace and loveliness.

Pierre Bouchard and prosecutor André Mornet worked together closely to convict Mata Hari of espionage on flimsy evidence. This photo was taken on the day of her execution. (Collection Roget-Viollet)

The last appeals and requests for pardons had failed; there was no other reason they would awaken her in the dark hours of that cold and foggy morning. She was to be shot at dawn. The nuns hovered in the background as she heard the dreadful news.

She had perhaps already decided to die as she had lived, with flair and courage. She had nothing left but pride and dignity. She would die as Mata Hari.

The men, except for Bizard, left the room while she dressed slowly and carefully for this, her last performance. She wanted to look her best, but she had no extensive wardrobe to choose from, only what her captors had allowed her. She asked permission to wear a corset, which was given. Most accounts say she also donned the only decent clothes she had been allowed, the ones she had worn to her trial: stockings, a low-cut blouse that showed off her beautiful shoulders under a two-piece, dove-gray costume, and fashionable ankle boots. A story from *The Little Parisian*—which would have appeared on October 16, 1917, had it not been suppressed by the censor—described her outfit as a very elegant one trimmed in fur. Sister Léonide and Sister Marie helped her dress, but soon their wrinkled faces streamed with tears and Mata Hari had to comfort them. Then she pinned up her unwashed hair carefully, slowly, as high and elegantly as possible. The gray hairs that she had once hidden with dye were beginning to show badly, which hurt her vanity. She would conceal the gray with her hat.

She felt no need for a last-minute confession, though Pastor Arboux accompanied her and the others to the execution. She was not a religious person. Even had she believed in the power of confession to wipe away sins, she had done nothing wrong in her view: she had only loved men and let them love her. Where was the harm in that? Hurriedly she wrote three last letters, one to her daughter and two to gentlemen friends, probably Vadime and Henri de Marguérie, the one whom she loved still and the other who had so kindly and bravely come to court to testify on her behalf. Naïvely, she trusted her captors to see to their delivery. She handed them over to the pastor, but the letters were never seen again. Her jailers were taking no chances of posthumous protest. She made no will.

She checked her hair, set a three-cornered hat upon her head and angled it just so, and drew on long, elegant, buttoned gloves. She threw a vivid blue coat over her shoulders like a cape and stood erect to look in the mirror. Her skin was sallow and wrinkled, her once-luxuriant hair now thin and dull, but her carriage was still proud. It would have to do.

With grave dignity, she thanked Dr. Bizard, who had tried to win better treatment for her during her miserable imprisonment. At this gesture, Sister Marie began sobbing like a heartbroken child.

"Do not cry," Mata Hari comforted the sister, wiping her cheeks. "Be cheerful like me. . . . Imagine that I am going on a long journey, that I will return and we will find each other again." They were words she might have spoken tenderly to a lover, to Vadime, but he had abandoned her in her troubles. Now she had only herself to rely on. The situation was familiar; she had made her life and now she would make her own death. "Besides, you will come a little way with me, won't you?" she pleaded with the sister. "You shall accompany me."

She walked down the dank corridor holding Sister Léonide's hand. She refused to let the warder touch her. Prison rats, their fur dark and matted with grease and filth, scurried past in the hallway. Their presence no longer made her shudder. She had become used to them over the months. She, who once lived in the best hotels and finest houses like a queen, did not flinch at mere rats.

At the door there were dozens of strangers: prison officials, journalists, onlookers jostling to catch sight of her. She wondered who they all were. "All these people!" she whispered to Sister Léonide cheekily, as if they were best friends from the theater, peeking out through a gap in the curtain to see the size of the audience. "What a success!" Whoever they were, they would be her audience, and she played her role to perfection. She let herself be led to a black car with its window blinds drawn, but she would not be hustled or hurried. The cortège of five identical cars sped rapidly through the still streets, losing the gawkers and journalists who tried to follow. The procession went to the Caponnière, the muddy fields near Vincennes that were used for drill practice by the cavalry. It was an apt choice. She had always favored military men.

The bleak autumn light of the coming dawn illuminated a somber scene. There was a firing squad of twelve from the Fourth Regiment of Zouaves, in their khaki uniforms and red fezzes, and the sergeant major from the Twenty-third Dragoons in his navy blue uniform with a black beret. She assessed them calmly. They all looked ridiculously young and nervous. In another time and place, she would have charmed and flattered them, made them feel like men of the world, won them over. Now she felt a little sorry for them; to be responsible for executing Mata Hari was going to be a burden to live with, she supposed. There was no time to think of that. She had a performance to give and it required all her nerve and skill.

She refused to be tied to the stake, and so she stood, lonely but regal, in the desolate field on her own. Dawn had broken just minutes before, and the light was still soft and pearly. When the senior officer offered a blindfold, she declined with a dignified movement of her head. "That is not necessary," she said graciously. She waved kindly to the two weeping nuns who had done as much as they could do to comfort her. Their kindness had been a great gift to her. She blew a kiss to the priest—just a moment of naughtiness, she couldn't resist—and another to her lawyer. She knew he was still in love with her. She knew he would think of her for the rest of his dull life.

Thibaut read out the sentence. "By the order of the Third Council of War the woman Zelle has been condemned to death for espionage." His words hung in the quiet misty air. Mata Hari awaited her fate like the magnificent heroine she was. They could take her life but they could not rob her of her identity.

"By God," the sergeant major of the dragoons said in quiet admiration, watching her. "This lady knows how to die."

He lifted his saber and the men shouldered their rifles. Then the sergeant major shouted, *"En joue!"* (Aim!), and then, after a long pause, *"Feu!"* (Fire!) The squad did their duty. No one knew which rifle shots killed her. She was proud and silent as the bullets struck, and then she slumped over, bleeding. Petoy slowly walked over to her flaccid body and administered the coup de grâce, firing one shot into her head. The act was a sort of macabre salute.

Mata Hari was dead.

Robillard, Thibaut, and Choulot signed the execution order, signifying that it had been duly carried out. Pitifully, no one came to claim her body. Her head was sent to the Institute of Anatomy museum in Paris for study with those of other criminals.

The next morning the French newspapers were full of stories about Mata Hari. One identified her as a "choreographic artist of foreign origin" and announced triumphantly:

The items that came into the hands of French justice demonstrated the evidence of the guilt of the accused and the value of the information handed over by her to the enemy.

On the day of the declaration of war, Mata Hari frequented political, military, and police circles in Berlin, [she] was in the service of Germany. She was enrolled under an organization number in the service of German espionage . . . [by] notorious chiefs of espionage, and received from Germany in the month of May 1916, important sums as remuneration for various missions and information she furnished.

Faced with material proofs, she admitted all of these facts.

Of course, she had admitted nothing of the kind, but the truth no longer mattered.

Although there was often an outcry about the secrecy surrounding executions—hundreds of convicted spies were executed during the war—one paper editorialized that the execution was given exactly the attention it deserved. "One does not ask for the crowd to attend such a horrible spectacle—a woman shot. But it must be that the traitors, whatever their sex, know what punishment awaits them."

Several Paris newspapers gave nearly identical reports because they were all following an official press release, which deviated from the truth in several particulars. One used an especially congratulatory headline: "The Spy Mata-Hari Paid Yesterday for Her Crimes." Criticisms of the execution or trial were strongly discouraged, and the official censor suppressed or modified some stories. The overall tone of the press stories was fervently, exaggeratedly patriotic. There was no suggestion of criticism of the French government or military.

Throughout the month of October, *The Times* in Paris ran a regular daily column entitled "Commerce and Intelligence with the Enemy," in which Bouchardon was frequently praised for his successes in achieving convictions of spies. His harsh treatment—and occasional abrogation of rights—of those accused was approved as being entirely necessary to keep France safe. Convicting Mata Hari had made Bouchardon a public hero.

Four days after Mata Hari's execution, Georges Ladoux was arrested as a German spy. It was Ladoux who had enticed her into the shadowy world of espionage; it was he who probably altered the contents of the telegrams that were the only solid evidence against Mata Hari. One of his own agents, Pierre Lenoir, had been arrested a few months earlier for defecting to the enemy. Lenoir protested that the Germans had manufactured evidence that he had been "turned"—all of his activities had been carried out for France, he said. Asked to name his accomplices, he pointed to Ladoux, who seems to have recruited and abandoned more than one agent.

Ladoux was immediately arrested, though the news was kept from the newspapers. Morale was dangerously low in France. News that the head of French counterespionage, the man who had done so much to convict Mata Hari, was in turn being investigated for espionage would be disastrous. Ladoux was suspended from the Deuxième Bureau, put under house arrest, and subjected to relentless questioning.

The case against Ladoux was dismissed on January 1, 1919, but he was rearrested on January 2. After the second arrest, he was imprisoned at Cherche-Midi, a grim military prison that may have been as horrific as Saint-Lazare. Ladoux was interrogated for four months, court-martialed, and finally acquitted on May 8, 1919. "All the world dropped me," Ladoux wrote sullenly of the period of his imprisonment and interrogation, an experience about which Mata Hari could have told him much. His defense was that his arrest was part of a clever plot, planned in all probability by the Germans:

> *At the beginning of August 1914, I was assigned to be a sentinel behind our lines by the greatest of our military chiefs and, as it was my duty, I have rung my alarm bells as soon as the danger appeared to me. It is thus not my fault if they have sometimes left me too exposed, so much so that I was used as primary target by the quiet enemy which approached, at the same time I was exposed also to the attacks which came from our own ranks and which have killed me off . . . [causing] my abrupt departure of the headquarters of the army in October 1917.*

How closely Ladoux's defense of himself against charges of espionage parallels that offered by Mata Hari and Lenoir! All three cases followed the same script: the undertaking of a dangerous job for France; the false accusation supported by false evidence, producing isolation, humiliation, and punishment. It may be that Ladoux himself was the original author of this scenario.

Ladoux's acquittal in May of 1919 may have been influenced as much by the end of the war in November 1918 as by the paucity of proof against him. His name was never fully cleared, however. Ladoux wrote:

> *The day after my acquittal, I asked Clemenceau—in a letter which was without a doubt sharp—what type of reparations he proposed to give me, he responded to me through one of the officers of headquarters, the commandant H———: "Say to Ladoux that he will*

stay in the service and that he will await his dirty turn for his fourth
stripe and his cross." But my comrade confided, he had added in a
voice less rude, "Ladoux has been punished to the end, but it is not
[right for] an officer to cover himself in shit. If he is finally splashed
[by it], too bad for him!"

Clemenceau's dismissal was bitter because Ladoux felt he had
done a superb job as head of the Deuxième Bureau. He bragged that
under his leadership they had arrested five hundred spies, "most of
which were shot, the others condemned to various punishments." If
Ladoux really managed to convict most of those he arrested, then
he had far surpassed the general conviction rate for spies, which at
the time was only about 10 percent. How was this possible? Either
French jurors had an astonishing willingness to convict on thin
evidence—which might have been true in those jingoistic times—
or Ladoux routinely enhanced the evidence against his suspects.

After his acquittal, Ladoux waited four long years to become a
major, at which point he retired from the service. He felt himself ill
used, but he was not convicted and shot as Mata Hari and Lenoir
were. Was Ladoux truly a double agent, working within the French
intelligence service for German advantage? Or was he simply a buf-
foon trying to draw attention from his own errors by using Mata
Hari as a scapegoat?

Though Ladoux probably manufactured evidence against Mata
Hari, even without the telegrams it seems likely that she would have
been convicted. The august judges at the tribunal "heard" Mata
Hari's guilt from Bouchardon and Mornet and never really entertained the idea that she might be innocent of espionage—because
she was surely not innocent of immorality.

Rudolf MacLeod was told of Mata Hari's execution by reporters
in Arnhem on the day of her death. He reportedly remarked,

"Whatever she's done in life, she did not deserve *that*." It was a very fair assessment.

Rudolf hoped she had left a will that would make their daughter, Nonnie, rich. He pursued the matter through the Dutch legation in Paris, fruitlessly. He found she had no will and many unpaid debts and that many of Mata Hari's valuable possessions were still in the prison warehouse. These were sold at auction in Paris on January 30, 1918. Rudolf tried diligently to find out how much money was raised by the sale of her possessions, but the French authorities were evasive. The auction of her possessions yielded 14,251.65 francs (almost $33,000 today), a sum far in excess of the tally of trial costs (335.56 francs, or about $775). The excess never reached Non. There was more than a suspicion of wrongdoing that revived in 1924, when the French newspapers announced an auction of items that had belonged to Mata Hari, especially jewels coming from the clerk of the prisons and the clerk of the Council of War.

Furnishings left in her house in The Hague were auctioned off on January 9 and 10, 1918, because the owners of the house were owed rent. Baron van der Capellan did not attend the auction. Non received nothing from the sale of her mother's possessions.

Non's only inheritance from her famous, infamous mother was congenital syphilis. On August 10, 1919, at the age of twenty-one, she died abruptly mere days before she was supposed to leave to become a schoolteacher in the Dutch East Indies. She had been examined and declared in perfect health very recently. The cause of death was said to be a cerebral hemorrhage or aneurysm, which can be a consequence of congenital syphilis. She was buried in Worth-Rheden, in a grave marked simply OUR NON. Rudolf did not want the tombstone to identify himself and Mata Hari as her parents, though such notations were common on Dutch graves.

Years later, after the Second World War, the prosecutor André

Mornet spoke to a writer, Paul Guimard, about Mata Hari. Guimard wrote: "He did not confide in me to the fundamental basis of the [Mata Hari] affair, but he told me with a supreme indifference, 'Between you and me, there wasn't enough [evidence] to flog a cat.'"

It is chilling that the prosecutor knew the evidence was insubstantial and yet did not desist. Being seen to convict spies, and being seen to punish them harshly, was more important than determining whether a suspect actually was a spy—except, of course, to the falsely accused spy herself.

MATA HARI'S ONLY OTHER LEGACY WAS a rich mélange of myth and legend that still persist. The iconic female spy—beautiful, seductive, utterly duplicitous—owes much to Mata Hari. Numerous rumors and fictional or grossly inaccurate treatments of her life, some written by purported eyewitnesses, have sprung up. The most lurid involve a fictional out-of-wedlock daughter, "Banda MacLeod," who followed her mother into espionage, or a last-minute salvation from the firing squad by a lover. Something about Mata Hari's exotic beauty and elusiveness fostered inventions and lies, during and after her life.

She also left a social legacy, more apparent today than in her own time, as a pioneering self-made and independent woman. She created Mata Hari, deliberately abandoning Margaretha Zelle MacLeod, and shaped her persona out of a talent—and a need—for pleasing men. She had no other way to live. A settled married life was a role for which she was completely unsuited. Even a husband fundamentally different from Rudolf MacLeod would have found her an impossible wife. She traded on her wits, her looks, her artistic talents, and her tremendous intuition about others to become a symbol of sexuality and pleasure that in some ways epitomized the

Belle Époque. When the more puritanical and xenophobic times of the Great War arrived suddenly, Mata Hari knew no other way to behave, to think, to be. The traits that brought her fame and glory were the ones that condemned her to death.

If indeed she was a spy, Mata Hari surely ranks among the world's most inept agents. Her ability to uncover secrets was questionable. Even before the police set tails on her, she was recognized everywhere, known everywhere, and was inevitably the center of attention. Her comings and goings, with whom she dined or danced, were the subject of newspaper gossip columns. She could not be clandestine, unnoticed, ordinary. Wherever she went, she attracted admiration from men and jealous glances from women. She knew what men wanted and needed, and she enjoyed giving it to them. While pillow talk might be seen as an effective means of learning secrets, her lovers were in universal agreement that she did not talk with them about the war. Indeed, it was a large part of her charm that she made them forget the war, the planned offensives, the numbers of men or planes or tanks to be sent to this battle or that. When she gathered a tidbit of information, her attempts at communicating it to her spymaster were the stuff of comedy. She sent uncoded letters to Ladoux through the ordinary mail; she telegraphed him openly; she called at his office repeatedly. She even sent intelligence to Ladoux by confiding it to a French diplomat she met by chance. What chance had such a woman of being a successful spy, much less a double agent?

She was convicted not for espionage but for her lack of shame, her frank admission of loving many men and preferring officers; this was the behavior that so damned her in the eyes of men like Bouchardon, Mornet, and the tribunal judges of the Third Council of War. Most of them were undoubtedly attracted to her themselves. Many may have indulged themselves with chic mistresses in the pleasure-loving years before the war. But having a mistress oneself and condemning a woman for being one were two different things. Officially, not one of the men at the tribunal had the courage to be less than rigidly moralistic.

During the hard days of the Great War, the politicians and military men of France cast Mata Hari in a larger role than that of the irresistible mistress. They demanded she play the femme fatale: a wicked and very sexual woman who brought men to their downfall. Unwittingly and unwillingly, she played the role to perfection.

Though she was unjustly put to death, there was only ever one possible ending to the story of Mata Hari. She was not a woman who could have grown old, lost her looks, and lived a quiet domestic life. Butterflies who live in the sun must die young.

References

For clarity, I refer to the subject of this biography as Mata Hari throughout the notes rather than whatever nickname she was using at the time of various documents. I have standardized spellings and modernized punctuation and format in quotations in the interest of clarity but have not changed emphases.

Many quotations are taken from the dossier "Mata Hari" of the Service Historique de l'Armée de la Terre (SHAT) in Vincennes, France. Most documents are numbered by *pièce* (piece or item), but some are numbered following the letter R (*résidu*, or residue) or S-DR (*sous-dossier résidu*, or under-dossier residue) and some are not numbered (non-cotée).

British government documents are cited by the number assigned by the Public Record Office (PRO) and, often, the Metropolitan Police (MEPO).

Many citations refer to a series of reports and documents in the archives of the former Ministry of the Colonies (Ministerie von Koloniën), now in the Algemeen Rijksarchief, The Hague. The general citation for these reports is *Verbaal*, followed by the date on which the memorandum, note, or other document was written, with the (different) date of publication, a number, and a page. The references and information are taken from a paper by Hanneke Ming, "Barracks-Concubinage in the Indies, 1887–1920," *Indonesia* 35 (April 1983): 65–93.

All details of Rudolf's military career have been traced through the *Stamboeken Officieren* (Register of officers) *1814–1929*, in the Nationaal Archief, The Hague, Inv. Nr. 624 (2.13.07), item 405, p. 110, and item 624, p. 98. This is the official source for all dates, postings, salary, and details of his career unless otherwise stated.

Books and articles are referred to below in full the first time they are mentioned in each chapter and in abbrieviated form thereafter.

Whenever possible, I have given the modern equivalents for monetary amounts using the excellent website http://eh.net/hmit. I first converted amounts and currencies into U.S. dollars of the day using a procedure published by Lawrence Officer ("Exchange Rate Between the United States Dollar and Forty Other Countries, 1913–1999," Economic History Services, EH.Net, 2002, http://eh.net/hmit/exchangerates/). Then I calculated the modern equivalent of that value in terms of buying power using another segment of the same website (John J. McCusker, "Comparing the Purchasing Power of Money in the United States [or Colonies] from 1665 to 2005," Economic History Services, 2006, http://www.eh.net/hmit/ppowerusd/). These conversions are not individually cited in the notes.

Notes

Prologue

2 *"There is something"*   SHAT, *pièce* 312, 5 June 1917.

Chapter 1 The Little Orchid

3 *think of herself as special*   Information about Mata Hari's early life from Sam Waagenaar, *Mata Hari* (New York: Appleton-Century, 1965), 5–11.

3 *an orchid*   Ibid., 8.

5 *"an* amazing *bit of foolhardiness"*   Ibid., 6.

6 *27,000 inhabitants*   Russell Warren Howe, *Mata Hari: The True Story* (New York: Dodd, Mead, 1986), 5.

6 *declare bankruptcy*   Dossier Zelle, Centraal Bureau voor Genealogie, The Hague.

7 *violent quarrels*   Howe, *True Story*, 18.

8 *"This day it pleased"*   Dossier Zelle.

8 *"I was playing"*   Waagenaar, *Mata Hari*, 9.

10 *minimum height for men*   E. M. Beekman, "Alexander Cohen," in *Fugitive Dreams: An Anthology of Dutch Colonial Literature*, ed. E. M. Beekman (Amherst: University of Massachusetts Press, 1988), 184–209.

10 *five thousand florins*   Charles S. Heymans, *La Vraie Mata Hari: Courtisane et Espionne* (Paris: Étoile, 1936), 5.

10 *the headmaster, Wybrandus Haanstra*   Information about Haanstra and the school from http://www.deschoolanno.nl/S.inBeeld/sibjrg11_15/sib1102.htm, accessed 7 July 2005.

11 *"Such a job"*   Waagenaar, *Mata Hari*, 1.

11 *a sexual relationship*   Ibid., 11; Sam Waagenaar, "Mata Hari as a Human Being," ms., Fries Museum, ca. 1927, 4; Julie Wheelwright, *The Fatal Lover: Mata Hari and the Myth of Women in Espionage* (London: Collins & Brown, 1992), 10; Heymans, *Vraie*, 22; Bernard Newman, *Inquest on Mata Hari* (London: Robert Hale, 1956), 179.

11 *until his death*   Information from http://www.deschoolanno.nl/S. inBeeld/sibjrg11_15/sib1102.htm, accessed 7 July 2005.

12 *Mysteriously, there are no documents*   Personal communication, Michiel van Halem to Paul Storm, 21 January 2005.

Chapter 2 *Different Lives*

15 *Approximately 7,700 officers*   General information on the Atjeh War taken from M. C. Ricklefs, *A History of Modern Indonesia Since c. 1300*, 2d ed. (Stanford, Calif.: Stanford University Press, 1993), 144–46; also C. M. Schulter, "Tactics of the Dutch Colonial Army in the Netherlands East Indies," *Revue internationale d'histoire militaire* 7 (1988): 59–67.

17 *"December 6, already 302 sufferers"*   J. van Swieten, *"De waarheid over onze vestiging in Atjeh met een kaart van Atjeh en een plan van den Kraton (The truth about our settlement in Atjeh: with a map of Atjeh and a plan of Kraton)*) (Zaltbommel: Noman, 1879), 7.

17 *more than 8,000 soldiers*   Information from http://www.engelfriet.net/Alie/Hans/Aceh.htm, accessed July 2005.

17 *at least three-quarters of the enlisted men*   E. M. Beekman, "Alexander Cohen," in *Fugitive Dreams: An Anthology of Dutch Colonial Literature*, ed. E. M. Beekman (Amherst: University of Massachusetts Press, 1988), 196.

18 *a twelve-foot-long behemoth*   This cannon and several others are on exhibit at Museum Bronbeek—Museum ran het Koninklijk Tehuis voor oud-Militairen in the Netherlands.

18 *medical treatment was minimal*   See J. A. de Moor, "An Extra Ration of Gin for the Troops: The Army Doctor and Colonial Warfare in the Archipelago, 1830–1880," in *Dutch Medicine in the Malay Archipelago 1816–1942: Articles Presented at a Symposium Held in Honor of Professor De Moulin*, ed. G. M. van Heteren, A. de Knecht-van Eekelen, and M. J. D. Poulissen (Amsterdam and Atlanta: Rodopi, 1989), 133–52.

18 *"An expedition in the Outer Districts"*   Ibid., 140.

18 *"So every day"*   M. Van Adringa, "Geneeskundig verslag van de expeditie tegen Latoentoer, zuider en ooster afdeeling van Borneo" (Medical report of the expedition against Latuntur, South and East District of Borneo), in *Geneeskundig Tijdschrift Nederlandsch-Indië* (1862): 84, cited ibid., 147.

19 *A total of 1,052 men*   J. W. F. Herfkens, *De Atjeh-Oorlog van 1873 tot 1896* (*The Atjeh War of 1873 till 1896*), recast and completed by J. C. Pabst (Breda: De Koninklijke Militaire Academie, 1905), 72; similar figures given in Schulter, "Tactics," 62.

19 *"to remain in Atjeh for ever"*   Schulter, "Tactics," 62.

19 *"I have seen a mother"*   Colijn was later adjutant to van Heutsz and, still later, prime minister of the Netherlands. This letter is reproduced on http://home.iae.nl/users/arcengel/NedIndie/heutsz.htm, accessed July 2005.

20 *"Jan Fusilier"*   H. L. Zwitzer and C. A. Heshusius, *Het Koninklijk Nederlandsch-Indisch Leger 1830–1950* (*The Royal Dutch Indies Army, 1830–1950*) (The Hague: Staatsuitgevrij, 1977), 10.

20 *arak*   De Moor, "Extra Ration," 136.

20 *"fortifying provisions"*   Ibid., 140.

21 *They worked in the open air*   Report of Johannes Godfried Kerlen, 1873–9, of his experiences in the Atjeh War, reproduced in http://www.engelfriet.net/Alie/Hans/Aceh.htm, accessed July 2005.

21 *ran out of these vital medicines*   Xavier Brau de Saint-Pol Lias, *Chez les Atchés: Lohong* (*Among the Atjeh: Lohong*) (Paris: Plon Nourrit et Cie, 1884), 21.

21 *A mere 10 to 15 percent*   A. H. M. Kerkhoff, "The Organization of the Military and Civil Medical Service in the Nineteenth Century," in van Heteren et al., *Dutch Medicine*, 9–24.

22 *sinkhole or sewer of Europe*   Hanneke Ming, "Barracks-Concubinage in the Indies, 1887–1920," *Indonesia* 35 (April 1983): 65, citing *Verbaal*, no. 4 (20 January 1902): 6; and Beekman, "Alexander Cohen," 194.

22 "Orang Atjeh datang!"   J. R. Jacobs, *Neerlands Driekleur in Neerlandsch-Indië door Neerlands Dapperen bewaakt*: "Schetsen uit het Indische Krijgsleven; met Portretten opgedragen aan de Ridders de Militaire Willemsorde, benelef den rang van Officier door J. R. Jacobs, Kapitein der Infanterie van het Ned.-Ind. Leger" (*The Dutch Tricolor in the Netherlands Indies by Dutch Heroes*: "Sketches of the Indies Warbook, with portraits of the behavior of the Knights of the William's Cross, under the rank of officer by J. R. Jacobs, Captain of the Infantry of the Netherlands-Indies Army") (Rotterdam: Nijgh and Van Dilmar, n.d.), 44.

22 *a sharp defeat*   Brau de Saint-Pol Lias, *Chez*, 10.

23 *"stunned by the rapidity"*   Ibid., 8.

25 *"finagled" not to give it*   Sam Waagenaar, *Mata Hari* (New York: Appleton-Century, 1965), 13.

25 *He coyly asserted*   Charles S. Heymans, *La Vraie Mata Hari: Courtisane et Espionne* (Paris: Étoile, 1936), 12–13.

25 *Women comprised less than 20 percent*   A. Van Marle, "De Groep der Europeanen in Nederlands-Indië, iets over ontstaan en groei" (The European group in the Netherlands-Indies, its origin and growth"), parts 1–3, *Indonesië* 5 (1951/1952): 10.

25 *Indisches or Indos*   Roger Wiseman, "Assimilation Out: Europeans, Indo-Europeans and Indonesians Seen Through Sugar from the 1880s to

the 1950s," paper presented to the ASAA 2000 Conference, University of Melbourne, 3–5 July 2000.

26 *Those without concubines*   Ming, "Barracks-Concubinage," 70.

26 *"necessary evils"*   Ibid., 81, 83–87; and Beekman, "Alexander Cohen," 201–2.

26 *most of the male Europeans*   Van Marle, "Europeanen," part 3, 485.

26 *the right of a soldier to have*   Ming, "Barracks-Concubinage," 67, citing *Verbaal,* 4 August 1913, no. 71, Exhibitum 7 October 1912, no. 131: 17.

26 *By 1872, military regulations*   Anonymous, *Een onderzoek naar den toestand van het Nederlandsch-Indisch Leger, uit een zedelijk oogpunt beschoouwd, ter ernstige overweging aangeboden door de Vereeniging tot bevordering der Zedelijkheid in de Nederlandsche Overzeesche Bezittingen en de Nederlandsche Vereeniging tegen de Prostitutie (Research into the state of the Dutch Indies Army, from the point of view of moral considerations, for the serious consideration by the Society for the Promotion of Morality among Dutch Overseas and the Dutch Society against Prostitution)* (Press and publisher unknown, n.d.), 86. See also General Order no. 62 of 1872, cited in Ming, "Barracks-Concubinage," 70.

26 *Prostitutes living in the barracks*   Ming, "Barracks-Concubinage," 84, citing *Verbaal,* no. 89 (13 May 1902).

26 *fewer men who cohabited*   Liesbeth Hesselink, "Prostitution: A Necessary Evil, Particularly in the Colonies: Views of Prostitution in the Netherlands Indies," in *Indonesian Women in Focus,* ed. Elsbeth Locher-Scholten and Anke Niehof (Leiden: KITLV Press, 1992), 205–24.

26 *"The moral standards"*   Ming, "Barracks-Concubinage," 70, citing *Verbaal,* no. 47 (29 December 1903): 13.

27 *"Unnatural vice"*   Ibid., 69, quoting postscript to report of 18 March 1893, in *Verbaal,* no. T1 (21 January 1903).

27 *girls in military brothels*   Ibid., 70.

27 *from twelve to perhaps thirty-five* Ibid., 73, citing J. T. Koks, *De Indo* (Amsterdam: H. J. Paris, 1931), 53.

27 *a single visit to the brothel* Ibid., 71, n. 32.

27 *"women's sheds"* Ibid., 68, citing report of 18 March 1893, in *Verbaal*, no. Tl (21 January 1903).

28 *inspected weekly for signs* Ibid., 68; Hesselink, "Prostitution," 207.

28 *no effective cure for syphilis* Deborah Hayden, *Pox: Genius, Madness, and the Mysteries of Syphilis* (New York: Basic Books, 2003), 36; Claude Quetel, *History of Syphilis*, trans. Judith Braddock and Brian Pike (Cambridge, U.K.: Polity Press, 1990), 6, 142.

28 nyai Ann Solter, "Sexual Affronts and Racial Frontiers: European Identities and the Cultural Politics of Exclusion in Colonial Southeast Asia," in *Tensions of Empire: Colonial Cultures in a Bourgeois World*, ed. Frederick Cooper and Ann Laura Stoler (Berkeley: University of California Press, 1997), 199–237.

28 *"for that . . . is prescribed by* adat" Ladislao Székely, *Tropic Fever: The Adventures of a Planter in Sumatra*, trans. Marion Saunders (1937; Kuala Lumpur: Oxford University Press, 1984), 110, 112.

28 *a* nyai's *influence* Lily E. Clerkx and Wim F. Wertheim, *Living in Deli: Its Society as Imagined in Colonial Fiction* (Amsterdam: Vrije Universiteit Press, 1991), 18.

29 Nyais *ran the kitchens* Ming, "Barracks-Concubinage," 67, citing *Verbaal*, 4 August 1913, no. 71, Exhibitum 24 February 1913, no. 111: 8, and no. 109, and Exhibitum 10 July 1916: 2.

29 *"walking dictionaries"* Rob Niewenhuys, *Leven tussen twee vaderland* (Life between two fatherlands) (Amsterdam: De Engelbewaarder, 1982), 18–19.

29 *"And now, hurry up"* H. Veersema, *Delianen van de tafelronde* (*Deli tales around the table*) (Medan: Kohler, 1936), 158, quoted in Clerkx and Wertheim, *Deli*, 31.

29 *if they became pregnant* Madelon Székely-Lulofs, *De Andere werelde*

(*A different world*) (Amsterdam: Elsevier, 1936), 103, 133–34, 296; and *Rubber* (London: Cassell, 1933), 9, 10. See also Székely, *Tropic Fever*, 206, 236–37.

29 *their mother had no further rights*   Anonymous, *Een onderzoek*, 15.

30 *"The* nyai *are numerous"*   Ibid., 5.

30 *overwhelming probability*   See, for example, such Dutch colonial literature as Louis Couperus, *The Hidden Force* (1900), trans. Alexander Teixeira de Mattos, in *Fugitive Dreams: An Anthology of Dutch Colonial Literature*, ed. E. M. Beekman (Amherst: University of Massachusetts Press, 1988); P. A. Daum, *Nummer Elf* (*Number Eleven*) (1893; 's Gravenhage: Thomas & Eras, 1981).

30 *"because of illness"* and *"promotion during leave"* *Stamboeken Officieren* (Register of officers) *1814–1929*, Inv. Nr. 624 (2.13.07), item 405, p. 110.

31 *prolonged periods of . . . convalescence*   See, e.g., Jacobs, "Neerlands," 61.

31 *carried on a stretcher*   Waagenaar, *Mata Hari*, 13.

31 *Rudolf suffered from diabetes*   Erika Ostrovsky, *Eye of the Dawn; The Rise and Fall of Mata Hari* (New York: Dorset Press, 1978), 23.

31 *neither a reliable means of diagnosing*   Christine Ruggere, Institute of the History of Medicine, Johns Hopkins University School of Medicine, e-mail to author, 28 April 2005.

31 *usual nineteenth-century treatments*   C. Savona-Ventura, *The History of Diabetes Mellitus: A Maltese Perspective* (Malat: self-published, 2002), 6.

32 *provokes joint problems*   Jonathan Waltuck, "Rheumatic Manifestations of Diabetes Mellitus," *Bulletin of the Rheumatic Diseases* 49, no. 5 (2000): 1–3.

32 *"Everyone, including the few"*   A. de Knecht–van Eekelen, "The Debate About Acclimatization in the Dutch East Indies (1840–1860)," in "Public Health Service in the Dutch East Indies," *Medical History*, supp. 20: 70–85.

32 *early stages of syphilis*   Hayden, *Pox*, 319.

32 *W (wounded) and F (fever)*   A. H. M. Kerkhoff, "Organization,"

22; also J. van der Werff, "Beknopt overzicht der gescheidenis van der militair-geneeskundige dienst van het KNIL" (Brief historical survey of the military medical service in the KNIL), in *Handboek voor den Officier van Gezondheid van het Koninklijk Nederlandsch-Indische Leger* (Handbook for the Officer's Health in the KNIL), vol. 1, ed. J. M. Elshout (Bandoeng: Vorkink, 1938), 25.

32 *the diseases that killed*   Peter Boomgaard, "Morbidity and Mortality in Java, 1820–1880: The Evidence of the Colonial Reports," in *Death and Disease in Southeast Asia: Explorations in Social, Medical and Demographic History*, ed. Norman G. Owen (Singapore: Oxford University Press, 1987), 48–69.

33 *Malaria constituted 90 to 95 percent*   Peter Gardiner and Oey Mayling, "Morbidity and Mortality in Java, 1880–1949: The Evidence of the Colonial Reports," in Owen, *Death and Disease*, 70–90.

33 *V (venereal), O (ophthalmic)*   Kerkhoff, "Organization," 22; and van der Werff, "Beknopt," 1, 25.

33 *Syphilis was the third most common*   John Ingleson, "Prostitution in Colonial Java," in *Nineteenth and Twentieth Century Indonesia: Essays in Honor of Professor J. D. Legge*, ed. David P. Chandler and M. C. Ricklefs (Clayton, Australia: Centre of Southeast Studies, Monash University, 1986), 123–40, citing Anonymous, *Mededelingen, Burgelijk Geneeskundig Dienst van der Nederlandsch-Indië* (Communications, Civil Medical Service of the Netherlands Indies), part 2, 1939: 99.

33 *alcoholism and venereal disease*   Ming, "Barracks-Concubinage," 84, citing *Verbaal*, no. 89, Exhibitum 13 May 1902.

33 *Syphilis was "rampant"*   Boomgaard, "Morbidity," 51–52.

33 *twice as common in towns with*   Anonymous, *Onderzoek naar de Mindere Welvaart der Inlandsche Bevolking op Java & Madoera* (Study of the declining welfare of the native population on Java and Madoera), vol. 2 (Batavia: Drukkerij G. Kolff, 1912), 24.

34 *an average of 127 prostitutes*   G. H. Von Faber, *Oud Soerabaia* (Old Surabaya) (Surabaya: Gemeente Surabaya, 1931), 246.

34 *an astonishing 29.4 to 35.9 percent*   J. F. H. Kohlbrugge, "Prostitutie in Nederlandsch Indië"(Prostitution in the Dutch Indies), *Indisch Genootschap* 19 (February 1901): 2–36; S. Weijl, and W. H. Boogaardt, *Pro en contra: Het concubinaat in de Indische kazernes* (Pro and con: Concubinage in the Indies barracks) (Baarn: Hollandia-Drukkerij, 1917), IX, no. 6.

34 *vitamin-deficiency disease*   Information from http://www.mc .vanderbilt.edu/biolib/hc/nutrition/nh1.html, accessed July 2005.

34 *determining the cause of beriberi*   Information from http://nobel prize.org/medicine/educational/vitamin_b1/eijkman.html, accessed 21 July 2005.

35 *mechanized rice processing*   Even after the publication of Eijkman's work, there was considerable resistance to shifting back to unpolished rice and the problem persisted. See E. M. Beekman, "Alexander Cohen," and "Bas Veth," in Beekman, *Fugitive Dreams,* 182n20, 207. See also http://nobelprize.org/medicine/educational/vitamin_b1/eijkman .html, accessed 21 July 2005.

35 *a soldier's soldier*   Waagenaar, *Mata Hari,* 13.

35 *always wore his uniform*   Sam Waagenaar, "Mata Hari as a Human Being," ms., ca. 1927, Fries Museum, 5–6.

35 *told a salacious story*   Ibid., 5.

36 *She loved officers*   Philippe Collas, *Mata Hari: Sa véritable histoire* (Mata Hari: Her true story) (Paris: Plon, 2003), 306.

Chapter 3 Object Matrimony

37 *In 1894, Lombok*   Information from M. C. Ricklefs, *A History of Modern Indonesia Since c. 1300,* 2d ed. (Stanford, Calif.: Stanford University Press, 1993), 134–36; http://home.iae.nl/users/arcengel/ NedIndie/lombokengels.htm; and http://www.aboutbaliisland.com/ Article_Resources/endofkingdom.htm.

39 *"Officer on home leave"*   Sam Waagenaar, *Mata Hari* (New York: Appleton-Century, 1965), 15.

39 *men known to live with* nyais   A. Van Marle, "De Groep Europeanen in Nederlands-Indië, iets over ontstaan en groei" (The European
group in the Netherlands-Indies, its origin and growth), part 3, *Indonesië* 5
(1951/1952): 483; also Hanneke Ming, "Barracks-Concubinage in the Indies, 1887–1920," *Indonesia* 35 (April 1983): 65–93, citing *Verbaal*, a secret
circular by the National Christian Officers' Association, no. 111 (8 April
1913), Exhibitum 24 February 1913: 21, 22, and 26; Ming, "Barracks-
Concubinage," secret communication from General Boetje to Governor-
General in Mr. no. 685, 1904, Ministerie van Koloniën.

39 *concubinage must be gradually*   Liesbeth Hesselink, "Prostitu-
tion: A Necessary Evil, Particularly in the Colonies: Views of Prostitution
in the Netherlands Indies," in *Indonesian Women in Focus*, ed. Elsbeth
Locher-Scholten and Anke Niehof (Leiden: KITLV Press, 1992), 190;
Ming, "Barracks-Concubinage," 79, citing *Verbaal*, no. 7 (8 April 1913),
Exhibitum 7 October 1912, no. 131: 29.

39 *permission before marrying*   Ming, "Barracks-Concubinage," 80,
citing *Verbaal*, no. 23 (17 April 1909).

40 *For enlisted men or NCOs*   Ibid., 83–84, citing communication
of General Boetje to the Governor-General, 6, in Exhibitum 18 November
1903, no. 57.

40 *his manners had deteriorated*   Sam Waagenaar, "Mata Hari as a
Human Being," ms., Fries Museum, ca. 1927, 5.

41 *"Great Imitator"*   Deborah Hayden, *Pox: Genius, Madness, and
the Mysteries of Syphilis* (New York: Basic Books, 2003), 32.

41 *"rheumatism, arthritis, gout"*   Ibid., xvi.

41 *Rudolf showed at least four*   Ibid., 319–20.

41 *"Some years after M'Greet and Rudolf married"*   Mata Hari to Adam
Zelle, 3 August 1901, reproduced in Adam Zelle, *De Roman van Mata
Hari, Mevrouw M. G. MacLeod Zelle: De Levensgeschiedenis Mijner
Dochter en Mijne Grieven tegen Haar Vroegeren Echtgenoot* (*The novel of
Mata Hari, Mrs. M. G. MacLeod Zelle: The biography of my daughter and*

my grievances against her former husband) (Amsterdam: C. L. G. Veldt, 1906), 124–26.

41 *wisdom and ethicality*   "Alfred Fournier," in Claude Quetel, *History of Syphilis,* trans. Judith Braddock and Brian Pike (Cambridge, U.K.: Polity Press, 1990), 150; see also Alfred Fournier, *Syphilis et mariage (Syphilis and marriage),* 2d ed. (Paris: G. Masson, 1890); Paul Diday, *A Treatise on Syphilis in New-Born Children and Infants at the Breast,* trans. G. Whitley (London: New Sydenham Society, 1859); and Rolla L. Thomas, *The Eclectic Practice of Medicine* (Cincinnati: Scudder Brothers, 1907).

41 *Alfred Fournier*   Quetel, *History,* 134–35.

42 *"So yes, a hundred times"*   Ibid., quoting from Fournier, *Syphilis.*

42 *"An individual actually affected"*   Diday, *Treatise,* 207.

42 *"constitutional symptoms"*   Ibid., 210–11.

43 *"now he had an affair"*   Waagenaar, "Human Being," 6.

43 *"I know well"*   Mata Hari to Rudolf MacLeod, n.d., in, Charles S. Heymans, *La Vraie Mata Hari: Courtisane et Espionne* (Paris: Étoile, 1936), 15.

44 *Griet had always found*   G. H. Priem, *De naakte Waarheid omtrent Mata Hari (The naked truth about Mata Hari)* (Amsterdam: n.p., 1907), 32.

44 *"Those who are not officers"*   Emile Massard, *Les Espionnes à Paris: La Vérité sur Mata-Hari* (The Spies of Paris: The Truth about Mata Hari) (Paris: Albin Michel, 1922), 36.

45 *"your loving little wife"*   Heymans, *Vraie,* 15–16; also Mata Hari to Rudolf MacLeod, n.d., in Waagenaar, *Mata Hari,* 15–16.

45 *"You ask me if I am longing"*   Heymans, *Vraie,* 18.

45 *"I thank you for"*   Rudolf MacLeod to Mata Hari, 30 March 1895, ibid., 19.

45 *"Do not believe"*   Mata Hari to Rudolf MacLeod, early April 1895, ibid.

46 *The correspondence was so*   Heymans, *Vraie,* 22.

46 *"Oh darling, I feel"*   Mata Hari to Rudolf MacLeod, n.d., in Waagenaar, *Mata Hari*, 16–17.

47 *"Young but good-looking"*   Waagenaar, *Mata Hari*, 18.

47 *By military regulation*   "Koninklijk Besluit," dated 28 July 1871, no. 28, and the "Indisch besluit," dated 3 October 1870, no. 5, in "Het Staatsblad van Nederlandsch-Indië," no. 143, 1871.

47 *Ministry of Colonial Affairs*   Ming, "Barracks-Concubinage," 80, quoting *Verbaal*, no. 23 (17 April 1909); also Mrs. M. Gaspar-Raven, Bronbeek Museum, e-mail to author, 30 August 2005.

48 *Surprisingly, Rudolf's military*   Neither an application for permission to marry, submitted by Rudolf MacLeod, nor evidence of its granting is recorded in Rudolf's entry in *Stamboeken Officieren 1814–1929*, the authoritative source of information about a military man's career.

48 *"That happens in the best"*   Heymans, *Vraie*, 22.

49 *"I will give my consent"*   Ibid.

49 *"Johnie—don't do it"*   Waagenaar, *Mata Hari*, 20–21.

50 *a rather cruel trick*   Ibid., 21; Waagenaar, "Human Being," 8; and Erika Ostrovsky, *Eye of the Dawn; The Rise and Fall of Mata Hari* (New York: Dorset Press, 1978), 28.

51 *"a number of young men"*   Zelle, *Roman*, 31; Waagenaar, *Mata Hari*, 21.

51 *"Gentlemen, . . . that lady"*   Waagenaar, *Mata Hari*, 21.

51 *"We went to Wiesbaden"*   Priem, *Naakte Waarheid*, 35.

51 *living with Tante Frida was . . . unbearable*   Zelle, *Roman*, 25–26.

52 *"Have you ever heard"*   Priem, *Naakte Waarheid*, 37.

52 *"Well, [the marriage] did alter"* and *"Certainly, but it was also difficult"*   Ibid., 36–37.

53 *he had a date with two women*   Waagenaar, "Human Being," 8; and Waagenaar, *Mata Hari*, 22–23.

53 *apologized for being detained*   Waagenaar, "Human Being," 9.

53 *"the right guidance"* Ibid., 8.

53 *1895 Hotel and Travel Sector Exposition* Information about the 1895 Hotel and Travel Sector Exposition from http://parallel.park.org/Netherlands/pavilions/world_expositions/index.htm.

54 *Calisch loaned Rudolf three thousand guilders* Waagenaar, "Human Being," 9.

54 *half a year's pay* Mrs. M. Gaspar-Raven, Bronbeek Museum, e-mail to author 30 August 2005; also A. Kruisheer, *Atjeh '96* (Weltevreden: N. V. Boekhandel Visser, 1913), app. 13.

54 *"be nice"* Zelle, *Roman*, 44–47.

55 *letters from Rudolf and Griet often complain* E.g., Rudolf MacLeod to Louise Wolsink, 29 July 1900, in Heymans, *Vraie*, 56; and Mata Hari to Adam Zelle, 12 July 1901, in Zelle, *Roman*, 118–21.

55 *still-precarious health* Waagenaar, *Mata Hari*, 23.

55 *Tante Frida . . . continued to criticize* Zelle, *Roman*, 27, 32–33.

55 *reception at the Royal Palace* Heymans, *Vraie*, 28.

56 *"Norman John"* Waagenaar, *Mata Hari*, 23. The date of birth of this child is confirmed by the records in the Centraal Bureau voor Genealogie, The Hague. Thus, Norman was not conceived before his parents were married, contrary to claims by Heymans, *Vraie*, 26.

56 *"ladies" . . . "ice skating club"* Zelle, *Roman*, 43.

Chapter 4 Indies Life

59 *"Physically and morally"* Adam Zelle, *De Roman van Mata Hari, Mevrouw M. G. MacLeod Zelle: De Levensgeschiedenis Mijner Dochter en Mijne Grieven tegen Haar Vroegeren Echtgenoot* (*The novel of Mata Hari, Mrs. M. G. MacLeod Zelle: The biography of my daughter and my grievances against her former husband*) (Amsterdam: C. L. G. Veldt, 1906), 62.

59 *"You get acclimatized"* Madelon Székely-Lulofs, *Rubber* (London: Cassell, 1933), 93–94; similarly in Ladislao Székely, *Tropic Fever: The Adventures of a Planter in Sumatra*, trans. Marion Saunders (Kuala Lumpur: Oxford

University Press, 1984), 93–94; and Rob Nieuwenhuys, *Tussen twee vader-landen* (Between two fatherlands) (Amsterdam: Van Oorschot, 1959), 33.

60 *"A European, no matter"*   Wilhelm Leonard Ritter, unpublished notes, quoted in Rob Nieuwenhuys, *Oost-Indische Spiegel* (1856); reprinted in English, *Mirror of the Indies: A History of Dutch Colonial Literature* (Amherst: University of Massachusetts Press, 1982), xxv–xxvi.

60 *ugly demands for repayment of loans*   Zelle, *Roman*, 68.

60 *a totok, or newcomer*   General information on Indies manners and views from Jean Gelman Taylor, *The Social World of Batavia: European and Eurasian in Dutch Asia* (Madison: University of Wisconsin Press, 1983), 136; and Elsbeth Locher-Scholten, "Orientalism and the Rhetoric of the Family," *Indonesia* 58 (1994): 19–39.

61 *"indecorous in their speech and dress"*   Ann Laura Stoler, *Carnal Knowledge and Imperial Power: Race and the Intimate in Colonial Rule* (Berkeley and Los Angeles: University of California Press, 2002), 60.

61 *"It was precisely when"*   Taylor, *Batavia*, 136.

62 *"Nènèk Tidjah was my* liifbabu"   Rob Nieuwenhuys, "Het Indische kind dat ik was en ben" (An Indies child that I was and am), in Nieuwenhuys, *Tussen*, 18–19. Translated and quoted by E. M. Beekman in his introduction to P. A. Daum, *Ups and Downs of Life in the Indies*, trans. Elsje Sturtevant and Donald Sturtevant (Amherst: University of Massachusetts Press, 1987), 14.

63 "babu *Norman*"   For the names by which *babus* were addressed, see Beekman, "Introduction," 14–15.

64 *more than half (9,360)* and *"characteristic skin color"*   A. Van Marle, "De Groep der Europeanen in Nederlands-Indië, iets over ontstaan en groei" (The European group in the Netherlands-Indies, its origin and growth), part 3, *Indonesië* 5 (1951/1952): 484.

64 *three-quarters of the legally European*   Stoler, *Carnal*, 79.

64 *"Most of the* blijvers" and *(a) have enjoyed*   Van Marle, "Europeanen," part 2, 110.

65 *"if important objections existed"*   Ibid., part 3, 484.

65 *"disease as well as debased"*   Stoler, *Carnal*, 67–68.

65 *extent of criminality*   Ibid., 63, quoting A. de Braconier, *Kinder-criminaliteit in de Verzorging van Misdadig Aangelegd en Verwaarloosde Minderjaren in Nederlandsche-Indië* (*Child criminality in the care of criminal affairs and neglect of minors in the Netherlands Indies*) (Baarn: Hollandia-Drukkerij, 1918), 11.

66 *"I cannot bear the arrogance"*   Hanneke Ming, "Barracks-Concubinage in the Indies, 1887–1920," *Indonesia* 35 (April 1983): 78, citing J. ten Brink, *Oost-Indische Dames en Heeren, Vier Bijdragen tot de kennis van de zeden en usantiën der europeesche maatschappij in Nederlandsch-Indië* (*East Indies ladies and gentlemen, four contributions to the knowledge of the manners and customs of the European society in the Netherlands Indies*) (The Hague: Dienst der Volksgezondheid in Nederlandsch-Indië, 1881), 173–74.

67 *"[Indos] had an image"*   Tineke Hellwig, *Adjustment and Discontent: Representations of Woman in the Dutch East Indies* (Windsor, Can.: Netherlandic Press, 1994), 26.

69 *Gretha enjoyed . . . being high in rank*   Zelle, *Roman*, 73–74.

69 *On May 2, 1898*   Ibid., 75.

70 *low-cut gown in purple velvet*   Charles S. Heymans, *La Vraie Mata Hari: Courtisane et Espionne* (Paris: Étoile, 1936), 34; and Zelle, *Roman*, 77.

71 *Gunung Bromo*   Zelle, *Roman*, 78–81.

72 *slippers and characteristic color*   Taylor, *Batavia*, 145, 147.

73 *her husband's resentful "housekeeper"*   Lily E. Clerkx and Wim F. Wertheim, *Living in Deli: Its Society as Imagined in Colonial Fiction* (Amsterdam: Vrije Universiteit Press, 1991), 92; and Lulofs-Székely, *Rubber*, 127–29.

73 *"No, I have no more"*   Mata Hari to Adam Zelle, n.d., in Zelle, *Roman*, 81.

Chapter 5 The Fatal Move

74 *with the intention of making a fortune* Anna Laura Stoler, *Carnal Knowledge and Imperial Power: Race and the Intimate in Colonial Rule* (Berkeley and Los Angeles: University of California Press, 2002), 26ff.

74 *the Europeans in Medan* Regerings Almanak voor Nederlandsch-Indië *1899–1901* (*Government Almanac for Netherlands-Indies 1899–1901*) (Batavia: Landsdrukkerij, 1901), 12.

75 *one of the lowest percentages of married* A. Van Marle, "De Groep der Europeanen in Nederlands-Indië, iets over ontstaan en groei" (The European group in the Netherlands-Indies, its origin and growth), part 3, *Indonesië* 5 (1951/1952): 496.

75 *at most 2 percent* Hanneke Ming, "Barracks-Concubinage in the Indies, 1887–1920," *Indonesia* 35 (April 1983), 71, citing *Verbaal*, 8 April 1913, no. 71, Exhibitum 7 October 1912, no. 131: 19.

75 *civil servants, had little or no* Van Marle, "Europeanen," part 3, 486.

75 *"The white group defended"* Lily E. Clerkx and Wim F. Wertheim, *Living in Deli: Its Society as Imagined in Colonial Fiction* (Amsterdam: Vrije Universiteit Press, 1991), 99.

76 *"almost everyone went"* Ladislao Székely, *Tropic Fever: Adventures of a Planter in Sumatra*, trans. Marion Saunders (Kuala Lumpur: Oxford University Press, 1984), 50.

76 *"A Delian hari besar"* Clerkx and Wertheim, *Deli*, 21, quoting Veersema, *Delianen*, unknown page.

77 *in favor of continuing* Ming, "Barracks-Concubinage," 83, *Verbaal*, 8 April 1913, no. 71, Exhibitum 7 October 1912, no. 131: 2, 3, 17, 23, 26, 33.

77 *The women had little choice* See, e.g., Madelon Székely-Lulofs, *Coolie*, trans. G. J. Renier and Irene Clephane (Oxford: Oxford University Press, 1982), 92.

78 *In 1898 a mixed-marriage law* Van Marle, "Europeanen," part 2, 320–21.

78 *the family was the emblem* Stoler, *Carnal*, 101–5.

79 nyais *were sometimes forced*   Clerkx and Wertheim, *Deli,* 87ff.

79 *"One man, a Hollander"*   Van Marle, "Europeanen," part 3, 488, citing Edward B. Reuter, ed., *Race and Culture Contacts* (New York: McGraw-Hill, 1934), 74n1.

79 *one European man out of every thirteen*   Van Marle, "Europeanen," part 3, 488–91.

79 *Fully 28 percent*   Ibid., 492.

80 *"This category of children"*   Stoler, *Carnal,* 138, quoting Braconier, *Kindercriminaliteit,* 8.

80 *few Deli planters would employ* sinyos   Ibid., 28.

80 *"Already I have spoken"*   Van Marle, "Europeanen," part 3, 487.

81 *"for about a week"*   Sam Waagenaar, "Mata Hari as a Human Being," ms., Fries Museum, ca. 1927, 9–10.

81 *"It is strange to see this city"*   Rudolf MacLeod to Mata Hari, 28 March 1900, in Sam Waagenaar, *Mata Hari* (New York: Appleton-Century, 1965), 25.

81 *"becoming quite embarrassing"*   Ibid.

82 *"if a little bit frivolous"* and *"from being married"*   Waagenaar, "Human Being," 10.

82 *"You know always"*   Rudolf MacLeod to Mata Hari, 24 April 1899, ibid., 10; and Charles S. Heymans, *La Vraie Mata Hari: Courtisane et Espionne* (*The True Mata Hari: Courtesan and Spy*) (Paris: Étoile, 1936), 38–39.

82 *"You mention that"*   Rudolf MacLeod to Mata Hari, 24 April 1899, quoted in Waagenaar, *Mata Hari,* 25–26; and Heymans, *Vraie,* 38–39.

82 *"The thing that makes me"*   Op cit.

83 *"Who is that naval"*   Op cit.

83 *"I wanted to be bitten"*   Waagenaar, "Human Being," 10.

83 *"A puerile letter"*   Heymans, *Vraie,* 36–37.

84 *"I await your telegram"*   Rudolf MacLeod to Mata Hari, 2 May 1899, ibid., 38–39.

85 *"May God see"*   Ibid.

85 *"God knows"*   Ibid.

86 *about 40 percent of children*   Barbara Stegmann and J. C. Carey, "TORCH Infections: Toxoplasmosis, Other (Syphilis, Varicella-zoster, Parvovirus B19), Rubella, Cytomegalovirus (CMV), and Herpes Infections," *Current Women's Health Report* 2, no. 4 (2002): 253–58.

86 *"A child born with the germs"*   Paul Diday, *A Treatise on Syphilis in New-Born Children and Infants at the Breast*, trans. G. Whitley (London: New Sydenham Society, 1859), 85–86.

88 *"Experience shows"*   Ibid., 208.

88 *needing extra protection*   Stoler, *Carnal*, 55–57, 63–74.

88 *sinking into the moral morass*   Ibid., 63–74.

88 *"Good colonial living"*   Ibid., 71.

89 *"I am glad"*   Rudolf MacLeod to Mata Hari, 14 May 1899, quoted in Waagenaar, *Mata Hari*, 27.

90 *Rudolf was outraged*   Heymans, *Vraie*, 41.

91 *she refused to move forward*   Waagenaar, *Mata Hari*, 28.

Chapter 6 *Death of a Child*

93 *Rudolf noted that Norman's color*   Charles S. Heymans, *La Vraie Mata Hari: Courtisane et Espionne* (*The True Mata Hari: Courtesan and Spy*) (Paris: Étoile, 1936), 41.

93 *"How she makes"*   Rudolf MacLeod to Louise Wolsink, 10 June 1899, quoted ibid., 42–43.

94 *The most detailed account*   Heymans, *Vraie*, 45–46.

95 *"Hair of my only son"* and *"Day of the death"*   Ibid., 46.

96 *"Rudolf refused to permit"*   Ibid., 48.

96 *"Ah, Louise"* and *"Gretha is at the end"*   Rudolf MacLeod to Louise Wolsink, 4 July 1899, quoted ibid., 51.

97 *"The 28th of July"*   Mata Hari to Adam Zelle, 27 July 1899, quoted in Adam Zelle, *De Roman van Mata Hari, Mevrouw M. G. MacLeod Zelle: De Levensgeschiedenis Mijner Dochter en Mijne Grieven tegen Haar*

Vroegeren Echtgenoot (*The novel of Mata Hari, Mrs. M. G. MacLeod Zelle: The biography of my daughter and my grievances against her former husband*) (Amsterdam: C. L. G. Veldt, 1906), 62.

97 *"My child has been poisoned!"* Ibid., 87–88.

98 *versions of the death* Heymans, *Vraie*, 49; and Sam Waagenaar, *Mata Hari* (New York: Appleton-Century, 1965), 28.

98 *A slightly different account* J. H. Ritman, "Ik kende Mata Hari . . ." (I knew Mata Hari), *Tong-Tong* 5 (15 September 1964): 7, 19.

98 *"Greta was a high-spirited"* Ibid., 7.

99 *For a* babu *to thus attack* Tineke Hellwig, e-mail to author, 9 February 2005.

100 *"nyais poison or otherwise kill"* E.g., see Rob Nieuwenhuys, *Tussen twee vaderlanden* (Between two fatherlands) (Amsterdam: Van Oorschot, 1959), 182, 218.

100 *between 1894 and 1899, only fifteen* *Kolonial Verslag* (Colonial report), app. A, 1899 Principal Illnesses.

100 *Fatal doses are tiny* M. Amini, "Arsenic Poisoning: Not Very Common but Treatable," *Shiraz E-Medical Journal* 3, no. 2 (2002); S. M. Bradberry, W. N. Harnson, S. T. Beer, J. A. Vale, "Arsenic Trioxide: A Monograph of the National Poisons Information Service," n.d., available online at http://www.intox.org/databank/documents/chemical/artrxide/ukpid43.htm.

101 *blowing a dried powder of* Datura Carl H. J. Brockelmann, "Vergiftungen durch einheimische Heilmittel und Giftpflanze in Indonesien" (Poisonings by native cures and poisonous plants in Indonesia), *Zeitschreift fur Tropenmedezin und Parasitologie* 12 (1961): 300–7.

101 *Norman's death . . . attack on a white* Ibid., 306.

102 *"Our darling NORMAN JOHN MAC LEOD"* *Deli Courant*, 28 June 1899.

102 *the number of Europeans in eastern Sumatra* *Regerings Almanak voor Nederlandsch-Indië 1899–1901* (Government Almanac for Netherlands-Indies 1899–1901) (Batavia: Landsdrukkerij, 1900), 12.

103 *Norman was the only European*   *Kolonial Verslag (Colonial Register)*, app. A, 1899.

103 *accidental food poisoning*   Glenn Bruce, e-mail to author, 23 March 2005.

104 *According to modern medical texts*   S. T. Kolev and N. Bates, "Mercury: A Monograph of the National Poisoning Information Services, U.K.," 1996, available online at http://www.intox.org/databank/documents/chemical/artrxide/ukpid43.htm.

104 *Children are notoriously*   D. L. Britt and J. M. Hushon, "Biological Effects, Criteria and Standards for Hazardous Pollutants Associated with Energy Technologies" (1976): 6–38; Lars Friberg, Gunnar F. Nordberg, and Velimir B. Vouk, eds., *Handbook of the Toxicology of Metals*, 2d ed., vols. 1 and 2 (Amsterdam: Elsevier Science Publishers, 1986), 41.

104 *"[a child's] gastrointestinal"*   Paul Diday, *A Treatise on Syphilis in New-Born Children and Infants at the Breast*, trans. G. Whitley (London: New Sydenham Society, 1859), 248.

105 *"So long as strength"*   Ibid., 260.

106 *he began their treatment*   Ibid. In animal studies, as little as 1–10 mg. ingested mercuric chloride per kg. of body weight has been found to be toxic, according to the U.S. National Toxicology Program, Acute Toxicity Studies for Mercuric Chloride, information available online at http://www.pesticideinfo.org/List_NTPStudies.jsp?Rec_Id=PC32890.

107 *The lock of hair*   Family of Rudolf MacLeod, telephone conversation with Paul Storm, 7 October 2005, 10 October 2005; Froujke Bos, e-mail to author, 28 September 2005.

108 *left on the S.S.* Riebeck   Stichting Indische Familie Archief, folder "MacLeod."

108 *Rudolf blamed Gretha ... and she blamed him*   Waagenaar, *Mata Hari*, 28; and Zelle, *Roman*, 87–88.

108 *"She was not beautiful"* and *"half joking"*   Ritman, "Ik kende," 7.

109 *"More than ever"*   Mata Hari to Adam Zelle, 2 December 1899, quoted in Zelle, *Roman,* 110–12.

111 *General Reisz . . . never promote him*   Waagenaar, *Mata Hari,* 30.

111 *"It is absolutely essential"* and *"a scum of the lowest kind"*   Rudolf MacLeod to Louise Wolsink, n.d., quoted in Heymans, *Vraie,* 53–55.

112 *"blacken his precious name"*   Ibid.

112 *"One has nothing"*   Rudolf MacLeod to Louise Wolsink, n.d., quoted ibid., 54.

113 *probably went to Kemloko*   In a letter, quoted by Waagenaar, *Mata Hari,* 29, Rudolf MacLeod refers to the plantation as "Kroewoek, near Ulingie." Plantations and the main houses on them were often known by different names. In any case, the Balkstras' Kemloko was also very near Ulingie.

113 *"As a friend of the truth"*   F. H. Roelfsema, Letter to Editor, *Algemeen Handelsblad,* 1936, quoted in Sam Waagenaar, "Mata Hari as a Human Being," ms., Fries Museum, ca. 1927, 12–13.

114 *"Two and a half months"*   Rudolf MacLeod to unnamed cousin, 31 May 1900, quoted in Waagenaar, *Mata Hari,* 31.

114 *Rudolf earned roughly* 700   A. Kruisheer, *Atjeh '96* (Weltevreden: N. V. Boekhandel Visser, 1913), app. 13.

115 *"My dear cousin"*   Rudolf MacLeod to unnamed cousin, 31 May 1900, quoted in Waagenaar, *Mata Hari,* 29.

115 *"Merciful God"* and *"After tomorrow"*   Rudolf MacLeod to Louise Wolsink, 29 July 1900, quoted in Heymans, *Vraie,* 55–56.

116 *the remarkable Paris Exposition*   Attendance figures from http://www.photoart.plus.com/expos/paris1.htm, accessed 14 October 2005; incident documented in Waagenaar, *Mata Hari,* 32.

117 *"Hello, darling"* and *"You can go to hell, bitch"*   Waagenaar, *Mata Hari,* 32.

118 *he could open and read*   Waagenaar, "Human Being," 16.

Chapter 7 Death of a Marriage

119 *"Ah, the Indies is a dirty"* Charles S. Heymans, *La Vraie Mata Hari: Courtisane et Espionne* (*The True Mata Hari: Courtesan and Spy*) (Paris: Étoile, 1936), 61. Only Mata Hari's mother was dead, so the statement that her parents were dead was made for effect and was not accurate.

120 *"As far as I can remember"* G. H. Priem, *De naakte Waarheid omtrent Mata Hari* (*The naked truth about Mata Hari*) (Amsterdam: n.p., 1907), 28–29.

120 *"I have received your letter"* Mata Hari to Adam Zelle, 28 June 1901, quoted in Adam Zelle, *De Roman van Mata Hari, Mevrouw M. G. MacLeod Zelle: De Levensgeschiedenis Mijner Dochter en Mijne Grieven tegen Haar Vroegeren Echtgenoot* (*The novel of Mata Hari, Mrs. M. G. MacLeod Zelle: The biography of my daughter and my grievances against her former husband*) (Amsterdam: C. L. G. Veldt, 1906), 115.

121 *"Honorable sir!"* Adam Zelle to Officer of Justice Batavia, 28 June 1901, quoted ibid., 116–17.

122 *abhorrence of impoverished . . . Europeans* Ann Laura Stoler, *Carnal Knowledge and Imperial Power: Race and the Intimate in Colonial Rule* (Berkeley and Los Angeles: University of California Press, 2002), 34–38.

122 *"And then I have to suffer"* Mata Hari to Adam Zelle, 12 July 1901, quoted in Zelle, *Roman*, 118–21.

124 *"Nothing else except the wish"*; *"But you had"*; and *"My doll!"* Priem, *Naakte Waarheid*, 47–48. Alfred Dreyfus, whose imprisonment on Devil's Island is referred to, was a Jewish captain in the French military who was wrongly convicted of spying for Germany against the French. On the basis of flimsy evidence—some of it forged—and widespread anti-Semitic sentiment, Dreyfus was stripped of his rank and given a life sentence to be served in the notorious prison colony known as Devil's Island, off of French Guiana, in 1895. After enormous controversy and public outcry on both sides, Dreyfus was finally pardoned in 1899 and made a Knight of the Legion of Honor.

125 *"At the end of my tether"*   Mata Hari to Adam Zelle, 3 August 1901, quoted in Zelle, *Roman*, 122–26.

127 *"[Rudolf] has a pension"*   Ibid. Rudolf's pension was, in fact, 233 guilders per month.

128 *Rudolf having fits of rage*   See Claude Quetel, *History of Syphilis*, trans. Judith Braddock and Brian Pike (Cambridge, U.K.: Polity Press, 1990), 160–75. See also Alfred Fournier, *Syphilis de cerveau (Syphilis of the Skin)* (Paris: G. Masson, 1879).

128 *"dictionary of medical sciences"*   A. Dechambre, ed., *Diction-naire encyclopédique des sciences médicales (Encyclopedic Dictionary of Medical Science)*, vol. 14 (Paris: Asselin, 1884).

129 *Rudolf forced Gretha, with a cat-o'-nine-tails"*   Zelle, *Roman*, 133–34.

129 *went down on her knees*   Heymans, *Vraie*, 61.

129 *"Think, to ruin my reputation"*   Rudolf MacLeod to Louise Wolsink, n.d., quoted ibid., 60.

129 *"With great sadness I received"*   Adam Zelle to Mata Hari, September 1901, quoted in Zelle, *Roman*, 134–35.

130 *"What woman cedes"* and *"very clearly annex"*   Mata Hari to Madame A. Goodvriend, 1 March 1902, quoted in Heymans, *Vraie*, 63–65.

130, 131 *"Naturally [Louise]"* and *"I am persuaded"*   Ibid.

132 *the family went to stay briefly*   Ibid., 66.

132 *MacLeods boarded the S.S.* Koningin Wilhelmina   Information from Stichting Indisch Familie Archief, folder "MacLeod."

132 *Her husband accused her*   Heymans, *Vraie*, 67.

132 *There Mr. Calisch*   Zelle, *Roman*, 144.

132 *He became violent again*   Ibid.

132 *Rudolf took Nonnie with him*   Julie Wheelwright, *The Fatal Lover: Mata Hari and the Myth of Women in Espionage* (London: Collins & Brown, 1992), 13.

133 *At the court of Amsterdam*   Zelle, *Roman*, 151–54.

135 *"On request of my brother"*   Ibid., 155, 222.

135 *"through the mud"* and *"like scum"*   Ibid., 155.

136 *The alternative version*   Heymans, *Vraie*, 68.

136 *"I have no more debt"*   J. H. Ritman, "Ik kende Mata Hari . . ." (I knew Mata Hari), *Tong-Tong* 5 (15 September 1964): 7.

136 *"WARNING"*   Heymans, *Vraie*, 69.

136 *on September 2, Gretha and Nonnie moved*   Zelle, *Roman*, 166–67.

137 *"I have suffered terribly"* and *"P.S. I am still"*   Mata Hari to Adam Zelle, 30 September 1902, quoted in Zelle, *Roman*, 168–69.

138 *"I am not well"*   Mata Hari to Adam Zelle, 10 September 1902, quoted ibid., 172–75.

140 *Zelle managed to send*   Ibid., 175–77.

140 *"I have thought long"*   Rudolf MacLeod to Adam Zelle, 13 October 1902, quoted ibid., 180, 222.

140 *he cared nothing for the ruling*   Ibid., 182–83.

140 *perilously close to becoming*   Heymans, *Vraie*, 71.

140 *"The idea that all is arranged"*   Mata Hari to Rudolf MacLeod, n.d., quoted ibid., 70.

141 *pointing out she had no winter clothes*   Ibid.

141 *"What a surprise"* and *"with big kisses"*   Mata Hari to Rudolf MacLeod, 1 November 1902, reprinted ibid., 71.

Chapter 8 The Birth of Mata Hari

143 *"Why Paris?"* and *"I don't know"*   Anonymous, "Mata Hari racontée par l'homme qui à fit la condamner," (Mata Hari told by the man who condemned her) *Paris Match*, 22 August 1953.

143 *she looked better with her clothes on*   Charles S. Heymans, *La Vraie Mata Hari: Courtisane et Espionne* (*The True Mata Hari: Courtesan and Spy*) (Paris: Étoile, 1936), 78.

143 *Rudolf threatened to have the police*   Ibid., 80; and Adam Zelle, *De Roman van Mata Hari, Mevrouw M. G. MacLeod Zelle: De Levensgeschiedenis*

Mijner Dochter en Mijne Grieven tegen Haar Vroegeren Echtgenoot (*The novel of Mata Hari, Mrs. M. G. MacLeod Zelle: The biography of my daughter and my grievances against her former husband*) (Amsterdam: C. L. G. Veldt, 1906), 188.

143 *he threatened to have her . . . state institution*   Adolphe Roberts, "The Fabulous Dancer," part 1, *Dance Magazine*, July 1929: 13–17.

144 *"Behold me, then"*   Mata Hari to unknown, January 1904, quoted ibid., 16.

144 *Ernst Molier had set up his circus*   Information from http://www.peopleplayuk.org.uk/collections/object.php?object_id=443&back=%2Fguided_tours%2Fcircus_tour%2Fcircus_acts%2Ftrickriding.php%3F, accessed 9 November 2005.

145 *"I never could dance well"*   Sam Waagenaar, *Mata Hari* (New York: Appleton-Century, 1965), 36.

145 *"Vague rumors reached me"*   Francis Keyzer, "The Parisians of Paris," *The King*, 4 February 1905.

147 *"Lady MacLeod is Venus"*   Ibid.

148 *The Malay phrase* mata hari   See, e.g., P. H. R. Beuming, *Schetsen uit den strijd op Groot-Atjeh* (*Sketches of the battle of Great-Atjeh*). (Amsterdam: Concordia, 1915), 48.

148 *a letter in 1897 . . . the name Mata Hari*   Waagenaar, *Mata Hari*, 38.

148 *Loge Mata Hari*   Information from http://home.hccnet.cl/wer.davies/fslogemh.html, accessed 5 April 2004.

149 *"In the beginning"*; *"I act as thousands"*; and *"The artistic cachet"*   G. H. Priem, *De naakte Warheid omtrent Mata Hari* (*The naked truth about Mata Hari*) (Amsterdam: n.p., 1907), 53–55.

152 *"My dance is a sacred poem"*   Pierre Bouchardon, *Souvenirs* (*Memoirs*) (Paris: Albin Michel, 1954), 310.

152 *"so feline, extremely feminine"*   *Le Gaulois* (The Gallic), 17 March 1905.

153 *"Lady MacLeod, that is to say Mata Hari"*   *Parisian Life*, 1905, quoted in Waagenaar, *Mata Hari*, 42.

153 *"She is tall and slender"*   Edward LePage, *Éclair* (Flash), 15 March 1905, quoted in Sam Waagenaar, "Mata Hari as a Human Being," ms., Fries Museum, ca. 1927, 20.

153 *"Mata Hari does not perform"*   Henri Ferrare, *La Presse* (*The Press*), 1905, quoted in Waagenaar, *Mata Hari*, 47.

Chapter 9 The Toast of Europe

155 *"She did not actually dance"*   Colette, *Figaro*, December 1923, quoted by Sam Waagenaar, *Mata Hari* (New York: Appleton-Century, 1965), 44.

156 *notorious lesbian garden parties*   George Wickes, *The Amazon of Letters: The Life and Loves of Natalie Barney* (London: W. H. Allen, 1977), 92; and Diana Souhami, *Paris, Sappho and Art: The Lives and Loves of Natalie Barney and Romaine Brooks* (New York: St. Martin's Press, 2005).

156 *Lady Godiva naked*   Waagenaar, *Mata Hari*, 49.

157 *"Who can Mata Hari be?"*   "Een Hollandsche danseres" (A Dutch dancer), *Nieuws van den Dag (News of the Day)*, 17 April 1905.

157 *"Mata Hari's real name"*   Henri De Weindel, "Une danseuse Hindoue à Paris" (A Hindu dancer in Paris), *Femme d'Aujourd'hui* (*Today's Woman*), no. 22, April 1905.

157, 158 *"Mata Hari! Strange"; "a tall and slender"*; and *"Suddenly she is no longer"*   *Nieuw Rotterdamsche Dagblad* (*New Rotterdam Daily*), quoted in Waagenaar, *Mata Hari*, 55–56.

159 *His intended was Elisabetha Martina Christina van der Mast*   Ibid., 64.

159 *he produced a photograph*   Ibid., 63–64; Charles S. Heymans, *La Vraie Mata Hari: Courtisane et Espionne* (*The True Mata Hari: Courtesan and Spy*) (Paris: Étoile, 1936), 97.

159 *The divorce was granted*   Adam Zelle, *De Roman van Mata Hari, Mevrouw M. G. MacLeod Zelle: De Levensgeschiedenis Mijner Dochter en*

Mijne Grieven tegen Haar Vroegeren Echtgenoot (*The novel of Mata Hari, Mrs. M. G. MacLeod Zelle: The biography of my daughter and my grievances against her former husband*) (Amsterdam: C. L. G. Veldt, 1906), 201.

159 *The grounds for the divorce were*   Heymans, *Vraie*, 98–100.

160 *"Mata Hari personifies"*   *Le Journal* (*The Journal*), 1905, quoted in Waagenaar, *Mata Hari*, 61.

161 *"One would need special words"*   La Presse (*The Press*), 1905, quoted ibid.

162 *"You ask me, Dad"*   Mata Hari to Adam Zelle, 8 October 1905, quoted in Zelle, *Roman*, 196–98.

163 *sued by a Paris jeweler*   Léon Schirmann, *Mata-Hari: Autopsie d'une machination* (*Mata-Hari: Autopsy of a fix*) (Paris: Éditions Italiques, 2001), 21; and Waagenaar, *Mata Hari*, 61–62.

163 *"discreetly voluptuous"*   Waagenaar, *Mata Hari*, 65.

163 *a romantic relationship with Jules Cambon*   Ibid.; and Schirmann, *Autopsie*, 22.

163 *ambassador to the United States*   Russell Warren Howe, *Mata Hari: The True Story* (New York: Dodd, Mead, 1986), 46.

163 *"true ambassadress of France"*   Ibid.

164 *"How happy I have been"*   Jules Massenet to Mata Hari, 1906, quoted in Waagenaar, *Mata Hari*, 67.

164 *"I remained three years"*   SHAT, *pièce* 363, 15 February 1917.

165 *"ladies who style themselves 'Eastern dancers'"* and *"Born in Java"*   Anonymous, "Coquelin and Charity," *The Era*, 3 October 1908.

165 *"Isadora Duncan is dead!"*   *Neues Wiener Journal* (*New Vienna Journal*), 1908, quoted in Waagenaar, *Mata Hari*, 73.

166 *"slender and tall"*   *Fremdenblatt*, 1908, quoted in Waagenaar, *Mata Hari*, 69.

166 *"His family having given him"*   SHAT, *pièce* 363, 15 February 1917.

167 The Novel of Mata Hari   Zelle, *Roman*.

168 "The Naked Truth About Mata Hari"   G. H. Priem, *De naakte*

Waarheid omtrent Mata Hari (*The naked truth about Mata Hari*) (Amsterdam: n.p., 1907).

168 *"A charming woman"*   Ibid., 22–24.

169 *"She spoke so calmly"*   Ibid., 29–30.

169 *"'Look,' she began"*   Ibid., 32.

170 *"Now I understand fully"*   Ibid., 56.

170 *"This beautiful 'novel'"*   Ibid., 44.

171 *"Certainly, this life"*   Ibid., 44–45.

171 *"I will absolutely not claim"*   Ibid., 68.

171 *"My only intention"*   Ibid., 72.

Chapter 10 Living Like a Butterfly in the Sun

172 "Star of the Dance"   Julie Wheelwright, *The Fatal Lover: Mata Hari and the Myth of Women in Espionage* (London: Collins & Brown, 1992), 28; and Sam Waagenaar, *Mata Hari* (New York: Appleton-Century, 1965), 81.

173 *"Saturday–Just today"*   René Puaux, "De Paris à Khartum" (From Paris to Khartoum), *Le Temps* (*The Times*), 21 March 1907, quoted in Adolphe Roberts, "The Fabulous Dancer," part 1, *Dance Magazine*, July 1929: 20.

173 *She campaigned vigorously*   Waagenaar, *Mata Hari*, 76–77.

174 *"a beautiful woman"*; *"very nice"*; and *"There was never"*   Ibid., 85–88.

174 *"she did not have a chance"*   Ibid.

175 *Antoine fired her and she sued*   Ibid., 82–84.

175 *In 1911, she and Rousseau moved*   SHAT, *pièce* 363, 15 February 1917; *pièce* 151, 9 May 1917.

175 *"Those who see her pass"*   Waagenaar, *Mata Hari*, 98.

175 *"a skirt-chaser"* and *"When at long last"*   Ibid., 89.

176 *the accusation that Rousseau*   Emile Massard, *Les Espionnes à Paris: La Vérité sur Mata Hari* (*The Spice of Paris: The Truth about Mata Hari*) (Paris: Albin Michel, 1922), 26–27.

176 *"My lover squandered"*   SHAT, *pièce* 363, 15 February 1917.

176 *"The part of Venus"*; *"an adorable creature"*; and *"very cultured"*   Waagenaar, *Mata Hari*, 94.

177 *"I wonder whether you know"*   Mata Hari to Gabriel Astruc, 8 February 1912, quoted in Waagenaar, *Mata Hari*, 97.

177 *she wanted to live like a butterfly*   G. H. Priem, *De naakte Waarheid omtrent Mata Hari* (*The naked truth about Mata Hari*) (Amsterdam: n.p., 1907), 36–37.

178 *Leon Bakst . . . found her figure . . . too matronly*   Waagenaar, *Mata Hari*, 98–99.

178 *Rudolf had separated*   Charles S. Heymans, *La Vraie Mata Hari: Courtisane et Espionne* (*The True Mata Hari: Courtesan and Spy*) (Paris: Étoile, 1936), 257.

178 *dismissed Anna with a curt word*   Waagenaar, *Mata Hari*, 91–92.

178 *if he could help her obtain . . . Berlin Opera*   Russell Warren Howe, *Mata Hari: The True Story* (New York: Dodd, Mead, 1986), 56.

178 *Photographs of one such event*   Anonymous, "Lady MacLeod Dances in the Light of the Moon to Her Friends," *The Tatler* 639 (24 September 1913): 376–77.

179 *"At a time that I cannot pin down"*   SHAT, *pièce* 151, 9 May 1917.

180 *"was an unforgettably radiant"*   Paul Olivier to Mata Hari, ca. 15 December 1913, Mata Hari scrapbooks, Fries Museum.

181 maisons de rendez-vous   Léon Bizard, *Souvenirs d'un médecin de Saint-Lazare* (*Memoirs of a doctor in Saint-Lazare*) (Paris: Albin Michel, 1923), 45.

181 *"talking animatedly"* and *"several hundred thousand [marks]"*   Waagenaar, *Mata Hari*, 109; also SHAT, *pièce* 363, 15 February 1917.

182 *a very respectable salary of 48,000 marks*   SHAT, *pièce* 363, 15 February 1917.

182 *"You will be there before then"*   Ibid.

182 *"We heard the noise"*   Ibid.

183 *On August 6, with hardly any money*   Waagenaar, *Mata Hari,* 116–18.

184 *In handwritten ink, the passport*   See photograph of the passport in Waagenaar, *Mata Hari,* between pp. 50 and 51.

184 *A remarkable anecdote*   The account that follows is taken from an interview with Maurice van Staen published in a Dutch newspaper on 20 March 1965, "Mevrouw Mata Hari" (Lady Mata Hari), 5. The copy I have does not include the name of the paper. The interviewer's name is given only as Willem.

185 *"Because I had only one chemise"*   Waagenaar, *Mata Hari,* 119.

185 *she entertained a Dutch banker*   SHAT, *pièce* 363, 15 February 1917.

185 *Baron Edouard van der Capellan*   Ibid.

186 *She rented a house*   Ibid.

186 *she moved in on August 11, 1915* and *hounded . . . by her creditors*   Waagenaar, *Mata Hari,* 126–28.

186 *"she was visited by Karl Kroemer"*   SHAT, *pièce* 404, 21 May 1917.

187 *the H of H21 indicated*   Léon Schirmann, *Mata-Hari: Autopsie d'une machination* (Mata Hari: Autopsy of a Fix) (Paris: Éditions Italiques, 2001), 33–34, citing Gempp report, Archives Militaires Allemande, vol. 8, Fribourg, 50.

187 *not in May 1916*   SHAT, *pièce* 404, 21 May 1917.

187 *"My 20,000 francs"*   Ibid.

188 *"A certain time after"*   SHAT, *pièce* 175, 13 June 1917.

188 *a scandalously low-cut white dress*   See photo, Mata Hari scrapbooks.

189, 190 *"I beg to report"* and *"Although she was thoroughly"*   PRO MEPO 3/2444 9666, Port of Folkestone, 4 December 1915.

190 *"Not above suspicion"* and *"most unsatisfactory"*   PRO MEPO 3/2444, W531.

190 *"Summary and description"*   PRO MEPO 3/2444 61207 ALIENS no. 30727/2. Information received from Folkestone Secret 61207/ MO 5 E, 9 December 1915.

Chapter 11 In Time of War

192 *"15,000 francs"*   PRO MI5 KV2/1, dossier 751 attached to memorandum MI5 no. 71637.

193 *"One suspects her"*   Ibid.

193 *"a liar and a first-class intriguer"*   Jeffrey T. Richelson, *A Century of Spies: Intelligence in the Twentieth Century* (Oxford: Oxford University Press, 1995), 12.

193 *expressed concern that the story*   PRO MI5 KV2/1 no. 74194.

193 *she was to be arrested*   PRO M6 3/2444, 22 February 1916.

194 *"Well-known Dutch artist"*   Telegram, John Loudon to Reneke de Marees van Swinderen, 27 April 1916, Nederlandse Gezantshap in Groot-Brittanie (en Ierland), 1813–1932 (Dutch embassy in Great Britain [and Ireland], 1813–1932), 849, Algemeen Rijksarchief, The Hague.

194 *"undesirable"*   Telegram, Reneke de Marees van Swinderen to John Loudon, 4 May 1916, ibid.

194 *a bizarre occurrence*   SHAT, *pièce* 366, 21 February 1917.

195 *"not even the intervention"*   Ambassade de la République Français en Espagne to van Royen, 17 June 1916, Dutch Legation in Spain, Algemeen Rijksarchief, The Hague.

196 *He committed suicide*   Russell Warren Howe, *Mata Hari: The True Story* (New York: Dodd, Mead, 1986), 271.

196 *the ferocious battle of Verdun*   Information taken from http:// www.firstworldwar.com/battles/verdun.htm, accessed April 2006.

197 *she complained to the bellboy*   SHAT, *pièce* 9, 21 June 1916.

197 *"très élégante"*   SHAT, *pièce* 8, 20 June 1916.

198 *she was seen in the company*   SHAT, *pièce* 17, 11 July 1916.

198 *why was she seeing these other men?*   SHAT, *pièce* 18, 12 July 1916.

199 *"Suffering from pains"*   SHAT, *pièce* 24, 18 July 1916.

199 *"We do not know"*   SHAT, *pièce* 26, 20 July 1916.

200 *They were observed together*   SHAT, *pièce* 27, 21 July 1916; *pièce* 28, 22 July 1916; *pièce* 31, 25 July 1916.

200 *"Around this time"*   SHAT, *pièce* 149, 9 May 1917.

200 *Mata Hari could not have known*   SHAT, *pièce* 37, 31 July 1916.

200 *"Abruptly, without my observing"* and *"In the days which preceded"*   SHAT, *pièce* 149, 9 May 1917.

200, 201 *He saw her on July 21, 22, 25, and 27* and *"very animated"*   SHAT, *pièce* 27, 21 July 1916; *pièce* 28, 22 July 1916; *pièce* 31, 23 July 1916; *pièce* 33, 24 July 1916; *pièce* 39, 1 August 1916; *pièce* 40, 2 August 1916; *pièce* 41, 3 August 1916; *pièce* 48, 9 August 1916; *pièce* 56, 17 August 1916; *pièce* 57, 18 August 1916; *pièce* 58, 19 August 1916; *pièce* 69, 30 August 1916; *pièce* 70, 31 August 1916.

202 *"too bleached blond"*   SHAT, *pièce* 149, 9 May 1917.

202 *she was with another officer*   SHAT, *pièce* 69, 30 August 1916; *pièce* 70, 31 August 1916.

202 *Vladimir de Massloff*   SHAT, *pièce* 35, 19 July 1916.

202 *in the Special Imperial Russian Regiment*   SHAT, *pièce* 36, 30 July 1916.

202 *they returned to the Grand Hotel*   SHAT, *pièce* 37, 31 July 1916.

203 *her permit was refused because*   Ibid.

203 *She also sent a note to Hallaure*   SHAT, *pièce* 38, 31 July 1916.

Chapter 12 The Tangled Web

205 *Joffre had appointed Ladoux*   Georges Ladoux, *Les chasseurs d'espions: Comment j'ai fait arrêter Mata Hari* (*The Spy-Hunters: How I Arrested Mata Hari*) (Paris: Librairie des Champs-Elysées, 1932), 7–8.

206 *"Counterespionage is not today"*   Georges Ladoux to Minister of

War Alexandre Millerand and Minister of the Interior Louis Malvy, 10 September 1915, no. 3036—SCR 2/11, reprinted ibid., 188–89.

207 *"It was in August 1916"*   Ibid., 231.

208 *"a fat man with very black beard"*   PRO MEPO 3/2444 9666, 16 November 1916, 11.

208 *"When I was slow to ask her"*   Ladoux, *Chasseurs*, 231–32.

209 *Although she was thoroughly*   PRO MEPO 3/2444 9666, Port of Folkestone, 4 December 1915.

209 *The second circular*   PRO M6 3/2444, 22 February 1916.

210 *"We have often spoken"* and *"With fliers"*   Ladoux, *Chasseurs*, 233–35.

210 *"And the strange creature"*   Ibid.

211 *"There, I was received"*   SHAT, *pièce* 366, 21 February 1917.

213 *reports from Monier and Tarlet show that*   SHAT, *pièce* 39, 1 August 1916; *pièce* 48, 9 August 1916.

213 *asked the hotel to tell Hallaure*   SHAT, *pièce* 40, 2 August 1916.

213 *On August 3*   SHAT, *pièce* 41, 3 August 1916.

214 *Later that day*   Ibid.

214 *Mata Hari accompanied Vadime*   SHAT, *pièce* 336, 19 May 1917; *pièce* 43, 4 August 1916.

214 *she asked anxiously*   SHAT, *pièce* 48, 9 August 1916.

214 *"a gift of silver"*   SHAT, *pièce* 170, 25 May 1917.

215 *The couple had not returned by 11*   SHAT, *pièce* 57, 18 August 1916.

215 *August 19, she told the hotel*   SHAT, *pièce* 58, 19 August 1916.

215 *The implication that de Marguérie*   SHAT, *pièce* 175, 13 June 1917.

216 *"Captain, in principle, I accept"*   SHAT, *pièce* 367, 23 February 1917.

216 *"an expedited telegram to the front"*   SHAT, *pièce* 60, 21 August 1916.

216 *she stopped at both the Russian embassy*   SHAT, *pièce* 63, 24 August 1916.

216   *On the twenty-ninth, she picked*   SHAT, *pièce* 68, 29 August 1916.

216   *On the thirty-first, Hallaure called*   SHAT, *pièce* 69, 30 August 1916.

216   *She left by train for Vittel*   SHAT, *pièce* 70, 31 August 1916; *pièce* 71, 2 September 1916.

216   *wore a bandage covering his left eye*   SHAT, *pièce* 72, 3 September 1916.

216   *"[Vadime] had been gravely injured"*   SHAT, *pièce* 367, 23 February 1917.

218   *"Vittel, 1916—In memory"* and *"To my dear little Marina"*   Sam Waagenaar, *Mata Hari* (New York: Appleton-Century, 1965), 140.

219   *Mata Hari asked the brigadier general* and *social snubs*   SHAT, *pièce* 77, 8 September 1916.

219   *"I was at Vittel"*   SHAT, *pièce* 173, 29 May 1917.

220   *"My doctor, Dr. Boulommier"*   SHAT, *pièce* 174, 30 May 1917.

222   *"a costume all of lace"*   SHAT, *pièce* 352, 2 June 1917.

222   *"a jewel of some value"*   SHAT, *pièce* 76, 7 September 1916.

Chapter 13 *Maelstrom*

224   *For mysterious reasons . . . Ladoux suspended the surveillance*   There is a gap in the surveillance reports; *pièce* 82 is dated 13 September 1916, and *pièce* 83 is dated 13 October 1916.

224   *"She had been the most docile"*   Georges Ladoux, *Les chasseurs d'espions: Comment j'ai fait arrêter Mata Hari* (The Spy-Hunters: How I Arrested Mata Hari) (Paris: Librairie des Champs-Elysées, 1932), 237–40.

225   *"I have already been the mistress"*   Ibid.

227   *there were cabarets in Berlin*   Phillip Hoare, *Oscar Wilde's Last Stand* (New York: Arcade, 1998), 32, citing Magnus Hirschfeld, ed., *The Sexual History of the World War* (New York: Panurge Press, 1934), 203.

227   *Hotel Meurice, where she had stayed*   SHAT, *pièce* 84, 14 October 1916.

227 *"From the beginning"*   SHAT, *pièce* 233, 2 April 1916.

228 *"Be serious"*   Ladoux, *Chasseurs*, 241.

229 *"Listen well, I am certain"*   Ibid., 243.

230 *"Do I go to Germany"*   SHAT, *pièce* 367, 23 February 1917.

230 *"Here is my plan"*   Ibid.

231 *she must have an advance*   SHAT, *pièce* 368, 24 February 1917.

231 *She asked if he had received*   SHAT, *pièce* 367, 23 February 1917.

232 *"No. That sort of trickery"*   Ibid.

232 *"Captain, I beg you"*   Ibid.

233 *Eventually she paid another*   SHAT, *pièce* 84, 14 October 1916.

233 *She also wrote to the Dutch consul*   Mata Hari to unnamed consul, 13 October 1916, bMS 1553, Houghton Library, Harvard University.

233 *She visited Ladoux*   SHAT, *pièce* 87, 17 October 1916.

233 *this pattern of visit and* pneumatique   SHAT, *pièce* 89, 19 October 1916.

233 *She moved into cheaper rooms*   SHAT, *pièce* 88, 18 October 1916.

233 *He had a brief leave*   SHAT, *pièce* 96, 26 October 1916.

233 *Mata Hari sent Vadime three letters*   SHAT, pièce 98, 28 October 1916.

233 *sent Vadime a money order*   SHAT, *pièce* 105, 4 November 1916.

234 *Mata Hari left Paris*   SHAT, *pièce* 106, 5 November 1916.

Chapter 14 Stepping into the Trap

235 *Upon our arrival*   SHAT, *pièce* 368, 24 February 1917.

236 *"She was one of the most charming"*   Sam Waagenaar, *Mata Hari* (New York: Appleton-Century, 1965), 154.

236 *"We found absolutely nothing"*   Ibid., 155.

236 *"MARGARETHA ZELLE MacLEOD"*   PRO MEPO 3/2444 9666, 14 November 1916, report from Falmouth, 22.

237 "As Madame MacLeod's story"   Ibid.

237 *"What do you want from me?"*   Waagenaar, *Mata Hari*, 156.

237 *The Grants had also permitted*   Ibid.

238 *"May I beg Your Excellency"*   Mata Hari to Reneke de Marees van Swinderen, 13 November 1916, Algemeen Rijksarchief, The Hague.

238 *Thomson held on to her letter*   Waagenaar, *Mata Hari,* 157.

238 *"For four days"*   SHAT, *pièce* 368, 24 February 1917.

238 *Captain Reginald Hall and his assistant*   Julie Wheelwright, *The Fatal Lover: Mata Hari and the Myth of Women in Espionage* (London: Collins & Brown, 1992), 56.

239 *"ACC: Did you ever"*   PRO MEPO 3/2444 9666 39, 15 November 1916, 38.

240 *"ACC: Just before you went"*   Ibid., 16 November 1916, 10.

241 *Mata Hari steadfastly denied*   Ibid., 8.

241 *"MZM: Now I have"*   Ibid.

241 *"He said, 'Go to Holland'"*   Ibid., 10–11.

242 *"You love a Russian officer"*   Ibid., 12.

242 *"It would be awkward"*   Ibid., 13.

242 *"I have the honor"*   Basil Thomson to Reneke de Marees van Swinderen, 16 November 1916a, Algemeen Rijksarchief, The Hague.

242 *"We have the honor"*   Basil Thomson to Reneke de Marees van Swinderen, 16 November 1916b, Algemeen Rijksarchief, The Hague.

243 *He sent a telegram in cipher*   Basil Thomson to Georges Ladoux, no. MA 22939, 16 November 1916, PRO MEPO 3/2444.

243 *"tall and sinuous"*   Basil Thomson, *My Experiences at Scotland Yard* (Garden City, N.Y.: Doubleday, Page, 1923), 201–2.

243 *"We were convinced"*   Ibid.

244 *"to give up what you are doing"*   Ibid., 183.

244 *"very large professional wardrobe"*   PRO MEPO 3/2444, 18 November 1916, 7.

244 *"Box with gilt clock"*   Ibid.

246 *"Understand nothing"*   Georges Ladoux, *Les chasseurs d'espions:*

Comment j'ai fait arrêter Mata Hari (*The Spy-Hunters: How I Arrested Mata Hari*) (Paris: Librairie des Champs-Elysées, 1932), 246.

246 *"Ref. our telegram"* and *"I'll BET he would!"* PRO MEPO 3/2444, marked B.C.I.—18-11-1916—marked "16/11/16 sent telegram asking if Ladoux employed her, sent in cipher."

247 *"to marry Captain Vadime de Massloff"* Wheelwright, *Fatal*, 61.

247 *"The compatriot had originally"* Reneke de Marees van Swinderen to Dutch legation Madrid, 1 December 1916, Algemeen Rijksarchief, The Hague.

248 *Arriving back in Spain* The date 11 December 1916 was stamped in her passport at the Dutch consulate.

248 *"What, they took you for"* SHAT, *pièce* 368, 24 February 1917.

248 *Cazeaux's response* Waagenaar, *Mata Hari*, 201–2.

Chapter 15 Secrets and Betrayal

251 *He ordered that all messages intercepted* Georges Ladoux, *Les chasseurs d'espions: Comment j'ai fait arrêter Mata Hari* (*The Spy-Hunters: How I Arrested Mata Hari*) (Paris: Librairie des Champs-Elysées, 1932), 146.

252 *She slipped into the envelope* The account of this meeting is taken from SHAT, *pièce* 369, 28 February 1917.

253 *"Him (in German)"* Ibid.

254 *"I can do what I wish"* Ibid.

254 *"Madam . . . I have never seen"* Ibid.

255 *"My colonel, calm down"* Ibid.

256 *"[Me:] Well, always tired"* SHAT, *pièce* 369, 28 February 1917.

256 *"Tell them . . . what sort of woman"* Ibid.

257 *"Him: Come here into the light"* Ibid.

259 *Kalle had given her 3,500 francs* SHAT, *pièce* 404, 21 May 1917.

259 *coy and sexual content* SHAT, pièce 181, 1 March 1917.

260 *"a person known to be hostile"* SHAT, *pièce* 370, 1 March 1917.

261 *She addressed a letter to him* SHAT, *pièce* 107, 3 January 1917.

261 *"Ah, yes, the military"* and *"Wishing desperately to see"*   SHAT, *pièce* 370, 1 March 1917.

Chapter 16 Caught in a Trap

263 *"4 January. My dear"*   SHAT, *piéce* 108, 4 January 1917.

263 *they did not record her second*   Ibid.

264 *was acting "bizarrely"* and *"In any case, you must"*   SHAT, *piéce* 370, 1 March 1917.

265 *Dr. Edmond Locard*   Julie Wheelwright, *The Fatal Lover: Mata Hari and the Myth of Women in Espionage* (London: Collins & Brown, 1992), 69; Russell Warren Howe, *Mata Hari: The True Story* (New York: Dodd, Mead, 1986), 138–39; and Edmond Locard, *Mata-Hari* (Paris: Flammé d'Or, 1954).

266 *"The first message"*   SHAT, *pièce* 237, 13 December 1916.

266 *More messages about H21*   SHAT, *pièce* 240, 20 December 1916; *pièce* 241, 22 December 1916; *pièce* 242, 25 December 1916; *pièce* 243, 26 December 1916; *pièce* 244, 28 December 1916; *pièce* 245, 28 December 1916; *pièce* 246, 29 December 1916; *pièce* 247, 5 January 1917; *pièce* 248, 6 March 1917; *pièce* 249, 8 March 1917. Note that *pièces* 238 and 239 are missing from the archives.

267 *"Tomorrow evening"*   SHAT, *pièce* 111, 7 January 1917.

267 *She visited a fortune-teller*   SHAT, *pièce* 110, 6 January 1917.

267 *She was seen weeping*   SHAT, *pièce* 112, 8 January 1917.

267 *She wrote Vadime loving cards*   SHAT, *pièce* 110, 6 January 1917; *pièce* 111, 7 January 1917; *pièce* 112, 8 January 1917.

268 *very worried about being tailed*   SHAT, *pièce* 116, 12 January 1917.

268 *she was taking many precautions*   SHAT, *pièce* 117, 13 January 1917.

268 *an incoming letter from Vadime*   SHAT, *pièce* 118, 14 January 1917.

268 *She complained to the concierge*   SHAT, *pièce* 119, 15 January 1917.

268 *on or about January 15*   Locard, *Mata-Hari*, 142–44.

269 *"What do you want of me?"*   SHAT, *pièce* 370, 1 March 1917.

269 *"If I am not ashamed"*   Ibid.

269 *to the Hotel Castiglione*   SHAT, *pièce* 231, 25–31 January 1917.

269 *she was spending 500 francs a week*   SHAT, *pièce* 218, 10 April 1917. In this document, Inspector Curnier reports that Mata Hari has spent 13,000 in Paris in various hotels since May of 1916. At first glance, this seems to indicate she spent 13,000 francs over almost 12 months, but Mata Hari was not in Paris for much of that time and, from February 13 until the date of the report, she was in prison and obviously not spending in hotels. According to the documents, Mata Hari spent roughly 26 weeks in Paris between May 1916 and February 13, 1917. This works out to about 500 francs per week, the equivalent today of $1,610 per week or a total of $41,860 in modern currency.

270 *Priolet ... and Henri Maunoury ... she was tailed*   León Schirmann, *Mata-Hari: Autopsie d'une machination (Mata Hari: Autopsy of a Fix)* (Paris: Éditions Italiques, 2001), 135–36.

271 *"The 6th or 7th of February"*   SHAT, *pièce* 329, 9 April 1917.

272 *"She showed me various photos"*   SHAT, *pièce* 148, 7 May 1917.

273 *a "dangerous adventuress"*   SHAT, *pièce* 306, 24 May 1917.

273 *the strongly worded caution*   SHAT, *pièce* 336, 19 May 1917.

274 *Denvignes had turned against her*   SHAT, *pièce* 306, 24 May 1917.

274 *"I wish to make known"*   SHAT, *pièce* 1, 10 February 1917.

276 *The warrant was stamped for execution*   SHAT, *pièce* 478, 10 February 1917.

277 *intercept her ongoing correspondence*   SHAT, *pièce* 176, 12 February 1917.

277 *Mata Hari did not appear naked*   Albert Morain, *The Underworld of Paris: Secrets of the Sûreté* (London: Jarrold, 1930), 217.

277 *"Seal Number One"*   SHAT, *pièce* 177, 13 February 1917.

Chapter 17 Grinding Her to Dust

279 *Ladoux had not yet confided*   Julie Wheelwright, *The Fatal Lover: Mata Hari and the Myth of Women in Espionage* (London: Collins &

Brown, 1992), 71; and Philippe Collas, *Mata Hari: Sa véritable histoire* (*Mata Hari: Her True Story*) (Paris: Plon, 2003), 279–81.

279 *a list of addresses for couturiers*   Collas, *Véritable*, 279.

280 *"Justice must know"*   Ibid., 284.

280 *"the Grand Inquisitor"*   Ibid.

280 *his name . . . was apt*   Ibid., 283, quoting *Annales politiques et littéraires* (*Political and Literary Annual*), 25 November 1917.

281 *she did not need one*   SHAT, *pièce* 362, 13 February 1917.

281 *"I am innocent"*   Ibid.

281 *"I saw a tall woman"*   Pierre Bouchardon, *Souvenirs* (*Memoirs*) (Paris: Albin Michel, 1954), 305–6.

281 *Bouchardon had recently*   Collas, *Véritable*, 302, 350; Adam Sage, "Misogyny and French Lies Killed Mata Hari," *Times* (London), 10 November 2003.

281 *"From the first interview"*   SHAT, *pièce* 422, 24 June 1917.

283 *Saint-Laʒare was dark, damp*   Sam Waagenaar, *Mata Hari* (New York: Appleton-Century, 1965), 179; and Wheelwright, *Fatal*, 72.

284 *"Yes! A telephone"*   León Bizard, *Souvenirs d'un médecin de Saint-Laʒare* (*Memoirs of a doctor at Saint-Laʒare*) (Paris: Albin Michel, 1923), 45.

284 *"Was she, had she been pretty?"*   SHAT, *pièce* 422, 24 June 1917.

285 *"I expressly renounce"* and *"abandoned the conjugal home"*   SHAT, *pièce* 363, 15 February 1917.

285 *"I wish, for the rest of the questioning"*   Ibid.

286 *"she had taken hold of herself"*   Bouchardon, *Souvenirs*, 306.

286 *Mata Hari was examined by . . . Jules Socquet*   SHAT, *pièce* 124, 15 and 17 February 1917.

286 *"aged 40 years, tall"*   SHAT, *pièce* 125, 16 February 1917.

287 *moved from her first cell*   SHAT, *pièce* 126, 18 and 19 February 1917.

287 *Maître Clunet was present*   SHAT, *pièce* 366, 21 February 1917.

287 *"an old and somewhat"*   SHAT, *pièce* SDR 14, 5 May 1917.

287 *"it was a grand love"*   SHAT, *pièce* 366, 21 February 1917.

288 *"Already the official mistress"*   SHAT, *pièce* 422, 24 June 1917.

289 *"I again ask for my"*   SHAT, R 8, n.d.

290 *Astonishingly, Bouchardon ordered*   SHAT, R 3, 25 February 1917; R 7, 1 March 1917.

290 *Curnier even put in*   SHAT, R 6, 28 February 1917.

290 *"Dearest Marina"*   SHAT, *pièce* 182, 23 February 1917.

291 *"completely astonished"*   Ibid.

291 *"She asked me simply"*   SHAT, *pièce* 336, 19 May 1917.

292 *Bouchardon ordered an analysis*   SHAT, *pièce* 127, 23 February and 10 April 1917.

292 *Bouchardon called Mata Hari in*   SHAT, *pièce* 368, 24 February 1917.

292 *"REJET"*   SHAT, *pièce* 135, 26 February 1917.

293 *Germans could read the French ciphers*   SHAT, *pièce* 369, 28 February 1917.

293 *"Please I beg you"*   SHAT, R 3, n.d.

293 *He wrote a very reasoned*   SHAT, *pièce* 273, 5 March 1917.

293 *he wrote a very similar letter*   SHAT, *pièce* 274, 7 March 1917.

294 *"At the time of the examination"*   SHAT, *pièce* 130, 10 March 1917.

294 *his disdain for her immoral*   See, e.g., Wheelwright, *Fatal*, 74.

294 *oxycyanide of mercury*   SHAT, *pièce* 128, 10 April 1917.

295 *both potions could be diluted*   Ibid.

295 *Mata Hari sent an undated note*   SHAT, *pièce* 372, n.d.

296 *"No, I absolutely did not"*   SHAT, *pièce* 373, 12 March 1917.

296 *"I receive pitiful letters"*   SHAT, *pièce* 275, 16 March 1917.

296 *"I cried from fear"*   SHAT, R 4, n.d.

297 *The military governor*   SHAT, *pièce* 136, 16 March 1917.

297 *"physiologically depressed"*   SHAT, *pièce* 276, 16 March 1917.

297 *a pleading letter*   SHAT, *pièce* 138, 23 March 1917.

297 *Clunet petitioned*   SHAT, *pièce* 277, 26 March 1917.

297 *The terse second opinion*   SHAT, *pièce* 131, 26 March 1917.

297, 298 *"without regard to their rank"*; *"was organized"*; and *"a number of indications"* SHAT, *pièce* 233, 2 April 1917.

298 *"It was very shortly"* Ibid.

Chapter 18 Suffering

301 *"After studying the question"* SHAT, SDR 12, 4 April 1917; see also SDR 9, 11 April 1917.

301 *"I beg you"* SHAT, *pièce* 284, letter, 6 April 1917.

302 *Another appeal for provisional liberty* SHAT, *pièce* 140, 10 April 1917.

302 *Loudon sent a telegram* John Loudon to Dutch legation, Paris, and Paris legation to Loudon, 23 April 1917, Ministerie von Buitenlandse Zaken, Archives of the Embassy at Paris, 1866–1940, no. 1306 ("Mata Hari"), Algemeen Rijksarchief, The Hague.

302 *"Our question should not"* SHAT, *pièce* 399, 12 April 1917.

303 *"The fact that I had* relations" Ibid.

303 *"I assure you"* Ibid.

303 *"I am very astonished"* SHAT, R 6, n.d.

304 *Her toilet articles* SHAT, *pièce* 402, 14 April 1917.

304 *"As for the three officers"* SHAT, *pièce* 278, 13 April 1917.

305 *she wrote to him again* SHAT, *pièce* 231, 13 April 1917.

305 *"I have asked you"* SHAT, *pièce* 282, n.d.

305 *Clunet forwarded to Bouchardon* SHAT, *pièce* 286, 17 April 1917.

306 *"I am very grateful"* SHAT, *pièce* 288, n.d.

306 *"I must insist"* SHAT, *pièce* 289, 23 April 1917.

307 *"I thank you very much"* SHAT, *pièce* 294, n.d.

308 *open and dangerous mutiny* Jamie H. Cockfield, *With Snow on their Boots: The Tragic Odyssey of the Russian Expeditionary Force in France during World War I* (New York: St. Martin's Press, 1998), 115–200.

Chapter 19 *Telegrams and Secrets*

310 *In his report to Dubail*   SHAT, *pièce* 235, 12 April 1917.

310 *However, he sent transcripts of only nine*   Russell Warren Howe, *Mata Hari: The True Story* (New York: Dodd, Mead, 1986), 139–41, 165–71. Howe's analysis of these telegrams is persuasive; apparently both the numbers and contents of the telegrams were changed over time.

310 *"Agent H21 from the intelligence office"*   SHAT, *pièce* 236, *pièce* 235, app. 1, 31 December 1916.

311 *Kalle asked for instructions*   Ibid.

313 *On April 29 she wrote*   SHAT, *pièce* 195, 29 April 1917.

313 *"the most audacious comedy"*   SHAT, *pièce* 403, 1 May 1917.

313 *"Von Kalle can say"*   Ibid.

314 *Bouchardon . . . initiated inquiries and received confirmation of the arrest*   SHAT, *pièce* 251, 3/31 May 1917.

314 *he had a right to see her entire dossier*   SHAT, SDR 13, 4 May 1917.

315 *could not be trusted*   SHAT, SDR 14, 5 May 1917.

315 *Jullien responded*   SHAT, SDR 15, 5 May 1917.

315 *"The frightful women"*   SHAT, *pièce* 297, n.d.

317 *"This is what I will ask"*   SHAT, *pièce* 299, 10 May 1917.

317 *On May 15 she wrote again*   SHAT, *pièce* 300, 15 May 1917.

318, 319 *"It has been three months"; "I beg you, my captain"; and "Captain Ladoux was wrong"*   SHAT, *pièce* 302, 15 May 1917.

319 *"The brusque change"*   SHAT, *pièce* 304, 15 May 1917.

320 *"That which I have feared"*   SHAT, *pièce* 133, n.d.

320 *"serious physical affliction"; "an extremely nervous temperament"; and "One does not observe"*   SHAT, *pièce* 134, 24 May 1917.

320 *"I have decided"*   SHAT, *pièce* 404, 21 May 1917.

321 *"render them a service"* and *repayment for the valuable furs*   Ibid.

322 *"Whom have you served?"*   Ibid.

322 *"flirted not at all badly"*   SHAT, *pièce* 149, 9 May 1917.

322 *"Mata Hari never asked"*   Ibid.

322 *after being warned by a friend*   Ibid.

322 *she had not seemed sick*   SHAT, *pièce* 159, 19 May 1917.

323 *it was not gentlemanly*   SHAT, *pièce* 404, 21 May 1917.

Chapter 20 The Lowest Circle of Hell

324 *"We have recorded your confession"*   SHAT, *pièce* 405, 22 May 1917.

324 *"You cannot simply"*   Ibid.

325, 326 *"Captain Ladoux promised me"* and *"The captain was more affirmative"*; *"I didn't dare"*; *"One cannot give a mission"*; *"I said nothing"*; and *"We must make clear"*   Ibid.

326 *"The case was perfectly clear"*   Pierre Bouchardon, *Souvenirs (Memoirs)* (Paris: Albin Michel, 1954), 31.

326 *"My absolute conviction"*   SHAT, *pièce* 146, 4 May 1917.

327 *"A man of Colonel"*   SHAT, *pièce* 406, 23 May 1917.

328 *She begged Ladoux*   SHAT, *pièce* 265, 24 May 1917.

328 *To Bouchardon, she wrote*   SHAT, *pièces* 306 and 307, 24 May 1917.

328 *Mata Hari's sense that Denvignes*   Philippe Collas, *Mata Hari: Sa véritable histoire (Mata Hari: Her True Story)* (Paris: Plon, 2003), 396.

328 *"I have nothing to say"* and *"I am not guilty"*   SHAT, *pièce* 407, 30 May 1917.

329 *"Captain Ladoux . . . understands"*   SHAT, *pièce* 267, 31 May 1917.

329 *"You can menace me"*   SHAT, *pièce* 269, 31 May 1917.

330 *Clunet sent another*   SHAT, *pièce* 308, 3 June 1917; *pièce* 313, 8 June 1917.

330 *"There is still something"*   SHAT, *pièce* 312, 5 June 1917.

332 *"To forget that she was"*   Pierre Bouchardon, *Journal Excelsior*, 2 August 1919.

333 *On June 9, Clunet's appeal*   SHAT, *pièce* 141, 9 June 1917.

333 *Inspector Curnier compiled*   SHAT, *pièce* 218, 10 June 1917.

333 *on June 27 she received*   SHAT, R 12, 27 June 1917; *pièce* 320, 14 June 1917; *pièce* 323, 21 May 1917; and *pièce* 324, 23 May 1917.

333 *"I have the impression"*   Mata Hari to Dutch consulate in Paris, 22 June 1917, Ministerie von Buitenlandse Zaken, Archives of the Embassy at Paris ("Mata Hari"), Algemeen Rijksarchief, The Hague.

334 *"a case of* en flagrant délit*"*   Bouchardon, *Souvenirs*, 311.

334 *"As the situation is now"*   SHAT, *pièce* 414, 21 June 1917.

Chapter 21 *The Kangaroo Court*

335 *"descended on the Grand Hotel"*   SHAT, *pièce* 422, 24 June 1917.

336 *"a formidable adversary"* and *"after freshening up"*   Ibid.

336 *"Her long stories"*   SHAT, *pièce* 422, 24 June 1917.

338 *spies can rarely be convicted*   Butch Hodgson, FBI agent, to author verbally, 1992.

338 *"One can see that a woman"*   SHAT, *pièce* 422, 24 June 1917.

339 *"1. Entered the entrenched"*   Ibid.

340 *"one . . . just one for me?"*   SHAT, R 11, 25 June 1917.

340 *She also begged him*   SHAT, R 1, n.d.

341 *"Over the weeks . . . she wrote Mornet"*   SHAT, R 12, 27 June 1917; R 13, 30 June 1917; R 14, 2 July 1917; R 26 and R 25, 3 July 1917; R 16, 5 July 1917; R 20, 6 July 1917; R 27, 8 July 1917.

341 *It is shocking*   SHAT, R 9, n.d.

341 *"I am scandalously malnourished"*   SHAT, R 19, 6 July 1917.

341 *there had been a number of articles*   Ministry of Foreign Affairs, telegram to Edouard Clunet, 30 June 1917; Ministerie von Buitenlandse Zaken, Archives of the Embassy at Paris, 1866–1940, no. 1306 ("Mata Hari"), Algemeen Rijksarchief, The Hague.

342 *her blouse was rather low-cut*   F. Belle, "Mata Hari Condamnée à Mort" ("Mata Hari Condemned to Death"), *Le Gaulois (The Gallic)*, 26 July 1917; and Emile Massard, *Les Espionnes à Paris: La Vérité sur Mata*

Hari (*The Spies of Paris: The Truth about Mata Hari*) (Paris: Albin Michel, 1922), 36.

342 *Yet she still walked like a dancer*   Belle, "Condamnée."

344 *Vadime was among the wounded*   Léon Schirmann, *Mata-Hari: Autopsie d'une machination* (*Autopsy of a Fix*) (Paris: Éditions Italiques, 2001), 295, citing SHAT 16N 210 S5, Liste des blessés du 1er régiment russe (List of wounded of the First Russian Regiment), 104.

345 *unpopular officers had been attacked*   Details of the mutiny from Susan Everett, *The Great War* (Greenwich, Conn.: Dorset Press, 1980), 164–70.

345 *The Russian troops*   Jamie H. Cockfield, *With Snow on Their Boots: The Tragic Odyssey of the Russian Expeditionary Force in France during World War I* (New York: St. Martin's Press, 1998), 100ff., 112.

346 *Mata Hari faced seven men*   SHAT, unmarked *pièce*, 24 July 1917, Jugement 570, Article 140 du Code de Justice Militaire, minute de jugement, formule no. 16, no. 2793 d'ordre: date du crime or du délit, 1915–1916–1917 (Judgment 570, Article 140 of the Code of Military Justice, minute of judgment, formula no. 16, no. 2793 of the order: date of crime or offense, 1915–1916–1917).

348 *"On what is this person"*   Massard, *Espionnes*, 94–95, quoting Jean Chatin to Emile Massard, n.d.

348 *Bouchardon's report*   Schirmann, *Autopsie*, 190.

349 *"one of the most dangerous"*   SHAT, *pièce* 169, 24 May 1917.

350 *"The evil that this woman has done"*   Massard, *Espionnes*, 36.

350 *Jules Cambon*   Sam Waagenaar, *Mata Hari* (New York: Appleton-Century, 1965), 274–75; Schirmann, in *Autopsie*, 192, does not believe that Cambon testified. Since there is no official record of the trial, the truth is impossible to determine.

350 *"Andrée Messimy, née Bonaparte"*   SHAT, *pièce* 435, 23 July 1917.

350 *Louis Malvy . . . whose subsequent political*   Julie Wheelwright, *The Fatal Lover: Mata Hari and the Myth of Women in Espionage* (London:

Collins & Brown, 1992), 131–32; Schirmann, *Autopsie*, 191; and "Scandal Obliterated," *Time*, 3 May 1926.

351 *"Madame did not ask"* and *"We spoke of art"*   Massard, *Espionnes*, 52–53.

351, 352 *"a siren with strangely"* and *"My defense is"*   Ibid., 58.

352 *"It is frightful"*   Ibid., 58–59.

354 *she cannot have passed Kalle*   Schirmann, *Autopsie*, 123–24.

354 *She repeated this story to an Allied*   PRO MI5 KV2/1, Cazeaux report, 15 December 1916.

355 *"In the name of the People of France"*   SHAT, unmarked *pièce*, 24 July 1917, No. 2793 d'Ordre de Jugement (article 151 du Code du Justice militaire), Jugment Exécutoire de Condamnation (number 2793 of the Order of Judgment (article 151 of the Code of Military Justice), Executory Judgment of Sentence).

355 *335.65 francs*   Ibid.

355 *"It's impossible!"*   "Gazette des Tribunaux" (Gazette of the Courts), *Le Figaro*, 26 July 1917; and *Le Matin (The Morning)*, 25 July 1917.

355 *"a sinister Salome"*   Maurice de Waleffe, "Après le châtiment de l'espionne" (After the punishment of the spy), *Le Journal*, 27 July 1917.

Chapter 22 Waiting

357 *Sister Léonide brought her*   Sam Waagenaar, *Mata Hari* (New York: Appleton-Century, 1965), 282.

357 *"I cannot stand it"*   Léon Bizard, *Souvenirs d'un médecin de Saint-Lazare* (*Memoirs of a doctor at Saint-Lazare*) (Paris: Albin Michel, 1923), 45.

358 *all her letters were read*   SHAT, SDR 28, 11 September 1917.

358 *On August 17 her appeal*   Décision du Conseil Permanent de Révision de Paris (Decision of the Permanent Council of Appeals of Paris), 17 August 1917.

358 *"Here, I am without defense"*   SHAT, R 31, 10 September 1917.

358 *Milhaud's letters*   SHAT, SDR 24, 29 August 1917; SDR 27, 6 September 1917.

359 *one of the most outrageous letters*   SHAT, SDR 39, 11 October 1917, 539.

359 *"repugnant"*   SHAT, SDR 40, 15 October 1917.

359 *beg for a presidential pardon*   Mata Hari to Ridder van Stuers, 22 September 1917, Ministerie von Buitenlandse Zaken, Archives of the Embassy at Paris, 1866–1940, no. 1306 ("Mata Hari"), Algemeen Rijksarchief, The Hague.

359 *Poincaré never granted*   Julie Wheelwright, *The Fatal Lover: The Myth of Women in Espionage* (London: Collins & Brown, 1992), 95.

360 *"In the theater world"*   SHAT, R 45, 14 October 1917.

361 *The order for her execution*   SHAT, SDR 46, 14 October 1917.

361 *A tender story of dubious accuracy*   Bizard, *Médecin*, 98; Albert Morain, *The Underworld of Paris: Secrets of the Sûreté* (London: Jarrold, 1930), 224; and Emile Massard, *Espionnes à Paris: La Vérité sur Mata Hari* (*The Spies of Paris: The Truth about Mata Hari*) (Paris: Albin Michel, 1922), 63.

Chapter 23 *Dying Well*

363 *Her hated interrogator*   Sam Waagenaar, *Mata Hari* (New York: Appleton-Century, 1965), 290–94.

364 *A story from* The Little Parisian   *Le Petit Parisien,* 16 October 1917.

365 *Hurriedly she wrote three*   SHAT, R 53, 9 February 1918, and R 52, 31 January 1918; letter from Pastor Arboux.

365 *"Do not cry"* and *"Besides, you will come"*   Julie Wheelwright, *The Fatal Lover: The Myth of Women in Espionage* (London: Collins & Brown, 1992), 97–98.

366 *"All these people!"* and *"What a success!"*   Albert Morain, *The Underworld of Paris: Secrets of the Sûreté* (London: Jarrold, 1930), 225.

366 *from the Fourth Regiment of Zouaves*   SHAT, SDR 48, 15 Octo-

ber 1917; M. Georges Godot, "La mort de Mata Hari" (The death of Mata Hari), *Paris Match*, 12 October 1953.

367 *"That is not necessary"* "L'Exécution de Mata Hari" (The Execution of Mata Hari), *Le Figaro*, 16 October 1917.

367 *"By God"* Russell Warren Howe, *Mata Hari: The True Story* (New York: Dodd, Mead, 1986), 11. A similar sentiment was expressed by Maurice Halbin, the sole living member of the firing squad, in 1995. Julie Wheelwright, "Mata Hari's Exotic Dance Made Her the Toast of France," *Times* (London), 12 June 1999.

368 *"choreographic artist"* and *"The items that came"* "L'Exécution de Mata Hari."

368 *"One does not ask"* Ibid.

368 *"official press release"* SHAT, 5N 403, quoted in Léon Schirmann, *Mata-Hari: Autopsie d'une machination* (*Mata Hari: Autopsy of a Fix*) (Paris: Éditions Italiques, 2001), 221.

368 *"The Spy Mata-Hari"* "The Spy Mata-Hari Paid Yesterday for Her Crimes," *L'Excelsior*, 16 October 1917.

368 *Criticisms of the execution* Schirmann, *Autopsie*, 208, discusses a series of newspaper articles about the execution that had been censored, located in the collections at SHAT (folder 5N 510), some of these spoke of Mata Hari's courage and beauty; see also Marcel Berger and Paul Allard, *Les secrets de la Censure pendant la Grande Guerre* (*Secrets of the Censor during the Great War*) (Paris: Éditions des Protiques, 1932) 228.

369 *Georges Ladoux was arrested; One of his own agents; and finally acquitted on May 8, 1919* Georges Ladoux, *Les chasseurs d'espions: Comment j'ai fait arrêter Mata Hari* (*The Spy-Hunters: How I Arrested Mata Hari*) (Paris: Librairie des Champs-Elysées, 1932), 7–8.

369 *"All the world dropped me"* Ibid., 190.

370 *"At the beginning of August 1914"* Ibid., 9–10.

370 *"my abrupt departure"* Ladoux, *Chasseurs*, 17–18.

370 "The day after my acquittal" Ibid., 181–82.

371 *"most of which were shot"* Ibid., 220–21.

371 *general conviction rate for spies* Wheelwright, *Fatal,* 102, citing Ferdinand Tuohy, *The Secret Corps: A Tale of "Intelligence" on All Fronts* (London: Murray, 1920), 20.

372 *"Whatever she's done in life"* Howe, *True Story,* 271.

372 *He pursued the matter* SHAT, R 49, 26 January 1918; R 50, 1 February 1918; R 52, 31 January 1918; R 51, 2 February 1918; R 54, 6 February 1918; and R 53, 9 February 1918.

372 *The auction of her possessions; items that had belonged to Mata Hari;* and *Furnishings left in her house* Schirmann, *Autopsie,* 215.

372 *On August 10, 1919* Waagenaar, *Mata Hari,* 296; Howe, *True Story,* 272; Ameeta E. Singh and Barbara Romanowski, "Syphilis: Review with Emphasis of Clinical, Epidemiologic, and Some Biologic Features," *Clinical Microbiology Review* 12, no. 2 (1999): 187–209.

373 *"He did not confide"* Paul Guimard, in *Le roman vrai du demi-siècle: Du prèmier jazz au dernier Tzar,* ed. Gilbert Guilleminau (*The True Novel of the Half Century: From the First Jazz to the Last Tzar*) (Paris: Denoël, 1959), 240–74.

Index

Page references in *italics* refer to illustrations.